The Low Countri[illegible]

Cover: Pieter Saenredam,
Nave and Choir of the St Catharijnekerk, Utrecht (detail). Undated.
Panel, 116.8 x 95.8 cm.
Upton House, Banbury / Photo courtesy of The National Trust Photographic Library / Christopher Hurst.

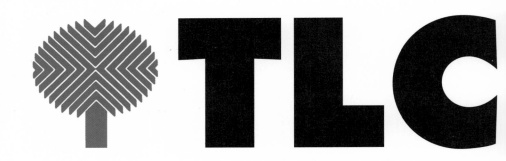

2002 Published by the

The Low Countries 10

ARTS AND SOCIETY IN FLANDERS AND THE NETHERLANDS

Flemish-Netherlands Foundation 'Stichting Ons Erfdeel'

Contents

Iconoclasms

11 Jozef Deleu
Foreword

12 Hans Cools
Tabula Rasa *The Iconoclastic Fury in the Low Countries*

21 Kees Fens
Not a Church Tower in Sight *The Secularisation of the Netherlands*

30 Peter Derkx
From 'Do you believe in God?' to 'What makes your life meaningful?' *Unbelief in the Netherlands*

36 Jan Kerkhofs S.J.
The Silent Iconoclasm in Flanders

42 Jeffrey Tyssens
The Road from Enlightenment to Indifference *Unbelief in Flanders*

48 Joris Gerits
How God Survived His Death in Books

56 Hans Ibelings
New Life for Old Churches *Reusing Religious Buildings in the Netherlands*

60 Jozef Deleu
'I'll Call You God, You Powers' *Fifteen Poems*
Poems by Joost van den Vondel, ?Hadewijch, Jacobus Revius, Guido Gezelle, Nikolaas Beets, Anton van Wilderode, J.A. dèr Mouw, Martinus Nijhoff, Maurice Gilliams, Gerrit Achterberg, Ida M.G. Gerhardt, Pierre Kemp, Leo Vroman, Hans Andreus and Jos de Haes.

70 Marc Dubois
Refurbishing the House of God *Adaptive Reuse of Religious Buildings in Flanders*

76 Brigitte Dekeyzer
Images of Christ *The Depiction of Christ in the Mayer van den Bergh Breviary*

84 C.G. Kok
Other Words, Another Sound *New Liturgical Music in the Netherlands*

89 Harold van de Perre
'Twixt Heaven and Earth *The Madonna in Painting in the Low Countries*

98 Th. van den End
Christianity in Indonesia, Past and Present

105 Valeer Neckebrouck
How the Congo Was Converted *Belgian Missionary Work in Central Africa*

112 Lammert G. Jansma
Religious Identity and Americanisation *Dutch Settlements in North America*

120 Pieter T'Jonck
A Seething Cauldron *Dance in Brussels*

126 Eddie Marsman
Room for Everything *The Photographs of Jacob Olie*

134 Rieta Bergsma
In Pursuit of the Moment *George Hendrik Breitner, Painter and Photographer of a Lost Age*

141 Hugo Brems
Poets Pick Things Up all over the World *The Poetry of Luuk Gruwez*
Five Poems by Luuk Gruwez

149 Johan Valcke
Flemish Furniture Design

160 Cyrille Offermans
Unstable Equilibrium *The Versatility of J. Bernlef*
An Extract and Four Poems by J. Bernlef

172 Cees van der Geer
His Own Protagonist *The Work of Teun Hocks*

178 Fred G.H. Bachrach
Encounters and Recognitions *English Landscapists and Dutch Old Masters – Then and Now*

187 Lori van Biervliet
No Victorian Disneyland *Bruges, the Past in the Present*

196 A.L. Sötemann
A Great Minor Poet *The Poems of J.C. Bloem*
Five Poems by J.C. Bloem

204 José Boyens
Opting for What Does not yet Exist *The Art of Carel Visser*

214 Hans Vandevoorde
On Yeats' Footstool *The Poet Karel van de Woestijne*
An Extract and Five Poems by Karel van de Woestijne

225 Marc Ruyters
Innocence Can Be Hell *The Art of Berlinde de Bruyckere*

230 Frans de Rover
Books Should Be Both Comic and Painful *The Work of Arnon Grunberg*
Extract from 'Phantom Pain' by Arnon Grunberg

237 Marie Christine van der Sman
Books in the Baron's House *The Renovation of the Meermanno-Westreenianum Museum*

244 Rudi van der Paardt
Paul Claes, a New Literary Wizard
An Extract and Four Poems by Paul Claes

252 Jozef T. Devreese and Guido Vanden Berghe
Simon Stevin, Flemish Tutor to a Dutch Prince

257 Peter Wesly
Johan Goudsblom: More than a Sociologist

Chronicle

Architecture

263 Koen van Synghel
Dasein, Empathic Architecture, or Poetry in Concrete? *The Architecture of Paul Robbrecht and Hilde Daem*

Cultural Policy

265 Filip Matthijs
A Temporary 'Naturalisation' *Translators' Houses in Amsterdam and Leuven*

267 Elly Cockx-Indestege
The Bookshop of the World

Film and Theatre

268 Jos Nijhof
Christ Recrucified *The Tegelen Passion Plays*

270 Wim de Poorter
How 'Royal' is the Royal Belgian Film
Archive?

271 Erik Martens
Where Angels Fear to Tread *The Discovery of
Heaven*

History

272 Reinier Salverda
Selective Affinities *Anglo-Dutch Relations,
1780-1980*

273 Fred G.H. Bachrach
A Passionately Dutch English King *The
Tercentenary of the Death of William III*

275 Lauran Toorians
The Commemoration of a Multinational *Four
Hundred Years of the Dutch East India
Company*

Language

277 Reinier Salverda
Languages in Competition

Literature

278 Annemie Leysen
The Ageless Writings of Bart Moeyaert

280 Luc Devoldere
Amsterdam, The Netherlands' Big Apple

281 Elsa Strietman
The Middle Dutch Arthur in his Rightful Place
at the Round Table

Music

283 Hendrik Willaert
Music of the People, for the People *Peter
Benoit, a Hundred Years On*

284 Jan Rubinstein
A Pioneer in Electronic Music *The Tonal Art of
Jan Boerman*

286 Vic de Donder
The Queen and the Violin *Fiftieth Anniversary
of the Queen Elisabeth International Music
Competition*

Philosophy and Science

288 Ger Groot
Face to Face with the 'Dalton Terror'
Philosophy between University and Journalism

289 Dirk van Assche
No Half-Measures *Peter Piot Leads the
Struggle against Aids*

Society

290 Willem Breedveld
Wim Kok, the Prime Minister from the Polders

291 Jos Bouveroux
The Lambermont Agreement: Another Step in
Belgian State Reform

Visual Arts

292 Hans Vanacker
Pieter Bruegel the Elder: The Master Drawer's
Comeback

294 Eric de Bruyn
An Enduring Fascination *The Boom in Bosch*

297 Wim van der Beek
Flexible Materials with Backbone *The Duality
of Sibyl Heijnen's Objects*

299 Johan de Vos
Variations on the Ordinary *The Photographs of
Rineke Dijkstra*

301 José Boyens
'A talent for art and a liking for mathematics'
The Sculpture of Norman Dilworth

302 Filip Matthijs
Short Takes

308 Bibliography of Dutch-Language
Publications translated into English (traced
January-November 21, 2001)

318 *Contributors*

319 *Translators*

Iconoclasms

Foreword

The iconoclasm which swept through the Low Countries in the sixteenth century had as its goal the degradation and destruction of the symbols of religious power. Images of Christ, the Madonna and the saints fell victim to its fury. Today, this Protestant revolt against Catholic authority has its sequel in an almost silent iconoclasm. This time the breach seems more definitive: the population is rapidly divesting itself of its Christian heritage. Church-going is in decline, very few new churches are being built, and many existing religious structures find themselves in a sorry state. Churches, monasteries and seminaries stand empty. They are being turned into museums, schools, offices, warehouses, residential complexes, even sports halls. Where writers after the Second World War still wrestled with questions of faith and the lack of it, these days God seems to have almost entirely disappeared from literature written in Dutch. And for some years now the confessional political parties, both in Belgium and in the Netherlands, have been out of power.

The Caermers monastery in Ghent, once a place of worship, now an exhibition room. Photo by Dirk Pauwels.

The secularisation of a society which once sent its sons and daughters out into the world to spread God's word is now an established fact. Flanders and the Netherlands have become more or less post-Christian areas, characterised by ideological eclecticism and increasing individualisation.

Yet those who have turned their backs on religion still feel a need for values and standards. This is apparent when we look at the history of 'unbelief' in Flanders and the Netherlands. Heaven has been stormed, the chains broken, Absolute Truth shattered, but all too often the new tolerance comes uncomfortably close to an indifference which many unbelievers also find repugnant.

Those who still believe are equally critical of the cosy inertia of old-style religion: what is needed is constant renewal, a contemporary setting for faith. And once again we see the emergence of writers and artists who deliberately characterise themselves as religious. Perhaps yet another iconoclasm is on its way.

From the next volume of *The Low Countries* the Chief Editor will be Luc Devoldere. I have every confidence that under his creative leadership the yearbook will continue to provide the English-speaking world with a reliable source of information about the Low Countries.

If after ten years of existence the quality of its content has made this publication to some extent indispensable, that is quite simply the greatest reward I could wish for as I take my leave of it.

Jozef Deleu
Chief Editor

Tabula

Rasa

The Iconoclastic Fury in the Low Countries

On 25 October 1555, Emperor Charles V handed over the government of the Netherlands to his son Philip II. The event made a deep impression on contemporaries, and later chroniclers have seen it as a major turning point in Dutch history. For the Emperor, who had been born in Ghent and raised in the Netherlands, was abdicating in favour of a distant 'Spanish' king. Moreover, all the major actors in the drama that was to unfold over the following decades now appeared on stage together for the first time. The scene has been described and depicted on countless occasions. Leaning on a stick, which he held in his right hand, and accompanied on his left by the young Prince William of Orange, Charles V made his way through the Aula Magna of his palace on the Coudenberg in Brussels. He looked tired as he told the assembled members of the States General that he felt too ill and exhausted to continue as ruler of these lands. Philip began his reign with an apology. He could not speak French (let alone Dutch). It was Antoine Perrenot de Granvelle, later to become Cardinal, who addressed the gathering on his behalf.

Louis Gallait, *The Abdication of Charles V in Brussels on 25 October 1555 in favour of his Son Philip.* 1841. Canvas, 485 x 683 cm. Musée des Beaux-Arts, Tournai.

Malaise

In spite of this apparent break with the past, in fact the problems which were to erupt with the iconoclastic riots of 1566 had been smouldering for years. The protracted war with France was costing the treasury a fortune and interfering with trade. This had led to a steep rise in taxation and in the price of food. Furthermore, during the last years of Charles' rule all who expressed doubts about orthodox Catholic doctrine were savagely persecuted by the Inquisition. William Tyndale, the translator of the Bible, had been burnt at the stake in 1536 in Vilvoorde. In short, there was a widespread feeling of malaise in the Netherlands during the 1550s.

The Peace of Cateau-Cambrésis between Philip II and the French King Henry II in 1559 brought little change. On 10 July that year Henry II died from wounds sustained in a joust that he had organised to celebrate the peace. After that, France rapidly sank into anarchy. Taking advantage of the temporary weakness of the monarchy, the leaders of both the Catholic and the Reformed or Calvinist factions tried to seize power. In this climate of religious polarisation, from the spring of 1560 Catholic churches throughout southern France were attacked by bands of Calvinist zealots. In 1562, after civil war had broken out, image-breaking spread to the rest of France as well.

At this time, in contrast to France, Reformed Protestants in the Netherlands could not openly confess their faith. But they did organise themselves clandestinely, certainly in the Southern Netherlands, in so-called 'churches under the cross'. Others fled abroad from the fierce persecution. In some places like London and Emden, the capital of East Friesland, groups of such emigrants from the Low Countries established 'refugee churches'. The Reformed community in Antwerp rapidly became the centre of a web connecting all these churches at home and abroad. From 1562 on, various synods were organised in this cosmopolitan port because the chances of Reformed Protestants being discovered and persecuted were far smaller there than elsewhere.

Meanwhile, the government of the Netherlands was dominated by a faction of magnates that was led by William of Orange and included Lamoraal, Count of Egmond and Philippe de Montmorency, Count of Horn. Only after they and their supporters had brought the apparatus of government virtually to a standstill did Philip II give way in 1564 to their demand that Cardinal Granvelle be recalled. Unlike the King and the Cardinal, these men did not believe it expedient to send heretics to the stake. But on this matter Philip II would not give way. Indeed, quite the contrary. In the notorious let-

Noblemen presenting their 'Compromise' petition to the Regent, Margaret of Parma, in Brussels on 5 April 1566. Engraving by Frans Hogenberg (1566).

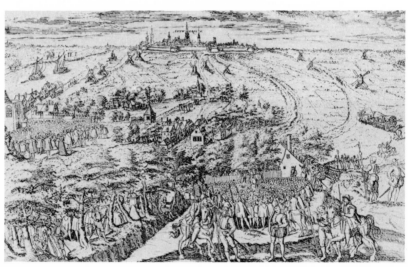

Hedge-preaching outside Antwerp. Engraving by Frans Hogenberg (1566).

ters he sent to Brussels from his Castilian hunting lodge at Segovia in the autumn of 1565 he commanded the governors of the Netherlands to enforce the anti-heresy legislation to the letter.

This news drove several of the lesser nobility into active opposition. From December 1565 they circulated a petition demanding the abolition of the 'inquisition', by which they meant the anti-heresy laws then in force. In the end, their 'Compromise' was signed by more than four hundred noblemen from every corner of the Netherlands, and on 5 April 1566 about two hundred of the signatories presented the petition to the Regent, Margaret of Parma, in Brussels. The despairing Regent did not dare to ignore so large an assembly of armed noblemen and the contested legislation was suspended until the King should finally decide the matter.

The more zealous reformers immediately seized their chance. The exiles

Iconoclasts 'on the job'.
Coloured engraving by
Frans Hogenberg (1566).

returned home. In June, at a synod in Antwerp, the delegates formally decided that from then on they would openly proclaim their truth. In the weeks that followed preachers addressed audiences in fields and meadows outside the walls of nearly every large town in the Southern Netherlands. And every week they attracted larger and larger crowds. More and more frequently, however, this hedge-preaching was being attended by armed men. Evidently it was felt that the audiences might need protection. The atmosphere was becoming increasingly tense.

Breakdown

The tension was greatest in the south-west of the Low Countries. On 1 August 1566 Sebastian Matte, an exile returned from England, appeared before the gates of Veurne accompanied by an estimated two thousand armed men. Their plan to take the town by force failed. But on 10 August the same Sebastian preached an inflammatory sermon just outside the walls of Steenvoorde. Nowadays this little town lies in France, but then it belonged to the Flemish seigniory of Kassel. After he had finished, a group of about twenty men led by Jacob de Buyzere, another returned exile and a former Augus-

Iconoclasts hit the Antwerp cathedral on 20 August 1566. Print by Gaspar Bouttats (17th century). Stedelijk Prentenkabinet, Antwerp.

tinian monk, forced their way into the church of the nearby monastery of St Laurence. There they smashed all the images and plundered the church treasures. The iconoclastic fury had begun.

In the days that followed, groups of image breakers moved from village to village and town to town. Within a week they plundered more than one hundred parish and abbey churches. On 16 August, for instance, these iconoclasts entered Ypres. They held the town for two days and not a single church was left undamaged. The image-breakers also rapidly crossed the boundaries of the old county of Flanders. In less than a week after the disturbances at Steenvoorde they were wreaking havoc in the area round Tournai. However, the iconoclasts were not always able to carry out their plans: the gates of Lille and St Omer remained closed to them on the orders of the town magistrates who had been forewarned of their approach. After about ten days the first wave of iconoclasm, which had radiated out from south-western Flanders, gradually subsided.

The second round

Meanwhile, the second round had already started in Antwerp, at that time the largest and wealthiest city in the Netherlands. On 18 August, as was customary on the Sunday after Ascension, the statue of Mary was carried in procession. On this occasion bystanders ridiculed it. Two days later there was a disturbance in the cathedral during Vespers. Almost immediately afterwards about two hundred men entered the church and destroyed its contents. Later that evening they split up into a number of smaller groups and spread through the city plundering the remaining churches, monasteries, chapels and religious houses. In Antwerp, then, unlike in south-west Flanders, the iconoclasm was carried out according to a preconceived plan. Leaders of the Reformed community had given precise instructions to the perpetrators, who were mainly from lower down the social scale. A number of merchants had even hired image-breakers to do the work.

Although news of the fury in south-west Flanders had already reached Antwerp on 16 August, the city magistrates had done almost nothing to prevent similar events in their city. So when the disturbance in the cathedral got out of hand, they were unprepared and reacted in panic. Fearing for their lives, they initially barricaded themselves into the town hall. Only after it became clear that the number of image-breakers was relatively small and that they were not plundering at random but deliberately targeting religious institutions did the magistrates attempt to regain some kind of control. On 27 August the first of the looters were executed. On the following day the magistracy declared that from then on anyone insulting a Catholic would be punished. They also made it an offence to disturb Catholic services, which had again been resumed.

But by then many of the Antwerp iconoclasts had already left the city and were taking part in the fury elsewhere. Antwerpers, for instance, destroyed the church of the abbey of St Barnabas near Hemiksem on 21 August. Antwerpers were also among the instigators of the image-breaking that broke out in Ghent on 22 August. And the same applies to the iconoclasm in Mechelen, Breda, Turnhout and Eindhoven. Often, too, news of the iconoclastic fury was spread by merchants. As early as 23 August, traders in the Amsterdam stock exchange were displaying fragments of marble and alabaster from Antwerp's statues and altars. And on that same afternoon, the baptism of some children at a Catholic ceremony in the nearby Oude Kerk (Old Church) provoked the destruction of saints' images. In a number of other places such as 's-Hertogenbosch, Middelburg, Leiden and Utrecht im-

Victims of iconoclasm: a heavily damaged sandstone altarpiece (c.1500) in Jan van Arkel's burial chapel in Utrecht Cathedral. Photo by Annemarie Deblaere.

age-breaking followed the Antwerp model. In these and many other towns in the core provinces of the Netherlands, churches were looted during the last week of August and the first week of September 1566.

Concessions

It was not until the second half of September that the iconoclastic fury reached the north-eastern provinces of the Netherlands: Gelre, Friesland, Overijssel, Drenthe, Groningen and the Ommelands. These lands had only become a part of the Burgundian-Habsburg territorial complex a few decades earlier and the central government in Brussels had relatively little control over the local administrators. Heretics could not yet be pursued as energetically as in the core provinces. Consequently, people with heterodox ideas could remain active within the traditional Catholic church for far longer, so that the crystallised doctrines of Calvin initially held little attraction for these border provinces. The nature of the iconoclastic fury was therefore much more random than in the core provinces. Where iconoclasts did force their way into churches, it was often at the instigation of the local authorities. Now that the already tenuous authority of the Brussels government appeared on the point of collapse, they dared to bring their Protestant sympathies into the open.

Towards the end of August, persuaded by the magnate faction and compelled by circumstances, the Regent Margaret of Parma made far-reaching concessions to the members of the Compromise. Protestants obtained the

Pieter Bruegel the Elder, *Massacre of the Innocents*. 1567. Panel, 116 x 160 cm. Kunsthistorisches Museum, Vienna. Some art historians consider this painting to be the artist's reflection on the Spanish repression following the religious revolt.

right to organise 'hedge preaching', but only in the vicinity of those towns where they had already been active before the Fury had broken out. The higher nobility, as stadholders of the various provinces, were supposed to supervise this condition and make sure that it was observed. Of all the stadholders, the Prince of Orange made the greatest concessions to the Protestants. On 2 September he granted both the Calvinist and Lutheran communities three plots of land within Antwerp's walls where they could hold religious meetings. Antwerp ministers, in contrast to their colleagues elsewhere, could now openly baptise children, conduct weddings and celebrate Holy Communion.

Restoring order

This arrangement in Antwerp was interpreted by Protestants throughout the Netherlands as presaging the universal legalisation of their church communities. But Margaret of Parma never sanctioned it. On the contrary, with the cooperation of Lamoraal van Egmond and others she was able gradually to bring the situation in the Netherlands under control. Supported by most of the higher nobility and many townsmen who had been shocked by the radical nature of the iconoclastic fury, Margaret withdrew her concessions to the Calvinists. In March 1567 her troops regained control of Valenciennes, the last Protestant stronghold. The coming of the Duke of Alva at the head of ten thousand troops with instructions from Philip II to restore order had in fact become superfluous. But Alva was already on the way with his army. Moreover, he believed that the troublesome Netherlanders needed to be taught a lesson. Many Reformed Protestants who had been involved in the Fury and feared reprisals again fled abroad. The more militant among them would later return as Sea Beggars or as soldiers in the army of the Prince of Orange.

Motives

These, then, were the main events; but one question still remains. What really motivated these iconoclasts? There is no simple answer. People from every level of society took part in the iconoclastic fury. Some were paid to break images, while others were well-to-do merchants or local dignitaries. Some were even members of the nobility.

Protestant preachers manipulated their audiences; and naturally they made the most of the prevailing discontent. There was a serious economic crisis in the summer of 1566. In the textile towns of south-western Flanders there was widespread unemployment, and after two failed harvests and the interruption of international trade food prices reached unprecedented levels. Sebastiaan Matte's criticisms of the Church's wealth struck a ready chord among hungry proletarian audiences. Calvinists did not storm the churches just because winter was approaching and they needed large buildings in which to meet on Sundays.

Certainly for the zealous and often well-educated preachers the fury had a deeper significance. Religious images can exercise a profound attraction for believers and this almost always develops into a cult. When ministers are unable to channel such a cult they see it as undermining their authority. The three great monotheistic religions all condemn in principle the worship of divine images. The actions of the Taliban against statues of Buddha show how deeply that aversion can be felt by religious leaders, even in the modern world. The objections of Jews and Christians to such worship is formulated in various parts of the Old Testament (e.g. Exodus 20.4 and Deuteronomy 4.15); and in their quest for scriptural purity preachers tried to follow all its injunctions. Naturally the symbols of transubstantiation, bread and wine, had to go. By pouring the liquid out of the cup and feeding the bread to the birds, the iconoclasts sought to destroy the power of those symbols and deprive them of all mystical content. As a result of this, the purged, almost naked, churches were forced to begin again. It was as if the centuries of corruption and idolatry that separated the early Christian era and the Reformation had been washed away. In short, by destroying images and desecrating the host the reformers drew a sharp dividing line between themselves and the rest of society. Their vision of their goal was unwavering, which is why during the decades that followed they would emerge as the most outspoken opponents of Philip II and resist every attempt to subject them again to his authority.

HANS COOLS
Translated by Chris Emery.

BIBLIOGRAPHY

CREW, P.M., *Calvinist Preaching and Iconoclasm in the Netherlands, 1544-1569* (Cambridge Studies in Early Modern History). Cambridge etc., 1978.

DEYON, S. and A. LOTTIN, *Les 'casseurs' de l'été 1566. L'iconoclasme dans le Nord.* Lille, 1986².

DUKE, A., 'De calvinisten en de "paapse beeldendienst". De denkwereld van de beeldenstormers in 1566'. In: BRUGGEMAN, M. *et al.* (eds.), *Mensen van de Nieuwe Tijd. Een liber amicorum voor A.Th. van Deursen.* Amsterdam, 1996, pp. 29-45.

FREEDBERG, D., 'De kunst en de beeldenstorm, 1525-1580. De Noordelijke Nederlanden'. In: FILEDT KOK, J.P. *et al.* (eds.), *Kunst voor de beeldenstorm. Noordnederlandse kunst, 1525-1580.* The Hague, 1986, pp. 39-68.

GOOSENS, A., *Les inquisitions modernes dans les Pays-Bas méridionaux (1520-1633),* 2 vols. Brussels, 1997-1998,

MARNEF, G., 'The dynamics of Reformed militancy in the Low Countries: the Wonderyear'. In: AMOS, N.S., PETTEGREE, A. and NIEROP, H. VAN (eds.), *The Education of a Christian Society. Humanism and the Reformation in Britain and the Netherlands* (St Andrews Studies in Reformation History). Aldershot etc., 1999, pp. 193-210.

SCHEERDER, J., *De beeldenstorm.* Bussum, 1978².

WOLTJER, J.J. and MOUT, M.E.H.N., 'Settlements: The Netherlands'. In: BRADY, T.A., OBERMAN, H.A. and TRACY, J.D. (eds.), *Handbook of European History. 1400-1600. Late Middle Ages, Renaissance, and Reformation. Volume II. Visions, Programs, and Outcomes.* Grand Rapids, 1996², p. 386-415.

Not

a Church Tower in Sight

The Secularisation of the Netherlands

Wim T. Schippers,
Drienerlo Tower. 1979.
Photo courtesy of
Universiteit Twente.

On 6 March 2001, the national Dutch newspaper *De Volkskrant* published an interview with the Archbishop of Utrecht, Cardinal A. Simonis. The interview was announced on the front page under a heading taken from a statement by the Cardinal himself: '*Purple is banishing religion*'. 'Purple' is the name given to the coalition of socialists, liberals and liberal democrats that has been governing the Netherlands since 1994, the first government since 1918 without any Christian representation. (The Catholic party, formerly a separate entity, merged with two Protestant parties in 1973 to form a single party, the CDA or Christian Democrats). The 'purple coalition' had come about as a result of the staggering losses suffered by the CDA in the 1994 elections. Simonis' complaint was that the government was ignoring the churches entirely; the Christian faith seemed to have not the slightest influence on government policy. So the Prime Minister and the Cardinal got together over a traditional Dutch cup of coffee to discuss the Catholic allegation. Not long afterwards, the mayor of Amsterdam officiated at the first gay marriage and the euthanasia act was passed in the First Chamber, the Netherlands' upper house, with the Christian parties and the smaller extreme left parties voting against.

The Cardinal was both correct and incorrect. The government is indeed failing to take Christian thinking into account, or rather the interests of Christian thinking as represented in Parliament by the Christian parties, which are in opposition. You might say that that's the way it goes in politics – if the government's disregard for the churches wasn't almost symbolic of the disappearance of every scrap of Christian influence, as represented by the churches, in public life. The Netherlands has become a pagan country, or to be exact a post-Christian country. There's no denying that, not even after two cups of coffee. The process of secularisation has taken about thirty-five years to complete, and it's most marked among the Catholics. According to recent data, only ten percent of the Netherlands' Catholics still go to church on Sunday. Among the Protestant denominations (there are two large Protestant churches and many smaller ones, varying in orthodoxy and strictness) that figure hasn't dropped quite so drastically.

Reconstruction of the altar in a hidden Catholic attic church in Amsterdam. Ons Lieve Heer op Solder, Amsterdam.

Closed ranks

For centuries, the Netherlands has officially been a Protestant country. Other religions, including the Catholic, were tolerated, but they were forced to live sequestered lives. It wasn't until the mid-nineteenth century, when the Catholic hierarchy was restored in the Netherlands (almost at the same time as it was in England and under as much protest), that Catholics could practise their religion openly and hold public functions. The Catholic faith became a religion of emancipation in the Netherlands; Catholics had to shake off centuries of deprivation. This not only drew the Catholic community together, it also filled them with enormous fervour. The character of the Dutch Church became highly ultramontane, with the Pope being the object of great devotion. The beliefs that were preached put great stress on morality, especially sexual morality. Priestly vocations were extremely numerous, and vocations to the religious life – for women and men – were equally so. During the first half of the twentieth century the Netherlands produced the greatest number of missionaries in proportion to its population, sending them all over the world. Countless churches were built in cities and villages, mostly in the neo-gothic style and many of them very large: the triumph over centuries of practising the faith in secret. The community of faith was a closed one; people segregated themselves among 'their own kind', especially in the north where, in contrast to the south, Catholics had always been in the minority. A comparable focusing on identity occurred among other population groups as well – Protestants and socialists. Thus developed the

typically Dutch 'pillar system', which was manifest in every area of life: politics, education, the radio (and later television), health care and even literature.

It could be argued that there has been very little development, certainly within the Catholic faith. Until the second half of the twentieth century, it was abundantly clear that its period of ascension had been the nineteenth. This meant that great emphasis was placed on observing commandments and obligations within the collective, under the authority of the clergy. There was hardly any appeal to the individual sense of responsibility, as there was among the Protestants. In such a closed community, self-satisfaction was no stranger.

Dutch Protestantism had already had a taste of modernism and had entered into a confrontation with the 'outside world' in the nineteenth century, exactly when the Catholics had just stepped into public life. The result was the separation of the more orthodox groups. Modernist tendencies had also manifested themselves in the Catholic Church at the start of the nineteenth century, but they were suppressed. The ranks were kept closed, which may have proved fatal: it led to isolation.

K.J.C. Verlaan, *Service of the Seceders.* c.1910. Canvas, 82 x 106 cm. Rijksmuseum Het Catharijneconvent, Utrecht. In 1843 a group of traditional Calvinists, led by a number of ministers, split from the Dutch Reformed Church – a move they regarded not as a separation but as a return to the old seventeenth-century Reformed Church of Dordrecht (see p. 144).

Porous walls

What applies to the Catholic Church as a whole applies to the Dutch Catholic Church as well: ever since the eighteenth century, the entire culture had

Drawing of a Dutch
Catholic procession, by
Petrus van Geldrop
(1872-1955).

been developing independently of the Church. This process continued
through the nineteenth century, and in the twentieth it moved so fast that by
the fifties the split between Church and what I call 'the world' was complete. The cultural language as it exists outside the church walls – in literature, in the visual arts, in music – is entirely different from the language
within. At the root of this situation is the fact that the break with major cultural traditions was never greater than in the twentieth century. The arts
seem to have started from scratch in many respects. Such a development is
certain to ignore church culture, which by its nature is embedded in a tradition encompassing the last twenty centuries. The isolation seems complete.

In the end, the emancipation of Dutch Catholics was one of the causes of
the Church's decline. No longer were the seminaries the exclusive, strongly
protective centres of secondary and higher education. Catholic secondary
schools were established everywhere, and in 1923 a Catholic University was
founded in Nijmegen. Growth isn't something you can tie down. Openings
to the outside world began to appear in the Church's intellectual and cultural isolation, and the faith proved unable to seal them back up. Its efforts only
made the openings bigger. Starting in the 1960s, great pieces of the wall –
which had become porous long before – began to fall away.

What very gradual process had led to this porosity? The massive abandonment of the Church that has been taking place since the late sixties cannot be explained without looking at prior history. I think one of the major
causes was the absence of any profound spirituality. The Catholic faith had
been reduced to a small number of obligations: attendance at mass on Sunday, confession and reception of Communion at least once a year (around
Easter), not eating meat on Friday and fasting on fast days, to name a few.
Simplifying the faith to the keeping of five commandments turns it into
a faith of externals – and of minimalism. No shirking of obligations without

the threat of punishment. That the obligations were able to survive for a long time was due to the fear of punishment and Hell. A system of obligations turns believers into a collective group, and very little was done to minister to individual spiritual needs. But the fear of damnation began to give way and it became possible to fulfil the so-called Sunday obligation on Saturday as well – a decision by Rome that may have had more far-reaching repercussions than any other because it made all the other obligations seem deferrable, too, until they were just swept aside, almost as a matter of course. It was then that Catholics began to leave the Church, not just individually, of course, but collectively. For many of them the religion of obligation had had little content, so that leaving caused them no pain. The only change was in their external circumstances. The big question may be whether their faith had ever meant as much to the Catholics as the success figures from the thirties, forties and fifties suggested. For many Protestants, with their personal responsibility and their personal relationship with God, abandoning religion was an agonising process, in keeping with the seriousness of their belief.

A people with a poor memory

For many, the cultural rift placed them in an almost schizophrenic situation. People felt that they belonged to two irreconcilable worlds, and the modernisation of the liturgy failed to bring about a reconciliation. Even worse, the high-handed approach to the search for new forms drove many more traditional believers out of the Church. An entire generation was in exile, churchless, left alone with their memories. A wilfulness similar to that involved in liturgical change became visible in the Dutch Catholic archdiocese. The Netherlands seemed to be leading the field in everything: in their view of the dominating central power of Rome (and only thirty years earlier

Catholic procession, Eijsden, 14 June 1998. Photo by Marie Cécile Thijs. (From *Roomse Rituelen*. Ad Donker, Rotterdam; mariececilethijs.com.)

The austere church of the Benedictine abbey in Mamelis near Vaals. It was designed by architect-monk Hans van der Laan.

the church had been ultramontane!), of the place of the laity in the Church, and of the value and worthlessness of priestly celibacy. Conclusions were drawn from the Second Vatican Council that were far from the conclusions being drawn in Rome. What was most devastating, in my opinion, was the questioning of the *sense* of almost everything. 'Sense' is easily identified with 'usefulness'. Not only are the Dutch a highly practical people, but their culture is characterised by the absence of a feeling for tradition – unlike that of, say, the English or the French. The Dutch have the worst memories in Europe. In fact, the Dutchman is a 'momentalist'. I believe that this momentalism, combined with the conviction that upon examination religious values and practices serve no useful purpose, has been partly responsible for the massive departure from the Church. It cannot be denied that the many priests and religious who have abandoned their vocations have impressed the laity with the seeming ease with which they did it.

Naturally, what happened in the churches cannot be separated from what was happening throughout the Netherlands from the mid-sixties on: a revolt against every kind of authority and a struggle to break free of it. As usual, the arts led the way. In revolutionary movements in poetry and the visual arts, traditions and norms that had seemed indisputable were done away with. These movements took place within a highly conformist society (in the Netherlands, the pre-war spirit seemed to have survived the war). It wasn't until the sixties that the freedom and anarchy of the arts got the society they had envisioned. The conclusions were drawn. The gentlemen's hats, professors' berets, policemen's caps and priests' and bishops' birettas were blown to smithereens. The word 'control' was the '*liberté*' of this revolution. Every group found itself participating in this craving for control, and pillarised Dutch society began to break down. The late date at which this all took place (in the Netherlands, the nineteenth century continued deep into the twentieth) explains the vehemence and somewhat exaggerated character of many of the movements involved. And the small size of the Netherlands is the reason why so many movements were affected. Amsterdam, a city with a mind of its own throughout Dutch history, did its best to set an example.

Religion *à la carte*

Society and the Church, always governed from above, began to feel the power from 'below' (and it goes without saying not for the first time). At first ecclesiastical authority – from the parish priest to the archbishop – was just under pressure; then it began to lose its power altogether. Increasingly, the Catholic Church found that its hierarchy seemed to be suspended in a vacuum. The grassroots had discovered personal responsibility, which developed into what I call a philosophical eclecticism, or a religious eclecticism as regards church life. This was reinforced by the growing sense of individualism during the 1990s, a quality whose influence is only absent today among football supporters (sport as the new church – that's a whole new chapter). Many people who say they're still religious are selecting from a variety of spiritual goods based on usefulness or on what matches their particular feelings. Many Dutch people have put together a religion *à la carte*, with choices made more from the dessert trolley rather than the main course menu. Most people are completely indifferent. Personally, I think that what is called tolerance is in fact indifference; and that ties up with the above-mentioned momentalism of the Dutch culture.

This entire history is necessary to understand the present situation. It all boils down to the fact that within the society and culture of the Netherlands today the churches have almost no authority, nor are they able to compel it, not even at the level of the religious leadership. It should also be noted that because of the very large influx of immigrants from Surinam, Turkey and Morocco and many other countries, Dutch culture is becoming more and more heterogeneous. It's far from simple. The whole world is represented, and both the Church and all of Christian culture occupy only a small place within it.

The only thing that has managed to remain intact in the Netherlands is anti-Papism, which seems fiercer than ever but at the same time betrays a Don Quixote character: more and more protest against something that no longer exists.

The last of the faithful

The history of a single place may be better at proving my point than theories

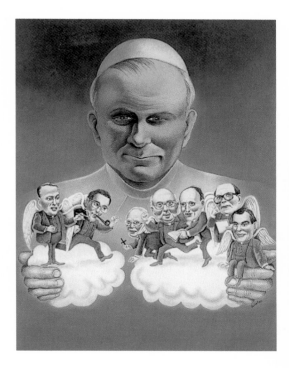

John Valentine's cover illustration for the Catholic weekly *De Tijd* (11 January 1980): the Pope tries to gather the Dutch bishops, his 'fallen angels'.

'*The feeling you want to share*': advertisement which was part of a campaign mounted by the Catholic Broadcasting Organisation KRO in 2000.

het gevoel dat je wilt delen

The Chinese Buddhist temple on Zeedijk in Amsterdam. It was officially opened by Queen Beatrix in 2000.

and speculations. I'll choose my most personal spot: the church of my youth. My church was located in a very densely populated neighbourhood of Amsterdam. It was built around 1924, and its first priest would later become bishop of Haarlem. The building seated eleven hundred. Many young Catholic couples came to live in the area around the church, my parents among them. Gradually, the church became the centre of the neighbourhood, regardless of the number of non-Catholics who came to live there. Nearby were a Catholic nursery school and girls' school, both run by nuns, who lived in great numbers in a huge convent. At late mass on Sundays the church was packed, attended by what in retrospect turned out to have been a largely faceless mass coming to fulfil their obligation. The church calendar imposed shape on time, both inside the church and at home. In the forties and fifties the church had five priests.

My mother, who remained in the neighbourhood for a considerable time, lived to see the beginning of the drop in church attendance. More and more of the eleven hundred places in the church remained unoccupied and the number of priests grew smaller. New people moved into the neighbourhood, people who had no contact with any church, and later many people from other countries who now even form the majority. About twelve years ago I went back to the church one Sunday. I sat there with only a handful of people, many of them reliable churchgoers whom I recognised from the past, now grey and elderly. These were the last of the faithful, the remains of what had been – or rather, had seemed to be – a blooming community (the number had been keeping up appearances far too long). The church is now closed, the convent was locked up years ago (religious communities now mostly consist of elderly members). Another decade, and all traces of what was once a vigorous monastic life in the Netherlands will have disappeared.

My church will be demolished, as so many other churches in Amsterdam, and indeed throughout the Netherlands, have been closed or demolished in recent decades, including some built less than forty years ago in new neighbourhoods. One of the largest mosques in Amsterdam was once a Jesuit church. Islam is the only religion that is growing in the Netherlands. On Friday evenings you can see many Muslim men on their way to the mosque. Sunday has changed from the Lord's Day to 'koopzondag' – 'shopping

Sunday'. And many people are completely ignorant of the meaning of most Christian holidays.

Not a word of regret

Perhaps the most bewildering thing is this: the ease and the noiselessness with which this total change has taken place. Naturally this applies to our whole social existence, in which the year of my birth, 1929, seems closer to the seventeenth century than to the twenty-first. And perhaps the noiselessness of secularisation is less bewildering than the way it was accepted as a matter of course. This must mean that the roots in the sacred soil did not run very deep. The process began with the defection of the working class, evident from early on, and later of the intellectuals. The middle classes held out the longest.

It's easy enough to say that material prosperity has taken the place of faith, setting economic riches against spiritual poverty. It's undeniable: the structure of life in anticipation of a hereafter remains the same, except that now the hereafter is what comes after one's working life is over. And advertisements which in every respect recall the language of the old-time sale of indulgences promote the paradise of the carefree life as up for sale. 'Enjoy life' – that's what it's all about. The notorious frugality of Calvinism seems to have disappeared.

The only possible explanation for what has taken place is that the structure of Church and faith have simply become historical. And since the structure is regarded as the substance, the faith disappeared along with the ageing of the structure. None of my numerous friends and acquaintances, once Catholic or Protestant, has ever uttered a word of regret. It was nice as long as it lasted. Their children still recognise the inside of the church, but they left it very early on. Their grandchildren will be the first with absolutely no memory of religion or church. Then secularisation will be complete. Not a church tower in sight. We'll be the Low Countries once and for all – except for the pointed towers of the minarets; they're growing thick and fast.

New towers in the Netherlands: the Sultan Ahmet mosque in Delft. This Turkish mosque was built in 1995.

KEES FENS
Translated by Nancy Forest-Flier.

ʻF^{rom}

‘Do you believe in God?’ to ‘What makes

your life meaningful?’

Unbelief in the Netherlands

In the sixteenth century perhaps 18,000 unbelievers were tortured and executed in the Low Countries. However, ‘unbeliever’ in these times did not really mean that one was an atheist. In pre-modern times the Dutch equivalents of ‘atheist’, ‘unbeliever’ and ‘infidel’ were often used to denounce people who believed in the Christian or Jewish God, yes, but not in the right way (according to the speaker, of course). The execution of heretics in the sixteenth century was ordered by the Roman Catholic Spanish Emperor and those concerned were Protestants, hardly atheists. Up to 1850 atheism, in the sense of publicly not believing in the Christian God at all, was very much an exceptional phenomenon in the Netherlands.

Before 1850 only a few individual Dutch men and women had concluded that the Jewish and Christian God did not exist. Mostly they continued to use the word ‘God’ to refer to something they thought really important, but this God had little to do with the God of almost all of their contemporaries. The seventeenth-century heretics Uriel Acosta, Adriaan Koerbagh and Baruch de Spinoza were some of the first and most important ‘unbelievers’. Spinoza’s *Ethica*, especially, influenced many later freethinkers. However important these individuals were in the history of ideas, they were controversial exceptions in their own society. They needed courage to be different and often had tragic lives (Acosta committed suicide after being ostracised and humiliated, Koerbagh died in prison because of his beliefs). Until the middle of the nineteenth century atheism and rejection of Christianity was something for individuals and very small groups. Only in the second half of the nineteenth century did atheism and leaving the Church become important social phenomena.

Johannes van Vloten (1818-1883), an early militant Dutch atheist. Part of photo opposite title page of: M. Mees-Verwey, *De betekenis van Johannes van Vloten. Een bibliografie met inleiding* (Santpoort, 1928).

Eduard Douwes Dekker (1820-1887) aka Multatuli, writer and hero of late nineteenth-century Dutch freethinkers and atheists, in 1875. Photo by Wegner and Mottu.

De Dageraad: an atheist David versus a Christian Goliath

De Dageraad, which means ‘dawn’ or ‘sunrise’, developed into the first atheist organisation in the Netherlands. It was founded in Amsterdam on 12 October 1856, and most of its founders were scientifically-minded deists. They felt that God will reveal Himself when nature is investigated scientifically and assumed, like Voltaire, that there had to be a God to explain the cosmos. In matters of politics they were conservative liberals. Once founded, De Dageraad developed quickly. Charles Darwin's *On the Origin of Species* (1859) proved to be a catalyst for the debate on science and religion, and after 1865 the Netherlands rapidly industrialised, leading to the rise of a socialist labour movement. By 1880 most of the members of De Dageraad were atheists, materialists who admired Jakob Moleschott, Ludwig Büchner and Ernst Haeckel, and socialists with Marxist or anarchist leanings. Often they thought science proved that God did not exist, and often they saw a connection between atheism and socialism. The teacher and social democrat Adriaan Gerhard was one of them. His view can be paraphrased like this: Freethinkers try to destroy the belief of the mass of the common people in a good God and in an afterlife in heaven. The freethinkers' efforts to raise the consciousness of the majority of humanity about their real situation are cruel, Gerhard thought, if at the same time we do not work hard toward a society in which a good life here and now is possible for everybody, not just for the happy capitalist few.

In its long history many courageous and important individuals have been active in and associated with De Dageraad. Apart from Gerhard we will mention only the militant atheist and Spinozist Johannes van Vloten, the important writer Multatuli (Eduard Douwes Dekker), the Darwinian H.H. Hartogh Heys van Zouteveen, the natural scientist and socially committed liberal Pieter C.F. Frowein, the anarchist and political activist Ferdinand Domela Nieuwenhuis, the physician and feminist Aletta Jacobs, the anarchist and anti-militarist Bart de Ligt, the philosopher Leo Polak and the journalist and anarchist Anton Constandse.

De Dageraad has a record as a strongly atheist, antireligious and anti-church organisation engaged in a battle with the Christian majority in the Netherlands. Among the issues it focused on are the importance of science and free inquiry, the non-existence of God, the dangers of religion and mind-policing churches, the separation of Church and state, the value of morals without God and the equal value of a non-religious and a religious oath in court or office. De Dageraad produced a large number of cheap pamphlets, some of which sold many thousands of copies. In the 1920s and 1930s De Dageraad, led by the cabinet-maker Jan Hoving, was able to organise large meetings in theatres where hundreds and hundreds of sympathetically-inclined people turned up. Membership rose to 2,500, 1,200 in Amsterdam alone. In July 1931 Hoving organised a much-publicised propaganda tour into the heart of the Catholic south. De Dageraad's activities were not only directed against religion, but also against capitalism, fascism and Hitler's Nazism. To the dismay of the rather authoritarian Christian government coalition (which wanted to remain friends with Hitler's Germany), in the 1930s the freethinkers of De Dageraad were among the most determined fighters against anti-Semitism wherever it reared its ugly head, in the Netherlands, in Germany, or in the Soviet Union.

De Dageraad's attitude has mostly been that of a minority in a hostile environment. In the latter part of the nineteenth century the number of people in the Netherlands who were not members of a church was very low indeed: 0.1% in 1869 and 2.3% in 1899. In the twentieth century it rose rapidly to 7.8% in 1920 and 17.1% in 1947. De Dageraad no doubt contributed greatly to the social and intellectual undermining of Christian belief in the Netherlands, especially before World War II. In 1957 De Dageraad changed its name to De Vrije Gedachte, meaning 'free thought'. Now it is a small organisation with less than a thousand members. After 1945 its role as the main organisation of 'unbelievers' was taken over by the Humanistisch Verbond.

Humanistisch Verbond: emancipation and identity

The Humanistisch Verbond (HV; Humanist League) was founded on 17 February 1946. The founders of the HV were of the opinion that De Dageraad put too much emphasis on the negative and unproductive fight against religion, whilst the main aim of the Verbond was to raise the consciousness of the non-religious part of the population to the level of a spiritually thought-out and morally justified world-view. De Dageraad had reached a dead end, and a new organisation was needed to unite and inspire the one and a half million Dutch who adhered to no religious faith. Membership of the new humanist organisation grew rapidly till it reached about 12,000 in 1956, and up to now it has remained between 12,000 and 16,000. Important individuals connected with the Humanistisch Verbond were the teacher and PvdA (Labour Party) politician J.P. van Praag, the social democrat and professor of Dutch Garmt Stuiveling, the radical socialist philosopher H.J. Pos, the first humanist spiritual counsellor Cees Schonk and the sociologist and prominent homosexual Rob Tielman.

KARAKTER EN AANLEG
IN VERBAND MET HET
ONGELOOF

DR. H. C. RÜMKE

TWEEDE DRUK

W. TEN HAVE N.V. · AMSTERDAM

Testimony to a bygone era: H.C. Rümke, *Character and Disposition in Connection with Unbelief* (Karakter en aanleg in verband met het ongeloof), second, slightly revised edition, Amsterdam, 1943. Rümke was a professor of psychiatry at the State University of Utrecht. The first edition of this popular booklet was published in 1939 as number 8 in the series 'The Psychology of Unbelief'. In opposition to Freud, Rümke defended the thesis that not believing in a personal God is a mental disorder. T.T. ten Have published an unbeliever's reply.

The history of the HV can be divided into two phases. In the period 1946-1965 it pursued a successful emancipation struggle on behalf of non-Christian humanists, and of atheists and agnostics in general. In 1965 this mission can be said to have been completed. Important to this success were the always very strategically formed board of the HV and its lobbying activities, but the decisive factor, of course, was the rapidly increasing number of people in the Netherlands who were not members of a church: 21% in 1960, 33% in 1966, 43% in 1979, 50% in 1980, 57% in 1991 and 63% in 1999. The Netherlands had ceased to be a Christian nation. Atheists were no longer regarded as second-rate citizens and as people without morals or conscience.

The period from 1966 to the present day can be characterised as the period in which the Humanistisch Verbond attempted to find a new mission, a new humanist programme. This was difficult because after 1965 Dutch society at large was very much a humanist society. J. P. van Praag, president from 1946 till 1969, tried – largely unsuccessfully – to present the struggle against nihilism, against not having any world-view at all, as the main task now, and one which would appeal to the general public. Personally he had always thought this to be the main issue, 'the big fight'. What was most important, he thought, is that people should have a conscious world-view, which can be humanist, Christian, Muslim or something else. The real danger is the mass of nihilists, 'unbelievers' in the true sense, who not only do not believe in the Christian God but who do not believe in any serious set of principles, values and purposes at all. In his view Hitler had come to power because too many people had no well-thought-out guiding principles and

J.P. van Praag (1911-1981), co-founder and president of the Humanistisch Verbond. Photo taken around 1975.

'*Believing in human beings starts with yourself*' ('Geloven in mensen begint bij jezelf'), a sticker distributed by the Humanistisch Verbond, probably in the second half of the 1980s.

had not made up their minds about what is really important in human life. While Van Praag's ideas may have been very sensible, the fact is that the Verbond did not grow to become the large organisation of 100,000 members he had envisaged. Rob Tielman's presidency of the Verbond (1976-1986) was probably the most successful one after 1965. He gave the HV a clear identity as the organisation which promoted a world-view centred on the principle of individual self-determination, and which crusaded in favour of legalising abortion and euthanasia and against discrimination against homosexuals. These moral and political priorities of the HV were very well adapted to the views of its members and leadership, which included leading politicians like the conservative liberal Frits Bolkestein and the social democrat Klaas de Vries. The humanists and the non-Christian political parties in the Netherlands were divided on important issues like the arms race or social inequality, but on desirable changes in laws and attitudes regarding abortion, euthanasia and homosexuality they were very much united. After Tielman's presidency this limited but clear and relevant identity of the HV lapsed into vagueness. The continuing search for a new mission became even more difficult (but perhaps also easier because it was now almost inevitable) when in 1994, for the first time since 1918, the Netherlands got a government coalition in which no Christian party participated. Many Dutch people were confirmed in their idea that there was no longer any need for a HV after the successful struggle for emancipation.

Comparing the Humanistisch Verbond with De Dageraad, one might say that the main difference is that the HV – and Jaap van Praag at its centre – always felt that it represented a large part and possibly the majority of Dutch society. The HV always wanted to be integrated into normal Dutch society, whereas De Dageraad was always kicking against other groups and what it saw as the dominant culture.

Frames of meaning today

The current social and cultural situation in the Netherlands is such that talking about belief and unbelief is reminiscent of a bygone past. It refers to a society in which Dutch men and women as a rule were Christian believers, and some exceptional people deviated from this norm. Dutch society at present is an inter- and multicultural society in which only 37% of citizens are members of a church or regard themselves as Muslims. Becker and De Wit forecast that in 2010 this percentage will have fallen to 33%. That 33% will be made up of 13% Roman Catholics, 13% Protestants and 6% Muslims (mainly of Turkish, Moroccan or Surinamese descent). But there is more. In 1999, 45 to 60% of church members only went to church a few times a year or not at all. Between 1979 and 1995 the number of men and women who were members of a Christian church but did not subscribe to the central tenets of the Christian belief, increased substantially. Since 1985 the group of non-believing church members is even larger than the group of traditional Christian believers in the churches.[1] We may be moving towards a situation in which the large churches have disappeared and what remains is a large number of smaller churches with a more conscious, convinced and 'orthodox' membership. And what do those Dutch people who are not members of a church believe? Less than 10% of them have traditional Christian beliefs. The others have (implicit) beliefs about what is important in life, about purposes and values, about maintaining some control over one's life, about retaining one's self-respect and personal identity. They are certainly interested in what makes their lives meaningful. They are no nihilists. They want to decide for themselves what they believe in. They belong to all kinds of organisations, but not to organisations which provide them with an all-encompassing world-view. One might say that they all have a 'frame of meaning' ('*zingevingskader*', as the Dutch call it), but only some have a 'world-view' ('*levensbeschouwing*'), to spell out the relative difference. A frame of meaning is a set of experiences, principles, values and views which makes the person concerned feel that her or his life is meaningful. This set may be largely implicit and have only a limited coherence, but it is there and it works. A world-view is a meaning frame which one is more conscious of, which is made more explicit, and of which one has tried to improve the internal consistency and external relevance. Frames of meaning and world-views may be highly personal, but to some degree they may also be shared by many others.[2] To say that most of the Dutch are 'unbelievers' does not make much sense. But their 'belief', 'faith', 'frame of meaning', 'life-stance' or 'world-view' is very hard to pin down, often also for themselves.

A few things can be said about the 'contents' of these frames of meaning. Research by Felling and others has shown that since 1979 the Dutch in general have come to regard traditional family ties and the traditional division of labour between men and women as less important. On the other hand they now judge to be more important: their own careers, freedom to enjoy life, freedom of speech and expression, and individual freedom in matters of life and death (think of abortion and euthanasia, both of which are now regulated by legislation that accords with the views of the HV). Late-modern Dutch 'believers' (atheists, agnostics and the majority of church members) welcome these changes in the climate of opinion. Traditional Christian believers have come to be the 'other-believing' minority and often object to these changes. David has become Goliath, and vice versa, and both have changed in the process.

PETER DERKX

NOTES

1. Traditional Christian belief here means that one believes in a God who concerns Himself with each human being personally, and also that one argues about and interprets the meaning of life, suffering, death and the problem of good and evil within the framework of this belief in God. See Felling, Peters and Scheepers (2000), p. 69.
2. Having defined these terms, we can now say that J.P. van Praag thought it very important for a society that most people should develop their largely implicit frames of meaning into conscious world-views, and share and discuss them with others.

BAUMEISTER, ROY F., *Meanings of Life*. New York, 1991.

BECKER, J.W. and J.S.J. DE WIT, *Secularisatie in de jaren negentig. Kerklidmaatschap, veranderingen in opvattingen en een prognose*. The Hague, 2000.

DERKX, PETER and BERT GASENBEEK (eds.), *J.P. van Praag. Vader van het moderne Nederlandse humanisme*. Utrecht, 1997.

DERKX, PETER, ULLA JANSZ, CORRIE MOLENBERG and CARLA VAN BAALEN (eds.), *Voor menselijkheid of tegen godsdienst?. Humanisme in Nederland, 1850-1960*. Hilversum, 1998.

FELLING, ALBERT, JAN PETERS and PEER SCHEEPERS (eds.), *Individualisering in Nederland aan het eind van de twintigste eeuw. Empirisch onderzoek naar omstreden hypotheses*. Assen, 2000.

HIJMANS, ELLEN J.S., *Je moet er het beste van maken. Een empirisch onderzoek naar hedendaagse zingevingssystemen*. Nijmegen, 1994.

HIORTH, FINNGEIR, *Secularism in the Netherlands, in Belgium, and in Luxembourg*. Oslo, 2000.

NADLER, STEVEN, *Spinoza. A Life*. Cambridge, 1999.

NOORDENBOS, O. and P. SPIGT, *Atheïsme en vrijdenken in Nederland*. Nijmegen, 1976.

PRAAG, J.P. VAN, *Foundations of Humanism*. Buffalo (NY), 1982.

SHADID, W.A.R. and P.S. VAN KONINGSVELD, *Moslims in Nederland. Minderheden en religie in een multiculturele samenleving*. Houten / Diegem, 1997[2].

∴ Don't look, boy, it's a secular humanist! ∴

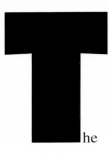
he

Silent Iconoclasm in Flanders

There is really little evidence of 'iconoclasm' as such in the religious life of Flanders today. 'A strange calm after the storm' would be a more apt description. While the year 2000, proclaimed a Holy Year by the Vatican, attracted approximately 30 million pilgrims or tourists to Rome, the number of Flemings among them was meagre indeed. Even before the Second Vatican Council (1962-1965), a noiseless dechristianising had begun in what was once the most Christian region of Europe. It all happened almost naturally, without a great deal of fuss, below the surface.

Most churches attract only a few elderly parishioners for Sunday services, except for funerals. As in almost every other country in Europe, priestly and

religious vocations have been reduced to a handful. Foreign aid workers have taken the place of the once so numerous missionaries. And the processions that used to wind through the streets are no longer a common sight, with Bruges, Veurne and Hasselt among the few rare exceptions. Empty churches are being converted into reception halls or offices.

Frits van den Berghe, *Sunday*. 1924. Canvas, 138.5 x 163 cm. Koninklijke Musea voor Schone Kunsten, Brussels.

Estrangement

This is not to say that the steady disappearance of a confessing 'Christianity' also means the end of the socio-cultural phenomenon known as 'Christendom'. Most people still prefer to mark occasions like birth, marriage and death with a religious rite, since society has not yet come up with anything better in the way of fitting ceremonial. In Flanders, most schools and hospitals fall under the 'Christian umbrella', though the priests and nuns have disappeared. And while most students and hospital patients are in fact no longer believers, most teachers still claim to be Christians – but they belong to an older generation. Even the three Catholic universities, including the University of Leuven, Belgium's largest, have become strongly secularised. The social organisations and movements continue to be overwhelmingly Christian in tone, but more and more of them are becoming open cultural organisations. This whole process has taken place in utter stillness, without shocks, without persecution. Public opinion was quite willing to accept that the Christian people's party (CVP, now CD&V) had declined from a majority party with an almost uninterrupted history of governmental power to a greatly weakened opposition.

How could all this have happened? The reasons are highly diverse and complementary, and some of them are to be found in the Church itself. Belgium has only one form of Christianity, Roman Catholicism, which once exerted a large degree of control over every aspect of existence, as it did in Ireland. But in Flanders this control led to an aggressive clericalism, followed by an equally aggressive anti-clericalism. The numerous new phenomena that could have stimulated creative responses were hardly considered at all. After the Second World War, attendance at secondary schools and especially at institutes of higher learning increased exponentially. The docile flock of the past lost its naïveté. The papal encyclical *Humanae Vitae* (1968), which prohibited the use of artificial contraception, was not in fact accepted, either by believers or by moral theologians or – though they were more cautious – by many bishops. Nevertheless, the encyclical greatly harmed the Church's credibility, even among practising Catholics. As a consequence, the Church lost both its traditional influence and its authority, not only in the realm of sexual life but also in the larger area of bioethics. The Abortion Act was passed by Parliament in 1990, despite the protest of pious King Baudouin. The majority of the population find euthanasia acceptable in terminal cases. The Church has remained silent in the face of widespread economic corruption. There has been no more dialogue between the Church and the scientific community – yet the theory of evolution is widely accepted, so that many people don't know what to make of the creation story and the doctrine of original sin. Furthermore, the results of modern exegesis have seeped into ordinary Bible discussion groups, and many people are beginning to wonder, 'What have they been feeding us, anyway?' A few regrettable cases of paedophilia among priests and religious have attracted media attention, further undermining confidence in

Penitents' procession in Veurne, 2001. Photo courtesy of Dienst voor Toerisme, Veurne.

Refectory, Primary School 'Dames van het Christelijk Onderwijs' (Ladies of Christian Education). Antwerp, 1992. Photo by Annie van Gemert.

Emile Claus, *Solemn Communion*. 1893. Canvas, 82 x 117 cm. Dexia Collection, Brussels.

a clergy already in a high state of alarm.

But it isn't only the attitude of the Church that explains why Christianity has been slipping away. Flanders has become one of the most prosperous areas of Europe, with a great deal of attention being focused on competition in the marketplace and the things money can buy. The Flemish travel a great deal to other parts of the world, and as a result of contact with other religions their own beliefs have become relativised. Because people are living longer they frequently put off asking questions about the meaning of life until they are mentally enfeebled. The average family size is less than two children, and these children enjoy an unprecedented level of prosperity. Christianity for them lies far outside their field of interest. The media – in Flanders more than elsewhere – present only sensational news about the Church, their religious programmes are broadcast outside prime time and they are almost completely silent about the actual religious feelings still present among most of the populace.

Naturally, this evolution is bound up with the profound shift in the political landscape. In the past the Church, both clergy and laity, exercised considerable influence on decisions of a political nature, either directly or through organisational channels. Today, however, the leadership has – quite correctly – stopped influencing political representatives, which in time will lead to a virtual separation of Church and state in almost every aspect of life. Although this may have a negative ring to it, it could become an asset and contribute to the Church's credibility where its essential tasks are at issue.

Confusing pluralism

In the meantime, everything points not only to a further estrangement from the Church but also to a confusing pluralism in the minds of most citizens. The Belgian analysis of the third European value study bore the title *Lost*

Certainty (Verloren Zekerheid, 2001), and with good reason. As in the neighbouring countries of France and the Netherlands, the unchurched are now in the majority. This is not to say that these people are unreligious. The majority vaguely acknowledge a mystery behind existence. They say they still believe in a god, but this god is less and less personal and is always more a kind of life force, an immanent spiritual reality. The number of convinced atheists actually remains very low (as in the rest of Europe, both East and West, where this segment of the population seldom amounts to more than five per cent). Yet the 'agnostics' – those who don't know whether they believe or not – are increasing in number. 'Evil' in particular remains a mystery. As it turns out, many more people claim they believe in sin than in Heaven or Hell. For them, sin means not so much a transgression of the Ten Commandments as a recognition of an inexplicable wickedness in life, the wickedness of other people. This doesn't mean that people who abandon Christianity find spiritual accommodation elsewhere. Free-thinkers are thin on the ground in Flanders, and sects or new religious movements are never successful. In contrast with France, conversions to Islam are very rare, even though sixteen percent of the 18-30-year-olds in Brussels, the capital city of Europe, are Moslems. There has been a trend towards religious syncretism among very small groups, with forms of Buddhism playing a role. One tenet of the 'New Age' movement is reincarnation, but here again, it is not as popular a belief among the Flemish as among other European populations. Most people cook up their own make-shift answer to questions of meaning and morality, without a trace of a solid, well-founded belief structure. Analyses show that a number of practising Catholics believe neither in God nor in life after death, while some atheists do. A considerable number of 'Christians' say they are no longer 'Catholic'. Among practising Catholics there is a rather high percentage who believe both in the resurrection and in reincarnation. In spite of numerous ecclesiastical pronouncements on ethical issues and many social encyclicals, the great majority insist that these documents provide no answers to their questions. Only a minority recognise that the Church ministers to their spiritual needs.

All this is not a specifically Flemish phenomenon; it characterises the whole of Europe. The Flemish religious sociologist Karel Dobbelaere entitled one of his works *The 'People of God' Astray* (Het 'Volk Gods' de mist in, 1988), and for good reason. A footnote is called for at this point. In an anthology edited by the American Lutheran Peter Berger, *The Desecularisation of the World* (1999), the contribution by the British sociologist Grace Davie bears the title 'Europe, the Exception that Proves the Rule'. She points out that, unlike Europe, the other continents are not undergoing a process of secularisation. Like all of Northern Europe at least, Flanders is deeply secularised. The result is undoubtedly an enormous spiritual vacuum characterising the younger generations in particular, while the older generations are struggling with doubt.

Quiet and unpretentious

Is there any light in the darkness? One initial conclusion is unavoidable. Everything that goes on within Christianity or the Church is happening on

A stall at Scherpenheuvel, a Flemish place of pilgrimage. Photo by Daniel Leroy.

a smaller and smaller scale. Attempts to copy major events such as the German Catholic Days invariably result in failure. People are seeking each other out in basic communities and Bible study circles, where belief is being re-interpreted and new forms of liturgy experimented with. The members of these groups experience religion in warm, interpersonal relationships. Some parishes are influenced by this activity and their churches are filling once again. People are visiting monasteries more than they used to, experiencing them as places of freedom and reflection. But these are still exceptions.

Since 1970 the Flemish Church has been running an Interdiocesan Pastoral Consultative Council (*Interdiocesaan Pastoraal Beraad*, or IPB). At first this body was meant to serve as the voice of everything taking place among believers. Then in 1980 disillusionment set in. The bishops, partly under pressure from Rome, refused to adopt any of the numerous proposals for renewal (such as opening up certain ministries to women). The IPB kept asking for more co-responsibility and just as frequently came away empty-handed, as if there were no 'reason' for the belief of the faithful, as if in the Church there could be no chance of a measure of democratisation, when as a matter of fact more and more generous lay people had been undertaking certain tasks themselves. The hierarchy clearly fear polarisation, and the population below the age of fifty regard the Church institution as bankrupt. This does not prevent some sideline activities from enjoying great success, such as the Lenten Action for the Third World, the Advent Action for the poor at home, and many initiatives to offer hospitality to asylum seekers and immigrants. A great number of inspired Christians continue to devote themselves to the aged and the disabled.

In fact there never was a storm. Everything has become quiet and unpretentious. Many are turning back to their circle of family and friends. Any activities that are carried out are generated by small cores of people who believe in the inspiration of the Second Vatican Council and dream of a really dynamic Vatican III. No one knows how the future will evolve, and sociologists are not prophets.

JAN KERKHOFS S.J.
Translated by Nancy Forest-Flier.

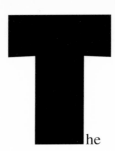he

Road from Enlightenment to Indifference

Unbelief in Flanders

Religious belief and non-belief are among the most complex and difficult phenomena for sociologists to pin down; and the problems are even greater for historians, who often have little or no data to work with. Moreover, even if data are available, this still leaves the question of whether social indicators can ever provide a reliable guide to the reality of religious conviction or its absence. A circumspect approach is therefore essential, especially when evaluating the invective which was once the stock ecclesiastical response to various kinds of nonconformist behaviour. The anathema of godlessness, for example, was frequently pronounced, but its target was not usually atheism as such, but anticlericalism. More specifically, the Church was concerned to discredit anticlericalist criticism of its abuse of religious discourse to obtain political power. As it was, the Counter-Reformation was so successfully implemented in the Southern Netherlands that no such criticism was heard again until the eighteenth century.

The Flemish Enlightenment

The Southern Netherlands were not immune to the impact of the Enlightenment on perceptions of Church and faith. In this connection it is important to note that the later, nineteenth-century, picture of Flanders – 'Poor Flanders'; obscurantist, and backwardly Catholic to the core – should not be projected on to the eighteenth century. At the start of the age of '*la critique universelle*'[1] regions such as Brabant and Flanders were enjoying a growth in agricultural production. Relative prosperity still prevailed, and led to a cultural blossoming. To a surprising degree, this blossoming was as much a rural as an urban phenomenon. The Enlightenment found fertile soil here, as is confirmed by contemporary Flemish and Brabantian private book collections and the host of small-town printers and booksellers who published and stocked both original and Dutch-language editions of Enlightenment literature. Voltaire proved a literary best-seller and was frequently to be found in the repertory of the many local theatre companies that sprang up all over the place.

Many historians do not hesitate to speak in terms of a 'Flemish Enlightenment'[2], as alongside the imported works a vernacular literature emerged, in which periodicals such as the *Vlaamsche Indicateur* stand out. An awakening civil society was stimulated by a series of *sociabilités*, which provided a forum for people from different social groupings to engage in relatively open debate and discussion. Reading circles, salons, literary gatherings and, above all, Freemasons' lodges, also fit into this framework. All of these tend to be perceived as vehicles for the spirit of the Enlightenment, but this generalised view requires some qualification, not least in regard to South Netherlands Freemasonry. Was Flemish Freemasonry really a torchbearer of free-thinking liberalism, or even of unbelief, as was retrospectively held? In fact, any such claim is an anachronism; even in the nineteenth century things were not always quite so cut and dried.

The Enlightenment in Flanders, as elsewhere, was not as a rule an atheist movement. This is borne out by the fact that the writings of Voltaire, a deist, had a wide circulation in the Southern Netherlands, while those of the atheist Diderot did not. Most Flemish and Brabantian followers of the *philosophes* were ideologically aligned with the so-called 'Catholic Enlightenment', then in vogue in Austrian court circles. But in the Southern Netherlands the Church authorities, as ever on the defensive against anticlericalism[3], greeted this trend with endless complaints about lax standards of censorship and rampant godlessness. Anti-clericalism was, of course, a recurrent motif in all Enlightenment literature, and the Southern Netherlands version was quite often extremely acerbic in tone; but one needs a microscope to detect any indication of atheist leanings. Sporadically, one does come across individual cases of someone abjuring God and His heaven and these become more frequent towards the end of the century when rejection of the last sacraments is also first recorded.[4] But this remained very much a marginal phenomenon and was not supported by specific organisations, not

Entrance of the grand temple of Les Amis Philanthropes in Brussels. It was built around 1880 in a kind of 'Egyptian' style. Eastern mysticism was among the interests of a lot of freemasons at the end of the 19th century.

even Freemasonry. The Southern Netherlands lodges, for all the Vatican's indictment of them, were solidly Catholic almost to a man. The fact that they took no notice of Papal bulls [5] did not mean that they were any more susceptible to radical Enlightenment ideas than the rest of society. Analysis of Freemasons' libraries confirms this. Equally revealing in this context is that during the French regime Freemasons were few and far between among the more rabidly anticlerical local jacobin factions.

Militant freethinking

The situation changed entirely during the nineteenth century, when the Masonic lodges did indeed develop into hotbeds of militant freethinking. But this did not happen overnight; until well into the century a surprising number of Freemasons maintained at least outward observance. This state of affairs continued into the 1830s, under mounting pressure from the Church, until a joint statement by the Belgian bishops in 1837 explicitly proclaimed the irreconcilability of Roman Catholicism and Freemasonry. In the end, therefore, the lodges did come to consist exclusively of liberals, who not only became progressively more entrenched in their anticlericalism, but in due course also came to disavow the religious tenets of a Church by which they were anathemised. As a result, Belgian Freemasonry has espoused so-

A la mémoire
d'ARTHUR COËL
époux de Dame Sophie QUÉVRIN
né à Menin le 28 Novembre 1875
et y décédé le 5 Avril 1917.

cial values closely aligned with those of the freethinkers' movement which came to the fore from the 1850s onwards.

The crux of this process of alienation from the Church was the fundamental question of attitudes towards death and final obsequies. Not only did non-believers define their identity by how they died and were buried, but their conception of mortality was often the catalyst in the decision to renounce Catholicism. This worked both ways, of course. On the one hand non-believers and the heterodox were free to repudiate the last sacrament and church burial, but by the same token the Church also had the option of repudiating any particular group or individual. For instance, it could withhold burial rites from a deceased Freemason who might have remained a practising Catholic but had at the same time refused to renounce his lodge membership. As burial in unconsecrated ground carried a social stigma and also posed considerable practical difficulties, it is no coincidence that it was this very issue which stimulated the establishment of the first freethinkers' unions.

The earliest such unions were by no means Masonic initiatives; L'Affranchissement, founded in Brussels in 1854, and its off-shoot Les Solidaires (1857), were both established by artisans with socialist ideas. Organised freethinking remained a mainly working class preserve until 1863, when in the wake of a tremendous rumpus about the secular interment of Pierre-Théodore Verhaegen, a socially prominent Freemason, a group of Brussels bourgeois liberals set up La Libre Pensée. All these associations existed primarily to organise their members' funerals.[6] The Church, predictably, regarded such activities as extraordinarily sinful, and the air was filled with the classic denunciations of them as godless, etc. In actual fact the philosophical motivations underlying repudiation of the last sacraments and church burial varied in their nature. Where the socialistically-orientated freethinkers' unions were for the most part atheist, their bourgeois counterparts were ideologically closer to a vague, masonically-tinted, spiritualism or an indeterminate agnosticism, into which atheism did eventually make headway, but only slowly and gradually.

Initially the spread of militant freethinking in Belgium was confined to the capital and was broadly speaking, though not exclusively, a francophone phenomenon. Among the founding members of L'Affranchissement, for instance, Jan Pellering stands out as a Fleming and native Dutch speaker, though he was by no means the only one.[7] Indeed, the Church authorities were perturbed to observe that the Brussels unions also had members in solidly Catholic Flanders. In due course, though haltingly to begin with, similar organisations started to proliferate in the Flemish cities, which culminated, in 1895, in the establishment of the Vlaamse Vrijdenkersfederatie (Flemish Freethinkers' Federation') and its organ, De Rede (Reason). The original support base was mainly centred in Ghent and Antwerp, but membership also steadily increased in smaller provincial cities such as Bruges, Geraardsbergen, Leuven, Willebroek, and Ostend. Though by the end of the nineteenth century Flanders by no means displayed the degree of secularisation which characterised the Walloon industrial basin, something was definitely fomenting in those regions of Flanders where the second industrial revolution led to the emergence of a young industrial proletariat and a budding socialist workers' movement.[8]

Memorial card of Arthur Coël (1875-1917), a leading Belgian freethinker. Photo courtesy of the author.

Collecting-box of 'L'Affranchissement'. Institut Emile Vandervelde, Brussels.

De Vrijdenker of 13 October 1935, a Flemish weekly for freethinkers, subtitled *'People's weekly for all sensible people'*. Photo courtesy of the autor.

The freethinkers' movement in Flanders spearheaded an alternative way of life which broke completely with ecclesiastical control over the conduct of life's major decisions and rites of passage. Not surprisingly, therefore, the second focus of the movement, after secular burial, became the annual freethinkers' youth festival. Furthermore, the freethinkers were in the vanguard when it came to promoting more liberal sexual mores, as they were also in the struggle for public education, secularisation of the state, and freedom of speech. The movement's membership in Flanders was never more than a small minority; but it created an enduring counter-culture which managed to hold its own through periodic setbacks and occasional patches of organisational weakness. After the Second World War, though, the freethinkers' movement lost ground more and more. In Flanders its traditional preserves were largely taken over by the Humanistisch Verbond (Humanistic League) established in 1951 on the Dutch model, whose guiding ideology focused less on militant atheism than on making a place in society for non-religious people in search of a positive system of ethics.[9]

Religious indifference

The input of the Humanistisch Verbond led to a proliferation of secular humanist associations with a range of activities. In 1971 the Flemish branches of all of these united under a single umbrella organisation, the Unie Vrijzinnige Verenigingen (Union of Secular Humanist Societies). The next major development came in 1993 when the Unie, in concert with its francophone sister organisation, secured the constitutional recognition it needed to put its humanist moral counselling services, which have operated professionally since 1981, on a firm footing. Though official recognition has heightened public awareness of freethinking in Flanders, this does not mean that the secular humanist movement is significantly more powerful than was the classic freethinkers' movement so many decades ago. This is somewhat paradoxical, given that according to 1998 figures [10] post-war secularisation in Flanders has caused church attendance to drop to a bare 12.7% and the number of people generally describing themselves as non-churchgoers (*'onkerkelijken'*) to rise to as much as 36.9%. Yet the situation is less clear-cut than this would suggest, as a considerable proportion of the population continue to practice their religion on an occasional basis, most notably as regards christenings (73.1%) and funerals (83.6%), which implies that some of the declared non-churchgoers do in fact adhere to these practices. Outright non-believers, those who describe themselves as freethinkers or non-believers by conviction, are fewer in number, accounting for only 17.3% of the population; and on closer scrutiny even this figure turns out to be too high.[11] It is striking that among the sample population surveyed no more than 1.1% were members of a secular humanist association. Contrary to what the Church might once have feared and freethinkers anticipated, organised secular humanism has not in fact gained those lost by the Church. Instead, as old ideological oppositions dissolve in today's secularised society, most non-believers see little or nothing of relevance to their everyday life in organised unbelief. Contemporary Flanders is characterised more by religious indifference than by any wide-spread conscious atheism.

JEFFREY TYSSENS
Translated by Sonja Prescod.

NOTES

1. HAZARD, P., *La Pensée européenne au XVIIIème siècle. De Montesquieu à Lessing.* Boivin, 1946, Part I, p. 3.

2. DHONT, L., 'Oost-Vlaanderen'. In: H. HASQUIN (ed.), *Het culturele leven in onze provincies in de 18e eeuw.* Brussel, 1983, pp. 133 ff.

3. See among others: VANDEN BERGHE, Y., *Jacobijnen en Traditionalisten. De reacties van de Bruggelingen in de Revolutietijd (1780-1794).* Brussel, 1972, Part I, pp. 102 ff.

4. As in the remarkable case of a certain Oomen, an Antwerp grocer's assistant who was known for his resolute atheism and was buried without religious rites in 1796. See: DE SCHAMPHELEIRE, H., *De Antwerpse vrijmetselaars in de 18e eeuw.* Antwerp, 1969, p. 96.

5. As none of these received imperial ratification they were not legally binding, though their content was, of course, public knowledge in the Austrian Netherlands.

6. The emphasis was on ensuring that members' testamentary wishes in this regard should be respected and carried out to the letter. More than a civil burial was at stake; members needed the support of their fellows lest in their final hour they capitulate to pressure from priests and family and, after all, consent to the last sacraments and religious burial. See: TYSSENS, J. and M.-P. VERHAEGEN, 'De dood van Pierre-Théodore Verhaegen'. In: *Pierre-Théodore Verhaeghen (1796-1862).* Brussels, 1996, pp. 151-169.

7. According to the testimony of French republican exiles who frequented these circles, Dutch was spoken quite extensively. See: SAINT-FERREOL, A., *Les proscrits français en Belgique contemporaine vue à travers l'exil.* Brussels, 1870, 2 vols., passim.

8. For the development of the freethinkers' movement in Flanders, see: TYSSENS, J., 'Vrijzinnigheid'. In: *Nieuwe Encyclopedie van de Vlaamse Beweging.* Tielt, 1998, Vol. III, pp. 3598-3599.

9. TYSSENS, J. and E. WITTE, *De vrijzinnige traditie in België. Van getolereerde tegencultuur tot erkende levensbeschouwing.* Brussels, 1996, pp. 111 ff.

10. DOBBELAERE, K. and L. VOYE, 'Religie en kerkbetrokkenheid: ambivalentie en vervreemding". In: DOBBELAERE, K. *et al.*, *Verloren zekerheid: de Belgen en hun waarden, overtuigingen en houdingen.* Tielt / Brussels, 2000, pp. 117-152.

11. The survey in question indicates that some Catholics also describe themselves as 'freethinkers'. See: *ibid.*, p. 120.

ow

God Survived His Death in Books

Epilogue

Really there's nothing I believe,
and I doubt everything, doubt even You.
But sometimes, when I think You do indeed exist,
then I think that You are Love, and all alone,
and that in like despair You seek for me
as I for You.

Gerard Reve
Translated by Tanis Guest

During the Second World War, whose end he would not live to see, the internationally renowned Dutch historian Johan Huizinga began work on his last book, without the aid of a library. It was published posthumously immediately after the war under the title *Violated World. Reflections on the Chances of a Restoration of our Civilisation* (Geschonden wereld. Een beschouwing over de kansen op herstel van onze beschaving, 1946). One of Huizinga's findings was that '*modern mankind in Europe and America is totally focused on acquisition and pleasure*'. He also wondered: '*Can we expect a revival of Christian faith?*'

He was not alone in his concern about materialism as a view of life and the acceleration of the process of secularisation, described at the time in terms of 'the abandonment of faith'. After the war authors of various denominations continued to respond, in writings that often included the word 'personalism' in the title, to nihilism in its various manifestations, from the tragic to the banal, to the Freudian reduction of the human mind to a bunch of sublimated instincts, and to the conviction that science makes any teleological or finalistic and metaphysical explanation of the existence of the world and man redundant and absurd.

Authoritative critics examined whether there was any role left for a 'Christian' dimension in literature, and if so, what. For example, in 1952

Mariusz Kruk, *Untitled*.
1991. Wood, porcelain,
linen, 400 x 450 x 800 cm
(exhibited in Watou,
West Flanders, 1998).

C. Rijnsdorp published *In Three Stages* (In drie etappen), a study of the role of Calvinism in literature. He found that the attempt to develop a separate Protestant literature had failed, both in the interwar period and after World War Two. In the same year A. Westerlinck wrote an essay on 'The Catholic Novel in Our Time' ('De katholieke roman in deze tijd'), in which he concluded that the Catholic novel had assumed a very problematic character. Should the Catholic writer 'edify' and avoid such tricky themes as religious doubt, sexuality and the power of evil, or should he explore them freely? The God who is present in the contemporary Catholic novel, writes Westerlinck in 1952, appears not to be primarily the God of the certainties handed down by the church hierarchy, but *'the God of Mystery and particularly the Deus absconditus, who, confronted with the conundrum of a gruesomely corrupt mankind, shrouds himself in secrecy'*.

In Flanders so eminent a Catholic author as Gerard Walschap (1898-1989) had attempted back in the 1930s to renew the Catholic novel and broaden its scope. His plea met with intense Church opposition and led in the pamphlet *Farewell Then* (Vaarwel dan,1940) to his departure from the Church and the loss of his religious faith.

Somewhat later Louis-Paul Boon (1912-1979) and Hugo Claus (1929-), standard-bearers of the generation of Flemish writers who made their debut during or soon after the Second World War, stressed the repressive force of religion in their work. This is a central theme in Boon's novel *The Bird of Paradise* (De paradijsvogel, 1958), which some commentators called a religious novel stood on its head. They saw Boon's book as a highly critical account of religious man. In it religion is unmasked as a human creation whose function is to oppress. Religion prevents man from living a paradisial, pagan life.

In the play *Friday* (Vrijdag, 1969) Hugo Claus demonstrates the transition from paganism to Christianity and the bankruptcy of Christian culture. The sense of sin and necessary penance is blown up to huge proportions in a play that is at once symbolic and visionary, anti-Catholic and anti-social. In 1970 Claus adapted De Roja's *La Celestina* as *The Spanish Whore* (De Spaanse hoer). The name 'Celestina' is a clear reference to heaven, in which the author locates an inhuman God, a strange hunter who cultivates His prey and kills His own progeny. Claus often refers explicitly to Christian rituals, which are an object of both recognition and rejection. In his symbolic novel *About Deedee* (Omtrent Deedee, 1963), adapted as a play, *Interior* (Interieur), in 1971 and in 1989 filmed as *The Sacrament* (Het sacrament), the annual Heylen family party, which flouts all bounds of decency, follows and parodies the ritual of a Catholic mass.

A donkey at the turning point

In 1951 Willem Frederik Hermans (1921-1995), who in his debut novella *Preserves* (Conserve, 1947) had been sharply critical of the both quantitatively and politically insignificant Mormons, had a serious clash with the Catholic community in the Netherlands, which felt insulted by the passage in his novel *I Am Always Right* (Ik heb altijd gelijk) where the drunken protagonist brands Catholics as '*the most squalid, crazy, grovelling, screwed-up part of our nation! But they fuck like there's no tomorrow! They multiply! Like rabbits, rats, fleas, lice*'. W.F. Hermans, who in his essays combats every form of absolute truth and dogmatic thought and regards belief in God as a dangerous threat to human freedom, was cleared on 20 March 1952 of having had the 'intention to insult' – as the indictment read – in *I Am Always Right*, since such an intention cannot be present in the utterances of a fictional character. A writer, in the view of the judge at the time, must always be free to create people with widely different natures and opinions.

In the rapidly secularising society of the 1960s other incidents of this kind were to take place. When in the spring of 1963 Jan Wolkers gave a reading of the story 'Artificial Fruit' ('Kunstfruit') from his collection *Candyfloss* (Gesponnen suiker, 1963), the deputy-mayor of Bergen ostentatiously left the auditorium because of the obscene nature of the story. A year later, in 1964, the previously mentioned Calvinist leader C. Rijnsdorp responded with shock to a crucifixion scene at the end of *The Obedient Deceased* (De gehoorzame dode, 1964) by Willem Brakman (1922-). Questions were later asked in the Upper House of Parliament by Senator Algra on the blasphemous nature of the scene. In 1966-1968 the same senator was to play a major part in the so-called 'Donkey Trial', in which Gerard Reve (1923-), then still known as Gerard van het Reve, was accused of blasphemy. In 'Letter to my Bank' ('Brief aan mijn bank'), included in the collection of letters *Nearer to Thee* (Nader tot U, 1966), the homosexual author had reflected that God, were he to be reincarnated, would assume the form of a Donkey and had then described union with Him through His '*Secret Orifice*'. Before the trial Reve was received with great ceremony into the Roman Catholic Church. The judicial process continued for two years. On 2 April 1968, after the case had gone to appeal, the highest court in the land upheld the previous acquittal by a lower court. In *Dutch Literature, a History* (Nederlandse Literatuur, een geschiedenis, 1993) Frans de Rover concludes: '*It would be wrong to see the Donkey Trial as a (final) backlash of the denominational spirit in the Netherlands against modern literature. The progress and conclusion of the trial are rather the affirmation of a liberal attitude, the new Zeitgeist: individualism, the right to freedom in one's spiritual and physical experiences – in short, the philosophy of "the Sixties".*'

The Old Brake Shoe

What image of God was it on which the authors of the so-called 'valedictory' generation in the Netherlands, Jan Wolkers (1925-), Maarten 't Hart (1944-), Maarten Biesheuvel (1939-), Jan Siebelink (1938-) – all from strict Calvinist backgrounds – and others, turned their backs?

It was an omnipotent, all-seeing, vengeful God, who demanded absolute obedience and submission to his commandments and decided arbitrarily who was to be elected or rejected for all eternity. In an interview Jan Wolkers recounted how as a child he asked his father whether he would obey if asked by God to kill his son, as with Abraham and Isaac, and how his father replied without hesitation: yes!

In the story 'White Chrysanthemums' ('Witte chrysanten') from the collection *Nightshade* (Nachtschade), Jan Siebelink's 1975 debut, we read: '*My father was not gloomy by nature, but it was the religion of the Veluwe that with its scrawny, wasted arms had choked off my father's joyful feelings.*' The God of Siebelink's father was not the God of love from the New Testament, but the avenging one of the Old Testament. In his substantial novel *The Other Side of the River* (De overkant van de rivier, 1990), as well as in his other collections of stories Siebelink describes again and again the suffocating weight and the terror of an extreme orthodox faith peddled by fanatical disciples.

In the autobiographical novel *A Flight of Whimbrels* (Een vlucht regenwulpen, 1978) Maarten 't Hart, the product of a rigid Calvinist upbringing, throws the Church elders out of the house when they come to lecture his mother even as she lies dying of throat cancer, adding the bitter reflection that God is a god who hates humanity so violently that He has invented throat cancer for them. In *Bearers of Bad Tidings* (De aansprekers, 1979) the son, who has lost his faith, says a moving farewell to his Bible-thumping father. For the writers of the valedictory generation, radical renunciation of the faith of their childhood by no means involves the complete denial of the culture and biblical texts that have shaped them. The residue of this is still felt in later work as a nostalgia for the past with which they may or may not have come to terms.

A strict religious upbringing often resulted in frustrations because of sexual taboos, in complete incomprehension in the face of a God who offers no help when it really matters, in complexes fed by fears of hell and damnation,

Gerard Walschap
(1898-1989).
Photo by A. Vandeghinste.

Gerard Reve (1923-).
Photo by Vincent Mentzel.

Hugo Claus (1929-). Photo
by Patrick de Spiegelaere.

Harry Mulisch (1927-) and
Pope John Paul II in Rome,
1999.

shame and a sense of sin. Rudy Kousbroek (1929-), who was born in Indonesia and spent his childhood in boarding schools and a Japanese internment camp, cites as his most dreadful memory the assurance of the headmistress of the boarding school that he, a boy of twelve, would die before dawn if he did not pray for forgiveness for the 'pornographic' stories he had told in the dormitory. The young Kousbroek refused, underwent paroxysms of terror as dawn approached, but found that he was still alive and saw it as final proof that God did not exist. In his essays, inspired by Neopositivism, among which the five collections of *Anathemas* (Anathema's, 1968-1984) appealed strongly to Dutch readers, the struggle against all kinds of manifestations of religious irrationality is a constant theme.

For the generation after Wolkers too faith in God remains a topic that provokes a resistance that has its roots in a Christian upbringing. In *The Garden of Mercy* (Het Hof van Barmhartigheid, 1996), the first book of the third volume of *Toothless Time* (De tandeloze tijd), the magnum opus of A.F.Th. van der Heijden (1951-), two of the principal characters, Albert Egberts, who has studied philosophy in Nijmegen, and Thjum, an actor in Amsterdam, have a long conversation about God. The Albert character, who has many similarities with the writer, has devised the name 'The Old Brake Shoe' for God. It is a metaphor for everything that frustrates, inhibits and opposes him, a blanket name for everything that is stronger than himself.

In his voluminous novel *The Task* (De Opdracht, 1995), Wessel te Gussinklo has the fourteen-year-old Ewout reflect on and question the existence of God, who has summoned his Dad to heaven without giving him the chance to say goodbye. It is obvious to Ewout that God does not really ex-

ist and that is precisely why the word God expresses '*the supreme, a vastness that linked all things together, giving them coherence and warmth*'. In his adolescent fantasies he too would like to achieve such divine status, but in the actual conversations with the other participants in the summer camp in the Veluwe National Park, he reveals himself with his ideas on power, leadership and superiority as expressed in his admired models – Jesus, Churchill, Roosevelt, even Hitler – as a sad, obsessed, paranoid young man.

Mulisch takes over from God

If God does not exist, man obviously feels the need for other interpretative systems such as Reason, Progress or History to explain the world and human existence. In the pamphlet *Farewell and Thanks* (Salut en merci, 1955) Gerard Walschap again argues that proofs of God's existence in fact prove nothing and that Christianity is an aberration that is perpetuated deliberately or otherwise. God is superfluous and to improve his lot man must trust in science and technology. However, Walschap's progressive optimism in *Farewell and Thanks* is strongly tempered by thoroughgoing cultural pessimism.

For W.F. Hermans too the exact sciences are the only universal rock for man to cling to. In *Sleep no More* (Nooit meer slapen, 1966) Professor Nummedal says that science is man's titanic attempt to free himself from his cosmic isolation by comprehending. Although Hermans is a great promoter of the study of nature, his vision of it cannot be called optimistic. The title *The Sadistic Universe* (Het sadistische universum), which he twice (in 1964 and 1970) gives to a collection of his essays, makes that all too plain.

Harry Mulisch (1927-), who with Gerard Reve, W.F. Hermans and Jan Wolkers is one of the giants of post-war Dutch prose, does not believe in God and agrees with Marx when, following Feuerbach, he says that it is man who has created God in his own image, and not the other way round. God's omnipotence has been transferred to technology and secularisation goes hand in hand with the technological revolution. The God who for centuries has kept mankind together in what the Catholic Church calls 'the mystical body of Christ', has been replaced by the Unio Technica. In his ambitious philosophical essay, *The Composition of the World* (De compositie van de wereld, 1980), though, Mulisch argues that the world of technology has become as hazardous for today's earth-dwellers as nature was for the Neanderthals. After the death of God he predicts the death of Man, who will vanish through the agency of the artefacts (cars, nuclear bombs, computers, etc.) that he himself has produced. The way in which , by deciphering the genetic code of DNA and with the help of biotechnology, man has almost succeeded in producing human beings, how through evolution he has appropriated almost all powers ascribed to the angels and is on the point of conquering heaven itself, is the theme of Mulisch's magisterial novel *The Discovery of Heaven* (De ontdekking van de hemel, 1992). In it God terminates his pact with man and ensures that the stone tablets bearing the Ten Commandments, the legacy of Moses, are taken back to their place of origin: heaven. In *The Discovery of Heaven* the God who created heaven and earth is replaced by an omnipotent narrator who rules over creation. The literary scholar and critic Frans de Rover comes to the conclusion that via the detour of this capacious novel God has his Word restored by the writer Harry Mulisch, thus turning the Judaeo-Christian God quite literally into a literary God.

After the 'death of God' the writing 'I' of the author himself takes God's place at centre stage. The author does, however, still rely on myths, stories, rites and symbols that have been handed down in religions to illuminate the precarious human condition. Marcel Möring (1957-), for example, in his novel *In Babylon* (1997), has created a first-person narrator who does not believe in God, but does believe in the explanatory power of stories. This Nathan Hollander, a writer of fairy tales from a Jewish family of scientists and clockmakers, believes that surrender to God leads to the loss of human dignity and self-awareness, but does not think that science provides an alternative. Science, after all, gives an insight only into the operation of things, whereas the only way of really knowing the world consists in the telling of stories. These retain their revelatory value even after postmodernism has proclaimed the end of the Great Stories.

Sincere pretence

The place occupied by God in the oeuvre of Gerard Reve is an odd one. Brought up in an atheistic family with dialectical materialism as his guiding dogma and initially tortured by his latent homosexuality, the author develops, from his much-discussed first novel *The Evenings* (De avonden, 1947) onwards, an image of God that runs completely counter to the trend towards secularisation. Reve's God is an immanent, incarnate God with whom man can be on confidential and intimate terms, and this was felt by some orthodox Christians, as outlined above, to be quite simply blasphemous. In contrast to the unapproachable God of the Calvinists, the God to whom Frits van Egters, the main character of *The Evenings*, appeals to behold the plight of his parents, is an accessible and understanding God. In *Mother and Son* (Moeder en zoon, 1980) Reve gives an account of the evolution of his faith which culminated in his official acceptance into the Roman Catholic Church. One can also read what Reve understands by the experience of faith in the correspondence with Josine Meijer which extended from 1959 to 1982 and was published in 1984 as *Letters to Josine M.* (Brieven aan Josine M.). The same applies to his poetry, collected in 1973 under the title *The Singing Heart* (Het zingende hart). The feminist literary scholar Maaike Meijer concludes an analysis of Reve's 'Religious Songs' in the Dutch magazine *Bzzlletin* with the following affirmation: *'Through the polemical retrieval of everything that has been suppressed in religion (sexuality, woman, evil) Reve restores expressive force to religious language.'*

The reciprocity of the relationship between God and man, in which, in Reve's view, God needs man just as badly as man needs God, since both are alone and long for each other, also manifests itself *mutatis mutandis* in the work of the promising writer Frans Kellendonk (1951-1989), who died prematurely of Aids, and who describes belief somewhere as *'sincere pretence'*. In 1986 his most important novel *The Body Mystic* (Mystiek lichaam) caused an uproar because of the supposedly anti-Semitic utterances of the protagonist, father Gijselhart, to the Jew Bruno Pechman, who has got his daughter pregnant. As had previously happened with Hermans, Brakman and Reve, some critics promptly identified the ideas of a character with those of the author. However, the core of *The Body Mystic* is the lost pact between God and human beings, heaven and earth, individual and community, of which the marriage between man and woman is a symbol. Homosexuals are excluded from that pact since they are not capable of procreation. Believing is therefore a kind of creativity. In an essay of 1983 called 'Image and Likeness. On God' ('Beeld en Gelijkenis. Over God'), Frans Kellendonk says that he imagines himself as God's blind helper, who through his work creates himself in His image and likeness, just as He creates Himself through him.

The experience of belief in the work of authors like Reve and Kellendonk is in stark contrast to the *'religion (that) in our literature (is) at best the virtuoso but impersonal discovery of a do-it-yourself, cut-out heaven'*, as Willem Jan Otten (1951-) cogently put it at the end of 2001 in the Dutch weekly *Vrij Nederland*. In recent years Otten himself, in the footsteps of his wife, the writer Vonne van der Meer (1952-), has turned increasingly towards the Church. Otten's background was even less religious than that of his wife, and yet he was baptised. Writers who had freed themselves by trial and error from the faith of their childhood were forced to look on ruefully as one of their colleagues, without their 'hereditary baggage', was received into the bosom of the Roman Catholic Church.

JORIS GERITS
Translated by Paul Vincent.

New Life for Old Churches

Reusing Religious Buildings in the Netherlands

Nowadays it is rare for an architect to be asked to build a church in the Netherlands. Over the past few decades, what used to be one of the main areas of activity in architecture has largely evaporated as a result of secularisation. This first became apparent in the second half of the twentieth century, when the construction programme for religious buildings came to a halt and churches ceased to be built as a matter of course in new residential areas, as they had been until the end of the 1960s. Until this time Dutch society was still strongly 'pillarised', which meant that every newly built residential area had at least three churches: Catholic, Reformed and Orthodox Calvinist. In the built environment, the first sign of the progressive decline in church-going became apparent from about 1970 onwards, when planners no longer regarded the church as an essential local amenity. Since then, new churches have been the exception rather than the rule.

Disuse and demolition

As the construction of new buildings for religious worship gradually ended, a further consequence of secularisation became apparent: more and more churches fell into disuse because they were no longer required for their original purpose. This also applied to monasteries but, since the Netherlands is a predominantly Protestant country with few monasteries, the phenomenon was only noticeable in the Catholic southern provinces of North Brabant and Limburg.

The church of the Vrije Gemeente on Weteringschans in Amsterdam symbolises the onset of this second phase of secularisation. Built by G.B. Salm in 1880, the church was granted a new lease of life in 1967 when it became a centre for the burgeoning hippie culture. The new centre was initially called the 'Kosmies Ontspannings Sentrum Provadya?' (Kosmic Relaxation Sentre Provadya?) and its name was even spelled according to the new hippie convention. The name supposedly referred to a Tibetan monastery, but happened also to strongly resemble that of the Provo protest movement. The story was that the Tibetan monks themselves were unsure whether the

Daf-architecten: the empty interior of the Roman Catholic St Isidorus church, redesigned to house a permanent exhibition of the history of Nagele (1998).

monastery actually existed; hence the question mark after the name. At the beginning of 1968 the centre was renamed Paradiso, and today it is still one of the main platforms for pop music in the Netherlands.

Converting the church of the Vrije Gemeente into a venue for pop concerts was a clever move because few modifications were required – little more than removing the pews and replacing the altar with a stage. The extent of the modifications needed to give a church a new lease of life is usually the main reason for demolishing it and replacing it with a new building. It is often difficult to find a new use for a church; the interior is likely to be too high and doors and windows inconveniently positioned. Heating and maintenance costs can also be prohibitive. This has led to the demolition of many churches, even today, despite a growing willingness to find a new use for them. That willingness comes from the growing awareness that religious buildings have architectural and historical value and, furthermore, that their central location and vertical silhouette make them an important feature of the urban landscape.

The most logical form of reuse – conversion into a mosque – is not even considered; it is simply out of the question. Religious communities are not prepared to hand over their empty churches to the only religion in the Netherlands whose adherents are increasing in number: Islam. Apparently the Crusades have not yet faded sufficiently from the collective memory to allow a Christian church to become a mosque. That is why Muslims initially worshipped in all manner of buildings, ranging from schools to garages, that were never intended for religious meetings. New mosques have only been built since the 1980s, their minarets and characteristic roofs lending an exotic flavour to the Dutch urban landscape.

The reluctance of Catholic and Protestant clergymen to hand over their buildings to the imams often makes it difficult to find a new use for a church. This is especially the case with 'everyday' church buildings; the most important Dutch churches, even if they are only occasionally used for religious services, are able to justify their existence by functioning as museums and sometimes exhibition centres. Examples of this are Amsterdam's Nieuwe Kerk and Jewish Historical Museum, housed in a former synagogue, and the Bergkerk in Deventer.

Forms of adaptive reuse

The Roman Catholic church in the centre of Nagele, a modern 1950s polder village, has also become an exhibition centre. On a large village green in the centre of Nagele, three churches and their three denominational schools are grouped together as symbols of pillarisation. The empty interior of the Roman Catholic church, with minimal alterations by the architectural firm Daf, now houses a permanent exhibition of the history of this unusual village.

The Daf approach represents one end of the spectrum, where as far as possible buildings are left intact. The Amsterdam offices of the firm Soeters Van Eldonk Ponec represent the other extreme. A photograph hanging on the wall in Sjoerd Soeters' studio is the only reminder that this building, now converted into sophisticated office accommodation, was once the Martin

Luther King chapel. Nothing about the building betrays that fact, except perhaps for the pontifical empty space at its centre. The 1960s brick and concrete facade has disappeared behind a cladding of corrugated steel. Next to the former church, an extension with apartments above it has further erased any trace of the original structure. The church is seen as a shell that can be adapted to any purpose.

The advantage of both these radical approaches is that they do not require the architect to consider the relationship between the old and the new, always a crucial consideration in every form of adaptive reuse. Where the building's new use derives directly or indirectly from its former use, a logical relationship can usually be found. The greater the gulf between the new and original purposes, however, the harder this becomes. The conversion of a traditional church into a women's refuge is an example of such a logical relationship. The church was built in the 1950s by H.P.J. de Vries and the conversion was carried out by the architects Duinker van der Torre at the beginning of the 1990s. The logic of the relationship exists at a conceptual level rather than in terms of use; never has a church so literally served as a sanctuary.

Trendy monastic cells

In 2001, a monastery in Vught belonging to the Friars of Tilburg underwent a similar conversion into a centre for contemplation and work. There is not a great deal of difference between a monastery and a spiritual haven intended for the working population of the Netherlands. The conversion has tempted the friars back to their old home and project architects Annette Marx and Ady Steketee have built a new house for them in the monastery grounds. The house provides accommodation for up to eight monks. The set-up is similar to a student house, and each occupant has his own room with a shower and balcony. There is a communal sitting room and kitchen and – the only feature not commonly found in a student house – a small chapel.

In the monastery itself Marx and Steketee made radical alterations to fit it for use as a venue for courses, lectures and retreats. Three main elements, in wood, cane and glass, have been added to the unspectacular building, which dates from 1905 and can at best be described as a textbook example of architectural frugality. One notable feature of this monastery for contemplation and work is the design of the guest rooms – a trendy variation on the monk's cell. With a single bed in the corner, a desk against the wall and a small bathroom, guests who come here seeking a meaning to their lives will not be bathed in luxury. Yet the decor is very contemporary: the desk – in yellow, orange, blue or green – is by Antonie Kleinepier and the continuous pipe, which functions as shower-curtain rail and toilet-roll holder, was designed by Kapkar.

Designers are a powerful presence elsewhere in the building too. Richard Hutten designed the dining room with its spartan wooden furniture and rudimentary chandeliers. The adjacent recreation room looks like a lounge with its colourful collection of second-hand chairs that have been stripped of their upholstery by Wendi Bakker. There is also an enormous wooden cocktail bar full of cupboards and drawers, designed by the Nigerian architect Ola Dele Kuku.

Sjoerd Soeters: his own offices (1989) in Amsterdam, once the Martin Luther King chapel.

Marx & Steketee: assembly hall in the Vught monastery (2000).

Respect or demolition

Examples such as these, where a building's new use is a logical extension of its old use, are few and far between. Churches have been given a wide range of new functions, from library to supermarket. In most cases, however, they are converted into homes or offices.

Two large neo-gothic churches in Amsterdam, the Posthoorn (1860) and the Vondelkerk (1870), both by P.J.H. Cuypers, have been converted into offices. Both buildings accommodate several businesses. The aisles have been brought into use and the nave – left largely intact – is used for receptions, conferences and exhibitions. What typifies both of these cases is that despite the churches' radical transformation, in architectonic terms the conversion is very restrained, as the subdued grey of the doors and windows clearly demonstrates.

A completely different philosophy informs the work of FAT (Fashion Architecture Taste), a British architectural practice that transformed a nineteenth-century neo-gothic church in the centre of Amsterdam for the advertising agency KesselsKramer. The result: a decorative, customised interior comprising many different architectonic elements, which, in the words of the designers, '*explicitly refer to the sort of commonly understood activities which advertising agents might use – football, holiday or landmarks. These are slotted between the original iron columns*'. However loud FAT's 'lad art' design may be, it nevertheless shows respect for the building's nineteenth-century architectural style.

The respect automatically shown to buildings of a certain age is not accorded to more recent church buildings. The newest churches in the Netherlands, built in the decades after the Second World War, are much less respected; moreover, being located in what were then new developments, they seldom enjoy the prominent position traditionally occupied by churches in the urban landscape. The fact that these newer churches were built in a style that was generally unpopular and very controversial in the post-war years does little to help them find a new role. And, of course, the churches most recently built are always the most likely to be pulled down. Only a few exceptions have been deemed worthy of preservation, one example being the Opstandingskerk (1958) in Amsterdam West, built by M. Duintjer. This church, also known as 'the coal-scuttle' because of its unusual spire, is a protected building and recently underwent complete renovation. A stone's throw away stands another church, St Josef (1952), designed by the architects G.H.M. Holt and K.P. Tholens. It is one of the first Catholic churches in the Netherlands to be built entirely from concrete, but even this is unlikely to save it from demolition within the next few years to make way for homes and offices. While it still stands, the church is being used for a very unusual but remarkably fitting purpose: it has been turned into an indoor climbing centre called 'Tussen hemel en aarde' ('Between Heaven and Earth').

HANS IBELINGS
Translated by Yvette Mead.

'Il

Call You God, You Powers'

Fifteen Poems Selected by Jozef Deleu

Joost van den Vondel (1587-1679)
From *Lucifer*

Chorus of Angels:
Who sits in this exalted place,
Bathed in unfathomable light,
Immeasurable in time or space –
No counterpart in rank or might?
Who on no other power depends,
A self-sufficient entity,
Whose nature fully comprehends
Of all things the identity,
That in and round it all rotate –
The pivot, hub and central strand,
Sun of all suns – life, spirit, state
And soul of all we understand,
Or seek to grasp but never shall:
The heart, the ocean and the spring,
The origin of blessings all
That flow from Him unwavering,
By virtue of His mercy, might
And wisdom, shaped from nothing, ere,
Above the spheres, on topmost height,
This heavenly palace glittered fair,
Where we, wings crossed to shade our eyes,
That gleaming Majesty revere,
Arousing Heaven with our cries
Of praise, submission or, in fear,
Fall on our faces at the sight!
Describe Him! What is He or Who?
His Name with quill seraphic write –
Or do both mind and tongue eschew?

Zang:
Wie is het, die zo hoog gezeten,
Zo diep in 't grondeloze licht,
Van tijd noch eeuwigheid gemeten,
Noch ronden, zonder tegenwicht,
Bij zich bestaat, geen steun van buiten
Ontleent, maar op zich zelve rust,
En in zijn wezen kan besluiten
Wat om en in hem, onbewust
Van wanken, draait, en wordt gedreven,
Om 't een en enig middelpunt;
Der zonnen zon, de geest, het leven;
De ziel van alles wat gij kunt
Bevroên, of nimmermeer bevroeden;
Het hart, de bronaêr, de oceaan
En oorsprong van zovele goeden
Als uit hem vloeien, en bestaan
Bij zijn genade, en alvermogen,
En wijsheid, die hun 't wezen schonk
Uit niet, eer dit in top voltogen
Paleis, der heemlen hemel, blonk;
Daar wij met vleuglen de ogen dekken,
Voor aller glansen Majesteit;
Terwijl we 's hemels lofgalm wekken,
En vallen, uit eerbiedigheid,
Uit vrees, in zwijm op 't aanzicht neder?
Wie is het? Noemt, beschrijft ons hem,
Met ene Serafijnenveder.
Of schort het aan begrip en stem?

Chorus of Seraphim:
'Tis God, the ageless Being, ever –
Lasting Source of what exists!
Forgive us if our praise is never
Adequate! His Might resists
Our puny powers of acclamation;
Pardon us, we're not to blame!
No symbol, word, imagination
Can define Him, who the same
Ever was, is and will be!
Angels' paeans – weak, inept –
Border on profanity:
Which of us would breathe, except
For Him – and who would dare address
Him by His Name or make so bold
As to His secrets claim access?
For what He is – unique, age-old –
Only the Godhead is aware –
The stream-bed of Eternity!
Such knowledge none of us may share:
Impenetrable Mystery!
What eye the Light of Lights dare face?
Such privilege, more wondrous yet
Than we've been blessed with through His grace,
Would overtax our limits set!
We age in immortality,
But God does not! He stays the same!
Without His Being, we'd not be:
So let us glorify His Name!

Hymn of Praise:
Holy, holy, holy Lord!
Three times be the Godhead blest!
He alone is our true ward.
Sacred, then, be His behest!
By its mystery be bound;
His command receive with trust!
Everywhere, His word let sound,
As Gabriel decreed it must –
And blew his trumpet loud and clear.
So let us God in Adam revere –
For all that God ordains is just!

Tegenzang:
Dat's God. Oneindig eeuwig Wezen
Van alle ding, dat wezen heeft,
Vergeef het ons; O nooit volprezen
Van al wat leeft, of niet en leeft,
Nooit uitgesproken, noch te spreken;
Vergeef het ons, en scheld ons kwijt
Dat geen verbeelding, tong, noch teken
U melden kan. Gij waart, Gij zijt,
Gij blijft dezelve. Alle englenkennis
En uitspraak, zwak, en onbekwaam,
Is maar ontheiliging, en schennis:
Want ieder draagt zijn eigen naam,
Behalve Gij. Wie kan U noemen
Bij Uwe naam? Wie wordt gewijd
Tot Uw orakel? Wie durft roemen?
Gij zijt alleen dan die Gij zijt,
U zelf bekend, en niemand nader.
U zulks te kennen, als Gij waart
Der eeuwigheden glans en ader;
Wien is dat licht geopenbaard?
Wien is der glansen glans verschenen?
Dat zien is nog een hoger heil
Dan wij van Uw genade ontlenen;
Dat overschrijdt het perk en peil
Van ons vermogen. Wij verouden
In onze duur, Gij nimmermeer.
Uw wezen moet ons onderhouden.
Verheft de Godheid: zingt Haar eer.

Toezang:
Heilig, heilig, nog eens heilig,
Driemaal heilig: eer zij God.
Buiten God is 't nergens veilig.
Heilig is het groot gebod.
Zijn geheimenis zij bondig.
Men aanbidde Zijn bevel
Dat men overal verkondig'
Wat de trouwe Gabriël
Ons met zijn bazuin kwam leren.
Laat ons God in Adam eren.
Al wat God behaagt is wel.

From *Lucifer*, in *Complete Works* (Volledige dichtwerken). Amsterdam:
H.J.W. van Brecht, 1937.
Translated by Noel Clark (in: 'Lucifer'. Bath: Absolute Classics, 1990).

? Hadewijch (c.1200 - c.1260)

Everything there Is

Everything there is
Is too cramped for me;
I am so wide!
For what's uncreated
I have reached out
In eternity.

I have held it fast.
It has opened me
Wider than wide.
I find all else too cramped;
You know that well,
You who've reached there too.

One is free
In that company
Undivided;
That's why it's his will
That it should be so
For both of us.

You may rightly grieve
Who still lag far behind
In that cramped place,
And have not advanced
To spiritual bliss
In that wide expanse.

For in that wide place
One can rejoice
In such boundless hope
That always there
One seems free from fear
Of eternal loss.

Translated by Tanis Guest.

Alle dinghe

Alle dinghe
sijn mi te inghe;
Ic ben so wijt:
Om een onghescepen
Hebbic begrepen
In eweghen tijt.

Ic hebdt ghevaen.
Het heeft mi ontdaen
Widere dan wijt;
Mi es te inghe al el;
Dat wette wel,
Ghi dies oec daer sijt.

Men es vri
In dat nabi
Ongesceden;
Daer omme wilt hi
Dat alsoe si
Met ons beden.

Ghi moecht sijn erre
Die noch achter verre
In dat inghe sijt,
Ende te groter vromen
Niet voert en sijt comen
In dat wijde wijt.

Want in dat wide
Es men blide
In hope so groet,
Datmen daer altoes
Scijnt sorgheloes
Van eweгher noet.

Jacobus Revius (1586-1658)

Temptation

I have prayed, O great God, for thy mercy,
But ah! thou hast denied it to me in my distress.
I have cried out for thy unstinting kindness,
But felt it not when things went ill with me.

Wrestled I have and striven to gain thy love,
But have awaited it in vain for all too long.
So many times I have sought thy compassion,
But to this very day nothing have I received.

How easily thy grace could turn my heart to thee,
Thy kindness and thy love draw me towards the good,
And thy divine compassion from all evil free me.

Alas! What am I saying, Lord! While my heart sought
To reach thy sweetness, within it there have wrought
Thy goodness and thy grace, thy love and thy compassion.

From In Thy Boundless Mercy *(In uw genade grondeloos). Hasselt: Heideland, 1967.*
Translated by Tanis Guest.

Aanvechtinge

Ik heb om uw genade, o grote God, gebeden,
Maar och! Gij hebt ze mij in mijnen druk ontzeid.
Ik heb geroepen om uw milde goedigheid,
Maar heb ze niet gevoeld in mijn ellendigheden.

Ik heb om uwe liefd' geworsteld en gestreden,
Maar hebbe tevergeefs daar lange naar gebeid.
Ik hebbe dik gezocht uw mededogendheid,
Maar en verneem ze niet tot op den dag van heden.

Hoe licht kost uw gena bekeren mijn gemoed,
Uw liefd' en goedigheid mij trekken tot het goed,
Uw mededogendheid van 't kwade mij bevrijden.

Eilaas! wat zeg ik, Heer! dewijl mijn herte tracht
Naar uwe zoetigheid, zo heeft daarin gewracht
Uwe goedheid, uw genâ, uw liefd', uw medelijden.

Guido Gezelle (1830-1899)

You Prayed on the Mountainside, Alone

You prayed on the mountainside, alone,
but... Jesu, there's no mountain, none,
high enough where I can climb
and find you there, alone:
the world purges,
wherever I go
or turn
or cast my eye;
and poor as I am there is none,
not one
who's needy and cannot complain;
hungry, and cannot beg; whom pain
tortures, and he cannot say
how bitterly!
Oh, teach this idiot, teach him how to pray!

Gij badt op enen berg

Gij badt op enen berg alleen,
en... Jesu, ik en vind er geen
waar 'k hoog genoeg kan klimmen
om U alleen te vinden:
de wereld wilt mij achterna,
alwaar ik ga
of sta
of ooit mijn ogen sla;
en arm als ik en is er geen,
geen een,
die nood hebbe en niet klagen kan;
die honger, en niet vragen kan;
die pijne, en niet gewagen kan
hoe zeer het doet!
o Leert mij, armen dwaas, hoe dat ik bidden moet!

From Collected Poems *(Verzamelde gedichten). Tielt: Lannoo, 1999.*
Translated by James Brockway.

Nikolaas Beets (1814-1903)
The Mulberry Trees Were Rustling

'The mulberry trees were rustling';
God was passing by;
Not passing, no, he tarried;
He knew what I had need of,
And spoke to me;

Spoke to me in the silence,
The still of night;
Thoughts which tormented me,
Which hounded and distressed me,
He quietly put to flight.

Over my mind and soul then
He spread his peace;
In his paternal arms enfolded
I felt cherished and protected,
And fell asleep.

The morning which awoke me
I greeted with a will.
I had slept so serenely,
And Thou, my Sword and Buckler,
Wert near me still.

From *Pine-Needles* (Dennenaalden). Leiden: A.W. Sijthoff, 1900.
Translated by Tanis Guest.

De moerbeitoppen ruisten

'De moerbeitoppen ruisten';
God ging voorbij;
Neen, niet voorbij, hij toefde;
Hij wist wat ik behoefde,
En sprak tot mij;

Sprak tot mij in den stillen,
Den stillen nacht;
Gedachten, die mij kwelden,
Vervolgden en ontstelden,
Verdreef hij zacht.

Hij liet zijn vrede dalen
Op ziel en zin;
'k Voelde in zijn vaderarmen
Mij koestren en beschermen,
En sluimerde in.

Den morgen, die mij wekte
Begroette ik blij.
Ik had zo zacht geslapen,
En Gij, mijn Schild en Wapen,
Waart nog nabij.

Anton van Wilderode (1918-1998)
The Time of God

The time of God, the final judgement day
when the world tumbles to annihilation,
the approaching downfall of all creation
scorched to a cinder by the sun's last ray

is now at hand. The time-honoured procession
of the seasons and the fixed company
of the constellations will steadily
be dislodged from their usual progression.

Then, from before the time when time held sway,
the empty, uncreated chaos will take over
where the harsh wind's blast is the only mover,
the time of God, the final judgement day.

From *Complete Work* (Volledig dichtwerk). Tielt: Lannoo, 1999.
Translated by Paul Vincent.

De tijd van God

De tijd van God, het grote eschaton
wanneer de wereld kantelt naar haar einde,
het nakende vergaan van al het zijnde
bij het verzengen van de laatste zon

komt naderbij. De eeuwenoude orde
der jaargetijden en de vaste stand
van de gesternten zullen overhand
aan hun gewoon verloop onttrokken worden.

Dan herbegint, van eer de tijd begon,
de leegte van de ongeschapen baaierd
waarin beweging komt van hevig waaien,
de tijd van God, het grote eschaton.

J.A. dèr Mouw (1863-1919)

I'm a Brahmin. But we haven't got a maid.
I do what little I can around the house:
Throw out my dirty water and fill up the jug;
But I've no cloth to dry with; and I always splash.

She says that that is no work for a man.
And I feel helpless, full of self-reproach,
When she pampers my long-humoured lack
Of practicality with her magic at the stove.

And I've always worshipped Him, who shows himself
In the wondrous pageant of world, art and knowledge:

When she gives me my little bowl of porridge,
And I see that her finger-tips are cracked,

Then I feel the selfsame burning adoration
For Sun, Bach, Kant, and her worn calloused hands.

'k ben Brahman. Maar we zitten zonder meid.
Ik doe in huis het een'ge, dat ik kan:
'k Gooi mijn vuilwater weg en vul de kan;
Maar 'k heb geen droogdoek; en ik mors altijd.

Zij zegt, dat dat geen werk is voor een man.
En 'k voel me hulp'loos en vol zelfverwijt,
Als zij mijn lang verwende onpraktischheid
Verwent met wat ze toverde in de pan.

En steeds vereerde ik Hem, die zich ontvouwt
Tot feeërie van wereld, kunst en weten:

Als zij me geeft mijn bordje havermout,
En 'k zie, haar vingertoppen zijn gespleten,

Dan voel ik ééenzelfde adoratie branden
Voor Zon, Bach, Kant, en haar vereelte handen.

From *Complete Work* (Volledig dichtwerk). Amsterdam: Van Oorschot, 1986.
Translated by Tanis Guest.

Martinus Nijhoff (1894-1953)
The Light

The light, God's white light, breaks up into colours:
Colours are actions of the light that breaks.
Life breaks up in the variegated event,
And my soul breaks up as it utters words.

Only he who accepts death can bear life:
Oh see my blood that leaks along the nails!
My window's open, open are my doors –
Here is my heart, here is my body: break!

The ground is soft with spring. Between the trees
There waves a haze of green, and people go
Walking in the grass alongside the ponds –

Being lashed naked on a post with cords,
Soul breaking up itself to love and words:
These are the actions I became man for.

Het Licht

Het licht, Gods witte licht, breekt zich in kleuren:
Kleuren zijn daden van het licht dat breekt.
Het leven breekt zich in het bont gebeuren,
En mijn ziel breekt zich als ze woorden spreekt.

Slechts die zich sterven laat, kan 't leven beuren:
O zie mijn bloed dat langs de spijkers leekt!
Mijn raam is open, open zijn mijn deuren –
Hier is mijn hart, hier is mijn lichaam: breekt!

De grond is zacht van lente. Door de bomen
Weeft zich een waas van groen, en mensen komen
Wandelen langs de vijvers in het gras –

Naakt aan een paal geslagen door de koorden,
Ziel, die zichzelve brak in liefde en woorden:
Dit zijn de daden waar ik mens voor was.

From *Collected Poems* (Verzamelde gedichten). The Hague:
Bert Bakker / Daamen NV, 1963.
Translated by James S Holmes (In 'De Kim', no. 5, 1955).

Maurice Gilliams (1900-1982)

Annunciation

When her flesh felt the touch of language,
of the fingers of the Holy Ghost,
a spasm shot right through her body
and the angel left her utterly alone.

She started to stroke herself gently,
she was little, fragile and inside
she carried the diamond-hard stuff
that was to harrow and sever her.

'Oh, let me be moved in a different way,
approaching cross, lament and wounds;
so the little mouth can taste sweetness right now,
my wine of love, oh, my dark juice of pain.'

She clasped herself so very tight,
with a strength born of madness and blame;
but her two hands were a wonderful sight,
almost like disembodied flame.

From Vita Brevis. Antwerp: C. de Vries-Brouwers, 1955.
Translated by Paul Vincent.

De boodschap

Toen zij werd aangeraakt met woorden,
die waren vingren van de Heilige Geest,
is door haar lijf een pijn geschoten
en de engel liet haar moederziel alleen.

Zij is haar lichaam zacht gaan strelen,
zij was de kleine tere en hier binnen
droeg ze 't diamanten harde goed
dat haar beschrijnen en doorsnijden moest.

'Ach, laat mij ànders zijn ontroerd,
toekomend kruis, geween en wonden;
dat proeve in mij het mondeken àl zoetigheid,
mijn minnewijn, ach, donker sap van pijn.'

Zij heeft zich zelve vastgeklemd
met een kracht van waanzin en verwijt;
maar wonderbaar waren hare handen,
bijna zonder lichamelijkheid.

Gerrit Achterberg (1905-1962)

And Jesus wrote in the Sand

Jesus wrote with his finger in the sand.
He stooped down low to write in the sand. We do
not know just what he wrote. He himself knew
not: engrossed in the words that came from his hand.

From scribes and scholars he had got the third
degree about somebody's wife (obsessed
by another man, and hot, by love possessed).
Those scribes watched from the sidelines how he erred.

'Go sin no more, I judge not, go on home,'
he said, 'and listen. Listen to the poem.'

And he stood upright. And those few words, brushing
their own wordiness aside, burned in the blushing

with which she went away: a child so light.
So heavenly a poem did Jesus write.

From Collected Poems (Verzamelde gedichten). Amsterdam: Querido, 1963.
Translated by Stan Wiersma (In 'Tourist does Golgotha'. Grand Rapids (MI), 1972).

En Jezus schreef in 't zand

Jezus schreef met Zijn vinger in het zand.
Hij bukte Zich en schreef in 't zand, wij weten
niet wat Hij schreef, Hij was het zelf vergeten,
verzonken in de woorden van Zijn hand.

De schriftgeleerden, die Hem aan de tand
hadden gevoeld over een vrouw, van hete
hartstochten naar een andere man bezeten,
de schriftgeleerden stonden aan de kant.

Zondig niet meer, zei Hij, ik oordeel niet.
Ga heen en luister, luister naar het lied.

En Hij stond recht. De woorden lieten los
van hun figuur en brandden in de blos

waarmee zij heenging, als een kind zo licht.
Zo geestelijk schreef Jezus Zijn gedicht.

Ida M.G. Gerhardt (1905-1997)

Green Pastures

We, who walk now in the light
of the kindly season,
with astonished faces turned
to the meadows' splendour, –
leading each other by the hand
through the green and lovely land –
for sure He will not part us.

Who has made our path to lie
by the cool waters,
pastured us in love and light
on the green margins, –
freed us from all tears and dread?
What fearfully had been awaited
Has come with diffidence.

In the margins of the light
we walk, we earthly two; –
coming before His countenance
at the end of days
we'll see at last, complete and whole,
what no earthly meadow can show:
Glory in glory, by glory ringed
in the green pastures.

From *Living Monogram* (Het levend monogram). Assen: Van Gorcum en Comp,
1955.
Translated by Tanis Guest.

Green Pastures

Wij, die wandelen in het licht
van het zacht getijde,
het verwonderd aangezicht
naar de pracht der weiden, –
elkaar leidend bij de hand
door het lieflijk groene land –
niet zal Hij ons scheiden.

Wie heeft onze gang geleid
langs de koele stromen,
ons in liefde en licht geweid
aan de groene zomen, –
ons van tranen en angst bevrijd?
Wat met schromen werd verbeid
is met schroom gekomen.

In de zomen van het licht
gaan wij aardse beiden; –
komend voor Zijn aangezicht
aan het eind der tijden
zien wij eindelijk, ongedeeld,
wat geen aardse wei verbeeldt:
Glans in glans, door glans omspeeld
op de groene weiden.

Pierre Kemp (1886-1967)

Night God

I'll call you God, you powers.
I know of no other name.
God then! I am so far from the flowers,
I press the window-frame.
I look at the starlight,
where children see You –
for me You're out of sight –
perhaps listening too?
I acknowledge I'm only a man,
bound to leap further than any man can.

From *Collected Work 3* (Verzameld werk 3). Amsterdam: Van Oorschot, 1976.
Translated by Paul Vincent.

Nachtgod

Ik zal U maar God noemen.
Ik weet ook geen andere naam.
God dan! Ik ben zeer ver van de bloemen
en zo dicht bij het raam.
Ik kijk naar de sterren,
waar kinderen U zien,
maar mij zijt Gij ver en
Gij luistert misschien.
Ik erken het, ik ben maar een mens,
bestemd voor de sprong ver over de grens.

Leo Vroman (1915-)

Creationette

Lord, could I only squeeze
You down to a gesture on my hand,
give You all the fuzz, the buzz bees,
beads and kittle-kittenese,
and You would weave them into one strand..

I'd close my fingers around You
and loving Your tickles while You do
Your Thing, I would have kissed,
gently, the outside of my fist;

and then, daring as You ordain,
would expose what You created,
and for evermore remain
staring at my empty palm, great
God
and never speak again.

From *126 Poems* (126 gedichten). Amsterdam: Querido, 1964.
Translated by Leo Vroman.

Scheppinkje

Kon ik Jou, Heer, tezamensponzen
tot een gebaartje op mijn hand
en gaf Jou alle kralen, donzen,
poesjesmiepsen en hommelgonzen
en Jij weefde het verband…

ik zou mijn vingers rond je sluiten
en Jouw gekriebel zó beminnen
terwijl Je scheppend was daarbinnen
dat ik mijn vuist héél zacht van buiten
zou kussen;

en als ik op een teken
Jouw werk voorzichtig zou ontbloten
nimmermeer zijn uitgekeken
op mijn lege handpalm, grote
God
en nooit meer spreken.

Hans Andreus (1926-1977)

Last Poem

This poem is the last I'll ever write,
now that I've almost reached my dying day,
and my creative urges ebb away
and cancer fills my body like a blight,

and, Lord (I'll use that name again, I fear,
though I can scarcely picture you at all,
but still I'd rather speak in someone's ear
than into thin air, so when I call

it seems the best way of making sense) –
what happens now, what good to me's that light
of mine, of yours, with the fall about to commence

to unexpected depths without a name?
Or will you find me a word none can write,
that even unpronounced remains the same?

From *Last Poems* (Laatste gedichten). Haarlem: Holland, 1977.
Translated by Paul Vincent.

Laatste gedicht

Dit wordt het laatste gedicht dat ik schrijf,
nu het met mijn leven bijna is gedaan,
de scheppingsdrift me ook wat is vergaan
met letterlijk de kanker in mijn lijf,

en, Heer (ik spreek je toch maar weer zo aan,
ofschoon ik me nauwelijks daar iets bij voorstel,
maar ik praat liever tegen iemand aan
dan in de ruimte en zo is dit wel

de makkelijkste manier om wat te zeggen), –
hoe moet het nu, waar blijf ik met dat licht
van mij, van jou, wanneer het vallen, weg in

het onverhoeds onnoemelijke begint?
Of is het dat jij me er een onverdicht
woord dat niet uitgesproken hoeft voor vindt?

Jos de Haes (1920-1974)

Delphi (1)

Navel of God's earth. From our seat
we hear thirsty sparrowhawks splashing.
It sounds as if metals are clashing
and melting in a bluish heat.

A serpent, the Creator's shame,
slides across flaking masonry,
or else lies there enduringly
amid baked clay pots and bones without name.

The camomile nipples as dry as dust
crumble between our lips.
Finally the savour slips
From taste buds dull with lust.

And then, your left hand in my right,
two last scraps of processed matter,
we ourselves are just food on a platter
in God's funnel, fireproof and bright.

From *Collected Poems* (Verzamelde gedichten). Bruges: Orion, 1974.
Translated by Paul Vincent.

Delphi (1)

Navel der aarde Gods. Wij zitten
en horen sperwers water drinken.
Dat is alsof metalen klinken
en smelten in een blauwe hitte.

Een slang, een goddelijke schaamte,
schuift over schilferende muren,
of ligt te blijven en te duren
bij kleibaksels en geraamten.

De droge tepels der kamille
verpulveren tussen onze lippen.
Het laatst zal ons de smaak ontglippen
uit de verzadigde papillen.

En dan, uw linker in mijn rechter,
twee laatste stofveredelingen,
zijn wij zelf eetbare dingen
in Gods vuurvaste trechter.

Carel Willink, *The
Preacher*. 1937. Canvas,
100 x 75 cm. Centraal
Museum, Utrecht.

Refurbishing

the House of God

Adaptive Reuse of Religious Buildings in Flanders

Building remains one of the most fascinating of human activities. A structure is always meant to satisfy a particular need. For all sorts of reasons though, the original function of a building ceases to exist, leaving it redundant. The Italian architect Aldo Rossi emphasised the fact that old buildings often outlive their original purpose. We do not demolish every redundant structure, but often find ingenious new roles for our architectural heritage. This continuous process is an essential part of the life of a town or city, and is precisely what gives it its fascinating complexity. Some buildings have been given a succession of new uses, reflecting the constantly evolving nature of society. Factories are transformed into homes or spaces for exhibiting art, offices become shops, and so on. For religious buildings, especially churches, however, the situation is less straightforward. Monastery complexes are usually located within urban conglomerations and therefore have many possible uses. Decisions about the reuse of a building are often based on fortuitous circumstances. Since 1975 there has been general agreement that finding a constructive new use should be a priority in conservation policy. Reuse is an essential aspect in the preservation of our architectural heritage because disused buildings represent self-destruction.

Can a church be given a new purpose?

Churches are undoubtedly the most problematic religious buildings when it comes to reuse. The decision to transform the Jesuit Church in Bruges into a venue for medieval-style banquets was heavily criticised. The decision was seen as scandalous, almost pagan. A church is set apart from other buildings by its typology, basic architectonic form, and iconography (among other things). Also important is the fact that a building does not become a church until it has been consecrated, that is: dedicated to God and worship. The church interior thus becomes a place of quiet contemplation, but at the same time it is an extension of the public space; it is a place that anyone may enter. A church building therefore belongs to the community, and not exclusively to a limited group of churchgoers; the deconsecration of

The church as exhibition space: Jan Fabre's *He'll Stand Forever with Feet Put Together* (1997) in Watou's St Bavo church. © SABAM Belgium 2002.

a church is far more than an administrative decision.

Churches are characterised by their spacious interiors. It is no coincidence that after the French Revolution confiscated churches were bought for use as stores, barns and stables. In the nineteenth century a church in Ghent was even converted into a textile factory. The structure of a church, with its large span, makes it suitable for such a purpose. Converting a church into offices involves dividing up that interior space with walls and flooring. The essence of the architecture is eliminated, leaving only the outer shell. From that moment, the church is reduced to nothing more than a large shelter, a shell that has been retained for economic reasons or in order to preserve the townscape. Churches are, after all, a focal point in the urban landscape.

When it is forbidden to partition a church interior, the possibilities for reuse are extremely limited. In such cases it is possible to use it as a museum, one example being the Beguinage church of Sint-Truiden which houses a permanent exhibition. A church may also be used for temporary exhibitions. The small village church of Alveringem, near Veurne, is used for art exhibitions during the summer months and so contributes to the tourist industry in Flanders' Westhoek.

The Catholic Documenta-
tion and Research Centre
in Leuven, KADOC: the
chapel, which is a protected
building, is used for small
concerts or academic
meetings. Photos courtesy
of KADOC, Leuven.

The Caermers monastery in
Ghent: its restoration was
completed in 2000 and the
building is now the Centre
for Art and Culture of the
province of East Flanders.
This is the exhibition room,
as it was set up for the
Joseph Plateau exhibition in
2001.
Photo by Dirk Pauwels.

The most obvious function for a building that is still used for religious worship is as a concert venue. The many organ concerts held every year in Flanders form an important part of cultural life. The well-known international Flanders Festival owes its size to the many churches and cathedrals in which concerts are held. Church interiors provide an ideal setting for the St Matthew Passion, but many people find them inappropriate for the profane music of Strauss. A church is still a church, and a concert hall is a concert hall.

Few redundant buildings

Finding new uses for parish churches is not yet a problem in Flanders since very few of them are redundant. The situation differs in several ways from that in the Netherlands, where in addition to a large number of Roman Catholic places of worship there are many that belong to the various Protestant denominations. The buildings are the property of the Dutch church and can

A former Dominican monastery became a school of architecture in Ghent. The restoration was carried out in several stages under the direction of architect Herman de Witte and finished in 2001. Photo by Marc Dubois.

therefore be put up for sale. In Belgium – and therefore also in Flanders – the relationship between the Catholic Church and the authorities is completely different. This means that the law regarding the ownership for church buildings is also fundamentally different. Civic responsibility for church property in Belgium dates from Napoleonic times. After the French Revolution, all church property was 'nationalised' and became the property of the Nation. From 1792 onwards a number of churches were sold. In 1801 Napoleon concluded a Concordat with the Vatican, and a decree of 1802 returned use of the churches to the bishops. The government is also responsible for the maintenance of this substantial ecclesiastical patrimony. Today, the churches are the responsibility of the Ministry of Justice, which funds church restoration. The churches are managed by church councils (called '*kerkfabrieken*'). Municipalities and cities are bound by law to provide financial support when a church runs into financial difficulties. It is simply a fact that the Church today has fewer resources available for conserving its patrimony. It is therefore understandable that, in the context of increasing laicisation, questions are being asked about this use of government funds. Indeed, there are people who would like a thorough review of the system. The church community itself is becoming aware that, in this age of secularisation, buildings preserved with public funds must play a wider role in the community. The concept of 'unlocking' means more than simply providing access.

The existing legal provisions mean that no parish churches are sold, but this does not apply to churches and chapels belonging to monastic orders and papal congregations. A monastery is considered to be the private property of the order or congregation in question. It is these churches that often become redundant, with no listed status to protect them from demolition.

In Flanders, unlike the Netherlands, there are very few examples of churches that have undergone a radical transformation and so acquired a new lease of life.

New uses for monasteries

This is not the first time in history that a decline in the number of persons entering monasteries and convents has resulted in disused buildings. In some cases, they continued to be used by small groups of clerics. The design of these buildings, usually based on a central cloister, makes them suitable for a range of other uses. In many cases, the architectonic quality of a conversion is not very high. This is because conversions are often seen as 'doing up', while the wrong approach can have disastrous consequences for the future use of a historic building. Nevertheless, Flanders has some interesting examples that show that with a little imagination a country's rich heritage can become part of its future too.

The chapel of devotion in Leuven's Vlamingenstraat is an inspiring example. The baroque octagonal central structure with its dome was designed by Joris Nempe and consecrated in 1705. In 1873 the chapel became the property of the Franciscans, who added a monastery complex. After the Second World War, however, the number of monks declined sharply. In 1987 the Catholic University of Leuven acquired the complex to house its Catholic Documentation and Research Centre, KADOC. The cloisters are used for exhibitions, the cells have become offices and workrooms, and the refectory and kitchen have been converted into a reading room. The chapel, which is a protected building, is used for small concerts or academic meetings.

The city of Ghent has a rich patrimony of monasteries. The former Dominican monastery near St Michael's Church had become a run-down residential building. In 1963 the complex was acquired by the University of Ghent and, after thorough restoration, became the venue for official university functions. The Abbey of St Peter, also in Ghent, was given a new lease of life as a cultural centre, and has functioned as a *kunsthalle* for temporary exhibitions since the 1960s. The Abbey even provided a suitable venue for the European Summit in October 2001.

The Caermers monastery is part of the compact medieval street pattern of Ghent's Patershol quarter. The monastery consisted of two quadrangles and was virtually derelict. The imposing two-aisle church had been used for some time to store theatrical scenery. The restoration was completed in 2000 and the building is now the Centre for Art and Culture of the province of East Flanders. One of the quadrangles is intended for private residential use, and this part of the monastery has yet to be restored.

The Poortackere monastery at Oude Houtlei in Ghent is a large neo-Gothic complex. The religious use of this site dates back to 1278. In 1999 the architect Romain Berteloot converted the complex into a hotel and restaurant and venue for seminars. The monastery, tucked away behind other buildings in the heart of the city, is a quiet, peaceful place. The diversity of its many rooms allows it to accommodate a wide range of activities. The neo-Gothic chapel, for example, provides an ideal setting for small concerts.

From monastery to school of architecture

The finest example of reuse can be found in another Dominican monastery in Ghent. This imposing complex from the early eighteenth century is again hidden away in the very centre of Ghent, almost invisible from the public thoroughfare. A listed building since 1981, it is a haven of peace at the heart of the historic city. Restoration work began at the end of the 1980s and in the early 1990s the St Luke Higher Institute for Architecture acquired the site on a long lease. The former monastery thus became a school of architecture. More than five hundred students choose to study at this historic location. The restoration was carried out in several stages under the direction of architect Herman de Witte. The final phase, in 2001, was the restoration of the Abdissenhuis (Abbesses' house). A number of small modifications have adapted the complex to its new educational purpose. The fine cloisters are used as an exhibition venue and meeting place, and allow people to circulate freely between the different areas. Thanks to the vision of former director Walter Steenhoudt, this listed building, an important part of the city's architectural heritage, has been given a constructive new purpose that has saved it from further decline. In every case of adaptive reuse it is vital that the potential of the historic building should be properly assessed and incorporated into a vision for the future.

MARC DUBOIS
Translated by Yvette Mead.

mages

of Christ

The Depiction of Christ in the Mayer van den Bergh Breviary

On the day of the Transfiguration, Christ has ascended Mount Tabor with Peter, John and James the Greater. Suddenly his appearance changes. His face becomes radiant and his clothes shine like the sun. The disciples who had stayed behind at the foot of the mountain are dazzled by the all-pervading divine light. As their eyes become accustomed to the brilliance, they recognise Moses and the prophet Elias emerging between the wisps of cloud. They have barely recovered from their fright when God the Father speaks to them from the blazing sky: '*This is my beloved Son, in whom I am well pleased.*'

Transfiguration, Mayer van den Bergh Breviary, Ghent-Bruges, 1500-1510, fol. 506v. Museum Mayer van den Bergh, Antwerp / © Bart Cloet.

Vera Icon (detail), Book of Hours, Bruges, ca 1400., Hert. Ms.3, fol. 202v. Stadtbibliothek, Nuremberg.

'An imposing figure with features that command respect'

Along with portrayals of Mary and the saints, depictions of Christ in late medieval art are amongst the very finest. His likeness was recorded on both panels and parchment by the greatest artists of the Southern Netherlands. Christ appears as a new-born child in the Birth, the Circumcision, the Adoration of the Magi, the Flight into Egypt, the Presentation in the Temple and as a young boy of twelve amongst the scribes. In the early years he has no characteristic features and his physiognomy is no different from other young children. Only when the spotlight is turned on him as an adult does it become specific. Artists based their portrayal of Christ's face on the so-called Letter of Lentulus, which is attributed to Publius Lentulus, one of Pilate's predecessors. Anselm of Canterbury is the first to refer to the letter, in 1100. The description is as follows: '*He is of medium stature, an imposing figure with features that command respect. His smooth chestnut-brown hair forms soft waves beneath the ears and then falls in thick curls over his shoulders. His hair is parted on top in the middle, in the style of the Nazarenes. His forehead is regular and smooth, his complexion is rosy, with no blemishes or wrinkles. His nose and mouth are flawless, and he has a luxuriant full beard of the same colour, which is also parted in the middle. His gaze bespeaks wisdom and he has large blue-grey eyes with an unusual range of expressions, frightening when he rebukes, gentle and loving in exhortation.*'

Copy after Jan van Eyck, *Head of Christ*. 17th century. Panel, 33.4 x 26.8 cm. Groeningemuseum, Bruges.

These characteristics can be seen in the early portraits of Christ by the pre-Eyckian miniaturists, who were active between 1380 and 1420, as well as in the incomparably beautiful bust-length portraits of Christ by the Flemish panel painters. Painters like Petrus Christus, Dirk Bouts, Hans Memling and Gerard David indeed portray him as an imposing figure with '*features that command respect*'. They were inspired by a lost prototype by Jan van Eyck, who was himself clearly influenced by his predecessors.

However, it is not only the portrait busts that depict him like this. The narrative cycles illustrating paintings on panel and canvas, prayer books and books of hours, breviaries and other devotional writing portray him in a similar fashion, so that he is always recognisable and cannot be confused with the apostles or saints. Only his brother, James the Less, has more or less similar facial features. But through the use of attributes and the obviously inferior position he occupies compared to Christ, he can always be distinguished from his divine superior. In Dirk Bouts' *Last Supper* (Sint-Pieterskerk, Leuven) the contrast is striking. Christ sits motionless in the centre and blesses the sacred host. There is no movement; everyone present, both the apostles and the members of the Brotherhood of the Sacrament for whom the polyptych was created (the contract is dated 1465), is totally focused on the blessing of the bread. The mystery of Transubstantiation is central to the medieval Christian Church and Christ performs it in a manner that is utterly concentrated, deeply moving, but without movement. His face is divinely beautiful, as Lentulus' letter describes it. No wrinkles mark his complexion, no muscles are tensed, it is absolutely smooth and beautiful, and the

chestnut-brown hair hangs in gentle, shoulder-length curls. Here, too, are the centre parting and divided beard. And the so-called 'brother of Christ' sits at the far right corner of the table, an observer, inwardly moved by this manifestation of godliness. Like Christ he wears a simple, unadorned garment and, like all the apostles, he is shown barefoot. A similar scene, influenced by Bouts, can be found in the Mayer van den Bergh Breviary (*Breviarium Mayer van den Bergh*, Museum Mayer van den Bergh, Antwerp, inv. no. 946). Although the angle is different and the scene is less dense, the inspiration is clearly the same. Historically, after all, Dirk Bouts is the first artist to focus on the Transubstantiation rather than, like his contemporaries, the Communion of the Apostles or the Identification of Judas as the traitor.

Dirk Bouts, The Last Supper (central panel, detail). c.1464. Panel, 183 x 152.7 cm. Sint-Pieterskerk, Leuven.

Last Supper, Mayer van den Bergh Breviary, Ghent-Bruges, 1500-1510, fol. 331v. Museum Mayer van den Bergh, Antwerp / © Bart Cloet.

Stories in pictures

Narrative cycles with Christ as the protagonist were particularly popular in the late fifteenth century and the first decades of the sixteenth. They appear in paintings on panel and canvas and, especially, in breviaries, prayer books and books of hours. In contrast to panel paintings they are particularly suitable for the inclusion of narrative scenes, as they do not require complicated compositional plans. The different parts of the story can simply be depicted page by page on the manuscripts. Thus a continuous, progressive, narrative painting evolves around the sacred texts. Furthermore, the so-called Ghent-Bruges illuminators, who were active from around 1470, thought up an ingenious system that combines the different stages of a story into one picture. They create historiated margins around full-page miniatures, in which the story-line continues to unfold. The central scene captures the attention, but

the decorative margins complete the picture. This contrasts sharply with paintings on panel and canvas, in which the consecutive elements of the story appear on a continuous, fragmented background. For this reason Hans Memling's *Panorama with the Passion of Christ* (Turin, Galleria Sabauda) seems like a succession of stages on which the scenes of the Passion light up in a unified multiplicity. The direction in which the story is read cannot be guaranteed, for that particular painting reads from the left foreground to rear left, and then, fragmented and confusing, finally ends up in the background right. To compensate for this and facilitate interpretation the artists introduce letters or figures to clarify the development of the story – by analogy, perhaps, with the titles in illuminated texts and by association with saying a chaplet. A panel by an anonymous artist from Brussels, recently bought by the Stedelijk Museum Vander Kelen-Mertens in Leuven, is organised like this. In the end, however, these are mere expedients that serve to indicate the complexity of the visual material.

The Mayer van den Bergh Breviary is, without doubt, one of the gems of Ghent-Bruges book illumination from around 1500-1510 and the cohesion between its full-page miniatures and the surrounding borders is superbly effective. In the miniature of the Ascension the Roman soldiers, asleep or dazzled, remain oblivious to the living Christ, who rises from the grave, banner in hand, making the sign of the cross. Around it can be seen, consecutively, the three Marys beside the empty grave, the *Noli me tangere*, the men of Emmaus (in two scenes: first the meeting with Christ, and then the recognition) and the incredulous Thomas. Christ's appearance to the apostles, which takes place, chronologically, before the meeting with Thomas, is carried over to the opposite folio (the second scene, beginning from the top right hand). In the margin beneath, Christ is recognised by three of his disciples beside Lake Tiberias. In the top right hand corner he ascends into heaven. The series of appearances, proof of Christ's life after death, is thereby concluded. What comes next, according to the gospels, is Whitsun or the descent of the Holy Spirit, who was to give the apostles strength to preach Christ's word throughout the world. This scene is depicted about thirty folios further on in the breviary.

It is not clear whether one or more artists were involved in the creation of the 'Resurrection diptych'. The full-page miniature with its historiated decorative borders has been added to the quire and could perfectly well have been created by another illuminator. At the same time the medieval miniaturist created a remarkable harmony between the left and right wings, for the imitation wood frame decorated with scenes in golden-brown grisaille harmonises perfectly with those around the full-page miniature. The colours, the clothing and the faces, too, blend harmoniously. And yet closer inspection reveals differences in technique, because the striking white strokes, which afford the faces of the protagonists in the main scene their exceptional luminosity, are absent from the folio opposite. Furthermore, there is no recurrence of the black outlines used to finish off and define the figures in the full-page miniature. Different too is the atmospheric quality of the waterscape with the movement of the waves, the transparent strength of the sail, the sharp rocks covered in clumps of deep green grass and the leafless trees. In any case, the two scenes form a visual unity – a unity which extends throughout the breviary. Although recent research has shown that at least eight artists worked on the production of the Mayer van den Bergh Breviary, the 12 pages of the calendar, 29 full-page miniatures, 7 half-page miniatures, 20 smaller scenes, 9 historiated margins, 148 decorative borders and the innumerable richly decorated initials which the breviary boasts form an indisputable whole. It is clear that the artists, who include famous names from the Ghent-Bruges world of miniaturists, such as the Maximilian Master and the Master of James iv of Scotland, worked together closely to create this exceptional breviary. Little is known about the exact organisation since there is no documentary basis and archival research is very patchy.

In any case, the manner in which the figure of Christ keeps appearing in the breviary shows that the artists use the same models and are inspired by similar sources, which they cleverly adapt to the constantly changing context. The figure of Christ in the Resurrection, for example, is exactly like that in the Last Supper: the dark wavy shoulder-length hair combed back from the face exposing the ear, though the central parting, as described in Lentulus' letter, is less obvious. The high sloping forehead, the downcast eyes, the straight flat lips and the fine, parted beard are there, too. The rather bland faces are almost devoid of emotion, merely subdued witnesses of events.

Motifs and themes

Unlike the Resurrection diptych, the Last Supper is not surrounded by historiated margins. Instead, an equally characteristic Ghent-Bruges border decoration appears. Recognisable, utterly realistic and precisely painted flowers and acanthuses replace their stylised precursors from the Burgundian period. Furthermore they are not painted straight onto the bare parchment, but against a background of green, gold, blue, grey, red and black. By casting their shadows on the coloured surface they become tangibly realistic. Like a protruding frame they push the miniatures to the background and function like a window that invites an audience. The miniaturists are above all exceptionally imaginative in creating countless variations on the basic pattern. Insects with transparent wings alight on the flowers and acanthuses, snails glide slowly through the scenery, or birds fly after their prey. Shells, gems, jewels, pilgrims' insignia and decorative letters are added to other margins. Pottery and artefacts in silver and gold are displayed in painted cases. Sometimes the borders are even adorned with expensive brocades or peacock feathers. But illusionism reaches a peak with the depiction of wooden altarpieces, stone architecture and grand landscapes. The viewer is drawn into the scenery and feels at home in tangible, recognisable surroundings. Although at first glance these motifs are purely decorative, they are also important symbols. The pansy, for example, symbolises humility, the iris purity and the fly mortality. The scenery in the margin is more than a pleasure for the eye, it invokes the moral world ordained by God.

This realism is, of course, even more apparent in the miniatures themselves. They are presented so naturalistically that even the unpractised viewer with only a minimum of knowledge can interpret the religious themes. In the Seat of Mercy especially, the mimetic force works in an extraordinary fashion. God the Father, in a glittering gold tiara and with the dove of the Holy Spirit on his shoulder, displays his dead Son with visible tenderness. Enveloped in a kingly robe, whose folds in shades of gold and deep pink are set off quite deliberately against the pale background, God directs his gaze, slightly hesitantly, at the audience. His eyes have a melancholy force that provokes a sort of shudder in the viewer, whilst his dead Son, his limbs still somewhat stiff, shows the wounds in his hands, his feet and, in particular, his side. But the blue lips and closed eyelids emphasise the inevitability of what has happened. Through his death on the cross, through the spilling of his blood the world, which glitters crystal-clear at his feet, may receive absolution. In the main scene and in the architectural borders the angels sing and make music in his honour. He, the Father and the Holy Spirit are alpha and omega, the beginning and the end, as the golden letters on the green canopy emphasise: '*Ego sum alpha et omega.*' Here too, although the artist is not the same one who painted Christ in the Last Supper and the Resurrection, the characteristic traits described in Lentulus' letter can be seen. Compositions by the Master of Flémalle, alias Robert Campin, and Hugo van der Goes served as direct models and provided the illuminator, probably the panel painter Gerard David, with the inspiration for this breathtakingly fragile portrait. The other representation of the Trinity, which is, of course, far less dramatic since Christ is beside his Father, is much more basic and less refined. Although the facial type and robe are exactly the same, the entirety makes a slightly crude impression because of the hard folds in the shaded areas that are given depth with dark red hooked lines, hatching and dots. But as a whole this portrayal, too, is a perfect visual translation of the text. For whilst the Seat of Mercy translates into pictures the Trinity from the *temporale* (the only one of the period which includes a series of prayers for the most important holidays of the church year), the Trinity is

Seat of Mercy, Mayer van den Bergh Breviary, Ghent-Bruges, 1500-1510, fol. 326v. Museum Mayer van den Bergh, Antwerp / © Bart Cloet.

a perfect transposition of the first verse of psalm 109 (110 according to the current arrangement of the psalms). At the feet of the divine protagonists is written: '*Dixit Dominus Domino meo: sede a dextris meis*' ('The Lord saith unto my Lord, Sit thou at my right hand'). The Coronation of the Virgin in the presence of the angels and saints is also a wonderfully beautiful metaphor for '*Sing aloud unto God our strength: Make a joyful noise unto the God of Jacob*' from the first verse of psalm 80 (81).

A wealthy patron

In recent years a relatively large amount of research has been carried out into the profile of the patrons and recipients of such sumptuous manuscripts and paintings depicting Christ and the saints. They belong to a social, cultural and intellectual elite. For although manuscripts and paintings were created for less wealthy people as well, most of the works of art that have ended up in museums and libraries were commissioned by rich and powerful men and by Confraternities. That is certainly true of the Mayer van den Bergh Breviary, which was bought at Christie's in London in 1898 for the then record amount of £1,420. It is most likely that the manuscript was originally created for Manuel I, King of Portugal. The Portuguese text with instructions for calculating the variable date of Easter, the many Franciscan saints, several of whom are ardently venerated in Portugal (Saint Anthony and the five Moroccan martyrs, for example) and the depiction of Our Lady in the Snow point in this direction. Besides, Manuel I is known to have been a member of the third Order of Saint Francis and of the Confraternity of Our Lady in the Snow in Bruges. In addition, documents show that he owned a breviary, a type of book intended mainly for prelates or aristocrats with

Coronation of the Virgin, Mayer van den Bergh Breviary, Ghent-Bruges, 1500-1510, fol. 75v. Museum Mayer van den Bergh, Antwerp / © Bart Cloet.

Trinity, Mayer van den Bergh Breviary, Ghent-Bruges, 1500-1510, fol. 100r. Museum Mayer van den Bergh, Antwerp / © Bart Cloet.

court chapels and chaplains. With its magnificent ornamentation and often unforgettable pictures, which capture the attention of the viewer / believer like delicate icons, the Mayer van den Bergh Breviary testifies to the magnificent art produced in the Southern Netherlands that was coveted from the far North to the deepest South and quoted with amazing frequency by contemporary artists from neighbouring countries. Those keen to see a few pages of the breviary (dismantled in 1994) with their own eyes, can visit the exhibition of Ghent-Bruges manuscripts, to be held first in the J. Paul Getty Museum in Los Angeles and then in the Royal Academy of Arts, London, in 2003-2004.

BRIGITTE DEKEYZER
Translated by Lindsay Edwards.

BIBLIOGRAPHY

AINSWORTH, MARYAN, BERNARD BOUSMANNE, LORNE CAMPBELL et al., *Les Primitifs flamands et leurs temps*. Louvain-la-Neuve, 2000.

BELTING, HANS and CHRISTIANE KRUSE, *Die Erfindung des Gemäldes: das erste Jahrhundert der niederländischen Malerei*. Munich, 1994.

DEKEYZER, BRIGITTE and PETER DE LAET, *Breviarium Mayer van den Bergh*. Antwerp, 1997 (CD-ROM in four languages with reproductions of all the miniatures).

Flemish Illuminated Manuscripts, 1475-1550, exhibition catalogue, published by MAURITS SMEYERS and JAN VAN DER STOCK, Ghent, 1996: pp. 49-115.

GASPAR, CAMILLE, *The Breviary of the Mayer van den Bergh Museum at Antwerp*. Brussels / New York, 1932 (with reproductions of 73 miniatures).

MARROW, JAMES H., *Passion Iconography in Northern European Art of the Late Middle Ages and Early Renaissance: a Study of the Transformation of Sacred Metaphor into Descriptive Narrative*, Ars Neerlandica, 1. Kortrijk, 1979.

PANOFSKY, ERWIN, *Early Netherlandish Painting. Its Character and Origins*, 2 vols. Cambridge, MA, 1953.

RINGBOM, SIXTEN, 'Icon to Narrative. The Rise of the Dramatic Close-Up in the Fifteenth-Century Devotional Painting'. In: *Acta Academiae Aboensis*, Ser. A, Humaniora, Humanistiska vetenskaper, socialvetenskaper, teologi, 31.2, Åbo, 1965.

SMEYERS, MAURITS, *Flemish Miniatures from the 8th to the mid-16th Century: the Medieval World on Parchment*. Leuven, 1999.

ther

Words, Another Sound

New Liturgical Music in the Netherlands

Broadly speaking, until the 1960s there were two traditions in church music in the Netherlands: Protestant and Catholic. In the Reformed churches it was mostly psalms that were sung, in the rhymed version of 1773, together with hymns from the 1938 collection. Before 1773 the Protestants had had to make do with the psalms of Petrus Dathenus, a mediocre translation from the French of the Calvin Psalter (Strasbourg, 1545 / Geneva, 1562), in which the melodies were rapidly stripped of their original popular rhythms and dynamics.

But the 'new' 1773 version of the psalms was also in need of replacement. Serious work was done on the project in the 1950s and 1960s, as a result of which the *Songbook for the Churches* (Liedboek voor de kerken) appeared in 1973, with a new rhymed version of the psalms and an enlarged section of hymns from many centuries and countries, including a large number of new ones by well-known (priest-)poets. The exclusive strophic song form was retained. One of the poets, Ad den Besten, remarked that in many cases this was to the detriment of the song as a poem. There was further criticism. Many people were (and still are) of the opinion that the feel of modern life is insufficiently reflected in the Songbook. '*How can we today be expected to echo what our ancestors sang during the Thirty, Forty or Hundred Years War?*', wrote someone. Others set store precisely by the historical breadth of the Songbook: '*It would be unimaginably arrogant of late twentieth-century believers to think their theology or their faith was better.*'

The language of faith

In my view, the reaction above, and similar ones, show insufficient recognition of the need for continual renewal in the language of faith. Of course this is not about whether today's believers have a better theology or a stronger faith. It is about the fact that every era has the right to a contemporary expression of its faith. And in the twentieth century that faith has been severely shaken. After Auschwitz, believing can never be so steadfastly unquestioning as in earlier centuries. For many people born and raised as

Christians it has simply become impossible any longer to pray and to praise in a language that takes no account of the questions and religious doubts evoked by the great tragedies of the twentieth century.

Furthermore, from the time of the Bible onwards questions and doubt have *always* been part of Jewish and Christian tradition of faith. The psalms themselves bear witness to this. But that witness is often difficult to discern in the prevailing ecclesiastical-dogmatic language in which they have been enshrined and immured.

The Reformation itself arose from the need to relate the faith of the Bible more directly to life and experience. In 1523 the reformer Luther wrote to his friend Spalatinus: '*Following the example of the prophets and the old fathers of the Church we have decided to make psalms for the people in the vernacular. I wish you to avoid all unusual and high-flown expressions; the translation must be readily understood and adhere to the sense of the psalms translated. We must go to work here freely, and while preserving the meaning let the old words go and replace them with appropriate ones.*'

Thus the call for modernisation of liturgical language is not something new, something from the secular 1960s, but a necessary consequence of change in the world as experienced by those who use it. Language is as changeable as people.

Catholicism

Throughout the 1950s (Roman) Catholic liturgical singing haltingly followed two distinct traditions. On the one hand there was the ancient Gregorian chant, though nobody knew any longer just how it was originally sung. On the other there was the rich polyphonic tradition of part-sung masses, from Mozart to Perosi, and, of native origin, Andriessen and Mul. And all, of course, in Latin, an incomprehensible language. The texts had remained unaltered for at least four hundred years, often much longer, but most worshippers had little or no idea of what was being sung about.

In the 1960s, as a result of the Second Vatican Council, the greatest change in the field of liturgical language since the Reformation took place. It was decided at that time that the Roman Catholic liturgy must be brought up to date. *Aggiornamento* was the motto of Pope John XXIII. In 1963, after much discussion and opposition, the use of the 'vernacular' in the liturgy was permitted. Since then all sorts of developments have taken place in church music in the Low Countries. The most influential innovatory movement has been, and still is, that led chiefly by the Amsterdam priest and poet Huub Oosterhuis.

'The universe of the whole of life'

In the early 1960s the young Jesuit Huub Oosterhuis (1933-) began to write Dutch 'songs' for the liturgy of the Amsterdam Student Church, the student community established in 1960 to meet the demand among students for a contemporary form of liturgy. There were hardly any Dutch religious songs, apart from some pious songs about the Virgin Mary and a few triumphalist

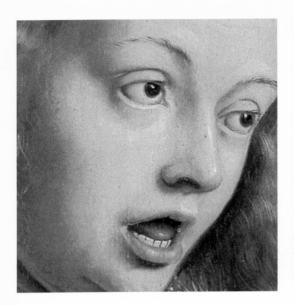
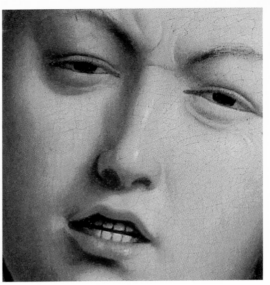

hymns whose purpose was *Propaganda Fidei* – the propagation of the Faith. And the culture of Protestant songs was totally alien to Catholic experience.

For the first few years Oosterhuis often wrote his songs to old Dutch folk tunes, which, on account of their rhythm and freshness, were quickly taken up by the numerous Catholic parishes that were looking for alternatives to Gregorian chant and polyphony. The little collections of hymns from Amsterdam went through reprint after reprint. What was it that was so different and so new about them?

In 1963 Oosterhuis said a lot about this on a number of occasions. I cite below a few lines from two (unpublished) lectures he gave in that year. They should be read as a sort of declaration of principle that still has not changed after forty years:

'It is impossible to imagine a service without live song. The demand is not for any old songs, but for songs that can function to best advantage within the entire liturgy of word and table (Eucharist) – for instance, songs as a way of explaining the Scriptures which are read.'

'Song as a form of life, that presents what is happening by way of good or evil, in a liberating manner; a word that internalises and revitalises the ever fragile faith, that keeps fortitude from flagging, ignites a flame, proffers sustenance, brings people together. Just as all poetry and all literature inspires people's lives by articulating life. Like any other poet the writer of religious songs must "seek to express the abundance of life". These eloquent words by the poet Lucebert unexpectedly and unintentionally describe the task of the new church song and the new liturgy, which is coming into being in all kinds of experiments, as an expression of contemporary religious awareness of life.'

'The old, mostly fossilised forms of ecclesiastical and monastic liturgy that have been handed down to us no longer portray existence as we live and ex-

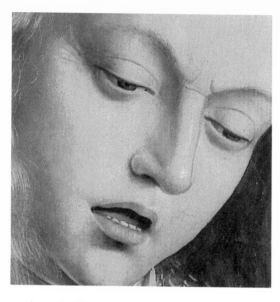

Singing angels on Jan and (?) Hubertus van Eyck's *The Adoration of the Lamb.* 1432. Cathedral of St Bavo, Ghent.

perience it. New means song and liturgy concerned with the now, the town where we live, man and wife, birth and death, right and wrong, ourselves in conflict with ourselves, hopeless, inarticulate people. Songs about light and darkness, about being born blind and being able to see. An old tale of love and death. Not a liturgy that fails to express how heart and body move, not a culture of forms too lofty in style to incorporate today's rhythm and ways of life in a recognisable form.'

'For this "the vernacular" is needed. Vernacular does not mean Latin in translation, for how many outdated theological views are embedded in the Roman Catholic missal? There is a need for comprehensible language and signs for people who are each other's equals.'

For platform and audience

It quickly became apparent that the one-sided form of the stanzaic song had insufficient liturgical potential. In the early 1960s Oosterhuis started working with the composer Bernard Huijbers S.J. The latter used his own Roman Catholic tradition of ecclesiastical music in a highly creative way. From the Gregorian chant he took the very close relationship between text and melody, in which the melody is not an autonomous element but expresses as directly as possible the meaning and feeling of the text. From the polyphonic tradition he took the part-singing. In a few years this led to a great variety of types of song in addition to the stanzaic form: recitative, canon, acclamation, psalmody, sung prayers. But what was really new – at least as far as Dutch church music was concerned – was that Huijbers wrote music that was specifically intended for both choir (and maybe a priest / precentor) *and* 'congregation' (community). Until that time, in the Catholic tradition it was mainly the choir that sang, often from a 'choir gallery' high up in the west end of the church, while the congregation listened. In Amsterdam the choir became the leader, the 'beautifier' and sometimes the second voice to the song of the congregation. The new religious music was to be sung '*by platform and audience together*', as Huijbers wrote in a small publication of the same title (*door podium en zaal tegelijk*). And it had to be 'elementary' music, that is to say: something lay people could sing without difficulty, in keeping with the meaning of the text and free from melodic, rhythmic or tonal capers. After Bernard Huijbers this new tradition has been carried on by Antoine Oomen and Tom Löwenthal.

In the last forty years a considerable 'Amsterdam' repertoire based on these principles has grown up; it now amounts to some five hundred very diverse liturgical compositions, some of which can be heard on twenty or so CDS.

Although the Amsterdamse Studentenekklesia (Amsterdam Student Church) became an independent organisation outside the official Catholic church as long ago as 1970, as a result of disagreements on celibacy and the celebration of the Eucharist (Mass), it is still a fertile source of new liturgical music. And this music is sung – in a most ecumenical manner – in ever more Catholic and Protestant communities. Not only in the Netherlands and Belgium, but also in English- and German-speaking countries. It is the poetic and biblical-theological power of expression of these texts that continually inspires the composers to new 'discoveries' and has gained widespread recognition among believers, though remarkably little in official church circles.

C.G. KOK
Translated by Sheila M. Dale.

HOW FAR IS THE NIGHT

Huub Oosterhuis, after Is 21:11–12
Translation by Tony Barr

Bernard Huijbers

How far is the night, how far, how far,___
watch-man?___ How_ far is the night, the night?
The_ morn-ing comes, says the watch-man,_ but_ still
it is night.

FURTHER INFORMATION

Stichting Leerhuis & Liturgie / Keizersgracht 96 / 1015 CV Amsterdam / The Netherlands
tel. +31 625 69 40 /
www.leerhuisenliturgie.nl

'Twixt

Heaven and Earth

The Madonna in Painting in the Low Countries

Today the Low Countries consists of Flanders (northern Belgium) and the modern-day Netherlands. And this political division corresponds historically to the world-famous Flemish and Dutch painting: Van Eyck, Bruegel and Rubens on the one hand, Rembrandt, Vermeer and Hals on the other, with as the one bridge between the two the North-Brabantine painter Hieronymus Bosch (see p. 294).

However, the same balance does not apply to the subject of this article, the portrayal of 'The Madonna'. Though an inexhaustible theme of Flemish painting for centuries, it is almost never found in Dutch painting. The main reason for this is the historical fact that Dutch painting is rooted in the Protestantism of the Calvinist North, while Flemish painting is a child of the Catholic Burgundian South.

A significant fact here is that Protestantism is regarded as a male religion, which gives precedence to 'the way of the head'; it recognises and worships only Jesus Christ as its Saviour and Lord. Christ is also the Saviour and the Son of God in Catholicism and in the Orthodox Church, but in His work to redeem the sins of the world a large and benevolent place is also reserved for Mary, His Mother. Consequently, the Catholic (and the Orthodox) Church is regarded as a female religion, which chooses 'the way of the heart'. And what touches the heart of mortal man more deeply than the image of his mother! This religious 'Mother aspect' is almost non-existent in the art of the Protestant regions, while it dominates the art of Catholic and Orthodox countries.

In the Byzantine art of the East and in the Romanesque and Gothic art of the West, the Mother of God or Madonna is depicted as 'the Queen of the Christians' and exalted in the hymn *Salve Regina*. Her royal status is expressed in the hieratic depiction of her maternal figure, radiating divine light. This hieratic, Byzantine element is still present in the late-Gothic painting of the Flemish Primitives, but to this divine immateriality is added a distinctly earthly corporeality. One might say that in the Flemish Madonna the icon and human warmth are merged in a highly creative manner. We find this Burgundian duality in the Madonna of the stable scene depicted by Hieronymus Bosch in the Bronchorst-Bosschuyse triptych (Museo del Pra-

do, Madrid). But Bruegel is already watching from behind the wall and over the roof of the stable.

The few depictions of Madonna and Child in Dutch painting lack this dual aspect and can be described as purely domestic. They are very much in keeping with the middle-class surroundings and sober observation so typical of the Dutch painters. The work of Vermeer and Frans Hals contains not a single Madonna. Rembrandt does portray Mary and her Child in the four paintings presenting 'The Holy Family', but the otherwise so visionary painter does not excel in any of the four, nor does he transcend the domestic genre. Though bathed in Rembrandt's own light, his Madonna displays no celestial élan, just the human intimacy between father, mother and child. How different from a 'Mary suckling her Child' by any Flemish Primitive! Even in Rubens' *Mary with the Child at Her Breast* the difference is fundamental: with Rubens, even the physical depiction of the Madonna has a mythical élan. Indeed, Flemish art is world famous for its unrivalled paintings of the nude or 'the flesh'. And it is this so pre-eminently voluptuous painting that surpasses the rest in its depiction of the Madonna. Perhaps for the Flemish painter the challenge is exactly this: to paint 'the nude' in a heavenly light.

Hieronymus Bosch,
Bronchorst-Bosschuyse Tryptich (central panel).
Late 15th century.
Panel, 138 x 33 cm.
Museo del Prado, Madrid.

Rembrandt H. van Rijn,
The Holy Family.
Canvas, 183.5 x 123 cm.
Alte Pinakothek, Munich.

'Mystic ground, my baroque earth, I feel like your child still, small and warm'

These words from a poem by Liliane Wouters embody the identity of Flemish art in general, and of the Madonna in Flemish art in particular. We will see the 'mystic ground' in the Madonnas of the Flemish Primitives, the 'baroque earth' in Rubens' Madonnas, and we will recognise the 'small and warm' not only in Bruegel's Madonnas but also in many popular Madonnas as well. This Flemishness of the Madonna becomes even more apparent when we compare her to the Italian Madonna of a painter like Raphael. His numerous Madonnas (who for centuries served as a model for Latin painters and those who worked in the Italian style) are so idealised and perfect, so utterly beautiful, that they do not belong to heaven and even less to earth, but rather to the neutral zone between the two. In contrast, the mystic contemplation of the Flemish Madonna is directed heavenwards and is anchored in the earth by her realistic and sensual depiction. In this 'typically Flemish' paradox she reveals the secret of her power and her beauty.

It is generally said that European painting begins with Giotto in the South and with Van Eyck in the North. In their works we also find the tendencies that distinguish Latin and Germanic painting. For example, Latin painting chooses an idealising style based on the ancient Hellenic example, while the Germanic is founded largely on realistic representation based on sensory perception.

At the beginning of this sensory realism we have the genius of Van Eyck whose influence in Northern Europe was inestimable. Yet his genius was preceded and prepared by the minute art of the Flemish miniaturists and by Robert Campin, alias 'The Master of Flémalle'. Campin abandons his miniature art for monumental panel painting and is the first to give prominence to the representation of the Madonna. In his *The Virgin and Child before*

Robert Campin, *The Virgin and Child before a Fire-Screen.* c.1440.
Panel, 63.4 x 48.5 cm.
National Gallery, London.

a Fire-Screen and *Salting Madonna* (National Gallery, London), he combines the sculptural and monumental style of the late-Gothic with the sensual and the intimate. The setting for his Madonna is a richly furnished Flemish interior.

With this new style of painting Campin becomes Van Eyck's teacher. And with Van Eyck the school of the Flemish Primitives begins, and achieves unprecedented heights with other geniuses like Rogier van der Weyden, Hans Memling, Hugo van der Goes and Dirk Bouts. Moreover, in addition to these truly outstanding painters, this school produces scores of lesser known 'masters' and anonymous or popular Flemish Primitives who reflect the genius of those they follow. Each at his own level, they all represent the characteristics we have already described as 'typically Flemish'.

Van Eyck has no equal when it comes to combining these characteristics. In his oeuvre there are no less than six (recognised as authentic) Madonnas of which *The Madonna with Chancellor Rolin* (Louvre, Paris) and *The Madonna with Canon Van der Paele* (Groeninghemuseum, Bruges) are the most famous. The Madonna in the latter work summarises Van Eyck's style brilliantly: Mary and her Child are at once detached and tender, inscrutable and immediate, untouchable and intimate. The same ambiguity is found in his realistic depiction of matter, even down to the minutest detail, and in the pyramidal monumentality of the central figure who exudes a divine majesty. In this majestic style – as in Egyptian images of kings –, along with the late-medieval piety, we also find the incomparable affluence of Burgundian court culture: the most magnificent cloaks and clothing in the rarest materials, the most beautiful carpets, the marvellous jewels, the brilliance of gold and of precious metals, ceramics, marble, crystal and glass. All this is translated into a visual language in which the richest graphic, pictorial and sculptural aspects are perfectly balanced. What Van Eyck manifests so massive-

Hugo van der Goes, *The Adoration of the Magi* (detail). Late 15th century. Panel, 150 x 247 cm. Staatliche Museen, Berlin-Dahlem.

Jan van Eyck, *The Madonna with Canon Van der Paele*. 1434-1436. Panel, 141 x 176.5 cm. Groeninghemuseum, Bruges.

ly and in such a concentrated form, we find diluted and humanised in his contemporaries.

The oeuvre of Rogier van Der Weyden contains no fewer than twenty representations of the Madonna, one of the most famous being the *St Luke Drawing the Virgin* (Museum of Fine Arts, Boston). While all the Madonnas by the Flemish Primitives might seem as like as peas in a pod, in fact nothing could be further from the truth. If we look closely at Van Der Weyden's Madonna, we notice a remarkable difference from that of the shining example Van Eyck. While in Van Eyck the forms are built up strongly and massively and exude a mysterious power, in Van Der Weyden the white cloth and the dark cloak fall around the Child and his Mother in subtle, rhythmic refractions. The fine Gothic hands with their elongated fingers – as if playing a harp – are no less aristocratic, the Child is drawn both playfully and hieratically, and the demure Mary looks with refined discretion at the subtle form of her breast. The painting of the fabrics and the subdued colours are equally diffuse and aristocratically refined, in contrast to the glowing fullness of Van Eyck's coloration.

Hans Memling, *Diptych of Maarten van Nieuwenhove* (left panel with the Virgin). 1487. Panel, 52 x 41.5 cm. Memlingmuseum, Bruges.

Rogier van der Weyden, *St Luke Drawing the Virgin.* 1435-1436. Panel, 137.7 x 110.8 cm. Museum of Fine Arts, Boston.

In the ascetic style of Dirk Bouts the hieratic Madonna figure reflects the austerity of a pared down, minimalist interior in *The Virgin and Child with Saints Peter and Paul* (National Gallery, London). The refinement of the mystical feelings and the softening of the forms continue in striking fashion in the oeuvre of Hans Memling. In fact, the Flemish Madonna reaches her highest point in Memling's works, appearing no fewer than thirty times. Particularly typical of him is the Madonna from the *Diptych of Maarten van Nieuwenhove* (Memlingmuseum, Bruges). In both content and form, every last detail of the small panel conveys an almost feminine tenderness and virginal purity: the folds of the mantle and the dress fall with courtly grace, the ritual gestures of her gentle hands suggest discretion, peace smiles in the introspective porcelain features, the light shimmers in the chaste little landscape, the celestial spheres sing in the soft Memling red and the pure Memling blue, green, yellow and grey.

Gerard David, *Rest on the Flight into Egypt.* c.1510. Panel, 44.3 x 44.9 cm. National Gallery of Art, Washington D.C.

Pieter Bruegel the Elder, *The Adoration of the Kings* (detail). 1564. Panel, 112.1 x 83.9 cm. National Gallery, London.

The human and popular are already very much in evidence in the work of Hugo van der Goes. In the Madonna in *The Adoration of the Magi* (Staatliche Museen, Berlin-Dahlem) the composition and traditional dress are still built up in late-Gothic style and worked out in the manner of Van Eyck, but in the details of the heads and hands we can see how realistic and popular, how warm and close the world is becoming. The mischievous Child Jesus underlines the contrast with Memling. This 'popular' aspect looks ahead to Bruegel and the sixteenth century; but before Bruegel, at the turn of the century, come the humanist painters Gerard David and Quinten Metsys.

Gerard David is described as the last of the Flemish Primitives. In the painting *Rest on the Flight into Egypt* (National Gallery of Art, Washington), the landscape, Mary's mantle and her chaste appearance still denote the late-Gothic world. The Gothic angularity, however, is so rounded, the colours so softened and diffuse and the features so subtly veiled that the ideals of the Renaissance are already heralded in the contours. The Renaissance and the Italianate style are even more manifest in the *sfumato* and in the idealised faces and hands of *The Madonna with the Pap Spoon*. Gerard David painted this subject three times, almost identically.

Virgin and Child Enthroned (Gemäldegalerie, Berlin-Dahlem) by the mannerist Quinten Metsys looks even more Italian. Though here, too, we still have the after-glow of the Flemish Primitives in the predilection for painting matter, the mannered poses of Mary and Child and the contours of their rounded and idealised forms undoubtedly allude to his Italian models.

Peter Paul Rubens, *The Holy Family*. 17th century. Canvas. Museo del Prado, Madrid.

In extreme contrast to this, a half century later Pieter Bruegel the Elder chooses the language of life. In his *Adoration of the Kings* (National Gallery, London), Mary is a robust working-class woman who bends amiably over her Child. A healthy peasant boy, he snuggles contentedly '*small and warm*' into the folds of the white cloth on his Mother's broad lap. Behind the Madonna stands the paunchy Joseph like a protective gate, while the villagers look on inquisitively.

In the next century, the great master Peter Paul Rubens dominates the Flemish baroque painting of Northern Europe. His Madonna representations tend to be at the centre of vibrant, religious creations suggestive of popular theatre. In the painting *The Holy Family* (Museo del Prado, Madrid) we recognise the pre-eminently Rubenesque Madonna. Like his nymphs, Venuses and nudes, she is a mythical Rubens woman, pulsating with life and radiating sensual abundance. Here '*the baroque earth*' from the verse by Liliane Wouters is triumphant.

Alongside Rubens, Anthony van Dyck paints no fewer than fifty representations of Mary and her Child. Totally different from the powerful Rubens, Van Dyck paints his Madonnas, like his portraits of noble ladies, in a frivolous (sometimes an almost decadent) style. Yet his finest Madonnas are of a standard comparable with the best works of the sophisticated Velasquez. In the *Rest on the Flight into Egypt* (Alte Pinakothek, Munich), the transparent brush strokes turn to chamber music with the soft, diffuse colours. In their sensual refinement, Mother and Child echo the same poetic dream.

Less poetic but essentially realistic are the Madonnas that Jacob Jordaens paints in harsh contrasts of dark and light, while the ordinary folk look on. In his type of Flemish Madonna the hieratic approach of Van Eyck and the mythical fashion of Rubens are transformed into a purely profane event, as in *The Adoration of the Shepherds* (Nationalmuseum, Stockholm).

Mother and Child forever

After the glorious baroque age, a period of economic adversity sets in for Flanders. Divided by the religious wars and deprived of its lifeblood by the closure of the River Scheldt, for centuries life is conditioned by poverty. And with this adversity, Flemish art dies a temporary death. Not until the second half of the nineteenth century, in neoclassicism and above all in neo-Gothic, are Madonnas painted again, but now in kitsch, retro forms.

The genius of James Ensor forms a bridge between the nineteenth and twentieth centuries and to modern art. There is a distinct absence of Madonna depictions in modern Flemish painting – save for Ensor's ambiguous allegorical *The Virgin of Consolation* (Tavernier Collection, Ghent) in which the image of the Madonna shifts from the foreground to the background, be-

James Ensor, *The Virgin of Consolation*. 1892.
Panel, 48 x 38 cm.
Tavernier Collection, Ghent.
© SABAM Belgium 2001.

coming merely an exotic little painting within a painting.

This shift illustrates perfectly the great change that had taken place: art and life have become secularised. In the once so Catholic Flanders secularisation has become a fact of life. Here, too, the depiction of the beloved Madonna is quietly moved from the beating heart of art to the otherworldly ateliers of liturgical art, where it dies a plaster death.

But 'breeding will out', and the image of Mother and Child apparently runs in the blood of the Flemish artist. These days the depiction of the Madonna is experiencing its sacred rebirth in the profane representations of artists who again look to the reality of life for inspiration and to the movements of their time. In the twentieth century there are two important Flemish artists in particular who, in the most personal way possible, testify to this age-old tradition. With their modern 'profane Madonnas', both represent the mystic and the earthly in Flemish art. The first is the sketcher and sculptor Georges Minne, who is fascinated by the mystic union of *Mother and Child* in their introverted embrace (Koninklijk museum voor Schone Kunsten, Ghent). The second is the great Expressionist painter Constant Permeke who in his powerful drawing *Motherhood* (Museum voor Schone Kunsten, Ostend) creates a monumental archetype that seems to be moulded out of granite and earth.

HAROLD VAN DE PERRE
Translated by Alison Mouthaan-Gwillim.

Constant Permeke, *Motherhood.* 1929. Canvas, 180 x 90 cm. Museum voor Schone Kunsten, Ostend. © SABAM Belgium 2001.

Georges Minne, *Mother and Child.* Early 20th century. Koninklijk Museum voor Schone Kunsten, Ghent.

hristianity

in Indonesia, Past and Present

Christianity arrived in the Indonesian Archipelago five centuries ago, with the Portuguese ships that sailed round the Cape of Good Hope. The Portuguese were drawn to the lands in the East by the luxury products to be obtained there; but their presence in Asia was also a military and a religious enterprise, a continuation of the Crusades that had freed the Iberian Peninsula from Moorish domination but had failed to make the Middle East Christian again. If the might of the Ottoman Empire made it impossible to defeat Islam by frontal assault, the Turkish flank could be turned and Islam attacked from the rear, in the Indian Ocean.

The Portuguese were a small nation; and in Asia they came up against great empires, ancient civilisations, established religions. Consequently, unlike the Spaniards in the Americas, they were able to establish themselves only in a few places and islands on the fringes of the continent. And this meant that, in South and South-East Asia at least, Christianity gained a foothold only in a few isolated locations. In the case of the Indonesian Archipelago these were the islands of Sangir and Amboina in the Moluccas and Timor and its neighbouring islands in the Lesser Sunda island group. Even today half of Indonesia's Catholics are to be found in the latter region, while the specifically Catholic identity that developed there was a strong factor in East Timor's resistance to its occupation by Indonesia from 1976 to the end of the 1990s. In about 1600 there were some 40-50,000 Christians in what is now Indonesia, out of a total population of about 10 million.

A merchant company as a Christian government

The Dutch too came to South-East Asia to pursue a war being fought in Europe. Their enemy was not Islam, however, but Roman Catholic Spain, whose King was at that time also King of Portugal. Between 1596 and 1613 the Dutch succeeded in ousting the Portuguese from most of their Asian possessions. In the majority of cases the local Christians were then protestantised. This was a fairly simple matter; since the Portuguese had trained no native priests, the Dutch had only to expel the Catholic missionaries and replace them with Protestant clergy. In new Dutch settlements, too, such as Batavia, which became the capital of the Dutch possessions in Asia, Catholicism was not tolerated while Islam and Chinese religion were. Only in the twentieth century has Catholicism in Indonesia won back some of the ground lost to Protestantism over the intervening centuries.

From 1602 until 1799 the VOC or Dutch East India Company exercised sovereign power in all Dutch possessions east of the Cape of Good Hope, and it took its task as a Christian government seriously. VOC ships carried the church ministers to their posts; the VOC funded their salaries and the buildings in which they held their services; the VOC paid all the costs of translating and publishing bibles, hymn books and catechisms. This solicitude was not confined to the Company's European subjects, but extended to Christian natives as well. The Company was also strong enough militarily to protect Christian communities from attack by their Muslim neighbours. As a result, these two centuries were a period of quiet consolidation. The VOC undertook very little missionary activity, though. Even when it became a great territorial power on Java it never attempted to establish missions among the Muslim Javanese. In the Moluccas the population of some small islands was Christianised, but no effort was made to follow this up. At the end of the eighteenth century the Christians in Indonesia numbered 100,000, of whom some 60,000 were Protestants.

Iconoclasm?

When the Dutch came to Indonesia they did not at first regard Islam as an enemy, but once the Portuguese had been defeated their relations with Indonesia's Muslim powers deteriorated. Despite this, however, the VOC

Church of the Portuguese-language Protestant community in Batavia (1695).

HET GEZIGT VAN DE GROOTE HOLLANDSE KERK TOT BATAVIA
TE SIEN VAN DE OVERKANT VAN DE GROOTE REVIER.

The Hollandse Kerk, Church of the Dutch-language community in Batavia (1643).

was never rash enough to attempt any persecution of the Muslims in its territories. Christian villages in the Moluccas were screened from Muslim influences for political reasons, but in the capital, Batavia, the Company tolerated the presence of several mosques. The city's Chinese population too was allowed to practise its religion openly, including holding processions in the streets. From time to time this situation drew protests from Batavia's church council, but these were ignored by the government. In fact, not even the church council would have wanted any physical persecution of the adherents of other faiths. The Church overseas, as in the Netherlands, would have been satisfied with having the public exercise of these religions suppressed.

Both Church and state took a less relaxed attitude to manifestations of tribal religions. As in the days of the Early Church, 'paganism' was equated with devil-worship. Villages that converted to Christianity therefore had to surrender all objects connected with their old religion. Any Christian caught practising the old ceremonies was punished; possession of an ' image of the devil' even carried the death penalty. However, this stern approach did not prevent the emergence of a syncretic variety of the Christian faith. This mix of seventeenth-century Christianity and magic, known as 'agama Ambon' ('Ambonese religion'), is very much alive today in the Moluccas and in other regions where it has been spread by Ambonese preachers working for Dutch missions.

A new missionary age

With the French Revolution came the separation of Church and state. But in religious matters, as in other areas, the new European model was not applied in the Indonesian colony. There the government established a 'Protestant Church' which included both European and native Christians, and continued to fund all its activities until the end of the colonial era; for a time it even financed missionary activity by this church, simply in order to prevent Islam gaining a hold among pagan populations. But somehow times *had* changed. Pietism and the Enlightenment had created an open space, outside the domains of state and Church alike, in which individuals could come together and pursue goals set by themselves. Between them, these movements also provided the motivation for bringing the Christian faith to non-Christian peoples.

In 1797, two years after the Dutch had their version of the Revolution with the French invasion of the Netherlands and the establishment of the Batavian Republic, the Dutch Missionary Society (Nederlands Zendeling Genootschap) was founded. However, its amalgam of pietism and rational Christianity led to conflict within the Society, with the result that over the course of the nineteenth century a number of other missionary organisations sprang up, each representing a particular element within Dutch Protestantism. In a sense, these organisations are comparable with the religious orders and congregations within the Roman Catholic Church. Like them, with a few exceptions they formed no part of the regular church organisation, but were bound together by a common purpose; like them, each had its distinct characteristics. Without exception they chose the Dutch colonies in South-East Asia as their sphere of operations. But since they lacked the resources to cover the whole of the Netherlands Indies, German and American missions were allowed to operate there also.

Frontispiece of a Malay edition of the Heidelberg Catechism (1730). The Christianised Malay has a distinct Arab flavour. Photo by Studio Beekpark.

The object of these missionary societies was to bring the Christian faith to the many areas untouched by the VOC mission, and to Java first and foremost. The Dutch government, fearing a Muslim backlash, at first refused to allow Christian missionaries on the island; but after the introduction of a liberal colonial policy it grudgingly permitted missionary activity. Thus, for the first time in history, an attempt was made to convert a Muslim population to Christianity by peaceful means. The attempt was not entirely unsuccessful: in 1942 Java's Christian population included some 60,000 Protestants and 45,000 Catholics who had converted from Islam, and by 2000 their combined numbers had risen to about two million out of the island's population of 120 million. Outside Java the missions concerned themselves mainly with peoples living in more or less isolated areas who did not belong to the Protestant Church and were as yet untouched by Islam. This led to the founding of a number of Protestant ethnic churches, which were granted autonomy between 1930 and 1966. The Batak Church in North Sumatra is the largest single Protestant church in Asia; it has three million members. But Eastern Indonesia is still the heartland of Protestantism in the region. In two of Indonesia's 26 provinces, Irian and Nusatenggara Timur, Christians form a large majority, while in North Sumatra, North Sulawesi and the Moluccas they make up half the population. But Eastern Indonesia is relatively thinly populated, so that in the country as a whole Christians form only a small minority. Today their numbers can be estimated at 15 million Protestants and 6 million Catholics, out of a total population of 205 million.

'Christianity and civilisation'

For all their differences and disputes, the Dutch and German missionary organisations active in the Netherlands Indies all belonged to the mainstream of continental Protestantism. They all took a rather positive view of the established order in state and society, and of modern science and civilisation. But they agreed with their contemporaries in regarding the indigenous peoples as backward or even degenerate. For this reason they accepted the colonial order, even if their close contacts with the native population made them more critical of that order's negative effects and more inclined to view it as temporary. The same can be said of their attitude to other aspects of European domination. Even the most orthodox and pietist of missionaries, who had gone into the mission field primarily to save souls from eternal misery in Hell, even they can be heard praising European civilisation and its introduction into the colony and criticising the government and their fellow Europeans only for introducing modern civilisation without the Gospel.

The other side of this positive attitude to modernity was a negative view of indigenous culture and religion. Throughout the nineteenth century these were more or less disregarded. To the orthodox they were 'pagan', and so nothing of them could be incorporated into the Christian community they sought to construct; while more liberal missionaries saw them as 'backward' and therefore irrelevant. Either way, the result was that new converts were isolated from their former environment. Often they were gathered into Christian villages, where their lives were supervised by the missionaries. Like the government, the missionaries – at this time mostly from the lower social classes, rather poorly educated, and with extremely limited funds at their disposal – made no attempt to provide opportunities for indigenous Christians to acquire a more advanced education, which would have enabled them to develop a Christian leadership and a new Christian culture.

The beginning of the twentieth century brought new ideas on the theory and practice of missionary work. Missions connected with the Netherlands Reformed Church (*Nederlandse Hervormde Kerk*), the largest Protestant church in the Netherlands, took a more sympathetic attitude to indigenous

Interior of the (former) Grote Kerk (Big Church) in Ambon.

culture. Some missionaries even became experts in the ethnography and linguistics of the Indonesian Archipelago and wrote books on those subjects which are still regarded as authoritative today. They sought to give indigenous culture, even indigenous religion, a place in missiological thinking and practice. In reacting to the negative attitude of their predecessors, however, they went to the other extreme and tended to regard indigenous language and culture as sacred. Attempting to shield their flock from modern influences, wherever possible they used the local language as the medium of instruction in education and deliberately founded no institutes of higher education. Only on Java, and only towards the end of the colonial era, was a theological college established (in 1934). Thus the christianised peoples of eastern Indonesia were turned away from modernity. This policy has to be regarded as one of the reasons for this region's present relative backwardness. It is ironic that the mission of the orthodox Calvinist *Gereformeerde Kerken*, which even in the twentieth century held to the negative view on 'paganism', actually did far more to prepare its converts for the future: by setting up an extensive Dutch-language school system it enabled them to participate in the political and cultural developments that took place after 1945. In some other Christianised areas, such as North Sulawesi and North Sumatra, indigenous Christians benefited from the extensive system of schools established by the state.

American missions

Until the end of the colonial era the Christian missions in Indonesia were almost exclusively the province of Europeans. Consequently, the large number of churches was due less to denominational differences than to the fact that most of them were ethnic in character, serving the region's many different races. The great majority of these churches joined the Indonesian Council of Churches (now the Persekutuan Gereja-Gereja di Indonesia or PGI) on its foundation in 1950. After independence, however, there was a strong American influence in politics and the economy and, increasingly, in religion as well. In 1950 about 1% of Indonesian Protestants belonged to churches with an American background; in 2000 the figure was 30%. The Americans were especially active in isolated areas which had remained unevangelised, such as the interior of Irian (New Guinea), and in the cities. These missions mostly belonged to conservative evangelical bodies and to the Baptist, Methodist and Pentecostal churches. They adopted an exclusive stance, refusing to work with each other and even more so with the churches with European roots. The result was that Protestantism in Indonesia became more and more fragmented. Nowadays, in addition to the PGI there are two other national councils of churches and over four hundred separate Protestant churches. American influences have also penetrated some of the older churches, in which charismatics now tend to look down on traditional Christians. The American-oriented churches themselves criticise their older sister churches not only for failing to maintain strict doctrinal orthodoxy and church discipline, but also for speaking out on political, cultural and economic matters. The result of all this is that Indonesian Protestantism is more divided today than it has ever been.

Increasing marginalisation

Right from the start, Indonesian Christianity had to face opposition from Islam. In the sixteenth century the antagonism between the two religions exploded into open war. The Dutch, much stronger militarily than the Portuguese, were able to impose the *Pax Neerlandica* on the Muslim kingdoms, but hostility to Christian missions never ceased. With the rise of nationalism Indonesia's Christians found themselves compromised by their association with the colonial power, though they were able to shed some of this stigma by joining the political and armed struggle for independence. When independence was achieved, the Christians were ahead of the Muslims in terms of education and so made a not insignificant contribution to the new nation's intellectual and economic development. But somehow they still did not feel safe. During the Sukarno and Suharto eras (1950-1998) they sought to prove their loyalty by following every ideological whim of those in power, from 'revolution' in the sixties through 'development' under Suharto to 'reform' in the late nineties. Most of them were quite content with the dominant role played by the military between 1966 and 1998 because it kept the Muslims from power. In those days Christians were able to deceive themselves that they had a role in the nation's affairs because Suharto played them off against the Muslims by appointing a relatively large number of Christians to senior positions in the state and the army.

In the nineties, when Suharto was making overtures to the Muslim majority, this policy was reversed. Moreover, the Muslim majority was now catching up educationally and claiming its due. Today, with the Muslim parties fighting for power among themselves, the Christians are suffering the same fate as have their co-religionists in every country with a Muslim majority, ever since the seventh century: they can only stand on the sidelines and await the outcome of the struggle, which will also decide what role – if any – is left to them in national life. Far from being able to call on the government to destroy mosques, as in the seventeenth century, they now have to watch their churches being destroyed in their hundreds by Muslim mobs and whole districts 'cleansed' of their Christian inhabitants.

The Meshid Raya or 'Big Mosque' in Kutaraja, built in 1879 by the authorities of the Netherlands Indies as a sign of peace. Two wings were added in 1936.

TH. VAN DEN END

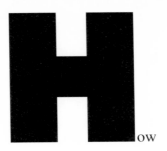

How

the Congo Was Converted

Belgian Missionary Work in Central Africa

For most Flemish people, the history shared by Belgium and an enormous territory in Central Africa begins with Leopold II. Few of them are aware that long before then Flemings and Netherlanders had been active in the area now known as the Democratic Republic of Congo. In 1482 the Portuguese Diogo Cao discovered the estuary of the River Zaire and made contact with the BaCongo people who lived along its banks. The evangelisation of the country, entrusted to various religious orders and members of the secular clergy, began in 1491. Although it enjoyed some initial success, the enterprise threatened to become bogged down because of the heavy toll in lives and the inhospitable nature of the territory. To prevent this, the Congolese king approached the Pope in 1618 with a request for missionaries from the Capuchin order.

More than a quarter of a century was to pass before the first members of the order disembarked in the black kingdom. None of them came from the Low Countries. The Portuguese, who had ruled the roost there for over a century and a half, had no wish to see immigration from other European countries. Particularly unwelcome were subjects of the Spanish crown, who at the time included the inhabitants of the Low Countries. This situation

In 1482 the Portuguese Diogo Cao discovered the estuary of the River Zaire. He left these inscriptions on the rocks at M'Pozo.

changed after 1641. As early as 1597, attempts at colonisation were made by groups from the Low Countries, referred to in the sources sometimes as Netherlanders, sometimes as Flemish. In any case, it appears that the majority of them were Protestants. Their power in the region grew steadily until in 1641 a fleet from Holland landed near Luanda and promptly occupied the entire coastal area. The power and influence of the Netherlanders became so great that Lisbon's authority was effectively ended. On the religious front it meant that Calvinist missionaries soon became active in the region and Catholicism lost its monopoly. Although the Flemish had previously been unwelcome in Portuguese territories because of their subjection to the Spanish crown, it now seemed advisable to send some to the region as missionaries. As Dutch speakers they would be well-qualified to mediate between the Catholic mission and the Calvinist authorities. That explains why by 1651 a number of Flemish Capuchins were working in the old Kingdom of Congo. The best-known of them is undoubtedly Joris van Geel, who was born in Oevel in 1617 and eventually murdered in a village by native converts after setting fire to traditional religious paraphernalia. Among Africanists his name is associated with the earliest known dictionary of a Congolese Bantu language. His annotations to the dictionary, which contain numerous references to his personal experiences and discoveries, are an important source of concrete information about missionary work at that time. In 1835 an anticlerical regime came to power in Portugal and proclaimed the abolition of all the religious orders active in Portuguese territories. This, together with the fact that civil war was making the region unsafe, led to the return of the Capuchins to Europe.

The Flemish Capuchin Joris van Geel, (1617-1652), killed in a village by native converts after he set fire to their traditional religious paraphernalia. Koninklijk Museum voor Midden-Afrika, Tervuren.

Belgian missionaries

It was not until 1865 that European Christians showed a renewed interest in evangelising the area. The first to do so was the originally French Congregation of the Holy Spirit, the Spiritans, followed hesitantly by other religious organisations. Meanwhile, through much diplomatic string-pulling the Belgian King Leopold II, who had had his eye on the territories for a number of years and had them surveyed at his own expense, succeeded in obtaining official recognition for his aspirations. In 1885 he proclaimed the birth of the Congo Free State and was granted permission by the Belgian parliament to assume the Congolese crown. Competition between the Western European nations was fierce at the time; all of them were equally greedy for a slice of the African cake. Seen in that light, it is understandable that Leopold was keen to ensure that, as far as possible, the missionaries in his territories should be exclusively Belgian. He even undertook a, largely successful, diplomatic offensive aimed at expelling the French Spiritans from the Free State. They were replaced by members of the mainly Belgian Scheutist Congregation and the massive involvement of the Belgian churches in Central Africa dates from that time. After the Scheutist missionaries (1888), who also supplied the first Apostolic Vicar for the new Congolese vicariate, other Congregations quickly established themselves on Congolese soil: Sisters of Charity from Ghent (1892), Jesuits (1893), Trappists (1894), Sisters of our Blessed Lady from Namur (1894), Priests of the Sacred Heart

Departure of the Sisters of
our Blessed Lady and
Jesuits on 23 July 1893.
Universiteitsbibliotheek,
Leuven.

A pioneering missionary in
his *pousse*. Archief Paters
van het Onbevlekte Hart
van Maria (Scheut),
Brussels.

(1897), Norbertines from Tongerlo (1898), Redemptorists (1899), Brothers
of the Sacred Heart (1904), Brothers of the Christian Schools (1909) etc.
Since Protestant missionaries were not subject to any centralised institution
that could be influenced by diplomatic initiatives, Leopold had far less control over them. But from the outset there were almost as many Protestant
missionaries, mostly of Anglo-Saxon origin, as Catholic.

Leopold's intention was to make the Free State first economically viable,
then profitable. To achieve this the enormous territory had to be occupied
and then opened up to Western civilisation, and what he mainly expected of
missionaries was that they should play a leading role in achieving this last
goal. However, the Congolese Free State did not survive very long. The interests of the great European powers were not served by allowing Leopold
to succeed. Rumours about abuses perpetrated by whites on the native population in building railways and tapping rubber gave France, Germany and
especially England a welcome pretext to unleash a smear campaign against
Leopold which would eventually destroy the humanitarian and philanthrop-
ic image that Leopold had built up. Pressure from international as well as

The Jesuits Liagre, Hanquet and Oddon with two lay assistants and two natives. Archief Paters Jezuïeten, Brussels.

domestic public opinion finally compelled him to give up his Central African kingdom. On 18 October 1908 the territory became a Belgian colony. After the First World War, Belgium took on additional responsibilities in Central Africa; on 21 August 1919 parts of the former German colonial territories to the east of Congo, notably Rwanda and Burundi, were mandated temporarily to Belgium. For the next fifty years a small Western European country would determine the fate of an area eighty times greater than the mother country and separated from it by thousands of miles. Congo became an independent Republic on 30 June 1960; Rwanda and Burundi followed two years later.

Originally, all missionaries had been members of religious congregations or organisations. But at the end of the 1950s an older tradition was revived whereby diocesan priests from Western countries were also sent out to missionary lands, the so-called *Fidei Donum* priests, named after an encyclical of Pope Pius XII (1957) that strongly encouraged the practice. The Belgian missionaries who departed for Central Africa, both at the time of the Free State and the Colony as well as after independence, had widely differing perceptions of the task that faced them. Many factors contributed to this diversity. Not only did each of the various congregations and institutions have its own specific appeal and forms of spirituality, individual missionaries also differed according to their country, region and language of origin as well as their own particular psychological make-up. Furthermore, views about theology and evangelism changed constantly throughout the period, while the missionaries themselves often developed new ideas and ap-

Father Mon Verbruggen and his boy scouts in Ntambwe Saint Bernard near Luluaburg. Archief Paters van het Onbevlekte Hart van Maria (Scheut), Brussels.

proaches between their arrival in Africa and the time when they either died or returned permanently to the mother country. Finally, perceptions of the relationship between Western states and churches and the non-Western world evolved in step with political, economic and social change. Consequently, the missionaries who worked in Congo, Rwanda and Burundi during this period cannot be regarded as a single undifferentiated and homogeneous group.

More than religion

An exceptionally large proportion of the region's contingent of missionaries came from Flanders. For example: in 1955, 65% of the primarily French Congregation of White Fathers working in the area were Flemish; of the Brothers belonging to the Congregation, 80% came from Flanders. It is probable that the percentages were even higher in a Congregation such as the Scheutists (the Immaculate Heart of Mary), not to speak of the smaller, mainly female, congregations that only recruited in Flanders. The objective of the missions was to spread the Christian gospel among peoples who had never, or in the case of the BaCongo had hardly, heard it before. The missionaries committed themselves to that goal in the firm conviction that their message was universal and uniquely relevant to all. However, the term 'preaching' which is usually employed to describe this type of activity can easily give rise to a one-sided and therefore incomplete and misleading impression of what the missionaries actually did. All of them were agreed that what mattered most was to preach the Gospel, teach the catechism, administer the sacraments, celebrate the liturgy and teach the principles of Christian morality to their converts. But these specifically religious tasks were preceded, accompanied and followed by a whole range of other activities that often consumed far more, indeed the lion's share, of their time and energy.

The first of these was the organisation of education which, almost until the end of the colonial era, the State left almost entirely in the hands of the Catholic Church. In fact, a kind of division of labour between Church and State developed fairly rapidly. The Church took responsibility for intellectual and moral education and also the medical care of the native population, in exchange for which the State offered the missionaries security and protection and provided the essential infrastructure. It also paid a small subsidy for schools that met the syllabus requirements laid down by the State. Initially this programme was confined to primary education, but later on technical and secondary education was developed and teacher training colleges and art colleges were set up. The educational efforts of the Church were crowned in 1954 by the opening of the University of Lovanium as a daughter institution of the Catholic University of Leuven. The following figures give an impression of the expansion of education in Congo in the colonial period. In 1935, there were 13,299 educational institutions in the colony, of which only 11 were set up by the state. A mere twenty years later, in 1957, the number had risen to no less than 30,514, of which 386 were independent of the missions. In the same period, the Congolese school population trebled from 599,601 pupils in 1935 to 1,732,769 in 1957. That means that at the end of the colonial period 10% of the population had completed primary school, while in Ghana, one of the best regulated of the English colonies, the figure was only 7% and in French Equatorial Africa only 3%. Africans who had been to school could join the army or be recruited as teachers, minor civil servants or clerks in large and small businesses. There were also specialised mission schools that produced large numbers of both male and female nurses and teachers. Furthermore, the Church did not neglect the training of native clergy, for which a number of minor and major seminaries were founded. The first priests in Congo and Rwanda were ordained in 1917. The first Episcopal consecration took place in 1952 when Mgr A. Bigirumwami became Bishop of Nyundo in northern Rwanda. This was followed four years later by the consecration of Mgr J. Malula, who eventually became Archbishop of Kinshasa and the first Congolese Cardinal.

The second task entrusted to the missionaries was health care. With financial and manpower support from the State, they established a network of medical institutions, ranging from unsightly dispensaries, clinics, field hospitals and leper houses to modern well-equipped hospitals, specialist centres for the blind, deaf, physically and mentally handicapped and psychiatric institutions. At the end of the colonial period in the Belgian Congo there were 4.4 beds per 1000 inhabitants compared with 2.7 in French Equatorial Africa, 1.2 in Kenya and 0.4 in Nigeria.

As well as education and health the missionaries also busied themselves in other fields of social development and services. Among these were their numerous and sustained initiatives and efforts in developing agriculture and animal husbandry, setting up orphanages, printing presses and publishing houses, and in some places even building bridges and roads. Several missionaries took an interest in the language, oral traditions, mentality, morality and customs as well as the pre-colonial history of the people among whom they lived, and emerged as pioneers of the region's linguistics, ethnography and ethno-history. J. van Wing, L. de Beir, N. van Everbroeck, P. Tempels, T. Theuws, G. Hulstaert, P. Boelaert, A. van der Beken and L. Verbeek are but a few names among many. They organised study days, even weeks, founded specialist journals and published the results of their research in learned books and articles.

Catholic *and* African

Such a wide range of activities was only possible because the missions could entrust much of the work of evangelisation in the strict sense of the word to an army of highly motivated and dedicated native catechists who took upon themselves the responsibility of spreading the Christian message. Through preaching and catechesis in the smallest and most remote villages they prepared the people for the sacraments and taught them the principles of Christian living. Often the Christian message and Catholic morality clashed with deeply rooted beliefs and the spontaneous inclinations of the African population. This was aggravated by the fact that only gradually and belatedly was it accepted that in conveying Christian belief and ethics some account should be taken of the individual cultural character of the African

Mgr J. Malula became Archbishop of Kinshasha in 1959.

peoples. A great pioneer of this approach, who acquired an international reputation, was Placied Tempels, a Flemish missionary in Katanga from 1933 to 1946 and 1950 to 1962. His book *Bantu Philosophy* (Bantoe Filosofie), first published in 1946, was translated into many languages and secured him a firm place in the history of African philosophy. He particularly wanted to apply his theoretical insights to missionary and pastoral work. With that aim he drew up a Bantu catechism and in the 1950s founded a spiritual movement within the Catholic church, the *Jamaa*, which would allow the Congolese to become Catholic without totally abandoning every aspect of their own culture and way of thinking. Even today, the *Jamaa* remains one of the most remarkable and profound attempts to give Christianity an authentic and original African countenance. His ideas and activities were far ahead of his time, and his presence gave rise to so many tensions that in April 1962 he had to leave the Congo at the age of only 56. Shortly after that, the Western missionary effort was plunged into deep crisis. The number of active Belgian Catholic missionaries in Congo had at first risen steadily. In 1903 there were 244, in 1924 1,013, in 1935 2,358, in 1949 4,559. But this trend went into reverse in the mid-1960s. By 1982 there were only 2,233 Belgian missionaries in Congo; in 1994 their number had dropped to 1,161 and in 2000 there were a mere 596. The causes of this decline in missionary dynamism in Belgium and Flanders are many and complex. It has undeniably had negative effects, but on the other hand it has not been entirely without positive consequences for the African Church. The Church in Central Africa has increasingly been compelled to stand on its own feet. Free of colonial reflexes and paternalistic tutelage, it now has the chance to develop its own identity and build a form of Christianity in which African Christians can feel comfortable, not just as Christians but also as Africans. Furthermore, they now face the challenge of becoming missionaries themselves.

VALEER NECKEBROUCK
Translated by Chris Emery.

A procession in Kisantu.
Archief Paters Jezuïeten,
Brussels.

Religious Identity and Americanisation

Dutch Settlements in North America

Compared with other European nations, the Dutch presence in North America goes back a long way. Dutch vessels had already appeared there in the late sixteenth century. The Dutch were interested in the New World first and foremost because of the trading opportunities it afforded. The main reason for their presence, then, was commerce; but commerce needed defensible trading posts, and so various settlements and forts were established in the northern parts of North America. The new colony near the mouth of the Hudson River was named New Netherlands, and New Amsterdam became its most important settlement.

The Dutch West India Company was granted a trading monopoly in the New Netherlands, and this meant that there were few economic opportunities for anyone except its stockholders. As a result, and because of restrictions placed on free settlement, very few Dutch people felt inclined to migrate to the new colony. Consequently, in 1639 the Company had to give up its monopoly of the fur trade and accept a more liberal policy on immigrants from the United Provinces. After that the population did indeed increase for a while, but its numbers were never great. By 1647, when Peter Stuyvesant became Governor, the colony's area had shrunk considerably: it now consisted only of the island of Manhattan and parts of Long Island, together with a few outposts. Under Stuyvesant's able leadership New Amsterdam began to prosper. The English, however, had always refused to recognise the Dutch colony's existence, and they kept pushing further into Dutch territory. In 1664 they captured the city, which had neither sufficient artillery to defend itself nor a population willing to do so. When the British took over the New Netherlands it is estimated that more than 10,000 settlers were living there. It was a cosmopolitan place: as well as the Dutch – the largest group – there were English, French, German and Swedish settlers and some of other nationalities. Very few Dutch settlers left the colony in 1664; those who stayed lived under British rule – with one brief interruption in 1673 when the Dutch recaptured New York (as New Amsterdam had now been renamed) – until American Independence in 1776. During this period immigration from the Dutch Republic came almost to a standstill. Dutch influence in New York did not cease, however. The Dutch language continued to be used in the courts, administration, trade and religion for a long time, not only in the city, but also in other parts of the old colony. The Dutch Reformed Church, in particular, played a very important role in maintaining Dutch awareness of their nationality and keeping the Dutch identity and language intact. The first Dutch Reformed congregation had been established in New Amsterdam in 1628 and congregations in other places soon followed. By 1664 there were eleven congregations and two 'stations'. The Dutch Reformed Church succeeded, not without a struggle, in staying relatively independent of the English Government, being responsible only to the *classis* of Amsterdam. Although this connection ended when America achieved independence, it continued to call itself the Dutch Reformed Church until 1867.

During the eighteenth century the Reformed Church expanded; by the time of the American Revolution it had a hundred congregations. This expansion continued in the early decades of the nineteenth century, even before the new wave of immigration from the Netherlands that took place in the 1840s. Over the course of the eighteenth century the Dutch language had had to give ground. By the end of the century English had become the main language, though Dutch was still used on occasion in services and continued to be spoken in private life. Prior to 1800 there was very little Dutch migration to Canada. What there was consisted mainly of a number of Loyalists of Dutch-American origin who fled to Canada, together with a few Mennonites whose pacifism had brought them into disfavour with the American revolutionists.

In the nineteenth century the great flood of immigration from the Netherlands, which started in the early 1840s, was directed towards the Northern Central states of America and the Midwest. In the last two decades of the century a small part of the stream of Dutch migrants also headed for Canada. Mention of the Mennonites shows that it was not only Dutch Calvinists who were settling in the New World. Other religious groups were allowed, albeit reluctantly, to settle in the New Netherlands. In the eighteenth century a variety of religious groups found their way to North America. In this brief article, though, we shall concentrate on those migrants from the Netherlands who were of the traditional Calvinist persuasion because they, who clung to their creed, migrated as groups and settled as a community, constructed a kind of Dutch-American identity that endured for generations. Protestants of other or more liberal persuasions were more inclined to become Americanised. The same goes for Roman Catholic immigrants of Dutch origin; as members of a universal church who could join a Roman Catholic parish in the immediate area of their new settlement, they assimilated rather quickly.

Migration between 1800 and 1914

In the first four decades of the nineteenth century only a handful of Dutch immigrants settled in North America, but from 1846 on huge waves of them arrived in the United States. These 'huge waves', though, need to be seen in perspective. Compared with the numbers of earlier Dutch immigrants to North America they are huge indeed, but compared with immigration from other European countries the number of Dutch immigrants is rather low. The main motive for migration was the lack of economic opportunities in the home country, with religious and political reasons in second place.

Migration from the Netherlands to the United States between 1840 end 1914 can be divided into four periods. The first was between 1846 and 1857 when the Calvinist Seceders (see next section) made up a substantial proportion of the migrants, the second in 1865-1873 when the ending of the American Civil War started a new wave, the third in 1880-1893 when the agricultural crisis in the Northern Netherlands sparked a new exodus, and finally the pre-war wave of emigration between 1902 and 1913. Most Dutch migrants were of rural or small-town origin, and they opted for the United States because of the availability of cheap farmland. Theirs can be described as a chain migration. Once settled in their new townships the first immigrants attracted others, mostly relatives and acquaintances from their places of birth, thus forging connections between Dutch villages and American communities – most of them in Michigan, Iowa, western New York State, New Jersey, Wisconsin and Illinois – from which they then dispersed across the United States in subsequent decades. As a result of this form of migration, certain parts of the United States still retain a strong Dutch character.

Seceders

The causes of migration in the 1840s were both economic and religious. The Napoleonic wars and the war with Belgium had left the Netherlands much impoverished. In the middle decades of the nineteenth century the Dutch economy was too weak to absorb the country's growing population. And in the field of religion the Dutch Reformed Church was attracting severe criticism. Accused of liberalism and rationalism, it was suspected of having moved away from the old truths of Calvinism. In 1843 a group of traditional Calvinists, led by a number of ministers, split from the Dutch Reformed Church – a move they regarded not as a separation but as a return to the old seventeenth-century Reformed Church of Dordrecht. The years that followed saw a steady increase in the numbers of these *Afgescheidenen* or Seceders, most of whom came from the lower classes. The Dutch authorities tried to suppress the Seceder congregations, banning or disrupting their services. Although official persecution ceased in the early 1840s, the Seceders were subjected to public discrimination for a long time after. Seceder leaders and their followers looked for somewhere they could practise their religion without being harassed. Under the able leadership of 'dominies' A.C. van Raalte and H.P. Scholte a large group of them emigrated to the United States. One has to bear in mind here that although these people did not come from the affluent section of the population, only a very few of them were from the poorest of the poor.

Most Seceder migration took place in the early years of this mid-nineteenth century wave. In 1846 and 1847 they made up three quarters of all overseas migrants; in 1849 they formed only 1.3% of the population of the Netherlands. But only in the beginning did they form the majority of Dutch immigrants. Over the nineteenth century as a whole the largest group were the Dutch Reformed, while the Seceders were outnumbered even by the Roman Catholics.

A.C. van Raalte (1811-1876). Archives, Calvin College, Grand Rapids (MI).

Those groups of Seceders who decided to emigrate to the United States did not go there unprepared. Their leaders had established contacts with ministers of the Dutch Reformed Church in America, and on landing in New York they were welcomed and helped on their journey to their still uncertain destination by members of the Church. The first group, led by Van Raalte, arrived in New York in November 1846. Van Raalte and some of his followers were trying to get in touch with people who could advise them as to the best place to create a little piece of Holland in the United States. Van Raalte had originally intended to settle in Wisconsin, but he became more and more convinced that Michigan would be a better choice. He himself scouted the region between the Kalamazoo and the Grand river intensively. Finally the Dutch decided to buy land near the Black Lake and along the Black River in Ottawa County. What they bought was mainly forest land; Van Raalte preferred this not only because it would provide the settlers with timber for houses, barns, fences and fuel, but also as a source of material for carpenters, furniture-makers and the like. But to turn a forest into a fertile prairie they had to begin by clearing the forest and building roads and cabins.

During the first two years the settlers suffered extreme hardship. The work was hard and both food and housing were inadequate. Many of them fell sick, suffering from malaria, smallpox and dysentery. Mortality was high in those 'bitter days', as they would later be remembered. But despite this the 'Kolonie', as it was originally called, grew. The years that followed brought a constant stream of new immigrants. By 1849 there were already a number of small villages: Holland, Zeeland, Vriesland, Groningen, Drenthe, Overijsel, Graafschap and Noord Holland (Noordeloos). In the 1850s the colony was slowly beginning to make some progress. Better houses were built, as were churches and public buildings, and connections with cities and towns in the surrounding areas were improved. As early as 1857 a visitor to the colony wrote that he was not a little astonished at the progress that had been made in only eight years. Connections both by land (roads and railroads) and by water were further improved in subsequent years. The communities founded by Van Raalte and his followers grew in size. Other settlements were established as the land-hungry Dutch pressed on into neighbouring counties and states.

Having come to the United States as a group that had split from the Reformed Church in the Netherlands, the colony formed the *classis* of Holland, an organisation independent of any church in the Netherlands or the United States. The old Dutch Reformed Church of America sought a union, but the people of the colony were reluctant to agree. Nevertheless, in 1850 the union took place and was in many ways beneficial to the colony. The settlers were given financial help during hard times and for the construction of church buildings, parsonages and schools. It also became possible to recruit ministers trained at the New Brunswick Theological Seminary in New Jersey. One small group did not approve of the merger with the Reformed Church. In their view it neglected to preach once each Sunday from the Heidelberg Catechism, tended to ignore the doctrine of predestination, preferred to sing hymns rather than psalms and, most importantly, accepted Freemasons as church members. In 1857 their discontent led to a schism and the establish-

ment of what was later called the Christian Reformed Church. Many congregations joined the new church because of its stand against membership of secret societies (i.e. Freemasonry) and it steadily increased in numbers. This was also an important reason for new Dutch immigrants of the Christian Reformed persuasion and of the Doleantie (a movement founded by the Dutch statesman and theologian A. Kuyper) to join the Christian Reformed Church.

From the outset the Reformed Church had been in favour of Christian education – not so much at the elementary level, but higher education. Colleges were established in both Holland and Pella. The Christian Reformed Church, stimulated by the ideas of the Doleantie movement, insisted from the beginning on establishing Reformed Christian education at all levels.

Van Raalte (Sod) Church in Thule, South Dakota. Built in 1886, the inside dimensions were 4.9 x 9.1 m. 2.1 m. high. The Reformed Church in America's congregation disbanded in 1905. Photo taken in 1891. Archives, Calvin College, Grand Rapids (MI).

Pella in Iowa

The Reverend Scholte came to America later, in 1847. Some of his followers were already there, having arrived in 1846. Like Van Raalte they were cordially welcomed by members of the Dutch Reformed Church. Van Raalte would have preferred Scholte and his flock to join the Michigan settlement, but Scholte refused. He knew that his followers wanted meadows, cattle and farmland as soon as possible, and that they had no taste for clearing forests. So he looked to settle on the prairie. Scholte's people were somewhat better off financially than Van Raalte's group, so they could afford to go straight to the prairie and buy the materials they needed. After scouting and taking advice Scholte bought some 18,000 acres of fertile prairie land between the Skunk and Des Moines rivers in north-eastern Marion County, Iowa. He named the new settlement Pella, after the city to which the Christians fled after the destruction of Jerusalem in 74 AD, so it was intended as a refuge for the faithful. Here log- and sod-houses were built and the prairie cultivated. New immigrants added to the population,

Christian Reformed church in North Dakota, perhaps Lark. Rev. Henry Ahuis, c.1900. Archives, Calvin College, Grand Rapids (MI).

Hendrik P. Scholte (1805-1868). Archives, Calvin College, Grand Rapids (MI).

stimulating trade and travel. The population increased steadily until 1870 and then stabilised. In its early years the town was a primitive prairie community. The only house with any display of luxury was Scholte's own. Not only a minister of the Gospel, he was a man of many trades: banker, real estate agent, notary public and editor of the *Pella Gazette*, among other things. Scholte wanted his people to become Americans and so he encouraged assimilation, and he wanted Pella to become an important centre. In fact Pella never developed into a large town, though it did become the centre of a rich agricultural area. Even in the 1860s some people in Pella thought that the area was overcrowded, and so new settlements were established in Iowa and further to the west.

Unlike Van Raalte, Scholte did not merge with the Dutch Reformed Church of America, not did he seek a connection with any other denomination. An independent Christian Congregation was established, based in part on Darbyist principles. However, it did not last long. Scholte had become an elder, not a minister, and even more a businessman, lawyer and politician. Consequently, the sheep felt that they lacked a real shepherd. After a while they sought contact with the Reformed Church in Michigan, and the union took place in 1856. Scholte continued for a few years as pastor of an independent Christian Church, but after his death the congregation disbanded. Pella became a mainly Reformed and Christian Reformed area.

Migration in the twentieth century

The First World War cut off virtually all immigration to North America. After 1918 it started again, but quota limits meant that the stream of migrants to the United States was greatly reduced. Since then most Dutch emigration has been to Canada, New Zealand and Australia. In the two decades following the Second World War, especially, the majority of Dutch immigrants to North America settled in Canada, mostly in Ontario, Alberta and

Scholte house from a photo c.1950. Archives, Calvin College, Grand Rapids (MI).

British Columbia and particularly in the urban centres in those provinces. In the 1960s Dutch migration to Canada, and to other countries, fell drastically; there was no longer any reason for the Dutch to leave the Dutch welfare state then coming into being. A high proportion of those who migrated after the Second World War were Gereformeerd, and many of these joined the Christian Reformed Church. Other traditional Calvinist groups also emigrated in smaller numbers and established congregations in Canada and the United States.

Adaptation and identity

During and after the First World War there was increased pressure on ethnic groups to become true Americans. The Reformed Church accommodated quickly to American life; it can be viewed as a mainstream church that stresses neither its Dutchness nor its Dutch Calvinist heritage. The Christian Reformed Church kept its Dutch character and remained an immigrants' church for longer. This was apparent in the years following the Second World War, when a substantial number of those migrating from the Netherlands to North America – this time mainly to Canada – chose to join it because it stuck closer to its Dutch origins and to orthodoxy than the Reformed Church. The approach of today's Gereformeerde Kerk in the Netherlands is regarded by the Christian Reformed Church as too liberal, both in theology and in practice.

The Dutch Calvinists' identification with their Dutch heritage was never based on ethnicity, however; it was based on religion. Traditional religion has led them to stick together and maintain a defensive attitude against Americanisation. That ethnic considerations were not important was again demonstrated after the Second World War. Dutch people emigrating to Canada tended to become Canadians as quickly as possible. They relinquished their language quickly. The Calvinist denominations, too, attached little value to retaining the Dutch language and identity. The issue is no

Marion County State Bank in Pella, Iowa. The town has capitalised on its Dutch heritage by remodelling and building new structures, like this drive-in bank, in a wide variety of Dutch and pseudo-Dutch styles. Photo by Dale Van Donselaar.

longer Americanisation, but how to preserve their identity as a church among other evangelical mainstream churches.

LAMMERT G. JANSMA

BIBLIOGRAPHY

BAKKER, U.B. (ed.), *Sister, Please Come Over. Experiences of an Immigrant-Family from Friesland / The Netherlands. Letters from America in the period 1894-1933*. Winsum, 1999.

DAAN, J., *Ik was te bissie... Nederlanders en hun taal in de Verenigde Staten*. Zutphen, 1987.

HINTE, J. VAN, *Nederlanders in Amerika : een studie over landverhuizers en volkplanters in de 19e en 20ste eeuw in de Vereenigde Staten van Amerika*. Groningen, 1928 (2 vols.).

GALAMA, A., *Frisians to America 1880-1914. With the Baggage of the Fatherland*. Groningen, 1996.

GANZEVOORT, H., *A Bittersweet Land. The Dutch Experience in Canada, 1890-1980*. Toronto, 1988.

HARINCK, G. and H. KRABBENDAM (eds.), *Sharing the Reformed Tradition: The Dutch-North American Exchange, 1846-1966*. Amsterdam, 1996.

KROES, R. and H-O. NEUSCHÄFER (eds.), *The Dutch in North-America. Their Immigration and Cultural Continuity*. Amsterdam, 1991.

LIGTENBERG, L., *De Nieuwe Wereld van Peter Stuyvesant. Vaderlandse voetsporen in de Verenigde Staten*. Amsterdam, 1999.

LUCAS, H.S., *Netherlanders in America. Dutch Immigration to the United States and Canada, 1789-1950*. Ann Arbor etc., 1955.

OOSTENDORP, L., *H.P. Scholte, Leader of the Secession of 1834 and founder of Pella*. Franeker, 1964.

PIETERS, A.J., *A Dutch Settlement in Michigan*. Grand Rapids, 1923.

SCHULTE NORDHOLT and R.P. SWIERENGA (eds.), *A bilateral Bicentennial. A history of Dutch-American Relations, 1792-1982*, Amsterdam 1982.

STEKELENBURG, H.A.V.M. VAN, *'Hier is alles vooruitgang.' Landverhuizing van Noord-Brabant naar Noord-Amerika, 1880-1940*. Tilburg, 1996.

STIGT, K. VAN, *History of Pella, Iowa and Vicinity*. Pella, 1897.

SWIERENGA, R.P., *Faith and Family. Dutch Immigration and Settlements in the United States, 1820-1920*. New York, 2000.

SWIERENGA, R.P. (ed.), *The Dutch in America. Immigration, Settlement, and Cultural Change*. New Brunswick (NJ), 1985.

VANOENE, W.W.J., *Inheritance Preserved. The Canadian Reformed Churches in Historical Perspective*. Winnipeg, 1975[2].

WEBBER, PH.E., *Pella Dutch*. Ames, 1988.

ZEE, HENRI and BARBARA VAN DER, *A Sweet and Alien Land. The Story of Dutch New York*. New York, 1978.

ZWAANSTRA, H., *Reformed Thought and Experience in a New World. A Study of the Christian Reformed Church and its American Environment 1890-1918*. Kampen, 1973.

A

Seething Cauldron

Dance in Brussels

Early in 2001, Steve Paxton was a special guest at a series of evenings of dance improvisations in the Flemish Brussels Kaaitheater. After one of the performances he remarked that the former brewery in Onze-Lieve-Vrouw-van-Vaakstraat, which for many years housed the studios of the Kaaitheater, was the birthplace of the current 'boom' in dance and dance improvisation in Belgium, and particularly in Brussels. And he was right. In the early 1980s it was there and in Leuven, during the first years of the Klapstuk dance festival, that a number of important Flemish choreographers made their debut. Since then names such as De Keersmaeker, Fabre, Vandekeybus have become famous all over the world. In the early 1980s important activity developed in other Flemish cities as well, such as Antwerp and Ghent, but in no time this work was performed on these stages too – and received substantial backing from them. Furthermore, both Kaaitheater and Klapstuk

Rosas, *Rain* (2001). Photo by Herman Sorgeloos / courtesy of Rosas vzw, Brussels.

were quick to acknowledge that a context had to be created for this new work, which introduced a completely new language of forms into the slumbering Belgian scene. That is why from the very beginning prominent avant-garde choreographers (mainly from the USA) such as Paxton, Brown and Childs were invited to work in Brussels and Leuven.

However, Kaaitheater was not entirely isolated in Brussels. At about the same time Frédéric Flamand launched a French-language initiative, Raffinerie du Plan K, based in an old sugar refinery in Molenbeek. Artists from all disciplines gathered here and Flamand presented his first multimedia dance experiments in collaboration with artists such as Marin Kasimir. Another small but commendable initiative, Contredanse, contributed to the revival of contemporary dance by providing trainee places.

In retrospect, this burst of choreographic creativity can only be attributed to the dialectics of progress. When it came to ballet as well as contemporary dance, at that time Brussels and Belgium were simply non-existent in the European context. Any kind of policy, let alone a sense of national artistic pride, was lacking in dance. Brussels was thus, artistically speaking, a suburb of European culture. Yet suburbs often prove to be the birthplace of new ideas. It is in garages and lonely attics, not in the spotlights of important stages that young artists with few resources and even fewer opportunities develop new insights. The one bright spot in the otherwise dismal Brussels situation was Béjart's Ballet of the Twentieth Century. Although his ecstatic form of aesthetics had had its heyday in the 1980s, in retrospect his presence has proved to be very important because of his MUDRA school for young choreographers. It was at MUDRA, for example, that a number of young dancers, who would later form De Keersmaeker's Rosas, met for the first time.

In the meantime, the situation was far from easy for these young Turks because the government failed to support them, even when they gained substantial international recognition. They survived by working closely with new autonomous organisations for the performing arts, which later evolved into arts centres with official recognition and support. Rosas (celebrating its twentieth anniversary in 2002) for instance had to threaten to move abroad for sufficient subsidies to be forthcoming. And history has a habit of repeating itself. When the American Meg Stuart moved to Brussels in the early 1990s, after pioneering performances such as *Disfigure Study* and *No Longer Ready-Made*, the government took so long to make up its mind that she looked for and found a 'second residence', this time in Zürich, where her nationality was less of an obstacle to obtaining substantial financial support.

Nevertheless, it can be said that the situation had changed radically since the 1990s: Flemish companies such as those of De Keersmaeker, Vandekeybus, Fabre and Platel were no longer the cuckoos in the nest, but had become leading figures on the Flemish-Belgian and European dance scene. However, the Royal Ballet of Flanders, technically outstanding but with very little artistic recognition, still received the lion's share of the dance subsidies of the Flemish Community, which decides in cultural matters concerning the Dutch-speaking part of Belgium. In French-speaking Belgium, however, the Ballet de Wallonie was wound up and replaced by Charleroi / Danses under the artistic direction of Frédéric Flamand from Plan K. Charleroi / Danses is officially charged with developing a contemporary dance

Meg Stuart / Damaged Goods, *Highway 101 (Vienna)*. Photo by Maria Ziegelböck / courtesy of Damaged Goods, Brussels.

policy in Wallonia; consequently, it swallows up most of the government subsidies. As a result, young choreographers looking for the chance to work have no choice but to ask Flamand for it. Organisations such as Contredanse have to be content with the crumbs from the subsidy table. Charleroi / Danses also maintains its own dance company which mostly performs Flamand's own work, a peculiar form of techno-baroque for which he invariably succeeds in seducing leading artists and architects into making a contribution. Despite its name, Charleroi / Danses, the artistic nerve centre of this organisation is again in Brussels, in the renovated Plan K studios.

The gap in the market

The presence in Brussels of so many prominent groups and institutions had two main consequences. The 1990s saw the beginning of a large-scale migration of young dancers to companies in Brussels and elsewhere in Belgium; in this rapidly growing colony all manner of new, small-scale partnerships were born. At the same time, those organisations which had from the outset supported and presented the work of young Belgian choreographers extended and reinforced their international networks. As a result, more and more international work was performed in Belgium. In the case of Meg Stuart and her Damaged Goods – which will receive structural funding from the Flemish Government for the period 2001-2005 – this even led to a permanent residency, while the outstanding English choreographer Jonathan Burrows regularly works in Brussels and Ghent.

The sense of euphoria created by this situation blinded people to the fact that it was largely due to happenstance. Some important movements abroad also went to some extent unnoticed by Belgian artists and spectators. Anne-Teresa de Keersmaeker was among the first to realise this. She is now resident choreographer at De Munt, the National Opera, just like Béjart before her. Inspired by the example of MUDRA, she worked with the Nat-

Milky Way, a project of third-year PARTS students (2000). Photo by Nathalie Willems / courtesy of PARTS, Brussels.

Meg Stuart / Damaged Goods, *Crash Landing*. Photo by Maria Anguera de Goyo / courtesy of Damaged Goods, Brussels.

An improvisation by Steve Paxton. Photo courtesy of Kaaitheater, Brussels

ional Opera to set up the Performing Arts Research & Training Studios (PARTS) in 1995. Didactically speaking, the training at PARTS broke the mould. In contrast to standard arts training programmes in Belgium, students have to apply for selection and are recruited world-wide. Also, PARTS provided training that goes beyond the purely technical aspects. The wide-ranging curriculum includes theoretical aspects such as general cultural history and theory, and the dance classes range from classical ballet to Trisha Brown's 'release technique'. Furthermore, the teachers are internationally acknowledged as the best in their field. The effect of PARTS was, in a short space of time, stunning. It filled a gap in the market. The first students to graduate quickly made a name for themselves throughout Europe. More importantly, young choreographers at the school formed an intellectual artistic network that survived their student days, if only because many students stayed in Brussels after completing their training and were given work opportunities in the buildings of Rosas, PARTS and Kaaitheater.

Radical research

In recent years, then, the pressure in Brussels has risen enormously, making it a seething cauldron of talent. No other European city has so many ambitious dancers and choreographers. And this comes at a crucial time. The model of theatrical dance that gradually evolved in Europe during the 1980s has been increasingly criticised during the past few years. The first indication of this was the renewed interest in improvisation that Meg Stuart's programme *Crash Landing*, among others, helped to bring about. These evening-length performances, where dancers and artists of every description meet and perform spontaneously, were conceived in 1995 during the Klapstuk Festival. The programme has travelled throughout Europe and attracted a wide following. It is no coincidence that leading figures from the experimental New York dance scene of the 1960s, such as Steve Paxton, took part.

Tom Plischke, *(Re)SORT*.
Photo courtesy of
Beursschouwburg,
Brussels.

Charlotte van den Eynde /
Ugo Dehaes, *Lijfstof*. Photo
courtesy of Kaaitheater,
Brussels.

At the same time, many young choreographers were seeking inspiration from the more radical conceptual experiments of this avant-garde movement. Philosophical discourse was suddenly 'in' again. Now, the tone is set by artists such as Jérôme Bel, Boris Charmatz, Xavier Leroy, Thomas Plischke, Vincent Dunoyer and, of course, Meg Stuart, who is an important bridge between the two generations. Their work is characterised by radical research into the working and presentational conditions of dance. Many of them work closely with the Brussels 'scene'. In Belgium itself, Alexander Baervoets, Charlotte van den Eynde, Ugo Dehaes, Thomas Hauert and many others are contributing to the shifting paradigm in contemporary dance. It is no coincidence that they all have (or have had) some connection with PARTS, or with one of the many companies in Brussels.

Remarkably, existing artistic platforms have been very slow to stimulate or provide an outlet for the capital's enormous artistic potential. Apart from the Kaaitheater, one of the few active institutions in this regard is the Beursschouwburg, which gives free reign to young choreographers. It does this in a number of ways – some of them quite radical – which can go as far as abandoning the concept of a completed performance as the *raison d'être* of the theatre. A fairly recent example of this is an amazing experiment by the choreographer Thomas Plischke, who invited selected friends and like-minded members of the public to live and work in the theatre for ten days, engaging in debate and performing finished and unfinished pieces. In the words of Meg Stuart: '*This is the hottest place in Brussels*'. Outside Brussels, Dans in Kortrijk is also taking up the challenge with its programme *Dans@Tack,* which aims to take everyday ideas and make them visible to audiences. The question we are now faced with is this: will the rest of the theatrical establishment in Brussels jump on this bandwagon before it packs up and moves on due to lack of interest?

PIETER T'JONCK
Translated by Yvette Mead.

FURTHER INFORMATION

Flemish Theatre Institute: www.vti.be
Rosas and PARTS: www.rosas.be
Meg Stuart / Damaged Goods: www.damagedgoods.be
Beursschouwburg: www.beurschouwburg.vgc.be
Kaaitheater: www.kaaitheater.be
Dans in Kortrijk: www.dansinkortrijk.be

Room

for Everything

The Photographs of Jacob Olie

Judging from the biographical data alone, one would hardly suspect that Jacob Olie Jacobszoon (1834-1905) was a photographer. Born at number 10 Zandhoek in Amsterdam, the son of a rafting boss in a family of rafting bosses. Apprenticed to master carpenter Lotz at 12A Bickersgracht at the age of 15. Instructed in physics and chemistry, building construction and mechanics at the private technical school run by architect Hendrik Hana. Carpenter and architect. Member of the Society for the Advancement of Architecture. Co-founder of the *Architectura et Amicitia* debating club, of which he was a member for twenty years, giving over 150 lectures on topics such as moveable scaffolding, the steam winch and the role of the concrete block in the construction of the North Sea Canal. At age twenty-six hired as drawing teacher at the Technical School of the Society for the Working Class, located on Oudezijds Voorburgwal. Appointed director of the school in 1867. In addition: at age forty-four married Carolina Augusta Blössman, who died in 1886 during the birth of their seventh child. Never remarried. Three of the children died at an early age.

A photographer?

On the other hand, why not? In the nineteenth century, photographers were rarely *just* photographers, certainly not the early practitioners of the art. Scientists, painters, bicycle makers, pharmacists and tinkers could all be found among their ranks. So why not the director of a technical school with a penchant for carpentry and drawing? Even an industrious and eventful life, with all its obstacles, has quite enough room for the making of 5,000 photographs (all of them preserved and meticulously restored in recent years in the National Photo Restoration Studio), of which 250 originals and enchantingly warm modern prints were exhibited in the Amsterdam Municipal Archives at the beginning of 2000.

But in Jacob Olie's case one can go further. Were it not for the small section of the exhibition devoted to his paintings, drawings and architectural designs (a gardener's house, an aviary, a 'country railway station' – never built but intended as a theoretical exercise for a competition among his colleagues), one might think that he had never been anything but a photographer.

The world at his feet

Olie probably produced his first photographs around 1860. That's a good twenty-one years after the public announcement of the invention of photography, but for the Netherlands it makes him a pioneer. It's not unlikely that Olie's introduction to photographs occurred at the first *Exhibition of Photography and Heliography* in the Netherlands, held in 1855 at the *Arti et Amicitiae* artists' club in Amsterdam. It included architectural shots and cityscapes by Edouard Baldus, the Bisson brothers, Charles Nègre and Henri Le Secq, images which, given his background, must certainly have made a deep impression on Olie.

Among the papers he left behind was a pocket notebook containing a little cut-out heart with the word 'Photography' written on it. The notebook opens with three pages of instructions for the making of 'negative plates', dated 1859. There's also a letter of thanks from the father of a pupil at the technical school which mentions a portrait: '*At first glance it seemed to me to look not at all like him, but the longer I looked the more I was charmed*

Jacob Olie, *Kalkmarkt, seen from Montelbaanstoren facing Prins Hendrikkade and Oosterdok.* c.1861. Gemeentearchief, Amsterdam.

127

Jacob Olie, *Prins Hendrikkade near Damrak*. 1890. Gemeentearchief, Amsterdam.

and saw in it something noble and good, truly quite different in his already budding individuality.' Olie never produced any drawn portraits, so the letter must have been referring to a photograph.

During the early months of 1862 he photographed second mate Gerrit Nicolaas Gerritsen, standing with tar brush and bucket on the deck of the frigate *Prins Maurits*. It's a self-conscious photo, a cross between a portrait of a man and a portrait of a ship, and in combining the two it affords a suggestive look at the tough, raw life on board. The date of this photo is fairly certain; the ship was sold to Norway in April of that year.

At around the same time he had three boys stage a fight under the gallery of the saw mill *De Steur*. Perhaps the boys were fighting over the frail girl sitting on a chair and observing the scene with amusement from under her straw hat – a strikingly *lively* photo for a time when photography still involved lengthy motionless posing. Just look at the portraits he made in the garden of his half-brother Carel Gustaaf, using as backdrop the fence on which he himself had painted a landscape with farms, trees and a brook meandering towards the horizon. These, by comparison, are stiff photos, a bit artificial even, in which gentlemen, ladies and children are taking visible pains to achieve immobility – as immobile as the city that stretched before him during the winter of 1861-1862, when he captured Oudezijds Voorburgwal with the Oude Kerk from the window of 'his' technical school in seven views, five of which would later be fitted together – though not without difficulty – to create a panorama.

Broad vistas appealed to Olie. In the same year, just before the construction of the new Halvemaan Bridge, he photographed the Amstel from the Munt to Vlooien Bridge in seven fragments taken from an attic window. And a year later, now from the medieval Montelbaan Tower, he recorded (in five parts) the expanse around Oude Schans: the Kalkmarkt, the IJ and Rapenburgwal – the world at his feet, stretching from the forest of ships' masts hazily delineated on the horizon to a passing vessel and the islands of tree trunks in the canal. Even now, it's as homely as it is sublime. You can stare at it forever: at the facades and the windows, at the building of the ships and the railings of the bridges. This was a world that Olie the *architect* must have known like the back of his hand, although everything must have looked quite new projected upside down on his glass plate. More then a century later, the enthusiasm generated by this is still palpable in the results.

The camera that was used for all these shots had been constructed entirely by Olie the *carpenter* from drawings of the earliest daguerreotype cameras: two wooden boxes fitted inside each other with a lens on one side and on the other the ground glass plate and a recess for the cassette with the negative. He cut the glass for the negatives himself from window glass, and he prepared his own photographic paper.

He would take hundreds of shots with this device, first between about 1860 and 1864, and then, after a twenty-five-year interruption taken up with work, worries and difficulties, between 1890 and 1900. Only during this later period would he switch over to a more modern, manageable camera that

Jacob Olie, *Binnen-Amstel River near Nieuwe Doelenstraat.* c.1890. Gemeentearchief, Amsterdam.

Jacob Olie, *Tweede Weteringplantsoen, seen facing Vijzelgracht.* April 1902. Gemeentearchief, Amsterdam.

could hold several glass plates at a time and contained a viewfinder so he could define his image at a single glance.

The results, all told, are 3,700 negatives and 4,000 prints (5,000 photographs, if you count the overlaps) – the largest completely preserved oeuvre of any nineteenth-century photographer in the Netherlands. Most of the shots are cityscapes, photographs that speak for themselves in all their clarity and simplicity, saturated with light and love. Some of them seem to be repeats of the same shot, yet each has something slightly different about it. No two facades are the same, no two streets have the same curves, no two doors make the same promises.

A back garden explorer

Olie made his first photographs with what were called wet collodion plates, a laborious procedure in which a mixture of gun cotton dissolved in alcohol and ether had to be poured out evenly across a glass plate, and the plate then placed in a bath of silver nitrate just before the shot was taken in order to make it light-sensitive. The plate had to be developed within a few minutes of exposure or the emulsion would spoil.

Perhaps, as photographer Hans Aarsman suggests in the introduction to his book of Olie's later city photographs published in 1999, he ran down the street with those plates from his darkroom to his waiting camera. That's the sort of story that fits right in with the folklore of a city chronicler. Or perhaps, as photo curator Anneke van Veen believes (her extensive biography of Olie was published to coincide with the exhibition), he used a portable chemical kit. Whatever his method, we know for certain that during his years as a photographer Olie was an explorer in his own back garden.

And this included Westerdok, Bickerseiland, Brouwersgracht, Herenmarkt, Zoutkeetsgracht – in short, the harbour and industrial area bordering on what were then the outskirts of the city. There was plenty to see: barges loaded with barrels and crates, the windmill known as *De Otter* on Achterweg, the ocean-going vessels that lay in the Westerdok for repairs, the Haarlemmer Houttuinen seen from the same Westerdok, children playing in Grote Bickersstraat, mothers in doorways, fathers taking breaks from their work. The illustrated walking guide also published in 1999 allows one to explore the area, with Olie's photographs as handy reference material. And whether it's because of the era portrayed or the photographs themselves, the famous prayer of the Dutch writer Nescio thrusts itself upon today's explorer, as instinctive as it is inevitable: that God may bless those responsible, preferably with a heavy hand.

Democratic gaze

By the time Olie resumed his photography after his retirement in 1890 wet collodion plates had been replaced by dry plates. This gave him more free-

Jacob Olie,
Weteringschans, seen from the Paleis voor Volksvlijt.
1892. Gemeentearchief, Amsterdam.

Jacob Olie, *Bokkinghangen, children in the alley next to the De Kat house.* c.1860. Gemeentearchief, Amsterdam.

dom of movement, so that now he could photograph all of Amsterdam and beyond: Nieuwer Amstel, Abcoude, Bussum and along the Vecht.

The city had changed profoundly. Entire residential districts had grown up outside the seventeenth-century city walls, canals had been filled in and streets widened. Hotels, offices and department stores had appeared in the northern part of the downtown area around the new Central Station which had opened in 1889.

He recorded it all, just for himself (he never published or exhibited anything during his lifetime): the Binnen-Amstel near Nieuwe Doelenstraat with a Venetian gondola; steam rising from the funnel of a freighter at the quay; the facade of the Stedelijk Museum; the still muddy wasteland of what later became Paulus Potterstraat; the tangle of horse-drawn trams, coaches and pedestrians on Dam Square; the Nieuwe Vaart with two interwoven three-masters against a background of smoky activity; three young ladies in hats smothered with feathers out for a walk in the Tweede Weteringplantsoen after a shower of rain; a hot air balloon above the Paleis voor Volksvlijt.

When you see them all together, they suggest a unique and, equally, a broad picture of a city at the end of the nineteenth century. But on closer inspection, such a characterisation lies a bit *outside* the photographs themselves. What really distinguishes them is their style: the comprehensive expanse of their high viewpoints, which causes the street noises to evaporate

Jacob Olie, *Self-portrait with hat and cane.* c.1860. Gemeentearchief, Amsterdam.

and gives each object its own place, from the freight barges and the handcar to the street lamps and playing children. It is an essentially democratic gaze that makes room for everything, from the church on the horizon to a lady's hat, from the mooring posts in the water to the white aprons of the maidservants in Grote Houtstraat – and room for straightness and proportions, as if everything had been laid out with a spirit level.

And although he clearly orchestrated things a bit now and then, directing the crew standing on the deck of a barge, placing the millers' men at the wheel on the mill gallery and a servant with his broom in the middle of the swept quay, Olie is always a detached presence in his photographs – as if he himself wasn't there at all.

You can feel this already to some extent in the three self-portraits he made early in the 1860s against an awkwardly improvised décor of white screens. He depicts himself, with his dog, as a 'labourer' in cap and apron, as a serious young man and as a Sunday gadabout. Who was the real Jacob Olie?

He knew. It was the labourer. He made an ambrotype of this portrait, affixing the negative to a black background so that it looked like a positive. After all, that was the photo in which he could see the carpenter's eyes that took his pictures.

EDDIE MARSMAN
Translated by Nancy Forest-Flier.

BIBLIOGRAPHY

BAAR, PETER PAUL DE, *Jacob Olie, fotograaf van Amsterdam: drie wandelingen door de stad rond 1900.* Bussum, 1999.
AARSMAN, HANS, *Jacob Olie: Amsterdam gefotografeerd aan het eind van de 19de eeuw* Amsterdam, 1999.
VEEN, ANNEKE VAN, *Jacob Olie Jbz. (1834-1905), fotograaf van 19de-eeuws Amsterdam.* Amsterdam, 2000.

Jacob Olie on the Internet: www.gemeentearchief.amsterdam.nl

n

Pursuit of the Moment

George Hendrik Breitner,

Painter and Photographer of a Lost Age

The role played by George Hendrik Breitner (1857-1923) in the history of Dutch painting is comparable to that of Courbet or Manet in French art. The shocking realism and brutal technique to which they treated the French public was introduced into the Netherlands by Breitner. His aim was to paint the history of his own era, of ordinary people, of the man and woman in the street. He saw beauty in the everyday life around him. In the nineteenth century a rather unusual ideal for an artist. Today Breitner is recognised as the unrivalled painter of Amsterdam street life, but his fame as a photographer has also now been established.

Breitner took his first steps down the painter's path in The Hague. Although he attended art school, the influence of the impressionists of the Hague School proved far more important – artists such as Mauve, Mesdag and the Maris brothers, whom he regarded as masters. The painters of the Hague School left their studies and usually worked directly from nature. They were to reach great artistic heights mainly in the landscape genre and in depicting the simple lifestyle of farmers and fishermen.

Breitner himself took little interest in landscape painting. His preference was for equestrian themes. Armed with his sketchbook, the painter made several journeys to the coast and the countryside to witness the army's vast, spectacular manoeuvres. It was action and movement that fascinated him, the sensation of seeing an approaching troop of horsemen on the beach or the heath. But there were still-lifes and figure studies as well. During his Hague period (1876-1886) we see him to some extent anticipating his later reputation as a painter of Amsterdam city life. It was mainly the picturesque qualities of the big city that attracted him. Referring to Rotterdam, the city of his birth, he wrote: *'It's such a beautiful city, bustling, filthy and picturesque, especially the ramparts and the harbour districts.'* And for a short time he and Vincent van Gogh ambled together through the working-class areas of The Hague, making drawings.

One great well-spring of stimuli

George Hendrik Breitner,
The Yellow Riders. 1886.
Canvas, 115 x 77.5 cm.
Rijksmuseum, Amsterdam.

In 1886, Breitner traded the tranquil life of The Hague for lively Amsterdam, a city buzzing with activity and with a burgeoning cultural life. That same year he made a breakthrough with one of his equestrian paintings. The painting *The Yellow Riders*, a troop of horsemen tearing through the dunes and making straight for the viewer, was purchased by the state. This was quite extraordinary, since such luminaries of the Hague School as Jacob Maris and Anton Mauve were not yet represented in the Rijksmuseum. At a single stroke, Breitner's reputation as a painter was established with the

George Hendrik Breitner,
*Recumbent Nude on Red
Cloth*. Canvas,
20 x 30.5 cm.

George Hendrik Breitner,
*Four Jordaan Factory
Girls*. c.1893-1895.
Water-colour, 66 x 95 cm.
Private collection.

Amsterdam avant-garde: '... *indicating with a few deeply expressive lines
the action of a horse or a rider, and thereby imbuing them with life and
speed and character, is more exalted than faithfully recording line by line,
hair by hair, those details that we never notice anyway when we see a figure in motion or observe it for a split second...*' For these artists, modern art
was primarily expression of emotion. What was striking about Breitner's
work was the bold neglect of detail in favour of colour and impression. His

George Hendrik Breitner,
Lauriergracht in Winter.
c.1893-1895. Canvas,
100.5 x 200 cm.
Dordrechts Museum.

anti-academic notion of art, as well as his bohemian attitudes, appealed to the young generation who were shaping the face of modern Dutch art in the 1880s.

It was during these years that Breitner painted his many cityscapes and figure studies, shocking the larger public every now and then with his rough style and realistic approach to the subject. Nudes were striking not only because of their colour and composition, but mainly because of the theme's brutal representation. These canvases were very different from the smoothly painted, idealised female forms that the public were accustomed to – the 'Venuses' and other goddesses they saw at the exhibitions, the neatly disguised (and thereby legitimised) nude who was meant to suggest classical antiquity rather than herself.

Breitner preferred to paint Amsterdam street life, with its playing children, porters, servant girls and coffee graders. He was enthusiastic about the 'Jordaan' type, women from that well-known working-class district of Amsterdam. Breitner could portray their heads or facial features with just a few brushstrokes, or show them grossly distorted. Critics called him the Amsterdam Zola after the great French naturalistic writer whose novels were grounded in the laws of heredity, and who felt that human beings were governed by these laws and by the time and environment in which they lived. A contemporary Zolaesque description of Breitner's work drew the following conclusions: '*Here the human being is no longer a creature that observes Nature and enjoys or fears her; here the human being is himself a bleeding, torn-off shred of eternally fecund Nature, a roving beast, and the cities are the pens that the beasts have made for themselves but through which they pass, driven like slaves, thundering along with their horses and carts*'. Indeed, the human beings in Breitner's city are often little more than ciphers in the metropolitan decor. People and animals alike seem to be swallowed up in the great maelstrom of life.

Breitner's work is characterised by phases. Besides his impressions of hectic city life there are other works in which he focuses on the achievement

George Hendrik Breitner,
*Pile-Driving in Van
Diemenstraat*. 1897.
Canvas, 100 x 150 cm.
Stedelijk Museum,
Amsterdam.

of stillness, such as an abandoned shipyard, or on intimacy and tranquillity, such as the series of girls in Japanese kimonos. Here the artist's concern with depicting textures and detail approaches that of the masters in that field. The pleasure he takes in the decorative play of colour and surface is immediately apparent. He was one of the few painters at that time dealing with this theme and can therefore be compared with foreign artists such as Whistler and Alfred Stevens, who had earlier been inspired by Japanese art.

Yet the city and its inhabitants remained Breitner's greatest love. Amsterdam was one great well-spring of stimuli for the artist. He preferred the city during the evening hours or when it was snowing or raining – certain times of day or weather conditions that added an extra dimension to reality. His fascination with light and reflections was unparalleled. In *Kalverstraat on a Rainy Evening*, the shopping street and its passers-by are barely recognisable. It is the impression of a moment that the artist translates into this quivering vision in paint.

Amsterdam was a hectic, active city during those years. Industrialisation came later to the Netherlands than to its neighbours; it was not until the last decades of the nineteenth century that everything began gaining momentum, and the consequences became clear. The city grew enormously and became the economic powerhouse of the Netherlands. In the years between the 1870s and the 1890s the population doubled. The inner city became busier and busier and an urban proletariat emerged. In a very short time Amsterdam took on a whole new look due to urban expansion, the modernisation of the network of streets and replacement of old buildings by new ones.

Canals were filled in and facades broken through. Building was going on everywhere, but so was demolition.

'It doesn't last long, it's over before you know it'

All that expansion, demolition and excavation is evident in Breitner's work, as in *Van Diemenstraat*. Oddly enough, he never got around to the last stage of activity: the building of new offices and residential areas. He never chose these as the main subject for his paintings, for Breitner loved the old historic centre of town. He made countless drawings and paintings of the Dam Square, the heart of the seventeenth-century inner city, and the streets, canals and alleys that encircle it like a wreath. In his many views of the Dam we see the Old Stock Exchange but not Berlage's new Exchange, which took its place in 1903. The horse, which had been an object of fascination for him since his youth, is present in many of his cityscapes dragging a carriage or waiting for a tram. The electric tram, which began to dominate the city in 1904, is nowhere to be seen in his work.

Breitner's paintings and drawings, and above all the many photos he took, bear witness to the moment when a city was transformed into a modern metropolis. The artist walked the streets of Amsterdam making countless photos and drawings. He used the camera and the sketchbook primarily as aids in constructing his paintings. Sometimes the works appear to have been painted with tremendous ease and speed, but in reality they were the result of a great deal of preparation. The influence of photography is sometimes clearly recognisable, as when we are confronted with the snapshot-like image of a servant girl on the street, a close-up of an abandoned shipyard near the IJ or an elevated view of the Dam. The sketchbooks were used for direct studies to record impressions. They are filled with notes about colour, atmosphere and light. The camera was an ideal tool for studying movement, details, light / dark contrasts and position. Usually Breitner interpreted his subject by changing the composition, using particular elements or leaving out certain details. In his later work he leaned more and more heavily on photography. As indicated by the many negatives and prints that were not discovered until after his death, he had a special interest in photography although he rarely mentioned it during his lifetime.

'*The fact is that you make better things before your fortieth birthday than afterwards. When you're thirty it's not hard to produce a good painting. The trick is to still be able to do it when you're fifty*', Brietner once said. This seems to be the painter's own brief summary of his career. In 1901 the forty-four-year-old artist put on a large, succesful retrospective in Amsterdam. But afterwards his virtuosity and productivity would gradually wane. The painter had in fact already told his story, and in later years he just kept repeating himself. Breitner was not interested in the modern artistic trends that followed each other in such rapid succession in the early decades of the twentieth century. After 1914 he hardly painted at all, partly due to a rapid decline in his health. Things went downhill for Breitner financially as well as physically. In 1917 his friends set up a relief fund for him, and in 1923 the painter died. '*It doesn't last long, it's over before you know it*' appear to have been the last words of an artist who spent his whole life in pursuit of the moment.

RIETA BERGSMA
Translated by Nancy Forest-Flier.

oets

Pick Things Up all over the World

The Poetry of Luuk Gruwez

Luuk Gruwez (1953-).
Photo by David Samyn.

In an essay written in 1980 the Flemish poet Luuk Gruwez (1953-) drew a distinction between poets whom he likened to piano-tuners, and other poets whom he described as singers. The latter group, in which he included himself, '*emerge from their poems as people of flesh and blood, not as robot skin specialists*'. They are more concerned with the essence of things than with the essence of poetry.

Gruwez made this statement when he himself was at the beginning of his oeuvre, having come to the literary world's notice shortly before with a collection which was imbued with the somewhat misty romantic view of life which typified the late 1970s. The title itself hints at the contents: *Oh, Such a Soft Caress because of a Mild Sadness* (Ach, wat zacht geliefkoos om een mild verdriet, 1977). It was published under an equally illustrative motto, taken from the great romantic poet Victor Hugo: '*La mélancolie, c'est le bonheur d'une tristesse dont on a oublié l'objet.*'

At the time and in the context in which the essay was written, the distinction between singers and piano-tuners was to be understood as a polemic against poets who were exploring the relationship between language and reality in a variety of ways and for whom reflecting on their own craft was an essential part of their writership. In the face of this trend Gruwez, who was also speaking on behalf of a number of 'neo-romantic' poets of his own generation, called for a return to emotion, to a profession of beliefs, to the great themes in which the reader could recognise him or herself. '*I remain convinced,*' he wrote in the same essay, '*that a poet who professes his beliefs evokes the same response in the reader*'. And that is the reader he has in mind. That is also the primary function of poetry: to touch the reader, to move him or her, make them feel pain and joy simultaneously through a combination of beauty and emotion. Today, more than twenty years later, and standing outside all the trends and poetic fashions, it is apparent that this was a fundamental choice for Gruwez. The poet is a singer, who uses his artistry to interpret joy and sadness in himself and in those around him, just like the minstrels of old.

As I have formulated it here, it sounds rather corny and not so far removed from a sentimental tearjerker. And indeed, Gruwez' poems do sometimes flirt with the boundary between art and kitsch. But the aesthetic quality, the awareness of form, the strategic use of irony and, particularly in his recent work, the increasing objectification of emotion, prevents his work from straying over that boundary and becoming kitsch.

The art of pretence

The collections from the 1980s, *A House to be Homeless in* (Een huis om dakloos in te zijn, 1981) and *The Festive Loser* (De feestelijke verliezer, 1985) still consist primarily of first-person poetry, in which the poet is seeking to find the right stance to take on the great existential problems: infinite longings and human shortcomings, life and death, the unavoidable passage of time, the longing for perfect tenderness in a world full of pain, the loss of all that is dear. In the face of all that loss within and around him the poet has little more to contribute than the beauty of his language. '*La sensualité du style ne diffère nullement de celle d'un corps qui – s'abritant contre la mort – s'abandonne à l'amour*' is the motto of *The Festive Loser*. At best, art – poetry – can preserve what has been lost by turning it into something of beauty. A poem about the poet's deceased mother puts it like this: '*I commit her to paper word for word, / clothe her corpse with a proper context.*'

It is not only where reality falls short, but even where it is at its most beautiful, as in the presence of a swan on a lake, that reality has to give way to the portrayal of it, in the mirror and in the poem which is the reflection of the mirror: '*it is not the swan which is the most beautiful, but the water / in which the reflection of the swan merges with infinity*'. Poetry is then the art of pretence, of inventing that which we long for, but which always and necessarily falls short, as in the early verses of one of his best-known poems, 'Sourdine':

And if there is no longer any tenderness,
let us then pretend this tenderness
with blindfold hands and eyes half closed,
lying against each other like a frontier

A lot of body

From the beginning of the 1990s, when the collection *Fat People* (Dikke mensen, 1990) was published, an important shift took place in Gruwez' work. The style became more sober, less directed towards intoxicating aesthetic effects, though the flair and refinement remains. At the same time the ego is pushed into the background in favour of characters who are presented in a somewhat anecdotal, narrative context. What does remain is the theme of human shortcomings. The singer who is the poet spends less time interpreting his own suffering at the hands of life and more time concentrating on his compassion for the defencelessness and powerlessness of humankind, his love for those who cannot cope with the world. The opening poem, 'Biography' ('Biografie') is a description of that human being:

the body is a lonely thing
of plasma, bone marrow and grease
and hollow places full of secrets
and three or four glands with the power to please.
(...)

– a body is a lonely thing
which no-one wants to heal.

It is precisely their bodies that make human beings so movingly vulnerable; and fat people in particular have a lot of body. They are enlargements, as it were, of all that flesh: *'less than a hundred kilos nothing / that nobody will ever want'*. The portraits in this and the next collection, *Bad Manners* (Vuile manieren, 1994), of characters such as *'the cloakroom attendant'* who for lack of anything else has become infatuated with coats, a retarded niece, or the lavatory attendant 'Miss Pipi', *'the heavenly drudge of stench'*, whose only applause comes from the flushing lavatories, are portrayed in a way which is at once grotesque and endearing, in a mixture of ironic ridicule and loving identification. They are ridiculous because they so clearly portray human mortality; but the motivation for writing all this down and preserving it is love: *'only that which is defenceless and finite / deserves immortality'*.

A singer, not a piano-tuner

Gruwez' most recent collection, *Thieves and Loved Ones* (Dieven en geliefden, 2000), takes a few steps further down this same road, through the greater infusion of reality and anecdotalism, some of it in a number of long, more or less narrative poems. The loved ones of the title are both loved ones in the strict sense and all those defenceless people from the earlier collections, while the thieves are everything that robs us of those loved ones. In the final analysis they represent death, which right from Gruwez' earliest collections is portrayed as a jealous lover, a thief who seeks to possess all those mortal bodies more completely than any loved one ever could. In the long poem 'Advice to a thief' ('Advies aan een dief') the poem addresses the thief directly, actually invites him in and shows around his house, shows him his dearest possessions and memories. Finally they come to the room occupied by his beloved:

Here I keep my girlfriend captive.
In ropes with chains around her feet.
No-one knows the possessor of her body.

Or: do you want to know the real truth?
These twenty years I've lain next to her.
We're proud that we are growing older,
the last ones who believe in each other.
(...)
You must love me very much
that you wish to take so much from me.
But even if you take all I have,
leave her with me, and me with her.

After almost thirty years, Luuk Gruwez has acquired a unique position within the world of Dutch-language poetry. He is one of the most 'human' poets, who has fully realised his ambition of being a singer and not a piano-tuner. On the way, he has gradually freed himself of woolly romanticism, of a desire for aesthetic effect, and ultimately of a preoccupation with his own ego and his own emotional world. On the other hand, against the tide of prevailing fashions he has continued to believe in the ability of language and poetry to express and share an experienced reality, to interpret songs – even if they sound less sweet-voiced than in the past – which give expression to the listener's experiences. It is no coincidence that in his public appearances he manages to move his audiences more than most of his colleagues. He is after all speaking on behalf of them, on behalf of us, on behalf of everyone who sometimes feels lost and wants to be gathered up.

The poet then comes along to do that gathering up, picking things up just like children do, and putting them in the warmth of their trouser pocket – or in this case, the poem. Like children, the poet sets his face against the laws of oblivion and gravity:

All over the world children pick things up:
a pebble, a marble or a cast-off sock,
the leg of a dismembered doll.
(...)
not just to be given things,
but also to stop them falling.
They absolutely disagree
with the earth's gravitational pull.

HUGO BREMS
Translated by Julian Ross.

Five Poems
by Luuk Gruwez

Fat People

Fat people know everything about love,
up to the remotest corners of their body,
the catacombs of their own flesh.

Their belly is the foreign country where they live,
continuously yearning for the slimmest waists
that make their mouths water like pastry.

Nobody is more sincerely sad,
so cheerfully mournful in those distant guts,
those far toes and bulbous buttocks.

As if they just consist of remnants:
less than a hundred kilos nothing
that nobody will ever want.

From *Fat People* (Dikke mensen). Amsterdam: De Arbeiderspers, 1990.
Translated by Ria Loohuizen.

Dikke Mensen

Dikke mensen weten alles van de liefde,
tot in de meest verloren uithoek van hun lijf,
de katakomben van hun vlees.

Hun buik is buitenland waarin zij wonen,
aldoor verlangend naar de slankste tailles
die hen doen watertanden als gebak.

Er is geen mens oprechter droef,
zo goedlachs treurig in die afgelegen balg,
die verre tenen en die bolle billen,

alsof zij slechts uit overschot bestaan:
zo'n kleine honderd kilo niets
die niemand ooit zal willen.

Miss Pipi

Please protect this pale Cinderella,
who has been made for the splashing
from rapid and from languid bladders,
who has been made for the sport
of each client who toys with her.

She nods above her bowl
and dozes. It's her way of ageing slower.
So she lays all her wrinkles almost coyly
to rest on a formica top.

A sweetie that calls her Miss:
the heavenly drudge of stench
that longs for money and sentiment,
warming herself on a coffee pot.
Never beautiful, but unearthly. Spotless dragon.
– Only the flushing gives rapturous applause.

From *Bad Manners* (Vuile manieren). Amsterdam: De Arbeiderspers, 1994.
Translated by Paul Vincent.

Juffrouw Pipi

Behoed toch deze bleke assepoes,
die is geschapen voor het klateren
uit snelle en uit trage blazen,
die is geschapen voor de pret
van elke klant die met haar solt.

Zij knikkebolt boven haar schaaltje
en soest. Zo wil zij trager oud.
Zo legt zij al haar rimpels haast koket
te rusten op een blad van formica.

Een lieverd die haar juffrouw noemt:
het hemels sloofje van de stank
dat snakt naar poen en sentiment,
zich warmend aan een koffiekan.
Nooit mooi, maar bovenaards. Kraaknette draak.
– Alleen de spoeling is onstuimig met applaus.

On Picking Things Up

All over the world children pick things up:
a pebble, a marble or a cast-off sock,
the leg of a dismembered doll.
Whatever would happen to them
if they were once not to bother?
Then children and things
would cease to be themselves.
Only later will they lie still, the things.
Finally dead.

All over the world children beg,
from Marrakech to Wimbledon,
not just to be given things,
but also to stop them falling.
They absolutely disagree
with the earth's gravitational pull.

Only later, unbending giants,
do they really want those things.
But they lie low and far away,
too far away from their heads,
far too close to their toes.

It is at that moment that some
(strange, sad, endless children,
who completely on the sly
still wish to bend humbly down),
it is at that moment that some
start wobbling alarmingly.
They slump helplessly down from their heads.

One sees them – everywhere and nowhere –
sometimes lying about. Usually nowhere.
Still twitching like shot game.
They're the ones who've picked things up.
Have pity, bend and pick them up.

Over het oprapen van dingen

Overal ter wereld rapen kinderen de dingen op:
een kiezelsteen, een knikker of een oude sok,
het been van een vernielde pop.
Wat zou er hun toch overkomen
zodra zij dat één keer vertikten?
Dan zouden kinderen en dingen
ermee ophouden zichzelf te zijn.
Pas later blijven zij liggen, de dingen.
Eindelijk dood.

Overal ter wereld bedelen kinderen,
van Marrakesj tot Webbekom,
niet enkel om de dingen te verkrijgen,
maar ook om te verhoeden dat zij vallen.
Zij zijn het hoegenaamd niet eens
met de zwaartekracht van de aarde.

Later pas, onbuigzame reuzen,
willen zij die dingen werkelijk hebben.
Maar laag en afgelegen liggen ze,
al veel te ver van hun hoofd,
al veel te dicht bij hun tenen.

Het is op dat moment dat sommigen
(rare, trieste, eindeloze kinderen,
die zich volstrekt in het geniep
nog onderdanig wensen te bukken),
het is op dat moment dat sommigen
beangstigend beginnen te wankelen.
Hopeloos ploffen zij neer uit hun hoofd.

Men ziet ze – overal en nergens –
wel eens liggen. Meestal nergens.
Nog trekkend als geschoten wild.
Zij zijn het die de dingen hebben opgeraapt.
Heb meelij, buk, en raap hen op.

From *Thieves and Loved Ones* (Dieven en geliefden). Amsterdam: De Arbeiderspers, 2000.
Translated by Paul Vincent.

Together

You died simply to kill the time.
Dying suited you, in fact so well
that, turned to a thing with other lifeless things,
you scarcely seemed deceased.

And when it got that far and you so far away,
a gentleman came by with strings of prayers
who, intoxicated by his offered blessing,
wanted to bore you with eternal life.

But nothing could harm you in that
silent rapture, in which you lay and dreamed,
paid court to and fingered
by smoothly handsome, idiotic death.

And together at last and never so together,
the lightest fairy, who once bore me.
The first gentleman first loved
the last lady.

From *Unrestrained Poems* (Bandeloze gedichten). Amsterdam: De Arbeiderspers,
2000.
Translated by Paul Vincent.

Samen

Je stierf alleen maar om de tijd te doden.
Dat sterven stond je goed, zo goed
dat, ding geworden met de dode dingen,
je nauwelijks leek overleden.

En toen het zover was en jij zó ver,
toen kwam er nog een heer langs met gebeden,
die, zich beroezend aan zijn zegen,
jou nog met eeuwig leven wou vervelen.

Maar niets dat je kon deren in dat
stil vervoerde, waarin je lag te dromen,
het hof gemaakt en aangeraakt
door beeldig schone, idiote dood.

En eindelijk samen en nooit zo samen,
de lichtste fee, die mij eens baarde.
– De eerste heer beminde voor het eerst
de laatste dame.

Sourdine

And if there is no longer any tenderness,
let us then pretend this tenderness
with blindfold hands and eyes half closed,
lying against each other like a frontier.

A word may then no longer be called a word,
but a mouthful of comforting silence;
and longing no longer the length of an arm,
but further, and more distant than a panoramic view

full of summer birds, music by Mendelssohn, a *sfumato*
derived from Da Vinci. You will swop your most beautiful pity
for my favourite sorrow; I, carefully taking time
to explore more deeply the fading of your body.

O, if there is then still tenderness,
this tenderness should be dreaded
like a very old wound. So much tenderness
no man could ever stand.

From *Unrestrained Poems* (Bandeloze gedichten). Amsterdam: De
Arbeiderspers, 1996.
Translated by Greta Kilburn.

Sourdine

En als er geen tederheid meer is,
laten we de tederheid dan veinzen
met geblinddoekte handen en geloken ogen,
liggend aan elkander als een grens.

Een woord mag dan niet langer een woord heten,
maar een mondvol troostvol verzwijgen;
en verlangen niet langer een armslag lang,
maar verder, weidser dan een vergezicht

vol zomervogels, muziek van Mendelssohn, een *sfumato*
aan Da Vinci ontleend. Jij zult je mooiste medelijden
ruilen met mijn liefste verdriet; ik, voorzichtig talmen
om het tanen van je lichaam dieper af te tasten.

O als er dan nog tederheid is,
laten wij de tederheid vrezen
als een zeer oud zeer. Zoveel tederheid,
daar kon geen mens ooit tegen.

Flemish

Furniture Design

Furniture design in Flanders is blossoming as never before. Some of these creations belong more in the world of art, some take inspiration from architectural principles, while others draw on exceedingly durable traditions of craftsmanship, but in fact all three elements are present to varying degrees in all furniture. From the mid-eighties, several factors, such as the existence of a mature generation of designers and companies, the discovery, appreciation and commercialisation of the lifestyle phenomenon, more favourable economic conditions, and a clearer awareness of regional culture, combined to create a climate in which a contemporary 'furniture scene' was able to grow. International appreciation of a number of top creations – Maarten van Severen for Vitra (1999), Luc Ramael for Palluccoitalia (1996), Koenraad de Wulf for Frighetto (1994), etc. – has confirmed the excellence of these high-quality designs and products.

Pioneers

Interesting modern furniture was already being produced in Flanders in the 1950s, supported by a number of furniture manufacturers who welcomed designers with open arms. The leading location was Mechelen, at that time still the biggest name in Flemish furniture. Companies including Belform and Tubax collaborated with such designers as Alfred Hendrickx and Willy van der Meeren. However, furniture companies elsewhere were also active in the field, such as De Coene in Kortrijk and the design company Vandenberghe-Pauvers in Ghent. This boom in contemporary furniture lasted until the early 1960s and then just faded away. Interest waned because the original designs were simply copied again and again, with modifications, so that the design element was stretched too thin and no longer gave any added value to the products.

Two uncommonly exciting designers filled this gap. From the late 1950s to the mid-eighties, Emiel Veranneman and Pieter de Bruyne dominated the field with their highly individual views on furniture design. Veranneman made every piece of furniture into a precious sculptural one-off, usually

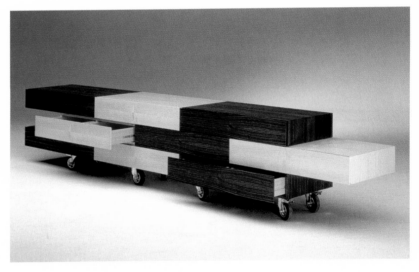

painted in vivid colours. He drew his inspiration from ancient Oriental furniture. De Bruyne's furniture was originally intended for industrial production. He endeavoured to design 'social furniture', but his aversion to compromise in the area of technology, and therefore form and construction too, led him to start up his own craftsman-based production company. Each piece was unique, composed in accordance with clear design principles. Towards the end of his life he explored the furniture of ancient Egypt.

Two figures stand out in the period between 1980 and 1995: Frans van Praet and André Verroken, who emerged from the shadows of their predecessors Veranneman and De Bruyne. They belonged to a generation of fascinating furniture designers that was active from about 1965 to 1980/85 but whose members stopped designing furniture for one reason or another. This was literally a 'lost' generation, whose work has been very little studied, except by Frans Defour in his book *Twentieth-Century Belgian Furniture*

André Verroken, *Kontener* cupboard (1995). Photo by Lieven Herreman.

(Belgische Meubelkunst van de XXe eeuw). Van Praet divided his attention between furniture and object design and interior design, and in the early 1990s concentrated mainly on the last two. In his furniture objects he combined playfulness of form with seriousness of craft and function. Some of them are unique pieces and others are suitable for commercial production. Near the lifts on the 'Departure' floor at Brussels airport are several of his somewhat controversial crystal stools, produced and cut in Val Saint Lambert. He also designed the Belgian pavilions for the world fairs at Seville and Lisbon, from which he retained his *Sevilla* benches, later used to furnish public spaces in several towns including Ghent. In the mid-nineties he largely withdrew from furniture design.

André Verroken blazed the trail for the current generation. He was the only one of the 'lost generation' who stubbornly persisted in designing furniture in a highly individual way. Now he is at the very top. He has created marvellous furniture such as the *Centipede* cabinet (1988), the *Homage to Eduardo Chillida* table (1994), the *Kontener* cupboard (1995), for which he won a bronze medal at the international *Design with Love, Life with Wood* furniture design competition in the Japanese city of Asahikawa in 1996. In 1997 Jan Hoet, the curator of the SMAK (Museum of Contemporary Art) in Ghent, commissioned a monumental conference table more than six metres long for his museum.

Even today Verroken remains active as an inventive pure furniture designer. He says his vocation only came late in life, and he always remains faithful to a number of artistic principles. The basis of his style lies in geometry and architectonics, and in constructivism. In the mid-eighties he gave shape to his ideas on the 'module' and 'stacking'. Ultimately, his creations are timeless and free forms, contrasting in colour (dark against light) and material.

Manufacturers and designers, styles and perceptions

In the mid-eighties a number of young designers made their appearance. There was an almost endless series of exhibitions of their work. Together they formed a generation which is today in full bloom. In addition to this, such furniture manufacturers as Bulo, Obumex, Extremis, Belgachrom, and even such bastions of tradition as Aurora, are once again, or even more, active in the design sector. In passing it is also worth mentioning those companies that produce contemporary light fittings (Modular, Kreon, Waco, etc.) for which they call in designers or set up their own design departments. In this way they too have considerable influence on the interior and design scene.

Various organisations also became involved. The design department of VIZO, a Flemish government institution, expanded its work on furniture design by giving both craft and industrial designers their due. This was achieved at the first and second Triennales for Design in Flanders in 1995 and 1998. At about that time, the professional federation Febelhout launched the necessary initiatives through Optimo, an economic grouping centred on design and furniture companies. Lastly there was the formation of Cepro, another economic grouping in the interior design sector, which resulted in

Luc Ramael, *Panorama*,
open bookcase in MDF and
metal (2000). Photo by Bart
van Leuven.

the highly successful F3 furniture display at the furniture shows in Cologne
and Milan in 2000. We must of course also emphasise the importance of the
well-known international Interieur Biennale in Kortrijk, which has been
blazing a trail for contemporary design for three decades. In short, it looks
as if the Flemish have suddenly become a race of furniture designers.

However, few common trends can be discerned in these contemporary
furniture creations, unless one counts the ever-changing cocktail of tradition, architecture and art, and perhaps a slight preference for minimalist
products. The creation and production of industrial, crafted and sculptural
furniture is carried on in parallel. It is usually the designers' individual
views that determine production, despite the unavoidable tug-of-war between the demands of the market, machine capability, managers' wishes and
designers' dreams.

There is a huge variety of styles and views: in fact there are as many styles as there are designers. In an attempt to see the wood through the trees,
I would like, on the basis of my personal view, to outline several major
'groups' who are linked by their training, methods, source of inspiration,
etc.

The architectural trend

There is no specific 'furniture design' course at any Flemish college or university. Students can become interior designers and architects, master sculp-

Bataille & Ibens, H_2O office furniture for BULO (1995). Photo courtesy of BULO.

tors, painters and jewellery designers, but not master furniture designers. However, an examination of their CVs shows that most furniture designers come from a background of interior design or architecture. Furniture design is to be found as an option or specialisation on these courses.

Several designers learnt their trade in one of these options. One recognises their architectural background in the construction, choice of materials and in the formal solution to the project and its aesthetics. The overall characteristics are austerity, rigid lines and a logical, 'less is more' composition. However, all these designers have their own style or emphasise particular aspects. I would like to look for a moment at Luc Ramael, who was already active in 1980 and in recent years has achieved recognition both at home and abroad. He was invited to be a member of the jury for the ideas contest at the seventeenth Interieur Biennale in 2000. He received his training as an interior designer, specialising in furniture design, from Rudi Verelst, a designer from the 'lost generation', who moved to Canada to lecture in design but did not feel at home in this field. Furniture design was the outlet for his own ideas: it was in his blood, especially since his father was a furniture maker. His designs are by no means those of a craftsman, however, but are destined for industrial production. Retail price, quality, feasibility and cost price are important factors in his work, and in this he differs from most other Flemish designers. Since 1988 Ramael has designed several pieces of furniture for a number of Italian companies: a standard lamp for Felicerossi (1988), a magazine rack for Steel (1992), the *Clips* table lamp for Foscarini (1994) and others. His *Abat-jour* standard lamp for Palluccoitalia dates from 1996.

There are of course also architects who design furniture. In fact there are probably no architects in Flanders who have never designed a piece of furniture. The best-known Flemish architect-designers are a couple, Claire Bataille and Paul Ibens. Since 1969 they have designed and produced light fittings (Light, 1986), the 'Palladio' glasses for Val Saint Lambert (1995), the H_2O line (1995) – office furniture for the Mechelen furniture company BULO – and among other products the 'Y Table' for Obumex (1999).

Maarten van Severen, Chair
03 (2000). Photo courtesy
of VITRA.

It is also striking that companies in or related to the furniture sector particularly like to employ architects or architecturally-trained designers. Few craft-oriented designers find a job with them. For example, BULO regularly has part of its collection designed by people from outside the company. Nor is it at all fazed by experiments, such as the production of the table by the fashion designer Ann de Meulemeester: a simple kitchen table, but covered entirely in white painter's canvas, so that when it showed too many signs of use it could simply be painted over. BULO clearly puts its faith in design as a sign of quality and as a sales argument, because they are setting up their own department of furniture design. OBUMEX in Staden is another company of international renown, specialising in kitchens. It also has its own design team, but often works with freelance designers like Bataille and Ibens, Maarten van Severen, John Pawson, Paul Smith and Jean de Meulder. It does not like routine. Its key word is innovation and the focus is on the quest for the best technological and aesthetic solutions. It recently brought out the WASH collection, a range of special washbasins. Suzon Ingber designed WASH1 and Vincent van Duysen WASH2.

There are a few other designers who combine a background as a furniture maker with training as an interior designer or architect, and who mostly design one-off pieces of exceptional originality which they often make themselves. Their pieces of furniture are frequently gems of expertise and virtuosity. The major difference from the previous category of designers lies in the research process. This takes place while they are making the furniture with their own hands, and not on the drawing board. A designer who opts for the path of craftsmanship is often faced with seemingly insoluble technical problems to which he has to find a solution. The lines of the piece are usually far from austere, as is its construction, which displays great technical ingenuity. The materials used are in most cases very straightforward, but are often worked with great (or excessive) virtuosity. One designer who produced interesting work was Koenraad Dewulf, but he ceased working as a furniture designer in the mid-nineties. He opened the 'Koen-Art' gallery in Watou. Another example is the smith Rudy van Geele who, after creating

Maarten van Severen,
Chaise longue (1995).
Photo by Bart van Leuven.

a series of almost 'living' fairytale iron cabinets and chairs, is now producing other special interior objects such as the mirror and chandelier that he showed at the VIZO Gallery in 2000. Van Geele studied to be an architect but became a smith and retrained himself as a craftsman furniture designer. His furniture has playful and bizarre organic shapes. They do not include any straight lines, which makes them the exact opposite of the 'architectural' tradition, but they are the perfect translation of the intrinsic force of forging, which makes metal soft and malleable. In recent years Van Geele has become known and appreciated in Paris and elsewhere abroad.

Other designers hover between architecture, art and furniture-making. It is a magical and artistic combination. These artists originally designed one-off craftsman's pieces, then developed towards series and finally to designs for large-scale industrial production, without really aiming for mass production. The lines are very often minimal, just like the volumes. The materials used are adapted to production processes, and *vice versa*. This means they may just as easily be in natural materials as in plastic.

Maarten van Severen is the great (and internationally celebrated) example of this sort of furniture design. For Vitra, the famous Swiss design company, he designed the 0.3 chair, for the Italian company Edra the blue sofa, for BULO a trestle table, etc. In this way he rose to the top rank of famous names in the design world. His name has for some time been synonymous with 'minimalist' design at an international level, together with Jasper Morrison and John Pawson. In the course of ten years (from about 1990 to the present time) Van Severen has developed a style that has stripped his furniture of all frills. He pursued this emphatically austere language of form in his choice of aluminium and natural oak as his chief materials, in the invisibility and sophistication of construction and in the overall, taut, self-effacing, no-nonsense form. Van Severen usually starts from a sketch, a pencil drawing, sometimes a single line, that summarises every aspect of the piece to be designed. The line does not obscure the form but flows, twists and turns, makes angles and intersections. But it remains a clear line that creates surfaces and volumes and thereby becomes architecture. He was evidently

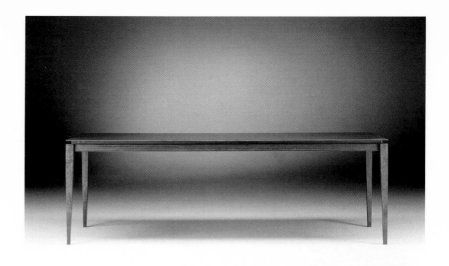

influenced, positively but unconsciously, by his father Dan van Severen, a painter of brilliant abstract works full of geometric figures that suggest space.

Idir Mecibah, Table from the *Fer 37* series (1999). Photo by Lieven Herreman.

Autodidacts

In this category, no real distinction can be made between the labels artist and designer, though neither term entirely fits their nature. Their work does not stick to a single line or fashion, except for a consistently personal approach, but is frequently founded on the mastery of a particular technique. These designers previously had little involvement with furniture, but they had their expressive vision, their urge to create. An urge that found form in the 'invention' of functional objects.

Idir Mecibah trained in smithing at various institutions. Two major contributions to his development were the courses he took under Albert Paley in New York and Vladimir Sokonevitsch in St Petersburg, two internationally renowned smiths. Up to 1998 he himself taught evening classes at the Royal Academy of Fine Arts in Antwerp. The use of rusted steel, in the form of discarded sheets, gave his designs a rough aspect. In 1996 he forged the 'Throne for the Devil' for the highly successful children's programme *Kulderzipken* on Flemish television (VRT). This gave him the opportunity to let the unpredictability of the fire that softens the iron play its part to the full. Rudy van Geele also employs this technique in his work. At a later stage, Mecibah 'encrusted' big blocks of rough wood with wrought iron parts, which gave his cabinets an extraordinarily sculptural appearance. In his collection *Fer 37, Fe 37, F37* (1998) he went one step further. He has not actually entered a new field, but has come very close to industrial design. The lines of the furniture in the collection have been refined, the baroque element has gone, and one sees areas bounded by straight lines. At first it appears as if there is no longer any craftsmanship, but Mecibah is not yet an industrial designer. This new furniture is still actually forged. He remains

Fabiaan van Severen, *Fold and Profile* table with stainless-steel top (1995-1996). Photo by Lieven Herreman / © VIZO.

faithful to his craft, in line with the purest Arts and Crafts philosophy, but at the same time makes sure that the objects continue to display considerable monumentality. In the meantime his name and reputation have crossed the ocean, bringing him two commissions for department store lighting in the USA: at Bergdorf Goodman in New York and Marshall Fields in Chicago.

Fabiaan van Severen's work is entirely industrial. It evolved from rigidly minimalist visual forms into an individual functional style. He is greatly inspired by architecture and like his brother Maarten unconsciously experiences and assimilates the influence of his father Dan van Severen, though in a pragmatic way. Fabiaan has created a whole series of objects that demonstrate his powerful versatility: screens, handbags, lamps, chairs and tables in metal, wood and leather. The fundamental idea underlying these designs is multiple production. Fabiaan van Severen does not present himself as an artist, but as an industrial designer.

Industrial designers

Occasionally, in the midst of all these designers with architectural training, one finds a real industrial designer who, unlike his fellows, devotes himself entirely to designing furniture. One such is Casimir. He himself retains control of the design and production of most of his furniture. The late Jan Kenis wrote of Casimir in *Kwintessens*: '... *he is a modernist in heart and soul. Every piece of furniture he designs is a reduction. Casimir reduces a piece of furniture to its essence but clearly does not simply settle for that as the very first Modernists did. He does not see any end to plainness, only a boundary that can be crossed. On the other side of this boundary of plainness lies a bizarre language of form. It is as if one takes a construction so far that it collapses under its own weight, and a new outlook on the concept of construction appears out of its ruins.*' One extremely successful and surprising design of his is the *Anna* wall cabinet. The surprise comes when you open it. Instead of just the front panel, the whole cabinet opens out on a big

rubber wheel. His one-man business has now expanded into a fully-fledged company. His activities include architecture, interior design, stand construction, product design and, more recently, graphic design. His name is an internationally registered trade mark. So it is now possible to buy a copyright-protected 'Casimir'. He was one of the partners in the successful *Forms from Flanders* event that promoted Flemish design at the furniture shows in Cologne and Milan. He recently developed a 'hothouse' called *GlassFlat*, a sort of verandah, for the MiniFlat company. The glass was specially developed by the Belgian Glaverbel company. Four of these hothouses were shown at the seventeenth Interieur Biennale. Each was fitted out by an internationally renowned designer: the Finn Ilkka Suppanen, the Swiss Argentine Alfredo Häberli, Karim Rashid, the new wonderboy of American design, and the Frenchwoman Matali Crasset, a former assistant to Philippe Starck. Each gave their own interpretation to Casimir's glass house.

Craftsmen and collectives

When it comes to crafts, one can train as a furniture maker, a woodworker or a carpenter. Furniture designers sometimes emerge from the everyday practice of the craft in the actual craftsmen's workshops. Dirk Meylaerts is one such designer. He was previously a dancer in a contemporary dance company, but was converted to the more concrete world of furniture. In his initial period he made what one might call classical, timeless furniture, preferring to use elements from the language of classical form as his basic principle. In comparison to the friezes and columns of the postmoderns, his creations were rather banal elements such as table legs. His furniture is linear, well-proportioned and often rounded in form. His next step was to create simple pieces of furniture clad in mirrored glass or metal, but then he gave up furniture making to work for architects and even to take his chance in the visual arts. But he gradually returned to designing furniture. His creations are now even more fundamental in form and line than before: severe, distilled to the essence and extremely ascetic. But their edges are softened by the felt trim applied to them.

In Limburg one finds a 'phenomenon within a phenomenon'. In the early eighties this was the birthplace of several progressive designers' collectives that stemmed from the interior design course at the Provincial Higher Architectural Institute (PHAI) at Diepenbeek. They received exceptional support and assistance from the province's Department of Culture. One often finds the same designers in each of these collectives, though in each case they accentuate different aspects of their work. Two examples are Het Labo and De Elf. Both work on the basis of an utterly surprising outlook. They implement a sort of intellectual assemblage. Their 'collective' brain sees links between materials and objects which other people do not. The most striking figure in De Elf is Patrick Reuvis. He makes a handbag from a pair of army boots or two irons, and a mobile display case from two transparent plastic rooflights.

It is clear from the above that one cannot possibly pin down any 'Flemish school' of furniture designers. There are few common stylistic features, and where they can be found they refer to the international scene rather than the regional. What one does find, however, is the constantly changing mix of tradition, art and function.

JOHAN VALCKE
Translated by Gregory Ball.

Leo Aerts, Glass case (1996). Photo by Johan Fieremans / © VIZO.

Unstable

Equilibrium

The Versatility of J. Bernlef

Quite a few covers of the books of J. Bernlef (1937-) feature photographs, usually in black-and-white or broken colours. The effect is unspectacular and the same goes for the subjects depicted: a few erratic stones, a coastline full of inlets somewhere in America (as can be seen from a flag), the blank wall of a hangar (or something else entirely), a lady's bike outside a station booking hall, a 1922 film star with a dreamy look in her eye. Apart from this last they seem to be random shots of random places, snapshots, nothing has been arranged for or by the photographer. Typical of this gaze that looks past, underneath and next to everything is the photograph on the back cover of a novel: a man, presumably the writer himself, leans slightly hunched over the railing of a kind of footbridge somewhere in the dunes; we do not see the man from the front but slightly obliquely from behind, what he is looking at is uncertain.

If those covers were not made to the author's instructions, it has to be said that the designers had a good intuitive grasp of his work. There is always something informal, casual about that work; the catch in the voice, the rhetorical flourish, the tarted-up pose are anathema to the author. So the same applies – we may assume – to the hard-selling, vulgarly eye-catching covers with which many publishers market their wares these days. Bernlef distances himself from them in advance, but not with a clenched fist: he turns his back or calls attention to other insignificant details. 'Insignificant' can be taken literally: from his earliest work onwards he is searching for things that have not yet been given significance, recorded and catalogued, for what is nameless in remote or written-off worlds – not, and that is decisive, to give it an indelible name before it is too late (and in so doing make a bid for eternal fame as the namer, creator or discoverer), but quite simply to observe it, without a plan or aim, and confirm its existence.

Open-air poet

At first sight, then, Bernlef is not a colourful writer. The colour that goes with him is a non-colour: grey. Some Dutch critics, who have never got beyond that 'first sight', use the word pejoratively. Grey is synonymous with flat, dull, indifferent. But at second sight there is no question of any of this. Indifference, said Proust, applies to everyone who does not – will not or cannot – see differences, and that may apply to the abused consumer's eye that is used to hopping about from place to place in reflex-like, uncoordinated movements, but it does not apply to Bernlef's.

The grey in his work is like that of the black-and-white photograph: it gives his texts an even quality, like in Baroque music, and that has an inviting, disarming effect. The reader has the feeling that he does not have to watch out for barriers of mysterious images, cryptic formulations or mysterious allusions that block his path, he is given the freedom to grope his way slowly from word to word, sentence to sentence so as to be able to understand how many nuances there are to that grey, hence also: how much life there is in it. It strikes him that what he had called 'grey' is no more than a facile and careless blanket term for all non-synthetic, natural shades, for which Bernlef has a predilection and which he certainly does name very precisely: brick-red and wine-red, cornflower blue and peacock blue, cement grey and mole grey, canary yellow, honey yellow, chocolate brown, rust brown, tobacco brown and rope brown.

These compound adjectives are more reminiscent of the neologistic vocabulary of impressionist poets (in the Netherlands, first and foremost Herman Gorter) than the harder and barer one of the modernists in whose footsteps Bernlef began. Yet that idiomatic affinity with impressionism is not that surprising to those who have followed his development: if in his early work Bernlef had focused mainly on isolated things in their chance manifestations – the *objet trouvé* of Dadaists and Surrealists – later, partly under the influence of Swedish authors like Lars Gustafsson, Tomas Tranströmer and Lennart Sjögren, he discovered the importance of space and light – central categories both for Impressionist poets and for the *plein-air* painters 'overtaken' by Modernism. Bernlef is an open-air poet. He does not present his protagonists – things, elements, plants, animals – in an artificial environment, lit from the wings. Rather, light and space are integral components of their manifestation, which as a result acquires a fleeting, transient quality, but also something that cancels out their isolation, although Bernlef would not dream of calling that 'something' metaphysical. Bernlef has a practised eye for these moments of vulnerability, these moments of happiness in which there is an unstable equilibrium between all that is separate and the universe, the writer observes it, holds his breath and chooses the most tentative words so as not to disturb that equilibrium prematurely.

Perhaps the finest Bernlef cover is that of *Cello Years* (Cellojaren), a collection of stories and sketches of 1995. It shows a detail from *Marthe*, a photograph taken around 1900 by Pierre Bonnard of his lover. The photograph is just as intriguing – in its vagueness and expectancy – as the book's title. It is part of a series taken deep in a wood, somewhere in a clearing, when Marthe was in her early twenties, Pierre a little older.

Bernlef: '*Marthe rolling off a stocking. The moment at which the sunlight catches one of the nipples of her forward-hanging breasts through the leaves, as if light is coming out of it. Marthe who – naked now – squats in the grass observing something. The curve from back to buttocks like a visualised caress. Her feet, somewhat too large, resting flat in the grass. And in all the photographs that background of dark and light leaves, in reality a rustling, seething mass. He did not record the moment when she took off her panties. Probably because he though the movement was too closely linked to current sexual representations. Because that was the last thing he wanted.'* And a little further on: *'She must have undergone it as something natural and mostly in silence, those endless hours when she posed for him, absorbed in her own body, or in minor domestic tasks like peeling potatoes or arranging flowers. And in all those paintings, which follow her life from the age of twenty-one to seventy-three, she stayed as young as ever. Malicious tongues maintained that it was she who demanded that of him. She was often ill and frightened of growing old. I don't believe it. In that case his paintings would have glorified her youth much more exuberantly. He never kept her prisoner in his paintings. She is engaged in some very simple task, usually indoors. At any moment she can change her mind or position. It did not matter to him that she changed outwardly over the years, that her body no longer radiated the firm perfection of the photos in the wood. He saw it, but his hands painted her as his body felt her.'*

Shadow reality

Bernlef, who made his debut in 1970 with poems and stories, has practised all literary genres from the outset. He has a preference for shorter forms: poems, prose poems, prose sketches, stories, essays. His first novels are modest in scale, later they become thicker and more complex. Bernlef is also an extraordinarily productive writer, publishing an average of two books a year. These include translations, of prose and especially of poetry (Marianne Moore, William Carlos Williams, Elizabeth Bishop and many more). Like his essays – on photography, film, the visual arts, jazz and literature – those translations are ways of appropriating. Bernlef makes no secret of his influences, he does not believe in creativity as a form of immaculate conception.

It is slightly surprising that this constantly expanding oeuvre is so consistent. Of course there are developments and shifts, but no radical breaks. All his books, regardless of genre, convey the same basic attitude. And in all his books you encounter identical or associated motifs, themes, ideas. This means that as a reader you can start anywhere. Just as Bernlef never concentrates on a single point per text, so the oeuvre as a whole has no privileged starting point or more or less compulsory routes, although unlike Cortázar, like him an improviser and jazz fan, he never mentions this expressly. In the meantime, Bernlef, without planning it, but true to himself, has written a series of books that form an unmistakable continuum, a shadow reality, which lies not so much *under* ordinary reality like the suppressed or forbidden realm of the Surrealists and Freud, but rather constitutes a dimension of it. For those with eyes and ears no *separate* sense is required.

And paradoxically that means: those with eyes and ears for the discontinuities, the blanks, the gaps, the threads, the mixed and transitional forms of existence. Bernlef seeks out those places, wants to know how much of that vagueness, how much loss he can take, whether and how he can keep his feet in those precarious circumstances. It almost always begins with a break: he places someone in a strange environment, often an island, or he gives him a physical or mental handicap, so that his relationship with his surroundings is systematically disrupted. In the novel with which he first reached a wide readership, *Out of Mind* (Hersenschimmen, 1984), the protagonist is an elderly man who falls quite rapidly into senile dementia and so loses his grip on his surroundings. In a previous novel, Under Icebergs (*Onder ijsbergen*, 1981), a Danish investigating magistrate visits an Eskimo settlement in Greenland in the hope of solving a baffling murder. To get to the bottom of the mystery he has to venture physically into similar conditions, just as the narrator in *Out of Mind* has to identify with the old man.

That is essential for the whole of Bernlef: ultimately, certainly in hazardous situations, he has less confidence in the instrumental potential of reason than in the mimetic one of intuition, of the spontaneous physical and sensory capacity to react. There are numerous places in his work – especially in his prose – where that confidence is rewarded, in which conscious loss of self, to the brink of madness and death, turns out to be the precondition for partaking in an unprecedented experience beyond language and reason. There are also numerous places – especially in the poetry – in which he observes fragments of life not covered by the protective but also mercilessly hardening and stiffening carapace of function, decency and convention. And the aim is always to capture those observations in words, to extract them from all-diminishing time, just as Bonnard photographed his Marthe when she took her clothes off deep in the woods – an extremely erotic situation precisely because they did not, in Bernlef's words, take '*the road to satisfaction*'. '*While he* (Bonnard, although Bernlef never uses the name) *developed the photos and saw her white figure emerging in the bath he must have hit on the idea – the thought of every lover who looks for a moment full of surprise at the body of the woman he loves* – she must stay like that forever, the sunlight must fall across her like that forever.'

The search for incidents nipped in the bud

Among the absolute peaks in Bernlef's oeuvre I include the large novel *Boy* (2000). The book is a synthesis of everything that he has written previously – and at the same time it is more than that. It is not easy to characterise the book succinctly, at any rate it cannot be assigned to any one genre. To begin with *Boy* is a historical novel, set in New York in the early years of the twentieth century. These are also the early years of silent films, the telephone, advertising, the car, which the minister inveighs against, and the typewriter, although at the *Flatbush Chronicle*, the paper for which the main character works, they still have to make do without that.

One can assume that it is mainly silent movies that attract Bernlef to this area, particularly to Coney Island. Coney Island is a seaside resort situated on the Atlantic Ocean at the southernmost point of Brooklyn, attractive because of its beach hotels and hippodromes, and especially because of its amusement park, then the largest in the world, which is also the birthplace of film. Bernlef evokes this now vanished world of faded glory – the place was ravaged by fires in the 1950s and later fell into terminal decay – with great expertise and very vividly. But since the perspective of the narrator remains limited to that of his characters, the atmosphere is more vital and expectant than nostalgic. Changes are everywhere in the air, everything is in a state of ferment and transition.

That also applies to the career of Polly Todd, an actress who wants to make it big but is murdered halfway through shooting on her film. She is found in her hotel room, naked on the bed. A deaf and dumb boy who is found in the wardrobe in the room seems the obvious culprit. But the book's main character, William Stevens, a reporter on the local *Flatbush Chronicle,* has his doubts. His investigation gives the book the features of a crime or detective novel, not for the first time in Bernlef's work. As well as this, and most of all, *Boy* is a love story in many variations; it goes without saying that the writer exploits the opportunities for a pastiche on the first, highly romantic film scripts, but – typical Bernlef – without distancing himself from them. Here too he leaves much unsaid.

Boy is a synthesis. In it the reader discovers countless motifs, ideas, formulations from earlier work. Bernlef had previously written a novel about a deaf mute, *Prodigal Son* (Verloren zoon, 1997), and also one about the strange, even weird world of Coney Island, *The White City* (De witte stad, 1992). He has also written poetry about Coney Island in decay. And William Stevens, in and outside the work of Bernlef, is of course no stranger either. He is based on the poet Wallace Stevens, to whom Bernlef is indebted – as is made explicit in *The Necessary Angel* (De noodzakelijke engel, 1990), but was apparent much earlier from his way of observing things. Like his namesake, the reporter Stevens is looking for *'incidents nipped in the bud'*, *'something wordless that without any adornment happened constantly and everywhere.'* A neat example of a thematic repetition is provided by the character of the half-blind hotelier in *Boy*, who makes up with his ears for what he misses with his eyes and consequently can hear *'each branch of a peartree'* as soon as it rains. Those strange feats of hearing of the hotelier had come up previously in a slightly different form in an essay on the Dutch painter Hans Giesen, a kindred spirit to Bacon, in *A Flick of the Wrist* (De losse pols, 1998), but in my view not very convincingly, since they are rather dragged forcibly into the argumentation of that essay, whereas in *Boy* they are meaningfully and organically embedded in the development of the action and especially the complex of motifs in the novel.

The secret tension between poetry and prose

Boy is more than a synthesis. It is also, more than in previous prose books, the proof that in Bernlef's case it is perfectly possible to write prose without denying poetry. What I mean is this: the ideal that the poet Bernlef has in mind he has formulated more than once as a state of unforced, unstable equilibrium, a state of calm in which everything is still possible. But that state is never granted a very long life in the prose of the real world, since everything and everyone is driven on by the maelstrom of time. Consequently in *his* prose, and certainly that of *Boy*, Bernlef is for the most part primarily concerned with the – ultimately inevitable – destruction of that state of equilibrium. The tension between the non-narrative and the narrative, between the sensory, descriptive and in a certain sense 'distracting' fragments and the fragments geared to the action and the passing of time, or: the tension between poetry and prose, is the secret theme of this novel, and perhaps of all his novels.

That is why Bernlef has such a pronounced preference for an early phase of technological and capitalist development, a phase in which nothing seemed to be fixed and which enables him to concentrate on phenomena in an uncertain transitional phase from 'poetry' to 'prose'. Here, for example, the replacement of the film consisting of separate, arbitrary images by the narrative film, a replacement which – and this is a constant for all transitions of this type – is accompanied by a conscious and systematic elimination of the element of chance. The most important transition relates to the work of William Stevens. Initially he, as the observer of 'poetic' moments that have so far escaped every subordinate, subservient function, is a very unusual and fairly unprofessional reporter, who with good reason is working for a small local paper. But when, driven by his obsession with Polly, he hopes to prove the innocence of the silent Boy (both represent the realm of poetry), he becomes of necessity the discoverer and inventor of a conclusive narrative – which hence *ex*cludes poetry, into which he consequently also finds his way.

In *Boy* Bernlef has achieved a rare equilibrium. On the one hand the reader is stopped in his tracks by countless 'poetic' descriptions, on the other he is almost imperceptibly sucked along by a story that turns all those still shots into happy passages. Accordingly Bernlef has no scruples at all in concluding his book somewhere between art and kitsch, with a happy ending. The deaf mute boy has committed suicide, but Amy, William's new lover, is expecting a child, takes William's hand and puts it on her belly. '*Something moved beneath his hand. He was about to say something. Smiling, she placed her finger on his lips.*'

CYRILLE OFFERMANS
Translated by Paul Vincent.

LIST OF TRANSLATIONS

Out of Mind (Tr. Adrienne Dixon). London: Faber and Faber, 1988 / Boston, MA: Godine, 1989.
Driftwood House (Tr. Scott Rollins). Francestown, NH: Typographeum, 1992.
Public Secret (Tr. Adrienne Dixon). London: Faber and Faber, 1992.
Eclipse (Tr. Paul Vincent). London: Faber and Faber, 1996.

An Extract and Four Poems
by J. Bernlef

Extract from *Boy*

Amy Faye had found Boy on the sands one Sunday three years ago, not far from the Brighton Beach Hotel. The boy with his dark hair had caught her attention because he seemed totally absorbed in the surging water in front of him, as if he were trying to take in exactly how much water he was looking at. His chubby cheeks were in constant motion. At first she thought he was chewing, but when she came closer she saw it was his thoughts that made his face so mobile. You often saw that in people who were not quite talking to themselves. You could almost read their thoughts in their faces. Even when she was close to him he did not so much as look up, as if he did not hear her approach. Sitting there right in front of the foaming advancing fringes of the waves, legs crossed in short trousers and with his hair blowing in the wind, he was just like a Buddha. Once she entered his field of vision he jumped up and ran away from her along the high-tide mark. Now and then he looked back. When he did she waved to him and smiled. Some way away he sat down in the sand again, with his face towards her. He waited motionless for her to arrive.

She had stopped in front of him and put out her hands. 'Come on. Stand up,' she had said. 'What's your name?' The boy looked at her lips but didn't answer. His brown eyes stared at her as if he could not believe what he was seeing. 'What's your name?' she asked again, but the boy did not react. 'Suit yourself,' she had said. 'I'll call you Boy.'

The boy had got up, brushed the sand off his bare knees and walked along with her. She had asked him if he had to go home. He had raised his hands to shoulder level, palms forward, as if he were surrendering and then clenched his fists. She had laughed and asked whether he had lost his tongue. But the boy had not replied and had pointed to the two seagulls flying seawards with languid wing beats.

When they arrived outside her house, the boy had stopped halfway down the garden, like a dog unsure whether the situation inside can be trusted. The shadow of the leaves of a pear tree fell across the worn patches of his grey jacket that had lost all of its buttons. 'Come,' she had gestured, 'come on with me.' She had left the door open and sat down at the table. The neighbours' goat had jumped over the fence and was now standing calmly grazing in her back garden, with its white goatee bobbing up and down. The boy had come in. He was holding on to the doorpost. With rapid eye movements he took in the room. Suddenly she saw that he really couldn't speak. He took in the room the way an animal would, making an inventory of all the escape routes and hiding places, curious and a little scared too. He had inched his way into the middle of the room. He stood there for a long time. She had said nothing either. She looked at him with her brown and her grey eye. The boy smiled, but not at her. He walked over to the piano against the side wall from which Amy had removed the front. The boy stopped in front of the open innards. It was as if he were counting the hammers and the strings, one by one. He had placed his hand carefully on the yellowish ivory keys. Perhaps he could not speak, but could listen. She went over to her piano stool and sat down at the piano. She played something from memory, Haydn's piano concerto no. 24. The boy had come and stood at the piano. He watched her hands, but did not react to the music, not even when she played fortissimo. The sounds did not get through to him. Yet he seemed to be enjoying her playing. After a few minutes he lay down on the floor and put one ear to the floorboards. Again she let the music rise to a crescendo. He raised his head from the floor, turned it towards her and smiled broadly. So he must be picking up something of the music. She smiled back and went on playing. When she could not play any more of the piece from memory, she took her hands off the keys. The boy made a gesture as if he were plucking something out of the air and holding it in front of his face. She shrugged her shoulders, uncomprehending.

She had got up and made him two sandwiches with sugar in. He had eaten them one after the other. He also greedily emptied two glasses of milk. She said he must take off his jacket, that she would put new buttons on. He looked at her in silence. Then she took off her own cardigan and pointed to the boy's jacket. He seemed to understand that. He slowly took off his jacket and laid it in front of her on the table.

She had got up, brought out her sewing box and sewn five bone buttons on the jacket. The boy had pulled a chair up to the table and taken the two extendable halves of the sewing box in his hands and pushed the drawers together like a harmonica. Then he had slowly pulled the two halves apart again. He had lovingly felt the hinges on the outside with his thin fingers. He looked at the sewing box as if it were a human being. Or rather, he looked at everything, people and things, in the same way. He had carefully taken in all the objects in the room. Standing in front of the knife tray, he had neatly put back a couple of forks that had found their way into the knife compartment by mistake. When evening came he had lain down on her bed and fallen asleep fully dressed. He must be dog-tired, he might have been wandering around for days.

Who could the boy belong to? She was now convinced that he was deaf and dumb. For a moment she considered going to the police, then dismissed the idea. The police would not know what to do with the nameless boy and would deliver him to some orphanage or other. Now and again she had got up to check whether the boy was still asleep. For now she was happy for him to stay.

The following day she had taken him to the Mélodrome. Art said it was OK for the boy to stay provided he did some work.

Boy had probably never been in a cinema in his life. The films brought him to a pitch of excitement. His face was a tense mask of concentration as he followed every movement on the screen. When the film was over he burst into a long series of movements, derived from the film he had just seen. Just as someone else recounts the story of a film, Boy would repeat all the gestures he had seen, precisely and in the right order.

From *Boy*. Amsterdam: Querido, 2000, pp. 97-100.
Translated by Paul Vincent.

J. Bernlef (1937-).
Photo by David Samyn.

Close

Prising a splinter
from the beam
laying on your fingertip
a feather-light splinter
from the old weathered beam
(there's not a breath of wind)

What use the beam served
– at the ends there are traces of threading –
why it is here
behind a shed, near to the water
nobody knows
nobody even asks.

The splinter is so new, so young,
beginning of all wood
at the tip of my little finger

It's too thin for a target
No nail can cope with it
It's really nothing but wood
wood itself – just.

Being so close,
a splinter's width,
no more, separated from wood
by my epidermis.

Dichtbij

Uit de balk
een splinter peuteren
uit de oude verweerde balk
een vederlichte splinter
leggen op de vingertop
(er staat geen zuchtje wind)

Waartoe de balk gediend heeft
– aan de uiteinden sporen van schroefdraad –
waarom hij hier ligt
achter een loods, vlak bij het water
niemand die het weet
niemand die het vraagt ook

De splinter is zo nieuw, zo jong,
begin van alle hout
op het topje van mijn pink

Zij is te dun voor doel
geen spijker kan haar aan
zij is alleen maar hout
hout zelf – nog net.

Zo dichtbij te zijn
op splinterdikte
alleen van hout gescheiden
door mijn opperhuid.

From *Still-Life* (Stilleven). Amsterdam: Querido, 1979.
Translated by Paul Vincent.

Silence

The melody worn at the sleeves
of the chords just a few
last flapping snatches

In empty shoes he walks on
past jerrycans and flats on his
way to waste ground.

Clearance makes him stronger
he thins his hairdo out down to
the last hair on which he floats

Something so light
was never so heavy; tone that, in love,
gives way under its own specific gravity.

Thus the dancer disappears in the dance
the angel in its necessity.

At last the silence can be cut with a knife.

Stilte

De melodie op de mouwen versleten
van de akkoorden alleen nog
wat wapperende flarden

In lege schoenen stapt hij voort
langs jerrycans en flats op weg
naar braakliggend terrein.

Kaalslag maakt hem sterker
hij dunt zijn kapsel uit tot op
de laatste haar waaraan hij zweeft

Zo zwaar is nog nooit
zo iets lichts geweest; toon die geliefd
zwicht onder eigen soortelijk gewicht.

Zo verdwijnt de danser in de dans
de engel in zijn noodzakelijkheid.

Eindelijk valt de stilte te snijden.

From 'Five Pieces about Steve Lacy' in *The Necessary Angel* (De noodzakelijke engel).
Amsterdam: Querido, 1990.
Translated by Paul Vincent.

Driftwood House

In his fight against city hall
he builds his house, board by board
day after day, with all the sea brought him

Latticework, seldom level, keeps the pane of
glass, the steps just that much in place,
there isn't a carpenter who could follow his act
                                        so topsy
                                        so turvy.

His house is a report about how it was yesterday
with a possible extension into today,
nails glistening in the grass

The daily harvest of driftwood determines
how things will go and what tomorrow will show
a fire escape or a new hiatus

For sometimes he dismantles something since
it turns out otherwise and driftwood, once picked up
and taken, has to be installed.

Drijfhouten huis

In zijn gevecht tegen de bierkaai
bouwt hij zijn huis, plank voor plank
dag na dag, met wat de zee hem bracht

Latwerk, zelden waterpas, houdt het vensterglas
zo'n beetje vast, de treden op hun plaats,
geen timmerman die het hem na zou doen
                                        zo schots
                                        zo scheef.

Zijn huis is een verslag over hoe het gisteren was
met een mogelijke uitbouw naar vandaag,
spijkers glinsteren in het gras

De dagelijkse oogst aan drijfhout bepaalt
hoe het verdergaat en wat er morgen staat
een brandtrap of een nieuw hiaat

Want soms breekt hij iets af omdat het
anders gaat en drijfhout, eenmaal opgeraapt
en meegenomen, moet worden ingebouwd.

From *Everything Recovered / Nothing Preserved* (Alles teruggevonden / niets bewaard).
Amsterdam: Querido, 1982.
Translated by Scott Rollins.

Winter Routes

Not just fox tracks, the partridge prints
pointing backwards in the snow,
but the winter routes as well,
narrow trails from the barn to the yard
not to be found on any map

Each and every house resting like a spider
in the middle of its own web of roads

A temporary language
like the barking of a dog
voices beyond the edge of a forest

Language that doesn't need to be understood
like a child's scrawl: a sign of
something that's behind you

When the winter routes melt
the assumption remains there's a map
under our feet

The first swallows high in the
empty sky, can probably read it
they follow other routes.

Winterwegen

Niet alleen vossensporen, de achterwaarts
wijzende patrijzenprenten in de sneeuw,
maar ook de winterwegen,
smalle looppaden tussen schuur en erf
op geen kaart te vinden

Ieder huis rust als een spin
in 't midden van zijn eigen wegennet

Een tijdelijke taal
zoals het blaffen van een hond
stemmen achter een bosrand

Taal die niet begrepen hoeft te worden
zoals een kinderkrabbel: teken van
iets dat achter de rug is

Wanneer de winterwegen smelten
blijft het vermoeden van een landkaart
onder onze voeten

De eerste zwaluwen hoog in de
lege lucht, zij kunnen hem lezen wellicht
zij volgen andere wegen.

From *Winter Routes* (Winterwegen). Amsterdam: Querido, 1983.
Translated by Scott Rollins.

H is

Own Protagonist

The Work of Teun Hocks

Teun Hocks (1947-) is an artist so individual that to call him original, or even unique, is no cliché. His work is not simply unlike anyone else's, but of a kind for which no formal name exists, though the term 'photo-painting', coined by one of the Dutch art press, certainly fits the basic principle of his working method. This consists of over–painting blow-ups of photographs which are subjected to a chemical bleaching process and mounted on panel before '*Hocks, the painter, gets down to applying his paint tubes and brushes to the black and white images*'.

But before this stage is reached the necessary preliminaries must be completed. First come preparatory sketches, fast jottings-down, which Hocks collects as personal memos to be used and developed as and when. After this

Teun Hocks, *Untitled* (Man on Rocking Horse). 1992. Black & white photo / oil paint, 123 x 170 cm (Edition 3 versions). Photo courtesy TORCH Gallery, Amsterdam.

Teun Hocks, *Untitled*
(SHOW Man). 2000. Black
& white photo / oil paint,
132 X 107 cm (Edition
3 versions). Photo courtesy
TORCH Gallery,
Amsterdam.

come the props. '*I was always handy,*' says Hocks, '*and quite capable of losing myself completely for a week just constructing a little mini-house. Immersing yourself in manual work is very restful. I get the same feeling when I'm painting my decors and assembling my props.*' After this Hocks, the actor, comes into the picture. '*If I like a scenario I start adjusting it, taking polaroids along the way. Only when I feel it's perfect do I set up the camera, and take my own place in the setting. Using a self-timer I go through eight moves; I always take eight pictures per setting.*'

Teun Hocks' preferred persona is that of an anti-hero, a bit of a bashful, whimsical simpleton reminiscent of the early Charlie Chaplin and Buster Keaton. This makes him a familiar, endearing presence, in spite of the bizarre situations with which he confronts us. Who but Hocks could carry off posing asleep in a giant nest high up in a tree, presenting himself in a tent in the middle of his living room, or standing waist-high in the water under a bridge in pouring rain? Or, even more extreme, it is hard to think of anyone who could emulate the image of Hocks striding through the universe with a shopping bag in either hand, capturing the everyday and the eternal in a single instant.

Teun Hocks, *Untitled* (Man in Hut). 2000. Black & white photo / oil paint, 150 x 132 cm (Edition 3 versions). Photo courtesy TORCH Gallery, Amsterdam.

Untitled

Right from his earliest works in 1979-1980, Hocks' hallmark has been a poetically-tinged absurdism through which he expresses paths of the imagination and of thought which no other artist would think of pursuing. Most people, after all (unless they wouldn't mind being put away for a spell), would shy away from admitting to looking out of their bedroom window at night and observing a meteor-shower of little white things – tiny buckles, screws, eyes, keys, paperclips – pass by. Connected with this image is *The Late Hour* in which Hocks, seated at an imposing desk, belabours with a flyswatter a host of angels and devils swirling over his head. Or are we perhaps being shown a new interpretation of Lucifer?

Hocks' early works still have titles; but since 1987 they have all been labelled *Untitled*, thus forcing the spectator to come to his own conclusions. And he is given every opportunity to do so. Viewing an assembly of Hocks' pictures one finds oneself becoming increasingly involved in the keynote little man who recurs in every picture, a pathetic and, above all, lonely figure. Only rarely is his isolation broken – and even then it is relieved only by the company of his *doppelganger*, leaving one unsure which is the 'real' Hocks and which the facsimile. This idea is played out in scenarios such as one little Hocks asleep in bed, and the other seated at the foot of the bed, which is laid as a dinner table, devouring a steaming hot meal. Allied to this image are two Hockses at a kitchen table, with one reading aloud what the other has evidently just typed out: a literary *perpetuum mobile*, it would seem; a permanent solution to writer's block. But otherwise, the little man is always alone, embroiled in situations which are at the same time dream and reality, but invariably pervaded by an undertone of poetic gentleness and mild self-irony. Indeed, it is Hocks' self-irony which most elicits sympathy, even empathy. His little man betrays no bitterness, no grudge against the world, although we get an occasional glimpse of an underlying fury or a barely restrained aggression. An example of the latter shows Hocks in a snowbound landscape, holding a gigantic axe, cogitating about whether or not to fell a minuscule pine tree. The selfsame axe also features in a picture showing little man Hocks, seated in an armchair, sizing up with a sinister eye a painting of three leafless trees. And what should we make of Hocks, bomb in hand, contemplating a miniature house?

What makes a Hocks a Hocks?

The answer to this must be: the originality of his ideas. Only very seldom is Hocks to be caught indulging in the now so-prevalent fashion for quotation. This is not to say that allusion is absent. For instance, the earthy, dark brown of his landscapes has something of the spirit of Van Gogh's early Nuenen pieces. Occasionally, too, there occurs an oblique quote, which is clearly conceived as more of a homage. An example of this is a (non-retouched or

Teun Hocks, *Untitled* (Man at Sickbed). 1989. Black & white photo / oil paint, 130 x 179 cm (Edition 2 versions). Photo courtesy TORCH Gallery, Amsterdam.

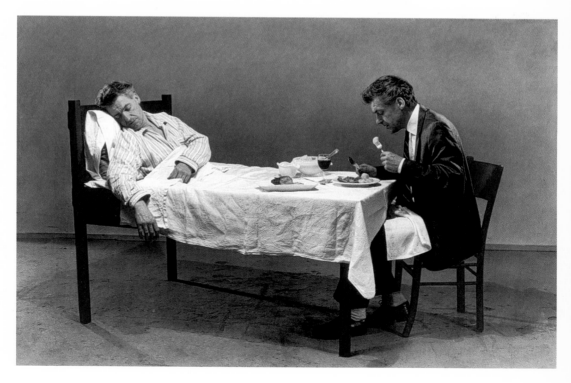

coloured?) photograph of a pair of black men's shoes peeping from under a red velvet curtain... Magritte? or not? Another example, where Hocks features himself in front of a party supplier's shop window, is beyond any doubt intended to honour James Ensor, who inherited from his parents just such a shop. Everything that makes a Hocks a Hocks is present in this particular picture: the perfection of setting and arrangement, the magnificent masks of his own making in the shop window, with one of them looking up at the man gazing in from outside, who sees his own reflection in the glass, unexpectedly crowned with a party hat.

Of all the evocative elements in this picture, the most impressive is the magnificent overall balance, which is so pitched that the spectator is torn between laughter and a sense of sadness.

Over the years Hocks has built up a huge oeuvre bearing his unmistakeable imprint. Aside from the protagonist, certain immediately recognisable images recur time and again, and these determine the emotional or intellectual mood of a picture. Typically *Hocksian* motifs are (smoke)clouds in various forms, flat brown landscapes, the moon, and shadows. These are particularly prevalent in the early work, such as a cycle of six works in which Hocks' shadow takes centre stage. In one of these Hocks stands with his back to a painting whose description he is reading in a catalogue; his shadow, meanwhile, studies the painting attentively. In the next episode Hocks and his shadow, hands outstretched, make each other's acquaintance. The sequence culminates with Hocks' shadow targeting him with a pistol.

In most of Hocks' set pieces one can work out how his tricks are done, but not always. In one picture, for instance, where the little man is shown toil-

Teun Hocks, *Untitled* (Cook with Pan). 1997-1998. Black & white photo / oil paint, 124 x 174 cm (Edition 3 versions). Photo courtesy TORCH Gallery, Amsterdam.

Teun Hocks, *Untitled* (Man in Shop Window). 1994. Black & white photo / oil paint, 134 x 178 cm (Edition 3 versions). Photo courtesy TORCH Gallery, Amsterdam.

ing uphill on his bike, all the while shedding books from his baggage carrier, we wonder how on earth Hocks managed to freeze those books in midair. In one work, however, he shows his way of working in detail. The case in point is a diptych, each panel depicting a path winding towards the horizon. On one picture he features himself at the start of the path, but in the companion photograph the illusion is completely dispelled, and we see that the landscape consists of a painted table behind which Hocks has positioned himself. This is the one time that Hocks takes on our role: that of the astonished spectator.

CEES VAN DER GEER
Translated by Sonja Prescod.

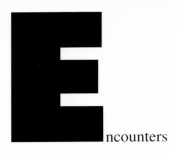ncounters

and Recognitions

English Landscapists and Dutch Old Masters – Then and Now

In June 1788 Thomas Gainsborough, perhaps the greatest English portrait painter of his time, burst out: '*I am sick of portraits and wish very much to take my Viola da Gamba and walk off to some sweet village where I can paint Landskip and enjoy the fag-End of my life in quietness and ease.*'[1] In May this wish had prompted him to confess, weak and ill though he was: '*I feel such a fondness for my first imitation of little Dutch landskips, that I cant keep from working an hour or two of a Day, though with a great mixture of bodily pain.*'[2] And in November 1828, John Constable, one of the greatest English landscape painters, wrote to a friend: '*I have seen an affecting picture this morning by Ruisdael, it haunts my mind and clings to my heart and stands between you and me while I am talking to you.*'[3] Between the two of them, these letters reflected what was happening in English art at the time, viz. that the traditional supremacy of history and portrait painting in the hierarchy of genres was fast becoming a thing of the past and that landscape painting, as the naturalistic rendering of chunks of Creation, was taking over. This was a uniquely English process, enhanced by the fact that, again and again, it recalled the astonishingly ubiquitous presence, both in private collections and at public auctions, of pictures by Dutch Old Masters – another uniquely English phenomenon.

Now here it is worth pointing out that 'landscape' was a Dutch term whose entry into the English language went back to the end of the sixteenth century. By the mid-seventeenth its usage had become so general that it gave rise to a passage in a popular instruction booklet for painting which opened the relevant chapter by informing readers that they were now about to be taught: '*An Art soe new in England, and soe lately come ashore, as all the Language within our fower seas cannot find it a Name, but a borrowed one, and that from a people that are noe great Lenders but upon good Securitie, the Dutch. Perhaps they will name their own Child. For to say the truth, the Art is theirs.*'[4]

Actually, when in the 1620s the 'illuminer' and herald-painter Edward Norgate wrote this in his *Miniatura, or the Art of Limning*, the genre still produced ideal rather than real landscape and in general merely as decor to socially or historically prestigious subjects. But the way in which the name of the above '*Child*' was introduced is revealing. For this was through a widely travelled and art obsessed '*student of physik*' from Oxford, one Richard Haydocke, a personal friend of Sir Thomas Bodley, recently Ambassador to The Hague. In 1598 Haydocke had felt he absolutely must translate Paolo Lomazzo's famous *Trattato del'Arte della Pittura* and, on finding himself stuck by the need to hit on an English equivalent for Italian '*paese*', had recalled the word '*landskip*' or '*-scap*' from conversations with painters in Holland. Clearly, once it had been explained to him, the derivation of its second syllable from the verb '*scheppen*' as meaning 'to create', had gripped him enough to adopt it unchanged. And when his *Tracte containing the Artes of curious Paintinge, Carvinge and Buildinge* proved a best-seller, the English vocabulary was enriched even to the extent that, from 'land'+'scape', soon enough 'seascape', 'cloudscape', 'riverscape' etc. came to be born – terms which one and all echoed the feeling of the Dutch that an artist who sat painting nature for her own sake was with his brush 'creating' new lands on his canvas, new seas, new clouds, new rivers.[5]

Depicting space not events...

In Britain, up to the eighteenth century, landscapes had regularly been painted under one alibi or another, i.e. always in a religious, mythologising or moralising context. In poetry, too, natural scenery had never been autonomous but always a mirror, often in imitation of the great Italians, and soon presented in a spirit of Burke's life-enjoying '*Beauty*' or death-defying '*Sublimity*'.[6] It was only in the works of such painters as Esaias van de Velde, Jan van Goyen and Jacob van Ruisdael that independent scenery had made its appearance before English eyes.

What was depicted, moreover, was no longer something happening, i.e. an event, but a space, even where this space was seemingly purely topographical and merely offering views of e.g. Leiden, or Delft, or Haarlem.

Of course, this development did not occur in a vacuum: there was the well-known socio-political background. In 1648, after eighty years of fighting its Spanish overlord, the area had become the independent Republic of

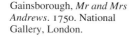

Gainsborough, *Mr and Mrs Andrews*. 1750. National Gallery, London.

the United Provinces, while in the same period the hereditary onslaught of the sea and the big rivers had been fought no less successfully. With and through it all, trade had prospered and refugees (often affluent) from tyrannies elsewhere had flocked in increasing numbers to the tolerant Dutch Republic as to a 'Bastion of Liberty'. In fact, an almost literally 'golden' age appeared to have started – an age in which painting and the decorating of one's walls with paintings from the thousands that were produced (and sold at extremely modest prices) came to be popular as never before, thereby no doubt functioning as so many trophies from their battles for land reclamation, military, political, as well as physical.

In the context of the social history of England, picture collecting became a dominant phenomenon and was no longer the preserve of Court and Nobility. In due course, world commerce and the Industrial Revolution were enriching merchants, bankers, factory owners and landed gentry alike – this, while at the same time paintings from the Continent were pouring on to the market partly as a direct consequence of the fate of private collections auctioned in London during the French Revolution and the Napoleonic wars. What proved to captivate the minds and hearts of English collectors, both old and new, was the realisation that *'the essence of Dutch art and the quality that set and sets it apart from the art of other times and other places was its truthfulness both about the world itself and the individuals who inhabit it.'*[7] This was something that fitted to perfection the feelings of the nature-loving and town-defying Romantics as first expressed by Wordsworth and Coleridge in their *Lyrical Ballads* of 1800.

Some Millennium exhibitions

Two centuries later, in addition to a spate of demonstrations by leading lights of our consumer society that the Millennium must mean something quite special, 'London 2000' offered the public some remarkable exhibitions. One was *Romantic Landscape. The Norwich School of Painters* (at what is now called Tate Britain); another was *Encounters. New Art from Old* (National Gallery)… Viewing these in succession proved truly fascinating. After all, not only did the so-called Norwich School, as led since 1803 by John Crome, show that its members openly acknowledged their indebtedness to the Dutch Masters, but such feelings were also manifested by a fair number of other artists of the Romantic Age, with at the forefront Constable and Turner.

Encounters was the National Gallery's ambitious attempt to connect contemporary artists with pictures of past masters from its own collection by inviting 25 leading moderns to each produce a new work inspired by one they had selected from the old. Its justification was that, as a press review recalled, art works were *'always both homage to and critique of the works that preceded them'*. There was no work that did not bear some relationship to prior art: *'manners changed, intentions belonged to a particular epoch and mentality, techniques and skills were lost and found, but no artist could ever appreciate another's work with innocence'*.[8]

In the *Romantic Landscape* exhibition the painters of the nineteenth century Norwich School and others like them could be found to also 'encounter'

John Crome, *Road with Pollards*. 1815. Castle Museum, Norwich.

Old Masters, but now what they saw in them was as a 're'-cognition (in the sense of 'knowing again') of a nature awareness that would always have been with them. It was this that enabled them as Romantics to create their landscapes without ever having been told of the etymology of the term or of the fact that in the Middle Ages 'shaped land' originally denoted 'land shaped by power of dominion' and only subsequently had come to be used for 'land shaped by power of imaginative depiction'. As to the localisation of the phenomenon in East Anglia and centring at Norwich, it was those coasts that Dutch fishermen and traders had long frequented, the latter plausibly including with their wares pictures many of which would have represented scenery strikingly chiming with that of an English county distinguished by the flatness of its surface. Moreover, the influx and settlement of the Dutch invited by Charles I to drain the Fens in the 1620s had a cultural impact on the region that is still visible today in its urban architecture. And in addition, there was the effect of the eighteenth-century upper-class Grand Tour custom which often started or ended in the Netherlands.

So if – following on Gainsborough's *Mr and Mrs Andrews* whose picture had so impressively introduced the importance of landscape *per se* – John Crome indeed uttered as his famous last words '*Hobbi[!]ma, oh my dear Hobbima, how I have loved you!*'[9], this was completely in character. Even a cursory glance at pictures such as his *Road with Pollards* will reveal as much, as will his son's *Yarmouth Water Frolic* – Yarmouth, incidentally, always being illustrative of the local connection with Holland as in e.g. John Cotman's *Dutch Boats off Yarmouth* or George Vincent's *Dutch Fair on Yarmouth Beach*. In the same way, although himself not hailing from the region, John Constable's London dwelling was not called 'Ruysdael House' for nothing. In addition to his striking panoramas, he painted numerous forest scenes with typical Dutch trees and his huge *The Haywain* is perhaps his most famous picture.

J.M.W. Turner, the 150th anniversary of whose death was marked by the Royal Academy's superb show of *The Great Watercolours*, reveals his indebtedness to the Dutch Masters not simply in a considerable number of his

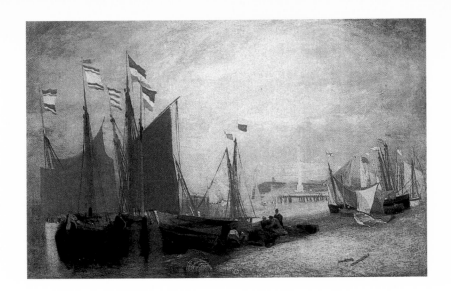

works, but also in some of his lectures as the Royal Academy's Professor of Perspective. As an example may be quoted: '*Cuyp, to a judgement so truly qualified, knew where to blend menutiae and forms in all the goldern colour of a dense Atmosphere, an illumined ambient vapour…*'.[10] But then, he also declared: '*How happily is the landscape painter situated, how roused by every change of nature…, that allows of no languor, even in her effects, which she places before him, and demands most peremptorily every moment his admiration and investigation to store his mind with every change of time and place*'.[11] And, of course, among Turner's most perceptive statements must be reckoned: '*Rembrandt depended upon his chiaroscuro, his bursts of light and darkness to be felt. He threw a mysterious doubt over the meanest*

John Cotman, *Dutch Boats off Yarmouth*. 1823. Castle Museum, Norwich.

George Vincent, *Dutch Fair on Yarmouth Beach*. 1821. Castle Museum, Norwich.

piece of common – nay, more, his forms, if they can be called so, are the most objectionable that could be chosen..., but over each he has thrown that veil of matchless colour..., that lucid interval of morning dawn and dewy light on which the eye dwells so completely enthralled, and it seeks not for its liberty, but as it were thinks it a sacrilege to pierce the mystic shell of colour in search of form'.[12]

Encounters, in its sumptuous catalogue, opened with the interesting query whether '*by the end of the twentieth century museums (were not becoming) the equivalent of shrines and spectacles, providing for modern tourists the equivalent of medieval pilgrimage routes to be visited with ritual devotion?*' Again, the point was that '*all the revolutions of modern art faced backwards as well as forward. Picasso (we were reminded) has slowly been transformed into the guardian of the past and his terrorist attacks on tradition turn out to be a way of rejuvenating not destroying our heritage*'.

Of the exhibition itself, after the extraordinarily provocative treatment by R.B. Kitaj of Van Gogh's *Chair* in painting a black, cigar-puffing *Billionaire* art-dealer sitting on it, the next item to be singled out is *Resonances after J.V.* by Claes Oldenburg and Coosje van Bruggen. These originally Dutch artists selected Vermeer's two pictures of *Young Woman at a Virginal* to be inspired by and the result is a kind of Vermeer-peepbox, i.e. a framed, three-dimensional impression of one of Vermeer's music rooms without any young woman but with a savaged viola da gamba prominently displayed on a tiled floor though half-hidden by a curtain; the voids in the instrument's soundbox represented by solids on its surface with a Cupid's bow suspended on the wall behind it. Into the calm of Vermeer's world, sexually creative disruption is thus entered and obviously aimed at undermining certainties while multiplying potential interpretations.

John Constable, *The Haywain*. 1821. National Gallery, London.

Vincent van Gogh, *Kitchen Chair*. 1888. Van Gogh Museum, Amsterdam.

R.B. Kitaj, *The Billionaire in Vincent's Chair*. 1999. Artist's collection.

If art is information, intelligence is what counts

The aim of the present essay was to draw attention to a particular set of phenomena in the English 'artscape' of the day by touching on the 'landscape' of Dutch civilisation of the past. The foreground of this artscape is filled by the Tate Britain exhibition built around the Norwich School, and its centre by the exhibition in the National Gallery. There, becoming aware of the double meaning of 'to encounter', as both 'to meet casually' and 'to meet in conflict', seems the point of the exercise. And this becomes even more obvious when two more exhibitions are now drawn in, viz. *Apocalypse: Beauty and Horror in Contemporary Art* with its echo of Hieronymus Bosch at the Royal Academy and *Intelligence. New British Art 2000*, characteristically under the same roof as *Romantic Landscape*.

Containing not simply pictures but many 'installations', sculptures, videos, sound distributors and vast (signed) emptinesses, these shows demonstrate how painting is now being seen by numerous artists as just one of many mediums available – in fact that their basis is the idea of art as a force for change and a space for a parallel world, often at the edge of perception and aimed at a reconciliation of the rational and irrational while freeing us from certainties. If art is information, what counts is the 'intelligence', in all the nuances of meaning with which we use it – with the artist as 'agent provocateur' or as 'secret agent'. Indicative of the basic approach to art is that *Intelligence* opens with *A Walk in the Park* by J. Opie, showing a big colour enlargement in vinyl of fallen leaves on the ground, '*their layers*', as we are told, '*creating a compressed rather than infinite sense of space*'.[13]

Johannes Vermeer, *Young Woman standing at a Virginal*. c.1670. National Gallery, London.

Johannes Vermeer, *Young Woman seated at a Virginal*. c.1670. National Gallery, London.

C. Oldenburg & C. van Bruggen, *Resonances after J.V.* 2000. Artist's collection.

J. Opie, *A Walk in the Park*. 2000. Artist's collection.

In a Britain of football-hooligans, a Dome fiasco, a 'wobbly bridge' (which was declared safe again in February 2002), a giant power-station turned into the Tate Modern museum, as well as mind-boggling exhibitions, for comparison's sake a very special significance may be attached to the fact that in Edinburgh the National Gallery of Scotland offered a superb show of some forty rarely seen instances of *Constable's Clouds*. Inevitably what comes to mind is Sir Joshua Reynolds's exhortation in the *Journal* of his visit to Holland in 1781: '*Painters should go to the Dutch School to learn the art of Painting, as they would to a Grammar School to learn Languages*'.[14] For the present author this amounts to his Q.E.D., i.e. to the fact that the full title of the Edinburgh exhibition could well have been *Recognition: the Norwich School of Romantic Landscapists*.

FRED G.H. BACHRACH

NOTES

1. Gainsborough to Jackson, 4 June 1788 (M. Woodall, *Letters of Thomas Gainsborough*, 1961, p. 115)

2. Gainsborough to Harvey, 22 May 1788 (id., p. 91)

3. Constable to Fisher, 28 November 1828 (R.B. Beckett, *John Constable's Correspondence*, 1962-69)

4. E. Norgate, *Miniatura or the Art of Limning, The Names, Order and Contents, both for Picture by the Life, Lan[d]scape, and History*, c.1620, p. 42.

5. Richard Haydocke, *A Tracte* [etc.]. Bk. 3, ii, p. 94.

6. See Edmund Burke, *A Philosophical Enquiry into the Origin of our Ideas of the Sublime and the Beautiful*, 1757.

7. Christopher Browne, 'Dutch Painting' (*The Low Countries*, vol. 1993-94, p. 192).

8. Adrian Searle in *The Guardian*, 5 June, 2000, p. 12.

9-12. Jerrold Ziff, 'Backgrounds: Introduction of Architecture and Landscape. A Lecture by J.M.W. Turner' (*Journal of the Warburg and Courtauld Institutes*, vol. 26, 1963, p. 146 ff.)

13. *Intelligence: New British Art 2000*, exh. cat., p. 32.

14. J. Reynolds, '*A Journey through Flanders and Holland in the Year 1701* (*The Works*, 1801, vol. II, p. 86).

Pieter Claeissens de Oudere (?), *The Seven Wonders of Bruges*. c.1560. Panel. Monasterium De Wijngaard, Bruges. This artificial townscape brings together the seven most important buildings. Foreground: the Waterhalle (middle), the Belfry (r.), the Church of Our Lady (l.). Background: the Poortersloge and Tolhuis (background, l.), the Zeven Torens dwelling (m.) and the Oosterlingenhuis (r.).

N_o

Victorian Disneyland

Bruges, the Past in the Present

On the afternoon of 28 May 1998, suddenly and for no apparent reason at all, all over the old city the bells began to peal in jubilation. Bruges had been named European City of Culture 2002. The city had of course been chosen for its image as a model city of monuments and museums and because of its well-preserved medieval centre. The city's culture and history were not the

Fernand Khnopff,
A Deserted Town. Canvas.
Koninklijke Musea voor
Schone Kunsten, Brussels.

A major politician but
a minor painter: Winston
Churchill at work in
Bruges, 1950s. Photo by
Brusselle. Brusselle-Traen
Collection, Stadsarchief,
Bruges.

only criterion, however; the selectors also looked for evidence of a dynamic and modern society. To meet this second requirement, Bruges' image was to be spruced up with a new concert hall (see p. 264). The prospect of 2002 provoked reflection, triggered an architectural debate and also revealed the need for a topical and lively art event in a city obsessed with the Flemish Primitives, a city whose architectural evolution had, according to some art critics, been stopped in its tracks by the neo-Gothic. The younger population, in particular, is anxious to bury the myth of *Bruges-la-Morte* and the corniness of the medieval city, which is in danger of becoming a stage set for mass tourism. To what extent, then, do the values of the past represent a resource or a stumbling block for the present and future of the city?

A medieval city

The medievalness of Bruges has become a cliché to which no one gave a moment's thought until a few years ago a sensational 'phoney Bruges' headline made the world press. In September 1997 Stephen Bates wrote in *The Guardian* that Bruges was an architectural fake and that no more than two medieval facades had survived the centuries. Fearing a slump in tourism, for a moment this attack on its authenticity had Bruges shaking on its medieval foundations. But it did not come to that. There was no let-up in the number of coaches and every day the streets of 'beautiful medieval Bruges' were packed with visitors.

Bruges is of course a city whose biography goes back a very long way.

The abundance of historical sources in the city archive, the archeological finds in the museum, the toponymy of the oldest streets and the city's extraordinarily rich artistic and architectural patrimony bear this out. But to what extent does the historical face tally with the city's actual appearance? Those who travel to Bruges by train or car are struck quite early on by the compactness of the old inner city with its distinct silhouette of low-rise buildings dominated by several prominent towers. This Bruges skyline is recognisable even in medieval miniatures and paintings by Old Masters. The city is still contained within its medieval fortifications. It covers 370 hectares and has been the same since the city walls of 1299 were built. Unlike most other cities, which demolished their city gates and ramparts on a massive scale with the abolition in 1860 of internal duties on goods, in Bruges they were largely preserved. The late-medieval ground-plan, too, with its network of streets, squares and canals has remained unquestionably medieval. Even the way in which the oldest urban nucleus developed in concentric circles from the old Burg is still clearly perceptible. The main approach roads run from the city gates to the very heart of the city, which consists of two squares, the Markt and the Burg, to what were the commercial and administrative centres in the Middle Ages.

The city is neatly arranged and the street pattern can be followed from the oldest city maps, of which the one drawn up by Marcus Gerards in 1562 is regarded as the most important. The explanation is that the urban fabric has never been seriously violated. Bruges was also fortunate enough to escape war damage. Moreover, there has been little large-scale urban development to damage the whole. Only the construction of the railway in 1838 left a still visible, and still lamented, scar in one place. Important medieval buildings with a symbolic function such as the Belfry, the Town Hall, St John's Hospital, the Church of Our Lady and other places of prayer have survived. They form part of the collective memory of the people and for each new generation they are anchor-points in the cityscape. It is true that several large buildings were demolished in the eighteenth century, including the imposing Waterhalle on the Markt and numerous monasteries and convents. Those spaces were however spontaneously filled by volumes of much the same size, even if they were divided up into dwellings. Some of the smaller canals were filled in to form streets in the eighteenth and nineteenth centuries, but this did not change the fundamental structure of the city. The canal network remained more or less intact. Practically nothing has been done to alter scale or volumes, as happened in other cities as a result of industrialisation in the nineteenth century.

Any areas suitable for development that appear on Marcus Gerards' map of 1562 have of course since been filled in. All available space in the city has always been filled, while expansion has taken place outside the city walls in the suburbs. Not only were new buildings constantly being erected, but above all they were rebuilt and from the eighteenth and nineteenth centuries onwards repaired and restored. Inventories show that Bruges still has a significant number of medieval houses, mainly because the Gothic style was retained until late in the sixteenth century, while the influence of new styles was mainly confined to ornamentation on the facades. Interestingly, when carrying out archeological research on houses, the markings on Marcus Gerards' map still often prove an accurate and reliable source. Usually

The Bruges Belfry. Photo by Lori van Biervliet.

The choir of the Gothic Church of Our Lady. Photo by Lori van Biervliet.

internal walls have been replaced in the intervening centuries and cabinet-work and woodwork renewed. In most cases the facades were adapted to the fashion of the day, but the old structure of the facade was nearly always retained. Moreover, many houses still have medieval party walls, original roof trusses and Gothic or even Romanesque cellars. Innumerable medieval wash-basins and wall niches have been preserved and sometimes medieval wall paintings are found under the plasterwork. All these features come to light when houses are investigated prior to restoration or renovation. It is clear beyond doubt that a great many buildings testify to centuries of life in the city; that the present rests on a very tangible past.

The neo-Gothic heritage

'*The word medieval is misplaced, and Bruges isn't really as Flemish as it looks*', wrote Max Borka in *The Bulletin* of 7 July 1994. He claims that only two authentic wooden facades have survived in Bruges and that '*the other buildings that seem to be of that period are nearly all "vieux neuf", imitation antique, built in the nineteenth and early twentieth centuries by British architects carried away by the Gothic revival, or by Belgian architects under direct British influence.*'

Such a claim is a grave distortion of the truth. Yet Bruges has not managed to shake off its image as a 'neo-Gothic Disneyland' and the city has been repeatedly portrayed as a stage-set for mass tourism. Art critics point accusingly to the Gothic revival in the nineteenth century, which they be-

A decorative 16th-century facade next to the Romanesque-Gothic and neo-Gothic Blood Chapel. Photo by Lori van Biervliet.

lieve stifled all new architectural styles and made an anachronism of the city. Moreover, in public opinion neo-Gothic is almost synonymous with ugly and is frequently regarded as a surrogate for the real Gothic. Yet neo-Gothic has as much right to exist as any other revived style. It has its own individuality and is not a retro style. Why is it, we wonder, that the neo-Gothic is a whipping-stock in Bruges and not elsewhere? Because here the historical significance, the scale and impact of that architectural style is more penetrating than in other historical cities.

In Flanders the neo-Gothic had its origins in the drive to preserve historic monuments and buildings after the French Revolution and sprang from a spirit of Romanticism and patriotism. Everywhere medieval buildings were restored and rebuilt as a matter of course in their 'own' style. The number of late-Gothic buildings was much larger in Bruges than in other cities and its inhabitants were proud of the admiration their medieval heritage inspired in foreign visitors. Striking tourist attractions such as the Gothic Town Hall and the Church of Our Lady were the first to be restored in the 1830s. After Belgian Independence, in the 1840s and 1850s the Catholic revival brought with it an explosion of new churches, cloisters and schools built in neo-Gothic style under the influence of the English Gothic revival. The Bishop of Bruges, Jean-Baptiste Malou, was a personal friend of Nicholas Wiseman and an admirer of A.W.N. Pugin, who in *True Principles* (1841) defined Gothic architecture as Christian architecture. Pugin visited Bruges on a number of occasions between 1837 and 1852. His theories were propagated there and applied by members of the English colony such as Thomas Harper King, John Sutton and William Curtis Brangwyn. Above all Pugin found a disciple in Jean Bethune who, together with Edward Pugin, built the episcopal palace of Sint-Michiels and Loppem Castle. In addition to that typical English architectural influence, in the 1860s Bruges was shaken from its slumber by the English antiquarian W.H. James Weale, who in his inimitable way instructed the people of Bruges about their medieval heritage and drew their attention to the need to preserve historic monuments and buildings.

That message could scarcely have fallen on more fertile ground. The inhabitants of Bruges have always been extremely proud of their city, and since the economic recession in the sixteenth century they have suffered from a chronic nostalgia for their magnificent past. In the nineteenth century that *Sehnsucht* was fed by the admiration of foreign visitors to the city. '*It is certainly the most perfect specimen of a town of the middle ages on this side of the Rhine*', wrote J. Emerson Tennent in 1841.

So the people of Bruges saw the neo-Gothic as a way of restoring their decaying city to its former glory. After 1872, when a Catholic city council took office, the 'restoration' of medieval Bruges became official policy. For years a campaign for reconstruction was conducted in the local press. The city was supported in this by government approval, by the King himself and not least by an increase in tourism. The specific form of late-medieval dwellings was studied, inventorised and published. Many new houses were erected in a typical Bruges style of the sixteenth and seventeenth centuries. Major new development projects such as the Provincial Government Palace (1887) on the Markt and the Rijksnormaalschool (state teachers' training college, 1882) in Sint-Jorisstraat even led to petitions to the King requesting that those complexes should be built in the '*elegant old architectural style*'. Around the turn of the century architectural competitions were organised in which preference was given to the local traditional brick architecture. The neo-Gothic supported the Gothic and promoted homogeneity in the cityscape. In 1902 Adolf Duclos published a book of styles, *L'art des façades à Bruges*, and two years later the Commission for Urban Beauty was founded. The neo-Gothic dream had become reality, and the care of individual monuments was replaced by concern for the general appearance of the city. Artists and art critics deplored the stagnation of the art scene. In 1892 Georges Rodenbach's *Bruges-la-Morte* appeared, followed five years later by *Le Carillonneur*. In both novels the neo-medieval city had degenerated into a spectre, a soulless past with no future. Nevertheless, almost a hundred years of government by the conservative Catholic party perpetuated the neo-Gothic in Bruges until after the Second World War. From 1877 to the pre-

The neo-Gothic
Rijksnormaalschool (1882).
Photo by Lori van Biervliet.

sent day 'skilful restoration' has been encouraged by grants from the City
Council.

Yet throughout the nineteenth century most of the building permits granted were for neo-baroque facades. The impact of the neo-Gothic on the Bruges cityscape is due not so much to sheer quantity, but to a handful of large-
scale projects whose location profoundly affected the city's appearance.
They bear witness to one of the most important periods in the history of the
city, when the inhabitants of Bruges sought to achieve an ideal cityscape
through a singular combination of retrospection and creativity. This sym-
biosis of Gothic and neo-Gothic makes the city unique.

193

It's alive!

In the city centre there are indeed relatively few examples of modern architecture because there are so few areas available for development; moreover, a large number of existing edifices have been made listed buildings and so have been preserved. Even so, it would be wrong to suggest that in terms of architecture the modernity of the twentieth century has passed the city by. Modernism manifests itself in the shopping streets, where the shop fronts have regularly been rebuilt; however, most examples of new architecture are to be found on the outskirts of the city. A boulevard was laid out on a small part of the old ramparts in 1885, surrounded by villas in revival, eclectic, art deco and cottage styles. An unusual dwelling to a design by the Polish architect Kaplansky dating from 1936 even shows the influence of Le Corbusier and the railway station built by the brothers J. and M. van Kriekinge in 1938 is a monument to modernism. New districts of the city around the Oude Gistfabriek (Old Yeast Factory) and the Nieuwe Molens (New Mills) reflect the influence of the Amsterdam School. The Gistfabriek, designed by V. Jockin in 1926, was a unique example of New Realism. Despite the protests of an action group, the factory was razed to the ground and only the office building was spared. In the new residential district of Christus Koning there are streets with quality inter-war architecture, including work by the Bruges modernist Huib Hoste. The garden city concept of the 1920s was adapted in Sint-Pieters and even in the old St Anna parish, though using traditional materials and the characteristic Bruges style. In the 1950s and 1960s typical examples of international post-war architecture sprang up in the inner city. In 1965 the Marcus Gerards Foundation reacted against that tendency towards 'stylelessness' and what was considered to be 'un-Bruges'. By purchasing, redeveloping and renovating run-down buildings, this action group championed the reappraisal of Bruges' architectural patrimony and fervently opposed the exodus from the city centre. In 1968, at the request of the provincial authorities, L. Devliegher published his inventory of dwellings in Bruges, which has since served as the standard work for the evaluation of the local housing stock.

In 1971, after the merger with the seven suburbs, a Municipal Department for the Preservation of Monuments and Historic Buildings and Urban Renewal was set up. Regulations were imposed governing protection, evaluation and subsidies and a master plan was drawn up for the inner city which specified above all that the urban fabric should remain intact. Demolition became the exception, re-use the rule. In the case of new buildings, a genuine contemporary architecture became the order of the day. Vehicles were banned from the heart of the city, car parks were constructed, streets and squares were re-laid and furnished with contemporary street accessories. Every effort was made to create public housing and residential areas where traffic was restricted. Architects experimented with 'infill' architecture, preserving the building's original skeleton, with postmodernism and new materials, and house fronts took on new colours. Tourism increased, and with it the number of hotels and restaurants. Property prices rose sharply. Bruges attracted international hotel and shop chains and developers. In the 1990s worried inhabitants expressed their dissatisfaction at living in a city where foreigners were buying up properties, scores of buildings were being sacri-

Sint-Annarei 11: an example of 'infill' architecture (1981). Photo by Lori van Biervliet.

The Bruges beguinage.
Photo by Lori van Biervliet.

ficed to the hotel and catering industry and some shopping streets had become a succession of lace and praline shops. Action groups such as 'Brugge die Scone' (Bruges the Beautiful) and 'S.O.S. Brugge' regularly defend their heritage against the threat of commercialisation.

By way of conclusion we might say that Bruges is unique because its remarkable past lives on in the present. The old buildings are well kept and retain their identity. The burgomaster and aldermen still have their seat in the Gothic Town Hall and marriages are celebrated there on a daily basis. The churches are still places of prayer and pilgrimage. The very fact that the Church of Our Lady has been home to Michelangelo's *Madonna* for centuries and that Hans Memling's paintings still hang in the old St John's Hospital serves to heighten their powers of expression. Authenticity and tradition create a form of security and trust to which people are extremely receptive. In December 2000 Bruges was added to the UNESCO list of world heritage sites, and in future an even more careful watch will be kept on the monuments and on the beauty of the old city. But there is also room for renewal, provided it is able to match the quality of the old. This is demonstrated by the monumental contemporary concert hall, the Concertgebouw by the Flemish architect duo Paul Robbrecht and Hilde Daem, and also by the futuristic visitors' pavilion built for 2002 by the Japanese architect Toyo Ito on the Burg, right in the heart of the city.

The city is alive and is there to be enjoyed by each generation in turn. So long as there are inhabitants who cherish their city and ensure that it continues to be a pleasant place to live, so long as young people stand up for their right to a place in this cityscape and so long as foreigners come and admire the city, old Bruges is assured of a future.

LORI VAN BIERVLIET
Translated by Alison Mouthaan-Gwillim.

Information about 'Bruges 2002': European City of Culture':
Tel. +32 70 22 33 02 / www.brugge2002.be

Great Minor Poet

The Poems of J.C. Bloem

The Netherlands is a country that does not cherish its literary heritage. The after-life of Dutch authors is usually of short duration. Even when they have enjoyed an impressive reputation during their life-time, they generally disappear from public view soon after their death. The collected poems of A. Roland Holst for instance, who was generally acknowledged and revered as 'the prince of our poets' in his time, have not been reprinted since their last publication twenty years ago (in an edition of 2000 copies); and the same holds true for the vast majority of his once-famous colleagues. A very small number of exceptions serves to prove the rule. All in all just a handful of poets from the last century (six or seven to be exact) survive and their work is regularly reprinted. One of them is Roland Holst's contemporary and friend J.C. Bloem (1887-1966). Forty-eight thousand copies of his *Verzamelde gedichten* (Collected Poems) have been printed since he died, and a paperback anthology *Doorschenen wolkenranden* (Translucent Cloudrims), selected by the poet himself, also sold many thousand copies.

When still at school young Bloem was fascinated by poetry and very soon he started writing himself, to the detriment of his formal education. He was the kind of boy who simply hated to learn and do things in which he was not interested. As a consequence it was not until he was 29 that at long last he became a LL.D. And his subsequent professional career was such that it is not unreasonable that, many years later, in 1944, he would wonder: '*Is this enough, a handful of poems, / to justify an existence, / wasted bit by bit in poorly fulfilling pointless duties / for an all too meagre living?*'

But between 1903 and early 1908 he did write about two hundred and seventy poems – an average of more than one a week – and became a skilled craftsman in his chosen field. Later on Bloem would observe that most of the poetry written in one's youth does not contain any real feelings and virtually all of it is merely '*reminiscence of literature*'. So it is not surprising that only four of them were ever published and not a single one included in his books. And, most remarkably, during the rest of his life his total production would not exceed two hundred poems altogether, of which he selected a hundred and sixty for his collected poems.

Having grown up as a spoilt child in a strongly tradition-bound family, with a French governess (he read French fluently at ten), it is no wonder that the young poet looked to his immediate predecessors for inspiration. In reaction to the messy cult of isolated images of their time, these 'poets of the nineties' had gone back again to well-constructed intricate sentences and formal stanzas. They were the impressive and influential poet P.C. Boutens and his Flemish counterpart Karel van de Woestijne (see p. 214), who wrote a complex and heavily adjectival kind of verse, of which clear traces can be found in Bloem's early published poems.

In 1913 our poet played an important role in the so-called 'debate on rhetoric'. In a review of the French poet Henry de Régnier's *Le miroir des heures* he admired its '*inspired rhetoric*', its '*lively formality*', '*the art of vitalising old forms and, in turn, discovering the soul in these forms*'. And in speaking of *Stances*, a collection by de Régnier's contemporary Jean Moréas, he realised '*how it is possible, by choosing the most common words and the most common images in the most common form, to write genuine and original poetry*'.

Two years after his *Miroir*-review Bloem published an essay that is generally considered to be not only a personal profession of faith but also a representative summary of the mood expressed in the work of other poets of his generation. It was called 'Het verlangen' ('Yearning'). He characterised this 'yearning' as a '*divine unfulfilledness that far from turning our lives into a burden, enables us not only to bear the otherwise unbearable burden of life, but even to love it more than anything else*'. It opens up a prospect of '*collective immortality*', it is '*the unshakeable centre around which (...) our dreams arrange themselves, eternal as life itself. It cannot be fulfilled on earth and is fully aware of this*'. Those who share this insight, Bloem writes, will be able to understand '*what one of the greatest men who ever lived among us wrote*'. And then he quotes Blake's '*Ah, Sunflower! weary of time ...*' A high-minded elitist declaration of faith by a frustrated transcendentalist in a fundamentally romantic spirit, one might say.

It would take Bloem another two years before he managed to cast off the influence of his eminent predecessors, their complicated sentences and their decorative adjectives, as well as the exalted romanticism of his literary environment. For the first time he found his own inimitable way of writing, exactly in the vein of his pronouncements on the French poets. It was a serene short poem 'Regen en maanlicht' ('Rain and Moonlight'), written in January 1917, a couple of months before his thirtieth birthday: '*All I have kept a secret all my life / Formless desire without a name / Has now become a warm and gentle rain / Beyond a silver window-pane.*'

Although he still wrote poems from time to time – all relatively simple and mostly short – he felt that his inspiration had run out. '*It has not been bad, but I have not become a Ronsard, not even a Charles Guérin*', he said. At that moment his friend the typographer J. van Krimpen, took control. He copied Bloem's scattered poems from the periodicals in which they had been published and with the cooperation of the poet turned them into a well-made '*burial mound of his youth*'. Two days after his thirty-fourth birthday, on 12 May 1921, Bloem's first book of verse was published, also called *Het verlangen*. It was favourably received by the critics and sold rather well.

Bloem once said: '*It is my ambition to know European poetry from the beginning of Romanticism to the first World War.*' And what he did not know of it was hardly worth mentioning. At first he was primarily interested in French poetry – together with Dutch poetry of course – but soon afterwards he immersed himself in the work of English poets. In his later verse we regularly remark his profound knowledge of nineteenth-century poetry. In 1958 he published an anthology called *Persoonlijke voorkeur* (Personal Preference) for which he made a selection of Dutch (27), English (33), German (17) and French (20) poems, each of them preceded by a short introduction. Most remarkable is what he writes about A.E. Housman: '*Housman, together with Hardy, is one of my three favourite poets. I am quite aware that he is the least important of them (the third one is [the Italian poet] Leopardi). The size of his work is not only smaller in quantity, but his field is much more restricted too. But in his field he is a master. He has expressed the reality of life, stripped of comforting but unrealistic fantasies, in such a perfect way that one keeps wondering whether in fact he is not a great poet.*' A striking indirect self-portrait of the critic himself!

During the next eight years Bloem wrote only five poems, two of which were not completed till 1929. Then, for no clear external reason, his inspiration suddenly returned and in 1931 Van Krimpen, who in the meantime had become a famous type- and bookdesigner, published *Media vita* (... *in morte sumus*, as a twelfth-century antiphony says: '*in the midst of life we are in death*'). And by now Bloem has clearly become a master of his craft. '*To me the greatest artist seems to be the one who is able to combine the greatest possible traditionalism with the greatest possible originality*' and '*a poem is all the better the less one notices its words*'. Bloem had discovered that '*writing poetry means unlearning*'. All these pronouncements have been put into practice in the twenty-three poems brought together in *Media vita*. Compared with his contemporaries he now writes a kind of verse that looks un-literary and deceptively simple in its choice of words. Although the poems contain many images, these are hardly ever spectacular. From a formal point of view they all appear equally simple: all but one consist of four-line stanzas, in most cases containing lines of five iambs with an alternating rhyme scheme. The line-endings nearly always coincide with the end of a sentence or with a natural pause. One fellow-poet let himself be taken in by the apparent simplicity of Bloem's new poems and praised their '*elegant spontaneity*'. Much nearer to the truth was another colleague, J. Slauerhoff, who wrote: '*Superficially considered these poems consist of very simply phrased feelings, nature-impressions and meditations; on closer scrutiny however, they reveal themselves as poems of a very subtle wordcraft. I hardly know of any poems in Dutch in which every word occupies its unique right position in such a deceptively self-evident and nevertheless resolute way. Nearly all of these poems are perfect and vital at the same time.*'

From the very beginning Bloem had always been an exclusively lyrical poet. Although a separate group of poems in *Het verlangen* is called 'Gestalten' ('Figures'), containing pieces called 'De avonturier' ('The Adventurer'), 'De bedelaar' ('The Beggar'), 'De eenzame' ('The Lonely One') etc., his colleague P.N. van Eyck correctly suggested that these too were only thinly-veiled personae of the poet himself in the vein of, say, Charles Guérin. Later Bloem admitted that the division between the sections 'Figures' and 'Lyrisch' ('Lyrical') was artificial and cancelled it. Still, there is a remarkable, even a fundamental gap between Bloem's first collection and

Media vita. The vast majority of the poems in *Het verlangen* are explicit 'I-poems' in which he writes about his experiences as referring exclusively to himself; and when he uses '*we*' he is including only the chosen few, those elected by the Muses. In his second book, however, the first person singular has virtually disappeared and when using '*we*' he only excludes '*the silly or mercenary crowd*'– who never care to think of what human life is about. Instead, the central subject of these poems has become '*the heart*' or '*life*'. In other words: he no longer writes about his private unique emotions, but about human life as it appears to everyone who reflects on his own and other people's experience.

And it stands to reason that at the age of forty-three he has lost the exalted yearning of his youth, having been confronted by the inevitable deceptions life has in store for nearly everyone, and especially in his particular situation: a none too successful marriage, a legal desk job as a clerk of the court that gives him no satisfaction, his life in a Frisian village which he experiences as a place of exile. So it is not surprising that in 'Spiegeling' ('Reflection'), one of the very good poems in *Media vita*, the poet's summary of life is: '*'t Was first an endless longing, a wandering here and there, / and then a daily sense of lack, and then not even that.*' In all its apparent simplicity this poem of sixteen lines – eight distichs – turns out on careful consideration to be a highly sophisticated piece of craftsmanship. The 'reflection'-theme is present throughout; on the level of sound of course: inconspicuous rhymes (mainly assonance and consonance), vertically and horizontally; in the metrical basis of the lines: the second half reflects the first one ($\cup - \cup - \cup - \cup / \cup - \cup - \cup -$), and structurally: the second part of the poem is a reflection of the first half, in images as well as content, albeit in a minor key. And also of course in its subject matter: the sky is reflected in the sea, the environment in the soul, the past in the present. Remarkably, in spite of the inevitable disillusionments of life summed-up in the lines quoted, the '*pigeon-feathered sky*' of the first line has changed into a '*pearl-black*' one in the final line: some of the initial lustre has been preserved. It is a pity that the subtle complexity of this poem makes it impossible to provide an adequate translation ('*Traduttore traditore*', the Italians say: a translator is – inevitably – a traitor). Perhaps these characteristics may serve to give an impression of Bloem's inconspicuous mastership.

Apart from a few poems such as 'November': '*Always November, always rain / Always this empty heart, always.*', the majority are never entirely gloomy. There are some situations where, in spite of the oppressive present, he manages to realise '*that the early dreams have not died behind the years*', or where he is able '*like a lad, with clear eyes / To look at the inexpressible sky*'. In most cases, however, the positive elements are denied, as in 'Grafschrift' ('Epitaph'), where the deceased one had been '*to no high seat o'er some unthreatened region, / exalted - to no radiant altitude*'. And by evoking this kind of non-existent situation he introduces an essential internal tension into most of his poems that saves them from becoming depressive or disconsolate.

After several bitter experiences (divorce, the death of his beloved mother and the final disappearance of his family home, and a period of unemployment and poverty), in 1937 Bloem published a third book: *De nederlaag* (Defeat). Understandably, the majority of these poems are even more disillusioned than the preceding ones, but in spite of that in many cases the internal tension has been preserved. And in several respects the poet has succeeded in subtly renewing his verse: it is rhythmically more flexible, the stanza-forms more varied, the imagery more specific. But at the same time he remained his unmistakable self, in accordance with his lifelong ambition '*to express some essential dimensions of life in such a way that it could have been done only by me and by no-one else*'. At fifty Bloem had not in the least lapsed into self-repetition as so many of his colleagues do at that age.

In 1942 a small collection appeared: Enkele gedichten (*A Few Poems*), just before the Germans made publication impossible for authors who did not agree with their ideology. Apart from one piece, 'Keats', that glorifies '*the immortal poem*' defeating the transitoriness of human life, nearly all the other ones are negative: '*There is no escape from a life that has become a failure past retrieval.*' And then, at the very moment the town of Zutphen, where Bloem lived, had been liberated, '*while still the neighbouring air / Reverberate[d] with war*', he wrote a sublime sapphic 'Ode', afterwards called 'Na de bevrijding' ('After Liberation'), by general consent considered to be the most impressive poem written in our country during the five years of German repression: '*[it] Is worth it all, the five years on the rack, / The fighting back, the being resigned, and not / One of the unborn will appreciate / Freedom like this ever*' (Tr. Seamus Heaney).

Of course several of the ten poems collected in *Sintels* (Cinders) a few months later, are in the same key as his earlier work, or at best display a sense of resignation, but most of them show a remarkable inner tension by opposing the present situation to past dreams of fulfilment: '*Incomparably clear the moon is shining*', '*When in the perfect light of the first nights of spring / Youth returns ...*'. And another aspect of this regained vitality is the fact that nearly all of them are written in different rhythmic and stanza-forms, an unusual phenomenon for this tradition-bound poet.

During his remaining years Bloem published three more slender volumes: *Quiet Though Sad* [a quotation from Milton], *Avond* (Evening) and *Afscheid* (Farewell) In these poems he not only maintained the level of his earlier work, but quite a number of them have attained proverbial status, for instance '*Thinking of death I cannot get asleep / And unsleeping I keep thinking on death*', '*Simply happy in Dapperstreet*' (a sombre street in an Amsterdam working-class area), '*And, then, it could have been so much worse*'. You can hear them quoted in the most unexpected places. And this is characteristic of Bloem's work. It is highly memorable and quotable, more so, I would say, than the verse of practically all his colleagues. Yet he was never 'popular' or facile.

Bloem was a superior craftsman, as I hope to have made clear. He has written quite a number of poems about human life that are both very personal and generally valid. From this point of view there is good reason for calling him a great poet. That, nevertheless, I have called him a great *minor* poet, is because his range is so clearly limited: exclusively lyrical and even that in a restricted sense. The poet himself was fully aware of these limitations and openly said so. But, as I wrote at the very beginning of this article: his work is still very much alive, in spite of his own epitaph on his tombstone: '*Past, past, oh and forever past*'.

A.L. SÖTEMANN

Five Poems
by J.C. Bloem

Mirroring

A pigeon-feathered sky is mirrored in the sea.
Blue light steams between sky and tranquil sky-reflection.

On one and the other side rounds the blade of the shore
Towards a faint horizon of sea, sky, land and haze.

Now memory awakes of a beauty that is lost;
An old feeling returns out of a long dream.

A dream of voices and of faces and of idle sound
And ever-increasing tiredness that one calls life.

't Was first an endless longing, a wandering here and there
And then a daily sense of lack, and then not even that.

– The hour is getting later, the dark grows through the grey.
And still a pearl-black sky shadows the twilit sea.

1930
Translated by A. Verhoeff.

Spiegeling

Een duivenveren hemel weerspiegelt in de zee.
Blauw licht dampt tussen hemel en stiller hemelbeeld.

Ter ene en andre zijde rondt zich de kling der kust
Naar een vervloeiden einder van zee, lucht, land en mist.

De erinnering wordt wakker aan een verloren schoon;
Een oud gevoel keert weder vanuit een langen droom.

Een droom van stemmen en gelaten en gerucht
En steeds vermoeider worden, en dien men leven zegt.

't Was eerst een eindloos hunkren, een dwalen her en der,
Werd toen een daaglijks derven, en toen ook dat niet meer.

– Het uur wordt later, 't duister groeit door het grijze heen.
Een parelzwarte hemel schaduwt de schemerzee.

Epitaph

Nameless among the nameless that are legion,
to general sameness seemingly subdued;
to no high seat o'er some unthreatened region
exalted – to no radiant altitude –

The safely sheltered ever and anon
bore with him, or forgot him, but none saw
the shadow of two wings that drove him on,
and in his bent neck the relentless claw.

And now, after desire, tired and outworn,
and lifelong patience under restless strain,
a tombstone, cracked by weeds, and weatherworn
letters and figures filled by the slow rain.

1931
Translated by A. Roland Holst.

Grafschrift

Een naamloze in den drom der namelozen.
Aan de gelijken schijnbaar zeer gelijk,
Door geen vervoering stralend uitverkozen
Tot heersen in een onaantastbaar rijk –

Wie van die hem vergaten of verdroegen
Ontwaarden uit hun veilige bestek
De schaduw van twee vleugels die hem joegen,
Den fellen klauw in zijn gebogen nek?

En nu, na het begeerde, het ontbeerde,
Na de onrust en het levenslang geduld:
Een steen, door 't groen gebarsten, en verweerde
Letters en cijfers, die de regen vult.

After Liberation

Sheer, bright-shining spring, spring as it used to be,
Cold in the morning, but as broad daylight
Swings open, the everlasting sky
Is a marvel to survivors.

In a pearly clarity that bathes the fields
Things as they were come back; slow horses
Plough the fallow, war rumbles away
In the near distance.

To have lived it through and now be free to give
Utterance, body and soul – to wake and know
Every time that it's gone and gone for good, the thing
That nearly broke you –

Is worth it all, the five years on the rack,
The fighting back, the being resigned, and not
One of the unborn will appreciate
Freedom like this ever.

April 1945
Translated by Seamus Heaney.

Dapper Street

Nature is for the empty, the contented.
And then: what can we boast of in this land?
A hill with some small villas set against it,
A patch of wood no bigger than your hand.

Give me instead the sombre city highroads,
The waterfront hemmed in between the quays,
And clouds reflected in an attic window –
Were ever clouds more beautiful than these?

All things are riches to the unexpectant.
Life holds its wonders hidden from our sight,
Then suddenly reveals them to perfection.

I thought this over, walking through the sleet,
The city grime, one grey and drizzly morning,
Blissfully happy, drenched in Dapper Street.

October 1945
Translated by James Brockway.

Na de bevrijding

Schoon en stralend is, gelijk toen, het voorjaar
Koud des morgens, maar als de dagen verder
Opengaan, is de eeuwige lucht een wonder
Voor de geredden.

In 't doorzichtig waas over al de brake
Landen ploegen weder de trage paarden
Als altijd, wijl nog de nabije verten
Dreunen van oorlog.

Dat beleefd te hebben, dit heellijfs uit te
Mogen spreken, ieder ontwaken weer te
Weten: heen is, en nu voorgoed, de welhaast
Duldloze knechtschap –

Waard is het, vijf jaren gesmacht te hebben,
Nu opstandig, dan weer gelaten, en niet
Één van de ongeborenen zal de vrijheid
Ooit zo beseffen.

De Dapperstraat

Natuur is voor tevredenen of legen.
En dan: wat is natuur nog in dit land?
Een stukje bos ter grootte van een krant,
Een heuvel met wat villaatjes ertegen.

Geef mij de grauwe, stedelijke wegen,
De' in kaden vastgeklonken waterkant,
De wolken, nooit zo schoon dan als ze, omrand
Door zolderramen, langs de lucht bewegen.

Alles is veel voor wie niet veel verwacht.
Het leven houdt zijn wonderen verborgen
Tot het ze, opeens, toont in hun hogen staat.

Dit heb ik bij mijzelven overdacht,
Verregend, op een miezerigen morgen,
Domweg gelukkig, in de Dapperstraat.

The Nightingales

I 've never hoped for bliss that life would bring.
The search for happiness is bound to fail.
What matter? – The immortal nightingale
Is singing in the chilly night of spring.

May 1947
Translated by A.L. Sötemann.

De nachtegalen

Ik heb van 't leven vrijwel niets verwacht.
't Geluk is nu eenmaal niet te achterhalen.
Wat geeft het? – In de koude voorjaarsnacht
Zingen de onsterfelijke nachtegalen.

All poems from *Verzamelde gedichten* (Collected Poems).
(16th [=20th] ed.) Amsterdam: Athenaeum-Polak & Van Gennep,
2001.

W. Schuhmacher, *Portrait
of J.C. Bloem.* c.1948.
Pencil, 46 x 31.5 cm.
Collection Letterkundig
Museum, The Hague.

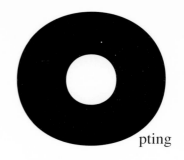pting

for What Does not yet Exist

The Art of Carel Visser

Carel Visser is probably the most influential and innovative of the post-war generation of Dutch sculptors. He was born into a large, prosperous family in 1928. As a devout Protestant, his father, a civil engineer with wide artistic interests, read aloud from the Bible every day. It was almost always the hieratic language of the Old Testament that the family heard.

At the age of ten Carel drew a lot, and especially animals; he became increasingly skilful at this as the years passed.[1] He dropped out of his Structural Engineering course in Delft after little more than a year, and out of his course at the Royal Academy of Art in The Hague after barely two years. The fact that he picked up the art of welding by watching the skilled craftsmen in his father's contracting firm was ultimately of greater moment in his development as an artist. He did his first sculptures, in wood and iron, when he was about twenty.[2] In the winter of 1948 he saw the *Thirteen Paris Sculptors* exhibition at the Stedelijk Museum in Amsterdam, and this made a deep impression on him and on all the other up-and-coming young sculptors in the Netherlands. To Carel Visser, who only moved to the Academy in The Hague in December 1949, the stars of this show were Brancusi, Giacometti and Gonzalez. This exhibition was the revelation that helped him decide on his future.

The Spaniard Julio Gonzalez was the first to systematically explore the potential of iron as a sculptor's material. In *La Montserrat* (1936-1937), which Sandberg, the museum's director, purchased after the exhibition, Gonzalez composed the figure of a healthy young woman with a child on her arm. The weld points and joints and the hammering marks on the iron sheeting were shown openly, and they enlivened the work with their technical perfection. This symbol of strength, which expressed his position regarding his native country of Spain, then racked by civil war, seemed to have been conceived in stone but was executed in iron.[3]

One of Visser's earlier sculptures, *Dying Horse*,[4] probably done in 1949, is made up of sheet iron and pieces of iron pipe. Its composition is much more open than *La Montserrat*. Based on a childhood memory, the horse is depicted at the moment when, bracing all four legs to stand up, it finds its strength fatally inadequate. The oversized head with open jaws reinforces

Carel Visser, *Dying Horse*.
c.1949. Iron, 130 x 135 x
115 cm. Kröller-Müller
Museum, Otterlo. Photo by
José Boyens.

the expression of this moving sculpture. Visser is just a beginner when compared to Gonzalez' mastery of welding; but Visser deliberately opts for the undelicate, as in the 'cover plates' for the knees. The philosophy behind this work appears to be that the more intense the means, the better the purpose of expression is served.

Emotion strictly channelled

Auschwitz, a sculpture from 1957, owes its existence to Sandberg, the active director of the Stedelijk Museum in Amsterdam. He adopted an initiative, originating in the countries of the Eastern bloc, of erecting a monument to all the victims of Auschwitz concentration camp. A great many artists from various countries took part in the open competition for the assignment. To clarify the significance of Auschwitz, Sandberg showed Alain Resnais' film *Nacht und Nebel (Crimes hitlériens)* to invited sculptors. The sober restraint of this film made a deep impression on Carel Visser, partly by its moving scenes of human beings reduced to skeletons and the gigantic pile of chil-

Carel Visser, *Big Auschwitz*. 1957. Iron, 220 x 300 x 300 cm. Kröller-Müller Museum, Otterlo. Photo by José Boyens.

dren's shoes; in fact he originally entitled his work *Nacht und Nebel*.

The design for *Auschwitz* is organically linked to other works Visser did in this period, such as *Double Form 3* and *Double Form 4*. These iron sculptures are composed of vertical and horizontal bars and rectangles in such a way that the upper half of the work mirrors the lower. This effect, an expression of perfect balance, is not to be found in *Auschwitz*.

The striking asymmetry of *Auschwitz*[5] is primarily the result of the single bar that projects high above the rest and symbolises the chimneys of the gas ovens. The horizontals represent the railway lines and platforms that fed into the death-trap. *Auschwitz* depicts the factory-like, impersonal manufacture of personal destruction.

In this work, it is no longer expression that is the means of achieving the form; emotion is strictly channelled. It is not so much Carel Visser the individual who is registering his resistance to the systematic humiliation and murdering of people, rather the sculptor who, in this taut image, is speaking for all those who wish to continue believing in human dignity. It is precisely the sculpture's abstract forms that raise it above the level of subjective outrage. *Auschwitz* is a memorial that has grown out of bewilderment rather than an indictment

The book spreads its wings

To many people Visser is best known as the sculptor of stacked bars, cubes, double forms, and for *Hole*, which appeared in the sixties. These works resemble the Minimal Art that arose on the east coast of America in about 1962. The resemblance lies in their geometrical, modular composition and the fact that many of these works were built by a construction company. The work that most appealed to Visser was that of Carl André and the special re-

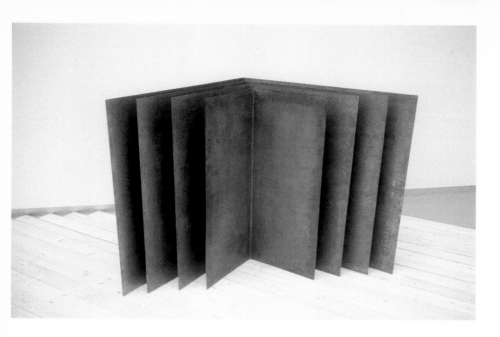

Carel Visser, *Four Plate-Books*. 1972. Sheet iron, 100 x 100 x 100 cm. Centraal Museum, Utrecht. Photo by José Boyens.

lationship it had with the floor and the earth. His admiration for Brancusi was also based, among other things, on this artist's demand that we focus our attention on the relationship between the sculpture and the floor. He gave the pedestal a value of its own. Another thing Visser admired in Brancusi was his quest for the most essential form, his preference for simplicity and his handling of materials. In the fifties, together with his fiancée and the young architect Aldo van Eyck, he visited the great master in his studio in the Impasse Ronsin in Paris. Not a word was spoken during the guided tour; some sculptures revolved slowly on mechanical turntables and Brancusi pointed out particular details with a cane.

In Carel Visser's work, the rigid, mathematical cube may symbolise an uncompromising father-figure, a paternalistic outlook on life and Calvinistic certainties (possibly illusory). One finds something of the spirit of the cube in the 1972 work *Four Plate-Books*,[6] in which four prefabricated steel sheets are arranged in perfect regular balance. However, compared to some cubes, this sculpture is more open and the steel is much thinner. Looking at this work without preconceptions, one sees that it comprises far more than four parallel sheets of steel: it also depicts an opening book. And since Carel Visser is not in search 'of *an* image, but *the* image', as he once put it,[7] *Four Plate-Books* is not simply a portrayal of any large book, but of the book of books, the Bible. After the mealtimes of his childhood, Visser's father was in the habit of saying, simply, 'Give me the book'. In addition to God's vengeance, the ensuing reading also preached life in the palm of God's hand. The *Four Plate-Books* – a title in which the material, the steel sheet, enters into a natural union with the Holy Scriptures – are open and welcoming to the viewer. The book spreads its wings for a flight of visual imagination.

Lyrical instability

When, in 1969, the strict authority of the iron cube had been broken down by such linear sculptures as *Open Cube* and *Soft Cube*, works that wobble at the slightest touch, the diversity of materials also expanded as an extension of this greater freedom of form. On this point, Rudi Fuchs wrote, '*The true reason for this development was that he had to follow his instinctive and lyrical preference for unstable motifs and combinations. Iron, being so heavy, started to be inhibiting. ... His technique is now so light that he can trace the paths of imagination more easily. In this way the technique fits in perfectly with the instinct.*'[8]

After the thin steel sheeting of *Four Plate-Books*, Carel Visser opted for leather, rope, untreated sheep's wool and birds' feathers. As well as animals' horns and bones, bales of straw, glass, paper and sand. '*The anecdotalism in this perception has thereby become very special and personal. Every feather and bone is a little story*', says Fuchs.[9] The fact that Visser was not dissociated from God in the choice of his material was proven by the catalogue published for the one-man show at the Kröller-Müller Museum in Otterlo in 1981; the artist included a passage from the Book of Daniel, describing a sculpture made of both precious and poor materials.

After the term *arte povera* (literally 'poor art') was coined by the Italian art critic Germano Celant in 1967, other artists also gradually started to use worthless material. This brought a radical change to the face of art. In the Netherlands Johan Claassen was already incorporating bone, textile and sand into objects in 1969. His work recorded the traces of work in the fields and life on and around the farm. It was also in 1969 that Ger van Elk waxed a triangle of parquet floor in the Boymans-van Beuningen Museum in Rotterdam. Sjoerd Buisman has been working on forms of growth since 1971: seeds, plants, leaves, fruit, shrubs and trees. Van Elk and Buisman's activities did not always leave them with saleable works of art. In this way *arte povera* and related movements were also an implicit opposition to the materialism of the art market.

The fact that Carel Visser moved to a farm in the countryside about two years before the retrospective in Otterlo was of great significance to his work. He kept animals there and was more frequently confronted with worthless material than in Amsterdam. In his case, however, the material is not the starting point for a sculpture, as in Claassen and Buisman's work; in Visser's case the idea comes first and then the search for the material that will express it most clearly.[10] Visitors to the exhibition could find there sculptures with such titles as *Ram, Eagle, Snake, Worm* and *Fish* and also *Landscape, Lightning* and *Rainbow*. To judge by their titles these works had taken the road back to nature. One feature of all the sculptures was that they sought plenty of contact with the floor. Just as in the work of Carl André, this was part of the sculpture itself.

The 1981 work *Worm* is characteristic of these sculptures. It is an 'unstable motif'. Two untreated sheepskins lie spread out on the floor. The square, dark tins[11] standing on them support the sheet of glass across which the worm crawls. The cow horns on the back provide an association with the prehistoric period; like the sheepskins they add vitality to the sculpture. The tonality of *Worm*, running from black to white with a great many natural intermediate tints, is a poetic element. This work is to some extent like an installation. This applies even more to *Rainbow*, also made in 1981, in which the pile of sand that forms its base has continually to be moistened so that the work does not evaporate into thin air.

Like some *arte povera* pieces, this work can hardly be included in a collection in this form. Carel Visser's work with poor material usually adopts a position midway between *arte povera* and art for the art market: for example, he combines bones or an ostrich egg with a silver fitting. In this way he ends up with a saleable object, even when it is such a piquant combination.

In 1978 Carel Visser made a statement of principle regarding his tendency to choose new approaches to each work: '*At a certain moment in your life you can opt to build on what you have achieved and to expand the positions you have occupied. But you can also opt for adventure. Either you choose what there is and must remain, or else that which does not yet exist and which may come, whatever it may be. In my work I ultimately react against what exists and opt for what does not yet exist.*'[12] In the Netherlands in the fifties and sixties Carel Visser pointed the way for the younger generation; even after about 1975 he continued to innovate and the inner freedom he displayed in both form and material kept pace with international developments. Younger artists then became the pioneers, though each one only for a short time. He continues to produce work of a consistently high standard which shows an uncommon sensitivity to the various materials he uses.

Carel Visser, *Worm.* 1981. Sheepskins, cans, glass, cardboard tubes, cow horns, rope, plaster, 90 x 320 x 245 cm. Private collection. Photo by José Boyens.

The wings of imagination

It is apparent from a 1988 work how highly Carel Visser values drawing, having himself drawn throughout his life. A one-and-a-half-metre high work is called *Sculpture for a Drawing*; the sculpture is topped by a drawing rolled up into a sculptural form. The restlessness and dark vitality of the work is calmed by the clarity of the drawing. Since his youth Visser has also kept scrapbooks in which, as an eager observer, he assembled the visual material that affected him.

One might see the colourful collages from the seventies and eighties as a combination of these two elements. In 1984 the walls of the Groninger Museum in Groningen provided solid support for their festive appearance. However fragile their paper-based cohesion – the technical structure was indeed light as a feather – they were a delight to the eye, so inventively were they composed, displaying the wealth of Mother Earth. The iconography of these collages seems a long way from a Calvinist childhood.

As early as the seventies, Visser was already using sheets of black 'coloured' paper as a background to the bones or feathers mounted on them. It is true that every bone and every feather is a little story in itself. In the nineties he mounted on them toads flattened by cars (1992), cows' hoofs (1993) and mussel shells (1995). In his orientation, he shows himself to be consistent and dedicated, even though in principle he opts for what does *not yet* exist.

However well such drawings fit into his sculptural work, Visser indicated in an interview for the *Paper for Space* catalogue in 1977 that: '*I make that sheet of paper completely black and thus it acquires a relationship with iron, with metal, becoming a sort of intermediate form between paper and sculpture, a sort of paper sculpture. And then I do something else in addition. I add something to it. ... I then take things from my surroundings (leaves, string, hair, eggs, arrows with feathers made by my son, etc.). The black sheet of paper dictates something to me, compels me to a certain way of thinking. I try to get away from the flatness of that paper – mostly 50 x 60 in size – for I am a sculptor after all. ... I denature the paper.*'[13]

A technical term still has to be invented for the series of drawings with animal objects which he did in 1988: they are not collages, because the parts have not been stuck on. They would be assemblages if the three-dimensional objects were joined into a single whole. But Visser preferred to create a tension in unframed confrontations between individual objects. One such work is *Drawings with Swan's Wings* from 1988.

The two drawings involved, both measuring 70 x 100 cm, are evenly covered with pencil so that forms and turbulences appear on the shining sheet of graphite. On the uppermost sheet these are, as a result of the direction of the pencil drawing, four half-diamonds. This sort of form gives the sheet an inner life. It appears that Visser finds it both enlivening and calming to spend a long time blackening a sheet of paper in this way. The result usually has a sonorous seriousness. The spread swan's wings give the work a poetic force, in the same way as the sheepskins in *Worm*. And so the viewer is carried off on the wings of imagination.

Carel Visser, *Drawings with Swan's Wings*. 1988. Pencil on paper, swan's wings, 200 x 200 cm. Artist's collection. Photo by José Boyens.

Solid sisters

Transparent material and bird's feathers, lightness and twinkling: this is what Carel Visser's work gained in the seventies and eighties. And yet his work retained a certain solidity. This is clear to see in *Water*, a 1981 iron sculpture for the Tropical Institute in Amsterdam. It comprises two parts whose organic internal forms reach out to each other longingly and suggest that they fit perfectly together. This work depicts in an erotic manner how much waters are inclined to merge.

In the *Sisters* or *Two Sisters* series, which extends at least from 1991 to 2000, there is no actual division because the two large forms are always linked together. Visser did several works as variations on the basic concept: mainly upright and monumental as for De Nederlandsche Bank in 1994, or

Carel Visser, *Two Sisters*. 1995-1996. Bronze, 100 x 200 x 70 cm. Private collection. Photo courtesy Kröller-Müller Museum, Otterlo.

smaller and tending more towards the horizontal as in *Two Sisters* from 1995-1996. This latter work gives the impression, because of the rough incisions, that the design was made in wood; in reality it was done in polyethylene and the incisions were made not by a chainsaw but by a red-hot electrified wire.[14] They were transferred into the bronze cast by means of the moulds. Visser had already ostentatiously displayed joints, such as those at the knees, as early as *Dying Horse* in 1949. Other Dutch sculptors, such as Herman Makkink and Sjoerd Buisman, also expressly show the technical process behind a work. The theory behind this attitude is probably their aversion to neatly finished hand-crafted products and the need, conscious or not, to distinguish their own work from them.

Some of the sculptures entitled *(Two) Sisters* – a rather witty title – are quite mathematically oriented, with linear and circular forms, as in one 62 cm version in solid steel done in 1992. In the *Two Sisters* measuring 100 x 200 x 70 cm illustrated here, as in all the 'sister sculptures', the right half more or less mirrors the left. Here too Visser remains true to his own work, in that in 1991 and subsequent years he revitalised the motif of mirroring, which was already to be seen in *Two Birds* in 1954, and which remained a guiding principle for the form of several works in the sixties. In 1954 he saw the two birds in reality, in 1991 the mirror motif developed out of the same need for harmony as it had almost forty years before. In the nineties, neither part of the mirrored form accurately reflects the other: the freedom ensuing from mature artistry permits all manner of modulations in the form and our attention eagerly focuses on them.

Like most of the sculptures in this series, the *Two Sisters* done in 1995-1996 is solidly bound to the earth on which it stands; on the right this bond is particularly emphasised by the suggestion of a form that weighs heavily upon the earth. This has also been a constant in Visser's work since the beginning: a concern for the right connection with the ground. *Two Sisters* is a sturdy, powerful sculpture, a classic in a classical body of work.

JOSÉ BOYENS
Translated by Gregory Ball.

NOTES

1. See Carel Blotkamp, *Carel Visser*. Utrecht / Antwerp, 1989, p. 34. This bilingual edition in Dutch and English is the most important study published on Visser (154 pp., 175 illustrations).

2. See note 1, pp. 36-40.

3. Statement made on 27th July 2000 by Carel Visser.

4. *Dying Horse*. iron, 130 x 135 x 115 cm. Otterlo, Kröller-Müller Museum.

5. The 1957 version, measuring 61 x 86 x 80 cm, which Visser welded himself, ended up in the Tate Gallery in London. *Big Auschwitz*. 220 x 300 x 300 cm, made by a construction company in 1967, stands at the entrance to the Kröller-Müller Museum.

6. Steel sheeting, 100 x 148.5 x 100 cm. Centraal Museum, Utrecht.

7. See José Boyens, 'Ik zoek niet naar een beeld maar naar hét beeld'. In *Ruimte in het beeld*. Venlo, 1991, pp. 51-71; quotation p. 60. The article appeared in a more concise form in *Ons Erfdeel*, vol. 32, 1989, no. 4, pp. 535-543.

8. Rudi Fuchs, 'De beelden van Carel Visser'. In: *Carel Visser, beelden in het Rietveldpaviljoen / Sculptures in the Rietveldpavilion*, exhib. cat. Kröller-Müller Museum. Otterlo, 1999, pp. 9-11.

9. See note 8, p. 11.

10. Statement made on 27th July 2000 by Carel Visser.

11. Carel Visser can become enthusiastic about an old, used oilcan.

12. Ad Petersen, 'Gesprek met Carel Visser'. In *Carel Visser, papierbeelden*, exhib. cat. Stedelijk Museum. Amsterdam, no date, no page.

13. Anonymous (Paul Hefting), 'Carel Visser'. In: *Paper for Space*. Amsterdam, 1977, p. 29, exhib. cat. by the Visual Arts Office for Abroad, Amsterdam, for a travelling exhibition of twelve Dutch artists. After the exhibition in the Stedelijk Museum in Amsterdam the collection went to Duisburg, Reykjavik and Antwerp, and possibly to Saarbrücken, Belgrade, Erlangen and Ingolstadt.

14. Statement made on 27th July 2000.

n

Yeats' Footstool

The Poet Karel van de Woestijne

In 2000 the Flemings were polled to discover which poem, out of a list of a hundred, they rated the best. Among those hundred poems there was just one by Karel van de Woestijne, one of the three poets of real stature that were born in Flanders in the nineteenth century. The poem in question, 'Fever-song' ('Koortsdeun'), comes from his first published collection, *My Father's House* (Het Vader-huis, 1903), but was probably written as early as 1895. Older poetry-lovers will be familiar from anthologies with its opening line, with its strong echoes of Verlaine: *'It's depressing that it rains in autumn'*.

Van de Woestijne ended up dangling somewhere near the bottom of the list, while his rivals Guido Gezelle and Paul van Ostaijen each had two poems in the first twenty. There are a few other poems by Van de Woestijne that still ring a bell, but they were not selected. It is difficult to believe that this was because the people who compiled the list barely knew of him. After all, Van de Woestijne still features prominently in histories of literature. His work had an enormous influence on early twentieth-century literature and attracted many imitators. Even the more independent talents that began to emerge in Flanders and the Netherlands around 1910 – from the Flemish poets Jan van Nijlen and Richard Minne to Jacques Bloem, Adriaan Roland Holst and Victor van Vriesland who were among the top literary figures in the Netherlands in the 1920s and 1930s – later acknowledged how much they owed to Van de Woestijne. Which makes it all the more puzzling that a writer who, despite his aristocratic attitude and baroque rhetoric, once enjoyed such boundless admiration should now be almost totally forgotten.

What happened? In my view, the reason for the poet's dwindling popularity is that attention has focused almost exclusively on his early work. The current impression of Van de Woestijne is of a poet who is passé, one who is decadent, overblown and gloomy. But when we concentrate on his later work – that from after the First World War – and set it in the context of its own time, it turns out to be surprisingly modern, with unexpected resonances for today's reader. And part of this essential historical and contextual approach is to compare him with contemporary poets from other countries.

The coppersmith's son

Socially, Karel van de Woestijne came from a less affluent background than those great turn-of-the-century writers, like Proust or Rilke, whose names have become household words. That he lacked private means, and unlike Yeats had no Lady Gregory to support him, may well have had a dramatic impact on his work and its *Nachleben*. Van de Woestijne was born in 1878 to a lower-middle-class family in Ghent. His father was a coppersmith with his own workshop. Some French was spoken at home, but at school Karel came into contact with the Flemish Movement, which was fighting for the rights of its own Dutch language. Consequently, it was in that language that he began to write; and so Dutch did not lose him to French literature, as happened with his better-off fellow-townsmen Charles van Lerberghe and Maurice Maeterlinck who were sent to the strictly French-speaking Jesuit college. In his youth Van de Woestijne became familiar with the two avant-garde periodicals of the day, *De Nieuwe Gids* in the North and *Van Nu en Straks* in the South. The latter appealed to him more, since it combined the individualism of the former with concern for the life and cultural advancement of poor backward Flanders.

Van de Woestijne never finished secondary school; yet in the 1920s he became a professor at Ghent University. Before reaching these heights, however, his life was dominated by a chronic shortage of money. His marriage – in 1904 – and growing family made it essential for him to earn a living. He became Brussels correspondent of the *Nieuwe Rotterdamsche Courant*, later combining this position with a post as a junior civil servant in a ministry. The First World War turned his life upside down. He joined the so-called 'passivists', those who refused to seek greater independence for Flanders while the country was under German occupation – an attitude which did him no harm at all after the war, even though he had in fact maintained contacts with Germans (among them the poet and translator Rudolf Alexander Schröder). He won rapid promotion in the civil service and eventually became a professor.

There are many ambiguities in Van de Woestijne's life and work. He was an 'ivory tower' poet, yet as a journalist he was at the heart of political life; he wrote introverted poetry, but his letters attest to a sense of humour and a great talent for gossip and scandal; he also championed the Flemish cause, though his cultural orientation was entirely French. He wrote his considerable oeuvre partly for money and partly because he had to. Writing came naturally to him; he was what was called a 'poetic animal', a born poet. But throughout his life he depended on publishing his poems to supplement his income. This was not always good for the quality of his work, but it does explain why, despite his many illnesses, he wrote so much.

His collected work comprises almost a thousand pages of poems and the same of prose, a sizeable volume of epic poetry and one of essays on the visual arts and literature. Then there is also the lengthy novel *Towers of Clay* (De leemen torens) which he wrote with Herman Teirlinck during World War I. For a long time this 'pre-war chronicle of two cities' (Ghent and Brussels) has been judged by standards derived from nineteenth-century narrative; and from this standpoint because of its digressions it cannot be considered a successful work. But read the book in a different way, for its portrayal of its age, its character as a roman à clef, its lyrical-ironic power, and you discover one of the most remarkable masterpieces in Dutch literature: still vivid, still challenging, worthy of a wider readership. Lastly there are the fifteen volumes of criticism and journalism written for the *Nieuwe Rotterdamsche Courant* – a goldmine for historians and cultural historians.

Van de Woestijne's poetry pleads to be read in the light of the social and cultural developments of his time. He saw himself as a '*son of the seeking and doubting, the complicated, the analytical nineteenth century*'. He belonged to the same generation as Paul Valéry and Hugo von Hofmannsthal, like him sharp observers of a self-fragmenting ego, but he died younger than either of them, in 1929, aged barely fifty. According to the general view, by then his poetic work – which falls into two trilogies, pre-war and post-war – was finished. Interestingly, though, at the time of his death he was planning a collection of odes similar to that by Paul Claudel.

A boy poet

Van de Woestijne was a prodigy, a 'boy poet' , who soaked up French symbolism like blotting paper and reflected it in his own way. Work dating from before his 1903 debut collection *My Father's House* bears the mark mainly of Verhaeren, Rimbaud and on occasion Verlaine. His first volume of poems also shows traces of minor symbolist poets like Henri de Régnier. Consequently, *My Father's House* is often described as mood-lyric or atmospheric lyric. As in Rilke's early poetry, the main concern is with musicality and atmosphere.

Only in a later phase do Van de Woestijne's poems move closer to Baudelaire, with whom he is most commonly compared. Catholic scholars especially have stressed the dualism of spirit and senses which he is thought to share with Baudelaire, with the fleshly element represented primarily by woman. This decadent theme is further reinforced by complaints of weariness and impotence, by narcissism and longing for death, so that one can characterise this second phase of his work as decadent symbolism.

With the war, however, came a radical change. Hardship and especially the lack of freedom stimulated introspection and a yearning for God. His spiritual bent, a smouldering presence even before the war, intensified. Asceticism and a preoccupation with grief and suffering gave his new lyric an ever-stronger mystical content. This mystical inclination showed itself first in his prose. After a volume of mainly whimsical stories in the style of Jules Laforgue, before and during the war he found his own material in hagiographies and the Bible. This he transmuted into a virtuoso descriptive art with a moralistic or speculative-spiritualistic tone. After the war, in 1925, the moralising which had always been part of Van de Woestijne found even stronger expression in what is perhaps his most typical prose collection, *Principles of Chemistry* (Beginselen der Chemie).

Van de Woestijne achieved his greatest virtuosity in his epic poems, of which he published three collections. They are reworkings of classical myths, full of splendid Homeric metaphors – a technique in which his translation of the *Iliad* had made him an expert. Like many other poets of his day, he took the story of Helen as the starting-point for his narrative poems, and like Rilke he also reworked the myth of Orpheus. Most characteristic, however, are his adaptations of the Heracles myth. Heracles becomes the archetype of the earthly seeker after the absolute.

For these versions of myths, too, Van de Woestijne found models in French symbolism. Again and again we see his attachment to symbolism, which in the early years of the twentieth century had spread throughout Europe. Together with the Dutch poets P.C. Boutens and J.H. Leopold and the Dutch poet and theoretician Albert Verwey, Van de Woestijne is the movement's leading representative in the Low Countries. And maybe, because he remained aloof from the Northern Dutch tradition and was geographically closer to France, he exemplified it more and better than did the Dutchmen.

'A silken rose'

Placing a poet in a movement can be a useful way of defining his individual characteristics. And comparison can bring out that poet's quality more clearly. That is certainly the case when one compares Van de Woestijne's later work with the later Yeats, Rilke or Valéry, all of whom had been influenced by the short-lived French symbolist movement in the last years of the nineteenth century. Already before the First World War they were publishing poems which showed a greater awareness of earthly reality than those of their predecessors, while still seeking to connect with a supernatural ideal. Almost all these poets retained the mysticism of their predecessors, but they no longer dwelt in an ivory tower; in Valéry's words, '*il faut tenter de vivre*'. Van de Woestijne did not resolve the conflict between himself and the world in his poetry, but neither did Valéry. In his poems the Fleming was searching for a universal humanity, and in this he came close to the neo-classicism of a writer like Jean Moréas, to whom he dedicated a cycle of poems on the occasion of his death.

The post-symbolist poets did not shrink from using modern subject-matter. Van de Woestijne, Yeats and the Russian Alexander Blok all wrote poems about airmen, though they were more interested in the fate of mankind, in the longing to transcend limitations or for death, than in the flying machines themselves. And like their predecessors they still saw themselves as magicians, as high priests of beauty; this is what differentiates them from the younger poets of the time, who were not averse to everyday language and topical subjects. The means to work that magic was sonorous musicality.

Apart from questions of influence, what Van de Woestijne has in common with the great post-symbolist poets is not only their turning towards life but, paradoxically, their evolution in later years to a more hermetic form of expression. This hermetic style indicates that they had become highly sensitive to the ambiguity of language. It seemed to them that this ambiguity better expressed the problems of existence than a simple naming of facts or events (realism) or the suggesting of a different reality through conventional or not-so-conventional analogies (symbolism). Their symbols – Rilke's angel is one example – were intended to denote entities from an intermediate world, and they became so personal that the reader can only grasp them intuitively. In this they were closer to Mallarmé than to any other symbolist poet.

The post-symbolists gave new and constantly changing meanings to old conventional symbols or created new ones, which were also surprisingly ambiguous. That Rilke, Yeats and Claudel made the traditional symbol of the rose into an emblem of absolute beauty is well known. No-one has yet investigated, however, how often it appears, usually in comparisons, in poems by their contemporary Van de Woestijne. '*Nothing that moves me more deeply than roses*,' he wrote in one of his short, succinct notes. From ancient times the rose has been a symbol of love and thus also of (feminine) beauty. In the Christian tradition, for instance in the mysticism of Jan van Ruusbroec, it is at the same time a symbol of Christ – who shed his blood for mankind – and thus also of the Resurrection. In poetry, however, it has also long been a symbol for the poem itself.

The rose derives its attraction from a combination of colour and scent with the danger it poses to humans – the danger of being pricked by its thorns and bleeding. Initially, Van de Woestijne associates roses both with the freshly dawning day and – entirely in line with symbolist preferences – with peaceful fading at night or in autumn: '*no lovelier rose than that which bloomed / in the slant, decay-bringing evening red*'.

In his late poems Van de Woestijne uses the symbol in more daring metaphors. In this bolder imagery it may retain its traditional connotations of tranquil transience: '*Oh ageing day, you taste of water and of roses*', '*I am the peace in which all roses wither*'; its connotations of love (for children): '*never has our dry mouth shone with sparks of dew / as does the rose of a child's open mouth*' and that of pain: '*There is no pain too great for us: / we gleam so much with happiness / that even the reddest, cruellest wound / adorns us like a rose*'. Unexpectedly, though, Van de Woestijne also gives the rose a very material meaning, as artificial beauty. In the poem 'Silence is the certainty' ('Stilte is de stelligheid') we come upon an embroidered silken rose!

Also, in a poem reminiscent of Rilke the rose becomes an almost mystical image, as a symbol of mankind's resurrection:

oh silent waters of the pools
which, sucked into the darkest earth
feel themselves ripen as they rise
up the veins within the tree;

– for: no waters will ever die
save in the furious bursting of a bud.
And I too shall not lose this life
Save as a rose in the eye of God.

The dark dancer

Other images too, less hackneyed than roses, are given mystical or esoteric meanings by Van de Woestijne and his contemporaries. The symbol of the dancer, for instance, derives from the old idea of the dance of the heavenly bodies. For the esoteric Yeats the dancer represents the unity of body and soul. It was the more intellectual Valéry who wrote most extensively about dance, in three of his longer texts. For him the dancer is an intermediary, at once physical and incorporeal in what his movements suggest, possessed of an autonomous beauty. In one poem Van de Woestijne, who was also fascinated by dancing couples and dance-halls, speaks of the dancer as fire and flame, an image highly reminiscent of a similar one in Valéry's 'L'âme et la danse':

And I have danced like a pillar of fire;
of bliss a fiery pillar I have been
that made its mighty blaze a festival,
where it could fill the universe with light
in the own fire of the all-consuming poem.

Because of its autonomy, for the late Van de Woestijne the poetic image becomes an intermediary between himself and God: '*image: panting dancer between God and me*'. For Van de Woestijne God is the perfect dancer, himself merely the '*mangy dancer*', sick and short of breath. In his story *Arnulphus* the saint performs a spiritual dance: '*This is what you had now become, Arnulphus: God's dancer. You could express your purified passion in dance, that was the manifest sign of your hard-won equilibrium. You had found your peace in the dance, you who had never known peace in all the years of your life, in the immobility of your solitude.*' Dance has now become, in Mathieu Rutten's telling observation, an image of '*inner, spiritual life*'.

Other images in Van de Woestijne's later poetry express the same introverted state, among them the strongly Rilkean image of the tree. The poet also forged symbols entirely his own such as that of the visitor, which somewhat resembles Rilke's angel. Van de Woestijne shared with his more famous great contemporaries a desire for independence, which for instance manifested itself in their highly individual way of expressing themselves. In these poets, though, conscious obscurity was accompanied – again paradoxically – by greater simplicity and directness of expression. In both Yeats and Van de Woestijne we find old ballads and refrains alongside poems with long-drawn-out phrases.

Unlike his great contemporaries, Van de Woestijne rarely dispensed with rhetoric. His poems were often plagued by exaggerated alliterations and over-elaborations, making them heavy and cumbersome. If a third of his work seems dated, it is because of this rhetoric. But even so, I have the same feeling when reading him as with the lighter, more volatile Gabriele d'Annunzio: in the best poems the deliberate thrust of the phrases adds an extra dimension to the already unique experience produced by this mix of life-weariness and vitalism, of a sense of sin and mystical intoxication. The result is the exaltation of the language.

Mario Praz once wrote in an essay on d'Annunzio that many people reacted to him as they did to '*the scent of the rose*': lazy perfumers have so devalued the rose scent that the slightest hint of its presence is enough to damn a perfume as crude and vulgar. These days, it seems, the merest whiff of ecstasy makes people hold their noses. Even though it was engendered by the finest of all fragrances.

HANS VANDEVOORDE
Translated by Tanis Guest.

Extract from *Roses*

19 July (1914)

Back through this hot summer luxuriance to Ghent, 'Flora's city', where an exhibition of roses calls to me. For I had not resisted the temptation; the one vivid recollection of last year's World Exhibition that lived in gentle splendour in my memory was of the *Floralies,* and though the present display of roses and other cut flowers – in the Great Hall of the Casino – might be more modest in scale, my urge to behold this new living beauty was no less.

Ghent lay baking in the fiery noon; the burghers were busy with their Sunday lunch, which is wont to engage their attention for hours on end; streets and squares were empty under the leaden-calm blaze of the sun, which did its summer duty with notable liberality. And so I came to Casino Square, quieter even than Ghent's other squares under a sky which seemed to have concentrated its calorific powers especially on this spot.

And from this white, mute dazzle, from the dust-smell that caught your throat, from the glare that made you feel that your own head was a sun radiating heat: suddenly into the blue hot-house atmosphere, into the subdued aquarium light sifting down from the lofty skylights with their lapis-lazuli-coloured stained glass, into the moist, balmy breath of thousands of roses…

This is not the triumphant, almost pompous, opulently decorative splendour of the summer flower-shows; you will not find here the bronze-clad majesty which, with bitter autumnal aromas, makes autumn flower-shows solemn and melancholy; this magic is that of the hour when the day cannot yet turn to dusk, but patient dusk already waits upon the weariness of the spent day – it is the magic of Armida's gardens.[1]

I am no Rinaldo – alas. But even as a busily note-taking journalist I feel that most sweet intoxication, which would inspire fear were it to last too long. These most wondrous children of the mysterious-dark earth, these incomprehensible whims of blind nature, which are fragrant and lure you, which astonish and sometimes frighten you, how shaken and moved one can stand before them, transported and suspicious… I go round the hall. The pale green walls disappear behind the gleaming, near-black green of the giant palms, with the blue light sliding down them, and the other, artificial-seeming blue of great hortensias like dull lamps in between. Below, on the tables, and lower still, among the pale gravel of the ground, the muted multiplicity of hues, stopping short of garishness, of the elegant borders in the hazy illumination.

And first of all the roses. Set against the curtains of red, of white, of yellow 'Crimsons' with fat bunches, like double daisies, of crazy little flowers on their canes, along the wires up which they climb, the crowded display of bouquets, of broad sheaves, of this one rare specimen, alone in its crystal vase. Some have plump, tight-closed buds, as though forbidden ever to open, as though, firm as young flesh, they were bound tight for ever; others are long and pointed as a hunting-spear, sharp as a lance, with their petals curling round them like barbs;

and then these, lolling wide open, lying like mother-of-pearl platters around the yellow fragility of their stamens, which are tired and languid and yearning for love.

Some are hard and brittle, fine and translucent as porcelain. Some are metallic, immutable, impregnable.

Some are soft and downy like the skin of a peach, soft and matt like a water-lily flower, soft and fleshy like the great chalices of magnolias.

Some are proud and strait-laced. Some are very much in love. Some are chaste and virginal, and these have no scent.

But all the stronger then is the fragrance of these amber-coloured ones that smell of amber too, these dark-red ones bathed in an aroma of tropical pepper and vanilla, these pale yellow ones which can light up a whole night with their clear glow and breathe the perfume of the golden, sun-warmed lemons of the Borromean Isles. There are some made to suffuse Autumn with the wildest longing; there's no summer that does not drowse in the calm, fruity scent of these others; every spring is shot through with this one's exhilarating perfumed darts. Modest and sharp as night-dew; blithe and open as a brisk morning; warm and blissful as a tranquil noonday; noxious and nauseating as the mud of an autumn pond in the ambiguity of early-falling dusk…

And the colours: here is Frau Karl Druschki, sturdy and white (she has the serene health and artlessly happy purity of a hospital nun); Marquise Jeanne de la Châtaigneraye is silvery-white with the faintest tinge of pink, like a real little marquise; Mademoiselle Simone Beaumez, surely you resemble the rose that bears your name, which is white as the skin on a girl's cheek and saffron-tinted like the skin of your swan-like neck. And you, Mevr. Second Weber, stately actress, rightly does this bloom bear your name since, elegant in its strength, it is the more alluringly rosy for not being very pure. You are paler and more sentimental, Lady Ashtown. While you, Caroline Testout, are magnificent in your vivacious pinkness.

And then there are the reds: vulgar red like brick, jaunty red like sour cherries, dark red like the velvet robes of kings.

And then there are yellow ones: acid-yellow like the hue of some Chinese vases; saffron-yellow like Eros' draperies; deep yellow like the most hidden gold in the secret palaces of Rajahs.

And there are even black ones; they are called Alsace-Lorraine; they look morose and resentful…

From *Nieuwe Rotterdamsche Courant*, 22 July 1914.
Translated by Tanis Guest.

NOTE

1. Armida is an enchantress in Tasso's *Gerusalemme Liberata*; the hero Rinaldo is enthralled by her gardens.

The Roses Are Musky, Dewy

The roses are musky, dewy
towards evening, pious and calm;
a purpler shadow stretches
around the chestnut-tree.

The pool gleams pale in vapours;
Comforting night is nigh.
Put on, put on the lamp now:
my terror wakes, my child.

1908

The Ladder and the Rope

The ladder and the rope; the straw; the chilly smoothness
of bowl and knife… The fearful morn dissembles, waits.
The air's inert. Each silence listens to the silence.
The house is deader than a snowy winter's night.
– The cauldron has been scoured where soggy swill once seethed,
the beast's outside. Sluggish wise fingers fumble;
the sow quivers; she stares askance… And the day is
like a dead woman whom I'm not allowed to love…
– The day is empty. Hear the horses stamping in the stable.
The day's a void; the hollow Christmas bells are sounding…

My God, I was the head where Thou didst show Thy grace.
They knew it. And they fed me, like this beast
that their desire did feed and that their lust will slay.
With their rancour they fed my yearning thoughts
and I grew beautiful, and had not grasped their envy…
Now is the time, my God, when they will slaughter me
and – naught that my resistance can fix its fear upon…

– The day's a void. The hollow Christmas bells are sounding…

1908

De rozen doomen en daauwen

De rozen doomen en daauwen
ten avond, vredig-vroom;
er waart een paarsere schaâuwe
om den kastanje-boom.

De vijver blankt in dampen;
de troostlijke nacht begint.
– Ontsteek, ontsteek de lampe:
mijn angst ontwaakt, o kind.

De ladder en de koorde

De ladder en de koorde; 't stroo; de gladde kilte
van teile en mes… De huiver-morgen veinst en wacht.
De lucht is lui. De stilten luistren naar de stilte.
Het huis is doover dan een sneeuwen winter-nacht.
– De ketel is gekuischt waar zwoele draffen brasten,
en 't beest is buiten. Logge en wijze vingren tasten;
de zeuge rilt; hare oogen loenschen… En de dag
is als een doode vrouw die 'k niet beminnen mag…
– De dag is ledig. Hoor ten stal de peerden stampen.
De dag is ijl; de holle kerste-klokken tampen…

Mijn God, ik was het hoofd waar Ge Uw genâ beweest.
Zij wisten 't. En zij voedden mij, gelijk dit beest
dat hun begeeren voedde en dat hun lust zal slachten.
Ze voedden van hun wrok mijn hunkrende gedachten
en ik werd schóon, en had hun afgunst niet verstaan…
Thans is de tijd, mijn God, dat ze mij slachten gaan
en – niets waar mijn verweer zijn angst weet vast te klampen.

– De dag is ijl. De holle kerste-klokken tampen…

All poems from *Collected Work I* (*Verzameld werk* I). Brussels: Manteau, 1948.
All poems translated by Tanis Guest.

Silence Is the Certainty

Silence is the certainty that never fails.
– I stroke your hair, my brother: and our sister
breathes deep of silence, since in the silence she
is more aware.

In the dusk she sews a silken rose, the which,
my brother, will never flourish in a fruitful sun.
It has a heart: there a dark bee will come
and tremble.

1923

A star: a Clump of Ice

A star: a clump of ice between my burning teeth.
While thou art hid from sight, oh sea that barely breathes;
while my heart's silent like an aged sister
comes this precise infinity to sear my lips.

– My nights were once a basket heaped with dreams;
my days the sum of all the apples that swell
in every orchard and on every laden tree.
I'd not fingers enough to count my riches.

Now: emptiness. The time is bleak, unmoved. The time
is like the chill and arid sea, that heaves nor moans.
I am alone; I press together my stiff lips
on naught but this great star, which scorches them.

1924

Stilte is de stelligheid

Stilte is de stelligheid die nooit begeeft.
– Ik streel uw haar, mijn broeder: onze zuster
dooraêmt de stilt', waar ze in de stilte leeft
bewuster.

Bij scheemren stikt ze een zijden roze, die,
mijn broêr, nooit in een vruchtb're zon zal leven.
Zij heeft een hart: daar komt een donk're bie
te beven.

Een ster: een klompken ijs

Een ster: een klompken ijs tusschen mijn heete tanden.
Terwijl ge onzichtbaar zijt, o zee, die naauwlijks hijgt;
terwijl mijn hart gelijk een oude zuster zwijgt,
komt deze stipte oneindlijkheid mijn lippen branden.

– Mijn nachten waren eene mand vol droom aan droom;
mijn dagen, 't vast getal der appelen die zwellen
in elken boom-gaard en aan elken zwaren boom.
Ik had geen vingren om mijn weelden aan te tellen.

Thans: ijlt'. De tijd is guur en onberoerd. De tijd
is als de kille en dorre zee, die zwoegt noch krijt.
Ik ben alleen; ik pers mijn strakke lippen samen
op eenzaam deze groote sterre, die ze bijt.

Like the Throbbing Lightning-Dash

Like the throbbing lightning-dash of engines
to which a human will has strapped itself,
seeking to penetrate the unfathomable void
to where it pierces the gaze of God's eye;

no, but like light in light: like to a candle
so meagre that the sun swallows it quite
from early green to final purple glow,
but which knows that its smallness cannot be snuffed out;

no, but like carp which in the densest ooze
gulp in some life, until Death finds them out
who only then, through rags of mother-of-pearl
lifts their blond bellies to the blowing light;

but no, oh no: like earth and like metal,
condensed by pressure and suction of the universe,
are inaccessible and secret rays
gathered together in one crystal tear;

no, but dead flesh, dissolved in sluggish streams
or richly blooming in a feast for worms;
no, only that flesh, that flesh and wretched oozing,
and the lowly beast that on the great beast dances;

no, no, oh God (I know not how to say;
I know not, God, I know not, but I say:
God);

like the…

like…

…

1921

Gelijk het gonzend bliksmen

Gelijk het gonzend bliksmen van motoren,
waaraan een menschen-wil zich-zelven riemt,
het ondoorgrondlijk-ijle wil doorboren
tot waar 't blik van Godes oog doorpriemt;

neen, gelijk licht in licht: gelijk een kaarse
zóó karig, dat de zonne haar doorvreet
van 't vroege groenen tot het late paarsen,
maar die haar kleinheid onverdoofbaar weet;

neen, gelijk karpers die ter dikste drabben
wat leven gapen, tot de Dood ze treft
die dán eerst, door de peerlemoeren schabben
hun blonden buik naar 't waaiend lichten heft;

maar neen, maar neen: 'lijk aarde en 'lijk metalen,
verdicht bij dringe' en zuigen van 't heelal,
worden verhole' en ongenaakb're stralen
vergaderd in één trane van krystal;

neen, dood stuk vleesch, vervloeid in logge beken
of weeldrig bloeiend in een wormen-feest;
neen, slechts dat vleesch, en dat vleesch en arrem leken,
en 't lage beest dat danst op 't hoge beest;

neen, neen, o God (ik weet niet hoe te zeggen;
ik weet niet, God, ik weet niet, maar ik zeg:
God);

gelijk de…

gelijk…

Gustave van de Woestijne,
Portrait of Karel van de Woestijne. 1910. Pencil.

Innocence

Can Be Hell

The Art of Berlinde de Bruyckere

Berlinde de Bruyckere,
*I Never Promised You
a Rose Garden*. 1991.
Metal, baskets, lead and
plastic, 260 x 250 x 120 cm.
Photo by Jan Pauwels.

A house or a tent could have provided shelter, but it could just as well have been a cage, a grid of steel. Baskets full of roses on a rack were given the title *I Never Promised You a Rose Garden*. These roses, a symbol of love, turn out to be made of lead, moulded from sorrow. Or hefty maces riveted to trees in the wood: the weapons were unusable and without danger, but they upset the composure of the woodland walker.

These are just a few of the early works by the Flemish artist Berlinde de

Berlinde de Bruyckere, *Untitled*. 1993. Eight haystacks on location, Kontakt Eupen.

Bruyckere (1964-). From the very beginning her three-dimensional work has had a fundamental duality. Her sculptures and installations can be quickly interpreted, in that a substantial part of each one can be 'understood' at first glance. But beneath this comprehensibility lies a complex tangle of content which in its turn is full of contrasts and extremes that affected and still affect each other.

Innocence Can Be Hell is the title of a work composed of two hundred blankets hanging from four gigantic drying racks. Each and every one had these words on its hem, and to some extent this reveals De Bruyckere's concept. After all, the blankets cannot keep the thunder and lightning away from any mortal being who hides beneath them in a storm. Innocence and disaster are closely related: it is often the innocent who are the greatest victims. Just as, in a later work, a heavy wagon loaded with blankets and brushwood was dragged into the museum only to become immobile there: flight had become pointless. Or, in yet another work, leaden roses frozen in ice on the sides of a goods wagon, on the way to death. Or blankets, piled up in a chapel that looked like a refuge for refugees or illegal immigrants, heaped more closely and oppressively the closer they were to the altar.

These blankets first made their appearance almost ten years ago and they were more or less to become a trademark of De Bruyckere's work: blankets to keep warm and be sheltered in, but also as a symbol of aid distributed after natural disasters or of endless streams of refugees. Or else they are piled up to make a 'blanket house', a den like the ones we built in our childhood as a place of protection: though at the same time they were utterly claustrophobic.

Berlinde de Bruyckere, *Talking*. 1999. Blankets, wax, polyester and polyurethane. MUHKA. Antwerp.

They also turned up in another of Berlinde de Bruyckere's best-known works, the haycocks. Here, the hay was kept 'warm' by all manner of blankets, possibly even to the point of spontaneous combustion. Haycocks were a familiar sight in the lowlands of Europe and inspired artists from Claude Monet to Emile Claus until they vanished from the landscape as a result of new mowing techniques and expanding urbanisation, and thus also from the childhood memories of De Bruyckere and many others.

Blanket women

Danger, the flight from violence, the loss of warmth, the yearning for a nest: these words bring us insidiously to the notion of 'woman'. The 'blanket women' have become a major feature of this blanket theme in De Bruyckere's work. The first version appeared in the mid-nineties: at first the visible parts of the figure were extremely true to life, because the 'reality content' was important. For example, in one piece two female figures were climbing upwards, while also covered oppressively in blankets. Or, in another, a woman was portrayed high on the branch of a tree, embracing the trunk, her head hidden under blankets; only her bare marble legs were visible. Or a woman face downward in a lake in a park, drowned (possibly a suicide) or strangled, and weighed down with a mass of blankets. Or another woman, so overloaded with blankets that it looked as if she were carrying her house. These women, even though they were largely invisible, seemed

Berlinde de Bruyckere,
In Flanders Fields. 2000.
Polyester and horseskin.

unutterably real: vulnerable, but at the same time indefatigable, desperately, doggedly crawling, climbing and hobbling.

For the last few years De Bruyckere has been working with more rough-ly formed figures: first she makes a cast in plaster, then she paints it with wax. This fits in better with the blanket that grows around the body. The blanket is now not only a covering or a (suffocating) protection, but has become a second skin, not only as a result of its constriction, but also because of its colour: it restricts the freedom of the body. The bodies are even distorted: arms, eyes or toes are left out, there are holes in the legs. And in fact this is De Bruyckere's view of humans: an erosion of humanness.
The figures which thereby come into being look more detached and abstract: they lose the anecdotal element that obtruded into the spectator's imagination in the earlier, more 'true to life' figures.

Sewn together

In preparation for these sculptures De Bruyckere does drawings and water-colours of the figures which are even more fragile and enigmatic than the sculptures themselves. Since 1996 they have become an oeuvre in themselves and are conspicuous for their transparency: there is no trace of anec-dote here, and the women have become frail figures. Yet even these water-colours have a dual nature, just like the sculptures. Some people see the positive side, others the negative, the beautiful or the ugly. Sometimes something sad is portrayed in a beautiful way, sometimes the reverse. Pleasant and unpleasant go together. How can they be absorbed into one another? By the way she makes her figures (but in De Bruyckere's work there is also a part to be played by the spectator: the way he looks at the figures is a contributory factor. The duality is there, but the spectator has to decide whether he opts for it or not. In this respect, one possible question is: how does the spectator feel at the moment when he or she is looking at the work?).

This is illustrated in an almost sublime way by a monumental work De Bruyckere made for the In Flanders Fields Museum in Ypres in 2000: she placed there the bodies of five horses in plastic, with real horse skin stretched over them. These horses lay like casualties, reflecting the fact that almost a century ago, during the First World War, horses (and soldiers) were sacrificed in trenches in the vicinity for a cause which most of the soldiers did not even understand. Some horses no longer had a head or legs: the corpses seemed to have been reduced to their essence: inescapable suffering and death. Several months later the same installation was on show at the Museum of Contemporary Art (MUHKA) in Antwerp, where its location in a clean, circular white laboratory-like room removed the last traces of anecdote that had obviously accompanied the work in the museum in Ypres, with its war-laden past. Yet, whatever the setting, the spectator involuntarily makes up his own story, one which is subtly guided by De Bruyckere in the direction of that single sentence, which can increasingly be seen as the thread running throughout her work: innocence can be hell.

In fact in the museum in Antwerp De Bruyckere took her 'sewing together' even further: it was there that she assembled her largest ever installation out of hundreds of toy animals, fluffy and otherwise, and hung them on racks and on the walls. These 'creatures' had all been subjected to the needle, had been manipulated and mutated: the legs cut off, the tail gone. They remained recognisable, but looked mutilated. Because of their numbers, one could not 'see' any single creature separately, because they formed a continuous whole. The inevitable consequence was that one again had those double feelings of childlike, innocent cuddliness on the one hand and uneasiness and disquiet on the other.

A dark image of man

The duality between covering and protecting on the one hand, and suffering and suffocation on the other, has become a cliché in almost all commentaries on her art. But De Bruyckere rejects the notion that her work is 'organic', since she does not actually sense that herself. The significance of the content is more important: her image of man goes against that of today's wealthy West, and that of everyone who wants to look absolutely perfect. All the fitness, lifestyle and fashion tricks available are useful in denying the decay of the body. But behind this facade lies the fear of loss, suffering and death. De Bruyckere's figures keep track of what is happening to man. She shows what humans today are anxious not to see, or what they push away from them.

Where will this end? Some of her recent sculptures are double figures sewn together. This inclines towards the positive again: people need each other. At present, man is manipulated to bits, but if you scrape together the best of those bits (look at the fluffy animals) you may be able to create a new human.

MARC RUYTERS
Translated by Gregory Ball.

Berlinde de Bruyckere, *Inge*. 2001. Life-size, wax, wood and horse hair. Photo courtesy of the artist.

Books

Should Be Both Comic and Painful

The Work of Arnon Grunberg

On the final pages of Arnon Grunberg's bizarre – cynical, but also very moving – novel *Phantom Pain* (Fantoompijn, 2000) the main character, writer-dreamer-swindler Robert Mehlman, writes in a letter to his son Harpo Saul Mehlman: '*My relationship with your mother, also known as Princess Fairytale, has survived a great deal. Too much to enumerate here, but I'll try anyway. Tumours benign, and less benign, literary flops and bestsellers, penury and seven-digit wealth, hotel rooms dirty and clean, extramarital affairs and platonic loves, neuroses, scores of suicides, a child, a marriage in Florida, my mother, shaving rash, gray hairs, gums that no longer function, mild alcoholism, burials and cremations, stench, fame and obscurity, and for the rest all those of my incompetencies, shortcomings and defects not mentioned above.*' This one sentence is a brief rundown of what has been presented in the over two hundred previous pages: the life story of Robert G. Mehlman under the title *The Empty Vessel and Other Pearls*. It is the poignant story of an unsuccessful writer who finally hits the jackpot as the author of a literary cookbook *The Polish-Jewish Kitchen in 69 Recipes*, subtitled *Cooking after Auschwitz,* the contents of which have been pilfered from an old Jewish woman, and of his hopeless affair with Rebecca whom Princess Fairy Tale consistently calls The Empty Vessel. On 29 October 2000 the novel was awarded the prestigious Dutch AKO Prize and Grunberg caused quite a stir by not being present at the live television presentation of the award. From his home in New York he replied by e-mail to questions put to him by the TV hostess and the audience; a woman friend accepted the 100,000 Dutch guilder prize in his name. '*I'm not going to fly for twelve hours to appear on TV for one hour,*' was his laconic commentary. The performance of his version of Erasmus' *In Praise of Folly*, commissioned by the publishing house Atheneum Polak to mark Rotterdam's year as Cultural Capital of Europe in 2001, did entice him to do just that.

A teddy bear with an Uzi

Since his remarkable debut *Blue Mondays* (Blauwe maandagen, 1994)

Arnon Grunberg (1971-) has been the *enfant terrible* of the Dutch literary scene, while at the same time being the embodiment of the mediagenic teddy bear: on his first appearance in a Dutch talk show he was presented as the Jewish kid who was often unflattering about his Jewish background, but who didn't actually mean any harm: in fact he was a rather '*pitiful case*'. But one that dares to be provocative: a daring that has given his work its charge since his debut. Grunberg continually undermines the notion of the victimised Jews and their collective past; he exposes the way in which in his parents' home non-Jews claim to identify themselves with their suffering. One of the most caustic scenes is in *Blue Mondays*: '*Then there was a group of women who wanted to become Jewish. They all looked as if they'd spent their youth being dragged through a hedge backwards. If you ask me, they probably had. They spent the whole time going on about how only Jews knew what real suffering was, but you could tell that what they really meant was that they were in the know as well. The world is full of ugly people, but I had never seen anyone as hideous as those women who wanted to become Jewish. If you ask me, they must have thought that once you're Jewish it doesn't matter if you're ugly. If I'd had an Uzi, I would have shot them all, out of pity. For aesthetic reasons, too, of course.*'

Arnon Grunberg (1971-).
Photo by Klaas Koppe.

Here we have the 'Jewish' writer Grunberg, who categorically rejects the epithet 'Jewish', at his most typical: throwing such niceties as political correctness and good taste – including literary good taste – to the winds. His way of dealing with the Jewish identity is far closer to that of an American writer like Philip Roth and his oversexed masturbating anti-hero Portnoy than to many a European author who complains so seriously (read: humourlessly) about the continuing effects of wartime suffering.

The sweet solace of slapstick

Sex and death are two subjects Grunberg likes to treat satirically anyway, as is demonstrated for example in a passage from *Phantom Pain* in which Robert Mehlman is on his way home with his Puerto Rican mistress Evelyn on the back seat of a limousine when just before Brooklyn Bridge they become involved in a pile-up with a number of deaths: '*I pushed her to the floor. Or else she fell to the floor. Maybe we both fell to the floor. The filthy floor of the limousine where people had puked, where liquor had been spilled, where it was sticky with unidentified substances (…) I saw two mosquito bites on her buns, I pulled her hair and then I held her buns tight. Her buns which she'd said were too fat, but she'd given up the fight. I pushed them apart, saw minuscule pieces of toiletpaper no bigger than cookie crumbs, no more than tiny white dots on a canvas of flesh. Why did she scream like that? Or were those the badly wounded outside who were still screaming? Do you scream before you die? And if you don't scream, how must you then die? (…) "You come so pretty," Evelyn said. "What do you mean?" "Your face is pretty when you come" "Thank you,"I said, "Thank you. But you mustn't keep an eye on me like that."*'

To explain his departure for New York in 1995 Grunberg made almost the same reproach: in the Netherlands he felt as if he were being watched. After his debut people kept asking him, where is your next book? New York meant living in anonymity; at the same time it provided a greater chance of creating myths about his life for his readers in the Netherlands. Yet he has never been anything but open about his childhood and adolescence in well-to-do Amsterdam-Zuid. He grew up in an irregular family. His father was almost sixty when Arnon was born. He had fled from Germany in the 1930s and survived by posing as a deserter from the German Army (according to Arnon Grunberg in the *NRC Handelsblad*, one of his saviours said after the war: '*If I had known you were a Jew I would never have taken you in.*') Arnon's mother survived Auschwitz. Both parents, with their pasts and their consequent inability ever to lead a 'normal' life, figure in various roles and periods in Grunberg's work. But the success of *Blue Mondays* was no doubt due to other elements as well: a recalcitrant teenager as hero (cf. *The Catcher in the Rye* in 1951), impudent adolescent exploits that nearly drive his teachers mad, a heartrending romantic desire for love, his first sexual experiences, prostitutes, escort agencies. In this connection Grunberg's reflections on his own work, on books by other writers and films are of interest. In 1998 he brought together a large number of assorted essays, reviews, and columns in *The Solace of Slapstick* (De troost van de slapstick). In it Grunberg gives free rein to his feelings on everything to do with the arts, especially their artificial tragicomic aspects. Significantly, the book opens with an essay about the silent film comic Buster Keaton. For Grunberg life is just one absurdity after another and everything can always be even worse. The only way to depict this sadistic universe is through a comic microscope. The caricature of Groucho Marx as God and Buster Keaton as his son is offensive to some people: '*Perhaps even in the form of slapstick the absurd is too hard to take.*' Grunberg has few illusions, he accepts fate in all its cruelty, and advises wandering seekers: '*And for those who may still be searching: there is no sweeter solace than that of slapstick.*' Such an outlook also implies a certain attitude towards the possibilities, or rather the limitations, inherent in depicting reality in a film or a book (Grunberg often mentions both arts in a single breath): '*Some people claim that reality is so complex that it can scarcely be adequately portrayed by a film or a book. The story and the characters in the films of Buster Keaton could not be simpler. The odd thing is that his films lose nothing of their credibility by being so simple, but become even more plausible. A not unimportant detail: an implausible film is a bad film.*' A not unimportant conclusion, and Grunberg's attitude towards writing in a nutshell, an attitude that he articulates in a variety of ways with terms like simple, straightforward, unambiguous, a tree is a tree is a tree. A writer is a good writer when he manages to build up enough tension to hold his readers' interest. At the end of last year he himself said: '*What I write need not be funny. It must be engrossing. I like a narrator who does not get carried away too much, who remains objective. Otherwise reading is like experiencing the suffering for the first time, keeping the wound open. Moreover, writing objectively about something horrible has a comic effect. But too much objectivity is no good either. It must remain painful.*' Comic and painful. For the comic effect Grunberg makes use of repetition, exaggeration, understatement, and at unexpected moments introduces absurdities in the form of asides, as if they help clarify the argument; which is one of the ambiguities that underlie the simplicity so praised by Grunberg himself.

A writer thrives on hard luck

Defining his position among his fellow writers, Grunberg compares his contemporaries with '*a sort of whopper, but the meat has been replaced by a mixture of soybean and beancurd. So really a veggie-burger*'. There is no denying that the three characters in the novel *Silent Extras* (Figuranten, 1997), a cinematic novel in both content and form, all have a high veggie-burger content: the visionary film director Broccoli (alias Michael Eckstein), the *femme fatale* Elvira Lopez (alias the future Marlène Dietrich of Hollywood) and the camp-follower / narrator (alias Grunberg's alter ego Ewald Stanislas Krieg, *schlemiel*). All three of them are dreamers and romantics through and through, all three convinced that a film career awaits them in America. In the end they all get no further than being extras in a virtual Hollywood hit film. The most vivid and appealing scenes in the novel are set in the Netherlands, in and near a fish restaurant on the coast where Broccoli's completely sozzled father, old Mr Eckstein, is their host: '*Anything will do, except pork. I am not a religious man, but it gives me a rash.*' Organising a streetwalker for the old man is the climax of the outing; Broccoli and Krieg stand with their backs to what is more a tragic sight than a comic one. '*It took a long time. It seemed like ages. Then we finally heard the girl say: "It's done". Broccoli was the first to turn around. Mr Eckstein was still positioned against the car like we put him there. He was sporting an erection, or something to that extent. So that's how erections look like when you're very old, I thought.*' In *Silent Extras* there are many scenes that seem to conform to Grunberg's view: '*Like God, sadism is in the details.*' Nevertheless Grunberg is neither a sadist nor a nihilist. Even in the most humiliating and grotesque descriptions – of which fathers are very often the victims – he shows too much compassion and melancholy, if only by way of the solace of slapstick. In his novels and stories Grunberg remains true to what he considers to be his fundamental task as a writer: hurting the human race, that is to say holding up to the reader a distorting mirror, in which he sees himself in his truly insignificant, despairing shape. Or as he puts it in his e-mail diary to the *Volkskrant* dated 21 October 2000: '*A writer does all sorts of things to his characters. I would say he dramatises hard luck. To be any good a story demands hard luck – whether disguised as a natural disaster, a neighbour with a knife, an illness, a bunch of worn out relations or a plane crash. Someone sees trouble approaching, thinks: get out of here – and only makes things worse. He thinks he can run away from hard luck, but runs towards it instead. That is such a strong theme, and so true too. A writer thrives on hard luck.*' It seems like a short discourse on classical tragedy; here too Grunberg's apparent simplicity is ambiguous and meaningful.

Silent Extras ends with a vanishing trick: Broccoli and Elvira fly ahead of Ewald to America and more or less disappear into thin air. After a delay of six years Ewald Krieg lands in the New World and sets himself up as a slum real estate agent in New York. The role-playing continues as he transforms himself into the caricature of the American immigrant: the money-grubber. It is at this point that the American period begins in Grunberg's work. As the gift book for the Dutch Book Week in 1998 but far removed from Dutch realism, he wrote a story from the perspective of two boys, who have migrated from Mexico to New York with their mother Raffaella. Their relative harmony is disturbed when the vulture Ewald Stanislas Krieg forces his way into their apartment and talks Raffaella into opening a Mexican take-away as 'Mama Burrito'. The boys distrust the braggart who claims to have written a book in his own country, earned a lot of money with it and become famous, but his curly hair charms their mother. Later she calls him an '*emotional terrorist*', but by then the damage is done. Grunberg teeters on the brink of sentimentality; such a simple story of New York, but how convincing it is: it seems like real life, so touchingly is it presented through the eyes of the two naïve young brothers.

This novella was the overture to *Phantom Pain*, Grunberg's most impressive novel so far (*Amuse-gueule*, a collection of early stories, is his most recent publication). He has never gone to such extremes, just like the leading character Robert Mehlman, who has, in his own words, climbed into a tree and didn't dare to come down again: it didn't seem right to call for help. So he behaved as if there was nothing he liked better than sitting in that tree, as if it was his aim in life. It was not his first choice to become a cookery book writer and fame is a leaking airbed, but he only realises that when he is in the middle of the ocean, so the blurb on the jacket tells us.

Phantom Pain is about illusory ways of finding fulfilment, deception, fraud, shame and ultimately an ignoble death. It is in the most literal sense a tragicomedy about the pain caused by loss. Numerous (semi)autobiographical elements are put into context with extreme skill. The pain does not hit the reader until he has finished the book. When he realises that the curtain has come down on the portrayal of the beauty of hard luck: a classical tragedy has come to an end. You can't wait to read Grunberg's next novel. Is a greater compliment to a writer possible?

FRANS DE ROVER
Translated by Elizabeth Mollison.

TRANSLATIONS

Blue Mondays (Tr. Arnold and Erica Pomerans). New York, 1997.
Silent Extras (Tr. Sam Garrett). New York, 2001.
A translation of *Phantom Pain* is in preparation (excerpts in this article translated by Sam Garrett).

Extract from *Phantom Pain*

By Arnon Grunberg

'I'm a natural for the royal family,' said Robert G. Mehlman one evening. We were sitting on the patio of the Hotel Santa Caterina in Amalfi. It was unseasonably cold. He had on his blue coat. Peanut crumbs were clinging to his lips. He smelled different. Of cellars where there's lots of dancing and no ventilation. There was a gravy stain on his white summer trousers, and his hands trembled like little birds that were trying to fly away, but kept falling back.

Mehlman had criss-crossed Europe with three steamer trunks and a huge bag of unopened mail. Now he'd taken up residence at the Santa Caterina, where he'd finagled a room with sea view at half-price because the season was somehow refusing to get underway.

He used to travel with his private secretary, but the secretary lit out on him.

When I first showed up, Mehlman refused to see me. 'Go away,' he'd shouted, 'can't you see the state I'm in?'

I'd wanted to leave right away, I hadn't travelled all that way just to be snapped at. But when I talked to my mother on the phone, she said: 'Stay there, he'll change his mind.' And the next morning at breakfast he had indeed changed his mind.

'What you've got on,' he said, 'you should throw away.'

Two waiters were staring sombrely at the grey sky. The season was three weeks late. An Austrian asked in bad Italian: 'When will there be a train going south?'

'There are no trains here,' the waiter said in English. 'If you want to go south you'll have to take a taxi.' The waiter moved over to our table. 'Am I right in assuming that you will be paying today, Mr Mehlman?'

Mehlman nodded, and the waiter said, staring at the sea: 'Yes, once a guest has settled in, there's no getting rid of him.'

The bag full of unopened mail was under the breakfast table. Mehlman rummaged through it, pulled out a bill, glanced at it, then tore it into tiny pieces. 'They can't find me anyway,' he said, 'and by the time they do, I'll be long dead.'

He wiped a little jam from his lips and ordered a glass of whisky. The waiter tried to walk away, but Mehlman stopped him. 'When I was your age,' he said, 'I had hair too, and you should have seen it.'

'Life certainly races along,' the waiter said, and kept staring at the sea.

The hair Mehlman still had was white and stuck out in all directions.

'It's been almost a year,' he said.

'What?' I asked. 'What's been almost a year?'

'Since my secretary disappeared.'

The Austrian got up. 'So are there any taxis around here going south?' he asked in a loud voice.

Everyone in the breakfast room looked at him. There weren't very many people, there were more waiters than guests.

An elderly gentleman sitting at the window with at least five foreign newspapers in front of him said in a mannered voice: 'I've been coming here for thirty years, I know more about this place than the staff does. If you need a taxi going south, I'll find one for you.'

A woman at the buffet, who was struggling to slide a slice of pineapple onto her plate, shouted: 'My parents used to come here, and I'm telling you, don't go south. There's nothing south of here, only poverty.'

But the Austrian wasn't waiting for any unsolicited advice. 'If I want to go south, that's my business.'

'Precisely,' said the gentlemen with the newspapers. 'And if you require a taxi, you should talk to me. I know everyone in this village.' He looked around triumphantly, and when no one said anything he went on. 'When I was sixteen my Latin tutor said: 'Henri, most people are dead, do not wake them.' But I paid him no heed, I have waked them wherever they were to be woken.'

'Should have let them sleep,' Mehlman mumbled. The lady who was still struggling with the slice of pineapple resumed her favourite theme: 'Further south the poverty starts, I've been there, first with my parents, then five years ago on my own, and nothing has changed.'

Mehlman was slowly spreading jam on his bread. I don't believe he was actually planning to eat the bread at all.

'I don't want to wake up,' the Austrian said. 'I want to go south, I need some sun. I have a bad back.'

A few of the waiters had already started setting tables for lunch. It seemed to me like a number of the guests did nothing but sit there all day, waiting for the next meal, returning to their rooms only after dinner. Maybe they went downstairs to the games room between five and six, to play a little table tennis.

'You have to die before you spend all your money,' Mehlman said. 'Not the other way around, otherwise you're just a burden on people. And they don't quite deserve that.'

Robert G. Mehlman is my father. Even though he has denied that during sudden fits of rage. 'Me, your father?' he shouted then. 'You know what your mother's like!'

When I was born, Robert G. Mehlman was at the peak of his glory. He was more than a major talent. But within five years there wasn't much of that glory left, and my mother sometimes compared him to a bunch of roses that had been in the vase too long without water.

I was probably conceived because my father, for once in his life, wanted to keep a promise. Because my begetters were in the midst of a crisis and didn't know what they were doing. But the important thing isn't why I was conceived, the important thing is that I was conceived. Even though my father would deny that as well. 'Every detail is important,' he would say. 'Nothing must escape our attention.'

But of course that's not the way it is. Many details are unimportant. Most details are unimportant. The important thing is that I was born on a cold January day in a hotel on Long Island.

At the outset of the pregnancy, my parents had discussed the advantages of having an abortion, but those discussions lasted so long that by the time they were done it was too late for any abortion. My mother, who was bent on having a child, had suddenly fallen prey to doubt. Giving birth seemed like a nightmare to her, but so did an abortion, and she decided in the long run that giving birth was the most bearable nightmare of the two.

My parents had taken a few days' vacation at Montauk. My father liked to work in hotels. The contractions started earlier than expected. They wanted to go to a hospital, but it was too late. Someone fetched a midwife. There wasn't much left for her to do.

During the birth my father got drunk in the hotel restaurant, which had an ocean view. According to the bill, which he saved and gave me on my fourteenth birthday, he paid that evening for two bottles of Chianti, four glasses of grappa and two bottles of champagne. I suspect that the Chianti and the grappa were from before I was born, and that the champagne was consumed afterwards.

That same evening, it seems – although readings differ on this point – he asked one of the waitresses to marry him. My mother wept, I shrieked like a banshee, the midwife slapped my buttocks and, two stories down, my father was proposing marriage.

From *Phantom Pain* (Fantoompijn). Amsterdam: Nijgh & Van Ditmar, 2000, pp. 9-12.
Translated by Sam Garrett.

Books

in the Baron's House

The Renovation of the Meermanno-Westreenianum Museum

From the Malieveld one can easily read the copper letters spelling out 'Museum Meermanno-Westreenianum' on the stately eighteenth-century mansion on The Hague's Prinsessegracht. This elegant museum, created around the private collection of Baron Willem van Westreenen (1783-1848), first opened to the public in 1851. Since then time seems to have stood still. The classical library, with its major collection of manuscripts and incunabula (early printed books), still breathes the hallowed atmosphere of the nineteenth century, when the museum was only open to the public for two hours

Nicolaas Pieneman, *Willem Hendrik Jacob, Baron van Westreenen van Tiellandt (1783-1848)*. c.1842-1843. Drawing. Museum Meermanno-Westreenianum, The Hague.

a day and one could study there at small tables while the keeper from the Royal Library kept a wary eye on things.

After 150 years the museum has been thoroughly restored with financial backing from the Ministry of Education, Culture and Science, whose property the collection is, and the State Buildings Department, which owns the building. A number of cultural funds subsequently made a contribution to the refurbishing of the renovated museum.

In February 2002 the baron's house was reopened to the public after a closure of more than a year. It is not only the Book Room, with its valuable collection of medieval manuscripts and incunabula, that has been reconstructed, but also the Back Room, which is filled with art objects and antiquities from the baron's collection. The nineteenth-century bookcases and display cases have been restored and the dark-red flock wallpaper cleaned. The shutters have been opened again and the windows allow in a diffuse light through a sophisticated system of blinds.

The first floor, which is used for exhibitions, has also had its former atmosphere restored. The renovation of the museum included the conservation of the rare and historically important eighteenth- and nineteenth-century wallpapers in the exhibition rooms. The baron's eighteenth-century furniture has been given a permanent location in the museum and a grandfather clock from 1700 is ticking again in the hall.

In keeping with the cabinets in the Book Room, the new display cases have been made entirely in mahogany and have modern unbreakable glass and contemporary lighting. The hall has been completely renovated and the basement has also had a facelift.

One can enter the adjoining property, which the state purchased in 1995, through a 'glass cube'. In this cube one can view the collection of medieval illuminated manuscripts on computer screens. The closure of the museum provided the opportunity to offer digital access to this valuable collection in the Royal Library. Since February 2002 it has also been accessible on the

Interior of the Book Room. Photo courtesy of Museum Meermanno-Westreenianum, The Hague.

The Friends' room with its medieval panels.
Photo courtesy of Museum Meermanno-Westreenianum, The Hague.

Internet. In the neighbouring house there is a large exhibition area and a screening room where films and videos can be shown.

The attic now contains workshop rooms, where the public is shown in three steps the development from the handmade book of the Middle Ages to today's printed books. One room contains the medieval scriptorium, where one can do calligraphy with a goose quill, like a monk. Next to this is the printing shop, where several printing methods are tried out. One learns hand typesetting and how to print a text under the supervision of an expert. The purpose of this is to gain an understanding of the invention of typography and the printing process as it developed thereafter. It focuses on the printing of books, but also looks at other printing techniques such as woodcuts and linocuts.

In the computer workshop one can draw up a design, add a digital illustration to it (such as a photo of oneself, which is first taken using a digital camera), do some typographic work and then merge the files and print them. The lessons and demonstrations always comprise two parts: an activity (in one of the workshops) is always combined with a hunt or a guided tour of the museum's permanent display. The tour goes from the medieval manuscripts and incunabula in the Book Room to the modern printed works in the new exhibit called *The History of the Book*, which opens in May 2002.

Those who wish to consult a manuscript or book can use the reading room in the former coach house. This involves a short walk through the garden, where one can in passing admire the graves of the baron's two dogs, Diana and Donau. This garden is one of the few methodically designed domestic gardens in the centre of The Hague. On weekdays it is an oasis of calm.

In the museum library, one can consult any of the 350 manuscripts, 1,500 incunabula, 30,000 old and 100,000 modern books, the museum archives and professional journals.

Outside the museum's opening hours, the reading room can be used for lectures and receptions. Above the reading room is the new, fully climate-controlled museum store-room: the most expensive part of the whole re-building scheme.

The Museum of the Book

It is no surprise that neither money nor effort have been spared in the transformation of the museum. The Meermanno-Westreenianum Museum is one of the twenty-six state museums that administer the Netherlands' precious national heritage.

The museum's origins go back to Baron van Westreenen van Tiellandt, born of a rich and noble family, who was a collector and bibliophile in The Hague. His father was a barrister at the Court of Holland. In 1848 Van Westreenen bequeathed his collections to the Dutch state on condition that his entire legacy be kept in his house. To this end the house would be fitted out as a museum. He chose for this museum the name 'Museum Meermanno-Westreenianum', linking his own name with that of his bibliophile relatives Gerard Meerman, a jurist, and Johan Meerman, a historian, who originated from a family of wealthy merchants in Leiden.

The core of the baron's collection consisted of a very sizeable set of manuscripts (largely from the Meerman Collection), incunabula and precious printed works from the sixteenth to the nineteenth century. He also had a substantial collection of coins, medals, prints and paintings. Of the latter, it is worth mentioning a number of Italian panels. The baron was the first to introduce this form of painting into the Netherlands. In addition he had assembled a small but exceptional collection of Egyptian, Greek and Roman antiquities and Italian majolica.

In his will, the baron stipulated that – with the exception of new issues of periodicals and annuals – nothing should be added to the collection. For this reason the Westreenen collection can be called complete. He also laid down restrictions regarding access to the collection. Visitors were only allowed into the museum on Prinsessegracht in small numbers. It is due precisely to this restful past that, a good 150 years after its founding, the original museum interior is still virtually intact, and that the private nineteenth-century collection has been retained almost in its entirety.

1935 saw an end to the museum's drowsy existence. A change in the law removed a number of stipulations that were regarded as restrictive. One of the changes was that pieces might be added to the museum's collection as long as they were kept separate from Van Westreenen's collection. Since 1935 several old printed items have been purchased which modestly supplement the existing works. The change in the museum's status only came in 1960, however, when the 'Museum of the Book' was established in the baron's house.

In the Netherlands there had for some time been the desire to set up a national museum of the book. The Meermanno-Westreenianum Museum and

Jean Humbert, *Johan Meerman (1753-1815)*. 1784-1785. Canvas, Museum Meermanno-Westreenianum, The Hague.

Petrus Comestor, *La Bible hystorians*, 1372. This page of this exceptional manuscript shows Jean de Vaudetar, who commissioned the book, offering it to King Charles v of France. The illumination is by Jean Bondol of Bruges. Museum Meermanno-Westreenianum, The Hague.

This book, entitled *Oostersch*, was printed by Jean François van Royen at his Kunera Press, using the 'Disteltype' typeface which he designed himself. The Hague, 1922. Museum Meermanno-Westreenianum, The Hague.

the Royal Library were proposed as possible homes for this institution. In the years preceding its establishment various collections were purchased or accepted as donations for the future museum.

Two major collections form the foundation of the present-day collection. The first is the bequest of the Dutch master printer Jean François van Royen (1878-1942), including the contents of his printing and typesetting shops, his archives and part of his library. The second collection is the Radermacher Schorer legacy, which comprises at least 4,000 books assembled by the Utrecht bibliophile and patron of the arts M.R. Radermacher Schorer (1888-1956). This collection offers a broad representative survey of the highlights of West European book printing from about 1890. Almost all the major private presses in England, Germany and the Netherlands are represented by several publications. It also provides an almost complete picture of Dutch book conservation between 1920 and 1950.

In 1954 the Royal Library bought a complete set of books produced by William Morris' Kelmscott Press at an auction in London. It was housed in a specially designed cabinet made at the Morris workshop. The cabinet and contents are now a permanent part of the museum's display.

Joint venture

The close collaboration with the Royal Library, which Van Westreenen had formulated in his will by stipulating that its director must keep an eye on events at the museum, remained undiminished over the years, though it became more relaxed. In 1987, the management of the museum was put in the hands of its own director, whereas previously it had been the task of a keeper overseen by the chief librarian at the Royal Library. As far as collecting

Jean Baptist Perronneau, *Gerard Meerman (1722-1771)*. c.1761. Canvas. Museum Meermanno-Westreenianum, The Hague.

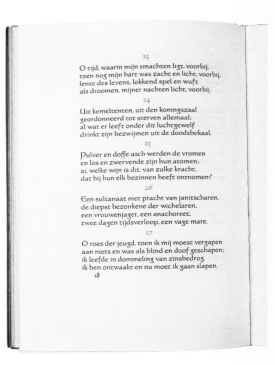

A book for Bruynzeel's factories in Zaandam. Designed by Vilmos Huszar in 1931. Purchased in 1999 with funds from the Society of Friends of the Museum of the Book. Museum Meermanno-Westreenianum, The Hague.

OOK HIER BRUYNZEEL DEUREN

CITROËN GARAGE   ARCH. JAN WILS   STADION

34

was concerned, a clear delineation of territory was maintained.

The museum became fully independent of the Royal Library in 1995, when the formulation of relations between state museums and the state authorities underwent a change. The collection and accommodation remained the property of the state, but the running of the museum was transferred to an independent foundation. It was however laid down that the director of the Royal Library should be a member of the Supervisory Board of the private museum.

The museum's collecting policy was largely rooted in the tradition of bibliophily, concerning itself with handsome volumes whose content was often of an elevating literary nature. Only in the last fifteen years has more attention been paid to the acquisition of ordinary reading books and the purchase of special books, such as those by contemporary artists. The ex libris collection has also greatly expanded as a result of a few significant purchases and donations from private individuals, and is now one of the biggest of its kind in the world. The museum has a modest purchasing budget for the expansion of the modern collection.

However, it can also count on the generosity of the Society of Friends of the Museum of the Book, which has 1,170 donors. They see to it that the annual purchasing budget is substantially increased for the acquisition of often expensive bibliophilic works or individual artist's books. At present there is a collective endeavour to expand the collection of books from between the wars (1918-1940) by means of selected purchases.

The opening of the museum was accompanied by the presentation of an exhibition entitled *Magnificence, Gravity and Emotion. The World of the*

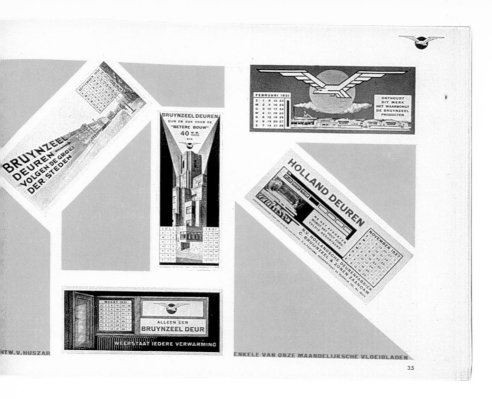

Medieval French Manuscript. This exhibition emphasises the importance of the combined collections of the Royal Library and the Meermanno Museum. Ninety of the best pieces from the two collections, supplemented by manuscripts from other Dutch museums and libraries, illustrated the role of the book in medieval society. It also focused on the book producers and their customers. In addition, this project showed once more how close the collaboration between the Royal Library and the museum still is, exactly as Baron van Westreenen intended.

MARIE CHRISTINE VAN DER SMAN
Translated by Gregory Ball.

FURTHER READING

BOER, TANJA DE *et al.*, *M.R. Radermacher Schorer 1888-1956: minnaar van het 'schoone' boek.* The Hague / Amsterdam, 1998.

BOER, TANJA DE, 'The Museum of the Book in The Hague'. In: *Art Libraries Journal*, 2000, 25 / 1, pp. 19-24.

EKKART, R.E.O., *Een boekmuseum verzamelt. Aanwinsten 1987-1991.* The Hague / Zutphen, 1992.

KORTEWEG, A., *Magnificence, Gravity and Emotion. The World of the Medieval French Manuscript.* Zwolle / The Hague, 2002.

LASEUR, W.A. and J. VAN HEEL, *Het museum Meermanno-Westreenianum 1848-1960: een bijdrage tot de geschiedenis van het museum en zijn bewoners.* The Hague, 1998.

ADDRESS

Museum Meermanno-
Westreenianum
Prinsessegracht 30
2514 AP The Hague
The Netherlands
Tel. +31 70 346 27 00
Fax +31 70 363 03 50
www.meermanno.nl

Paul

Claes, a New Literary Wizard

Until recently, the history of modern Dutch literature could boast only one wizard: Simon Vestdijk (1898-1971), who was given this honorary title by Menno ter Braak, the foremost Dutch literary critic of the 1930s. Admittedly, Vestdijk was at the time just emerging as a writer to be reckoned with, but Ter Braak, highly impressed by Vestdijk's versatility and near-maniacal level of production, predicted that his friend's literary output would continue to grow in both quality and quantity. History has proved him correct. Vestdijk practised nearly all literary genres: poetry, short stories, novels, essays, criticism, even studies with more or less scholarly pretensions. Drama was the only genre he did not try his hand at, although he did write the libretto for an opera by the composer Willem Pijper.

The post-war world of letters in the Netherlands and Flanders has occasionally felt the need to honour another writer with the title Ter Braak awarded to Vestdijk. There have of course been other prolific writers of great versatility, one example being Johan Daisne (1912-1978), who was called the Flemish Vestdijk because of his extensive oeuvre and related literary views. But no other author has more right to be called a 'wizard' than the Fleming Paul Claes (1943-). After his relatively late debut with a volume of scholarly essays called *Network and Nebula* (Het netwerk en de nevelvlek, 1979), in the 1980s and 1990s Claes let loose a flood of articles and more than fifty books and booklets. Like Vestdijk he feels at home in all genres, with the exception of drama. Nonetheless, in the midst of such diversity it seems possible to detect a core of unity, the point around which all his activities revolve.

Paul Claes – who now lives in Belgium in Kessel-Lo, near his home town of Leuven – studied classical philology in the 1960s at Leuven's famous Catholic University. In 1981 he received his doctorate, publishing a dissertation called *Moth-Eaten Myths* (De mot zit in de mythe), dealing with elements from classical antiquity in the work of the great Flemish writer Hugo Claus. Although Claes later studied modern literature as well (English and German), his wide knowledge of Greek and Latin literature nevertheless provides the basis of nearly all his work. His education plays an equivocal role in this. Its influence is positive in as much as it has put him in touch with such poets as Catullus and Horace, with Sappho and the tragedians, with the Greek and Roman writers of romances. It has also taught him to read closely, with an eye for detail. What the old-fashioned philology course could not give him was a mode of analysis and an interpretative method. His Flemish teachers tended to confine their instruction to finding solutions to the problems of authenticity, textual variants, historical background and the 'correct' translation. Following in the footsteps of his chosen guides, Ezra Pound and Hugo Claus, Claes broke with traditional notions of translation: his own poetical renderings entail – in addition to transposing from one language to another – adapting both the form and the cultural context, which requires a whole range of adaptations, deletions and additions. In his study on the art of allusion, *Echo's Echoes* (Echo's echo's, 1988), Claes gave such a lucid description of the series of transformations undergone by a text during the process of translation or adaptation that he even succeeded in providing his colleagues in the field of literary theory with a mode of analysis, thereby earning the right to be considered the founder of the discipline of intertextuality in the Low Countries.

'Make it new'

Claes' translations in the manner outlined above form an impressive body of work on their own. In the first place I should like to mention his contemporary version of Catullus' *Carmina* (1995) as worthy of closer inspection. This text is characteristic of Claes' approach in two respects. First, in the course of his translations and explications he offers new interpretations of various, often much-discussed poems, so that his translation and commentary together can stand as a scholarly work. (Awaiting publication is an auxiliary monograph, written in English, on this Latin poet's working method.) Secondly, he does not tone down the 'foul-mouthed' Catullus – he of the strongly sexual and obscenely aggressive poems – but lets him speak in fitting and equivalent Dutch. What holds true for Catullus also holds true for Claes' selection (1997) from the Greek *Anthologia*, a series of 150 epigrams selected from the ample supply available. In the field of contemporary world literature, he has done much the same with the poetry of Rilke and Rimbaud, Mallarmé and De Nerval. He has also made such lesser-known poets as Louïze Labé and José-Maria de Heredia more accessible by producing anthologies of their work, complete with an introduction and notes. His translation of James Joyce's *Ulysses*, done in collaboration with Mon Nys, was published in 1994. John Vandenbergh's Dutch translation of this text, roundly praised but long out of print, has been surpassed in every respect by Nys and Claes. Some critics have lamented the fact that the duo did not follow the example of their predecessor and supply the text with a commentary. Anyone who compares the translation with the original, however, will note that in countless difficult places Nys and Claes have incorporated implicit commentary in the text itself.

The annotated character of Claes' translations comes even more strongly to the fore in his Latin versions of classic Dutch poems. He has, for example, made translations which are brilliant and surprising – even for connoisseurs – of such canonical poems as 'Melopee' by Paul van Ostaijen and

'I try in poetic fashion' ('Ik tracht op poëtische wijze') by Lucebert. Many of these poems are not available in book form; others have never been in print. The volume entitled *Metamorphoses. Carmina poetarum recentiorum* (1991) is Claes' anthology of twenty-four Latin versions of great Western poetry, ranging from Shakespeare and Vondel to Eliot and Pessoa.

A feast of recognition

Claes' own poetry, and no less his fictional prose, can also be considered a form of commentary. His prose debut, *The Last Book* (Het laatste boek, 1992), contains stories in the style of pastiches recalling Proust, Kafka, Joyce, Nabokov and Borges. *The Satyr* (De Sater, 1993) is an extremely ingenious design for the prototypical romantic novel of classical antiquity. *The Son of the Panther* (De zoon van de Panter, 1996) rewrites the New Testament in twelve stories recounted by the twelve apostles, each offering his own vision of Jesus Christ. In *The Phoenix* (De Phoenix, 1998), a philosophical detective story in the style of Umberto Eco's *The Name of the Rose*, Claes manages in passing to make a mockery of the whole genre. And his most recent novel, *The Chameleon* (De kameleon, 2001), is again a historical novel, presented as the autobiography of Charles d'Éon. This French nobleman, born in 1728, made a lightning career in the diplomatic corps at the French Court and was also quite successful in a number of military enterprises; yet he died penniless and forgotten in London in 1810.

Of these prose works *The Satyr* was the most successful, possibly because the book bears a deceptive resemblance to the old-fashioned dime-store novel, with a pair of lovers who encounter seemingly insurmountable obstacles but emerge unscathed to enjoy the happy ending. As mentioned above, *The Satyr* is a reconstruction of the oldest novel in Western literature, currently held to be the *Milesian Tale*, a Greek text written in the first century BC by Aristides of Miletus, of which only one word has been preserved. Claes composed his reconstruction along the following lines: from the Greco-Roman tradition of romance – that of Longus, Heliodorus and others on the Greek side, and Petronius and Apuleius on the Roman side – he put together a package of motifs and stock situations which he sprinkled lavishly throughout the frame narrative as related by his protagonist-narrator, Endymion. The result – for readers acquainted with these antique romances – is one big feast of recognition. Claes embellishes his story with such freely acknowledged gems as 'Trimalchio's Banquet' and 'The Widow of Ephesus', both from Petronius, as well as 'The Festival of Laughter' from Apuleius' *Metamorphoses*. But Claes never includes such borrowings without introducing variations to the original text, at once contributing to the humour of the novel and lending it deeper meaning.

Perhaps such a transformation is best illustrated by the following example: just as in Petronius' *Satyricon*, Claes' main character finds himself on a ship, the *Eros*. Petronius, of all people, is also there (an impossible situation, in fact, because Petronius lived at least a century after Aristides; but this is not the only anachronism in *The Satyr*). Petronius now makes Endymion the victim of a rather complicated practical joke, the gist of which is as follows: the boy thinks that, in an attempt to help, he has accidentally killed Petronius and two of his slaves, though it turns out he has only pierced three wineskins (yet another borrowing, though this time not from Petronius' romance but from Apuleius' *Metamorphoses*, in which a similar fate befalls the hero of the story). Then comes the following fragment: 'The laugh stifled up to this time now burst forth. *Like dead men from their grave*, Petronius and his slaves appeared from within the command cabin. Several Adonises lifted me up and carried me around like the hero of the Festival of Laughter which was being celebrated that evening. Not knowing whether I should laugh or cry, I submitted to the passengers' roars of laughter, while reflecting on how quickly one's luck could turn: *Blood had turned to wine*, tears of sorrow had been magically transformed into tears of joy, *death had been converted into life.*'

Apart from the change of situation, it is mainly the italicised parts of the text which effect a transformation, touching upon the theme of Claes' novel: death and resurrection. This is, of course, a well-known theme: as Claes said somewhere, it is '*the most important of all Greek myths, which has come, via all manner of roundabout ways, to be our most important myth as well*'. That this theme is also typical of many romances of antiquity is a view now generally shared by specialists. It was introduced into *The Satyr*, therefore, to enhance the feeling of authenticity. It also lends unity to the oeuvre of Claes himself: in his dissertation on Hugo Claus (trade edition 1984), he was the first to make clear the debt Claus owed to Sir James Frazer's twelve-part study, *The Golden Bough*, in which the Scottish anthropologist elaborated upon the very same theme of death and resurrection. Claes has shown its influence on the work of other authors, especially in the Netherlands, in his recent study *The Golden Bough* (De Gulden Tak, 2000).

Pasticheur and scholiast

It goes without saying that, as a poet, Claes is the hermetic type, appealing more to his readers' experience of reading than to their experience of life. It was a long time, too, before any interest was shown in Claes' poetical work. His formal debut, *The Sons of the Sun* (De Zonen van de Zon, 1983), contains a series of translations of (and therefore commentaries on) one of his own youthful sonnets, rendered in English, French, German, Italian, Spanish, Latin and Greek. The critics found it an object of curiosity more than anything else. His real debut, *Rebis* (1989), in which the volume just mentioned is included, received few reviews, probably because such poetry did not fit easily into any existing framework. Given the alchemistic structure of this series of poems, a comparison with the fictional prose of someone like Harry Mulisch would be more appropriate. The volumes *Emblem* (*Embleem*) and *Mimicry*, both of which appeared in 1984, have something in common: they are both offshoots of well-known literary-historical genres. In the former text Claes gives us forty quatrains with the same number of illustrations, taken from the four arts of painting, sculpture, drama and photography. The commentaries on the paintings, in particular, are extraordinarily ingenious, prompting one to reconsider time-worn (and worn-out) art-historical value judgements. *Mimicry* contains fifty Dutch poems (as well as seven poems in other languages), which are attributed to great poets of Dutch and Flemish letters but are, of course, the work of Claes himself. The idiosyncrasies of the poets selected are often so aptly demonstrated that those in the know find the texts downright hilarious. This is reinforced by the commentary accompanying the poems: not infrequently, the information supplied intentionally misleads the reader, by referring, for example, to non-existent critical essays. In fact, Claes is gently mocking his predilection for explanatory notes and bibliographical information, even in the case of his own poems. The subtitle of *Mimicry* reads: 'The history of Dutch poetry in fifty pastiches' ('Geschiedenis van de Nederlandse poëzie in vijftig pastiches'), which pretty much hits the nail on the head.

Glow / Feux (Glans / Feux, 2000) is a combination of two earlier publications consisting of thirty-six poems in French and Dutch, printed on opposite pages, their position alone causing them to interact. The main theme is love (in all its facets, but most often that of erotic tension) between famous couples from Greek mythology, such as Orpheus and Eurydice, Theseus and Ariadne, Hades and Persephone, Amor and Psyche. There is, to varying degrees, similarity in content between the poems of each diptych, though formally they are different: the French poems are slimmed-down sonnets, the Dutch poems are elegiac distichs printed over four lines, which creates an optical contrast between verticality and horizontality. In the couple Cybele and Attis, for instance, the poems refer to the relationship between the mother-goddess Cybele and the beautiful shepherd boy Attis, who castrates himself after the goddess afflicts him with madness for his faithlessness. The subject is treated in detail by Catullus in his *Carmen* LXIII, which, though viewed in the past simply as an Alexandrine *tour de force*, is now generally thought to embody his main theme: the love for a motherly lover. In a way this also holds true for Claes: the relationship between mother and son occurs in all the genres he practises, including that of essayist. The combination of beauty and cruelty – of 'Beauty' and 'the beast' – is also a conspicuous constant in Claes' work, which is one reason why this paradoxical diptych can easily serve as a *pars pro toto* example of the rapidly growing oeuvre of this new literary wizard.

RUDI VAN DER PAARDT
Translated by Diane L. Webb.

NOTE

A complete list of Paul Claes' publications is to be found in Christine D'haen's *De zoon van de Zon* (Leiden, 1997). She treats the various aspects of Claes' work in exemplary fashion and conducts a remarkable interview with him about *Mimicry*.

For my analysis of *The Satyr* I have relied on my article 'Ernstig spel', published in Mark Pieters *et al.* (eds.), *Oude keizers, nieuwe kleren*. Amsterdam, 1997, pp. 25-29. I have written in more detail on Claes' dissertation and his other studies of Hugo Claus, in *Mythe en Metamorfose* (Amsterdam, 1991, pp. 168-172).

Extract from *The Phoenix*

The Deathbed

With the panting shadow of his secretary at his heels Count Giovanni Pico della Mirandola, Prince of Concordia, hurried to High Mass. The crowd of believers jostling in front of the bronze doors of the cathedral was even greater than on other Sundays. What prophecy would the preacher from Ferrara utter today about the fury advancing from the north?

The die was cast. A month ago the French king, Charles VIII, had begun his campaign in Italy. Fourteen years ago his father had inherited the kingdom of Naples, where a Spanish usurper still held sway. Now the son was coming to claim his father's rights by force of arms. But before he could topple the Aragonese bastard from his throne he had first to traverse the maze of dukedoms, counties and city states that awaited him behind the white rampart of the Alps.

Discord is the ruin of strength. On the peninsula political alliances were made and broken as casually as romantic liaisons. His enemies' jealous rivalry was the king's opportunity. Had not the clairvoyant preacher foretold that the Italian pitcher would soon shatter into a thousand pieces?

No sooner had Ludovico il Moro seized the ducal coronet of Milan than he inveigled the French king into his reckless campaign. While the condottieri dozed the Doge of Venice serenely looked the other way. For three months the Borgia Pope Alexander VI supported the new duke in the north. Then he betrothed his fourteen-year-old son to the daughter of the King of Naples. If the Papal States closed their borders the councillors would begin their chess-game. In the background loomed the menace of the French king and his artillery. One tower still barred the way to the south: Florence.

Pico della Mirandola had been presented to the king, then still under tutelage, nine years ago when he went to study theology at the Sorbonne. The twenty-two-year-old student and the fifteen-year-old monarch had gazed at each other's pointed noses and recognised that Power and Intellect had come together like Zeus and Hermes.

Less than three years later the king had had to protect his new friend from the papal inquisitors. When Lorenzo de' Medici subsequently offered Count Pico the hospitality of his territory the philosopher Ficino had exulted: 'Be glad that you can be a Florentine.' That was now more than ever debatable. King Charles VIII was before Genoa with eight thousand French nobles, five thousand Gascon crossbowmen and three thousand German halberdiers. The road to Florence beckoned. What was Piero de' Medici intending to do? Two cousins of Lorenzo's unloved son and successor had already gone over to the king. Who should Pico opt for: the Frenchman or the Florentine?

In the throng in front of the cathedral the good secretary Cristoforo di Casalmaggiore lost his master once and for all. Pico quickly found himself a place by the curtain that divided the men from the women like goats from sheep. Here every Sunday his soul found refreshment in the preacher's words.

Pungent incense cut through the reek of tallow candles and the sickly scent of flowers. High Mass began. A choir of angelic voices rose thinly to fill the cathedral's dome. Pico's weak eyes looked in vain for Angelo. Perhaps the canon was outside in the piazza, where hundreds of other devotees were still thirsting for the sermon.

After the lesson the door to the sacristy swung back. A black-and-white shade moved swiftly to the pulpit. The preacher mounted the steps and pushed back his hood. His black eyebrows, lapis-blue eyes and flesh-red bottom lip made his face look even paler. Today, Pico knew, 21 September 1494, his friend was celebrating his fortieth birthday.

Later he remembered how a shudder ran down his spine and the hairs on his neck stood on end when the Dominican began his homily in biblical Latin. *Ecce ego adducam aquas diluvii super terram.* Behold, I bring a flood of waters upon the earth to destroy all life under heaven. Thus He spoke, proclaiming the destruction of his own creation.

Once there had come a day on which the Lord repented that he had made man. He had said to Noah: 'The end of all flesh is come before me.' Such a day had now dawned once more. Did not the armies of the white lily threaten the city of the red lily? Was not a new Cyrus approaching the sinful Babylon that was Florence?

Women sobbed and men sighed. A gesture by the preacher calmed the turbulent waters below him. Where the Lord chastised, there He saved also. Had not the Lord bidden the patriarch to make a ship and to go into it with his wife and his children? Today the few remaining true believers must build another Ark and take refuge within it when the Lord should open the sluices of Heaven once more to engulf this city and all who dwelt in it.

From *The Phoenix* (De phoenix). Amsterdam: De Bezige Bij, 1998, pp. 14-17.
Translated by Tanis Guest.

Chiasmus

Your sighs
recall
my rise
and fall.

My call
replies
to all
your lies.

My groans
rehearse
your moans.

Your sighs,
my cries
converse.

From *Rebis.* Amsterdam:
De Bezige Bij, 1989.
Translated by Paul Claes.

Amor

Secretly coming and going
   I keep hiding my Soul:
should you happen to see her
   she would flee with your Love.

From *Glow / Feux* (Glans / Feux). Amsterdam: De Bezige Bij, 2000.
Originally written in Dutch ('Amor') and French ('Psyché') by Paul Claes;
English translation of 'Amor' by Paul Claes.

Amor

Heimelijk ga ik en kom
   en houd mijn Ziel zo geheim dat
als je haar eenmaal zou zien
   zij met je liefde vervloog.

Chiasme

Mijn stijgen
en dalen
herhalen
jouw hijgen.

Jouw zwijgen
vertalen
mijn dralen
en dreigen.

Jouw steunen,
mijn kreunen
wordt spreken.

Mijn beten,
jouw kreten
ons teken.

The Scar

O the red wound where
Heaven rudely maimed
Showed a sun inflamed
In a screaming air.

From the shaggy hair
Of a cloud has rained
Silent blood that stained
Desert with despair.

Not a single son
Of the blinded sky
Saw this setting sun

Without wondering why
Secrets had begun
With a scarlet cry.

From *Rebis*. Amsterdam: De Bezige Bij, 1989.
Originally written in English by Paul Claes.

Psyché

Je viens
Je vais
Vaurien
Discret

Qui tient
Ses traits
Si bien
Secrets

Que les
Scrutant
Un jour

Tu en
Perdrais
L'Amour

Paul Claes (1943-). Photo
by David Samyn.

imon Stevin,

Flemish Tutor to a Dutch Prince

Simon Stevin is best known for his introduction of decimal fractions, which later led to the establishment of the decimal system of weights and measures. But he was also the brains behind many technical inventions, of which the 28-passenger sailing chariot he built for use on the seashore was probably the best known to his contemporaries.

For those less familiar with Simon Stevin, he was born in Brugge in 1548, the illegitimate child of Anthuenis Stevin and Catelyne vander Poort. Recent research indicates his father may have been the youngest son of a burgomaster of Veurne. His mother was from a burgher family from Ieper (Ypres) with Calvinist leanings; she later married a merchant involved with the carpet-weaving and silk trades. Very little is known of Stevin's youth and education. His first job was in Antwerpen as a bookkeeper and cashier in one of the city's trading houses, where he became acquainted with business practice and methods. In 1577 he accepted a post with the financial administration of the *Brugse Vrije*, the region around the city of Brugge. A few years later we find him registered in Leiden, in the present-day Netherlands. Exactly why he emigrated to the North is not known; perhaps he disliked the Spanish oppression of the southern part of the Low Countries, or he may have had Protestant sympathies. In 1583 Stevin's name appears on the roll of the newly-founded University of Leiden, where the young Prince Maurits of Orange was attending courses.

A lifelong friendship developed between the two men. In Simon Stevin Prince Maurits found an excellent tutor and later a capable and loyal counsellor, while in return Stevin could count on the support and protection of his princely friend. When Maurits was elected Stadholder of Holland and Zeeland in 1584 he appointed Stevin to his personal service. According to some sources Stevin was Quartermaster-General of the State Army. A journal and a corresponding ledger have recently been discovered in the *Rijksarchief* (Public Record Office) in Den Haag. The ledger, which dates from 1604, has been identified as Stevin's practical application of his ideas on 'princely' bookkeeping; it includes an entry for Stevin's annual salary of 600 Dutch guilders – a considerable sum which confirms Stevin's high status at the Prince's court. In 1600, on the Prince's initiative, Stevin founded

Sailing chariot. Lithograph by J.G. Canneel (19th century).
Universiteitsbibliotheek, Gent. Photo courtesy of De Biekorf, Brugge.

a school of engineering at Leiden University; one unusual feature was that it offered courses taught in Dutch ('*Nederduyts*') rather than Latin. Several authors mention Stevin's extensive travels throughout Europe; unfortunately, though, we have only indirect evidence for these, such as city and harbour plans to be found in his works. Of the many journeys he presumably made there is only one known record: a visit to Danzig (now Gdansk in Poland), where he was invited to provide expert advice on harbour works. In about 1614, at the age of 66, Stevin married the much younger Catharina Cray. The couple had four children: Frederic, Hendrik, Susanna and Levina. The second son, Hendrik, published some of his father's works posthumously. Simon Stevin died in Den Haag some time between 20 February and early April 1620, probably in the house on Raamstraat which he had purchased in 1612 for 3,800 Dutch guilders.

Engineer and scientist

Simon Stevin has always had a special place in the collective memory of the people of the Low Countries, where there are many streets and squares named after him. In 1846 a bronze statue of him was unveiled in Brugge, his birthplace, amid great festivities. There are also a whole range of organisations that bear his name, including such diverse bodies as Simon Stevin sailing clubs in the Netherlands and in Belgium, a Simon Stevin student organisation for electromechanical engineers at the Technische Universiteit Eindhoven, several Simon Stevin observatories, a Simon Stevin technical institute for architecture, health sciences and management, as well as a Simon Stevin Foundation concerned with promoting the study, conservation and restoration of fortifications.

In addition, Stevin's influence can still be felt today in a variety of scientific organisations and instances. An international Simon Stevin exchange programme operates between eight History of Science Departments in the Netherlands, the United Kingdom and North America. Every year the Technologiestichting STW (Dutch Foundation for Technology) awards the prestigious title of *Simon Stevin Meester* (Simon Stevin Master) to an outstanding researcher in the field of technology. The individual so honoured also receives the generous sum of 1 million Dutch guilders . The education section of the BBC website devotes four pages to Stevin under the heading 'local heroes'. Then there is the Belgian scientific journal '*Simon Stevin, wis-en natuurkundig tijdschrift*' (Simon Stevin, Journal for Mathematics and Physics), now the Journal of the Belgian Mathematical Society. Distinguished authors included Stevin, along with such eminent figures as Pascal, Babbage, Hollerith, von Neumann and Zuse, in a list of some ten individuals whose work, vision and technological skill made possible the development of modern computers; and his *De Thiende* (The Disme) features in the famous Philadelphia list *Printing and the Mind of Man,* which highlights books that have had an impact on the evolution of Western civilisation – one of only 65 books listed for the sixteenth century. To mark the 400th anniversary of Stevin's birth in 1948 the Belgian Royal Academy of Sciences, Letters and Fine Arts devoted an entire 112-page issue of its journal to him. In 1995 an exhibition on Stevin's works was held in the Biekorf, the city library of Brugge and home to many unique historical manuscripts. And in 1998 the Central Library of the Universiteit Gent organised a Stevin exhibition, comparing works by him in the library's possession with those of his contemporaries. The catalogues that accompanied these exhibitions provide a good overview of current knowledge about the great scholar and scientist. On 11 and 12 December 1998 a *Simon Stevin Bruggelinck* (Simon Stevin of Bruges) Symposium organised by the present authors and Dr C. van den Heuvel, then from Den Haag but now in Maastricht, was held in Brugge, at which specialists from the Netherlands, Denmark and Belgium explored Stevin's importance for science in general, for the liberal arts and for technology.

In the last fifty years there has been no shortage of publications devoted to Stevin. It would take too long to list them all, so we shall mention only a few important examples. One of the most famous Dutch historians of science, E.J. Dijksterhuis, together with some of his colleagues, produced a very extensive study of Stevin's collected works in which a large part of his work is reproduced with a commentary and a modern English translation. Dirk Struik, a Dutch professor of mathematics at the Massachusetts Institute of Technology, gives his personal views on science in the Golden Age and also devotes a significant amount of space to Stevin. The volume *Geschiedenis van de wetenschappen in België van de Oudheid tot 1815*, (The History of the Sciences in Belgium from Ancient Times to 1815, published in 1998) deals extensively with Stevin's work, especially in the contribution by Prof. Paul Bockstaele.

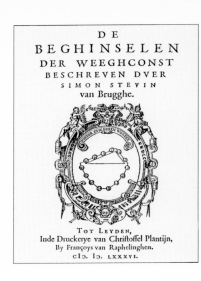

Title-page of *De Beghinselen der Weeghconst* (The Elements of the Art of Weighing, 1586), showing Stevin's

Innovative ideas

Many of Stevin's contributions and endeavours have long been recognised as pioneering or influential, and these still attract great interest today. One of the first books he published was *Tafelen van Interest* (Tables of Interest, 1582) which for the first time in Western Europe made interest tables available to all. Until then they had existed only in manuscript form, with copies being sold for very high prices to tradesmen, merchants and bankers. And Stevin was certainly the first to produce a complete description of decimal fractions and the operations that can be carried out with them in his pamphlet – mentioned above- entitled *De Thiende* (The Disme, 1585) in which he also dealt with their practical applications in surveying, the measurement of weights and the subdivision of money. Robert Norton's English translation of the pamphlet, *Disme, The Art of Tenths, or Decimall Arithmeticke. Invented by Simon Stevin* (London, 1608), inspired Thomas Jefferson's proposal of a decimal monetary unit for the new United States of America; to this day the tenth part of the American dollar is called a dime. The Scottish mathematician and theological writer John Napier also drew on Stevin's work in his invention of logarithms. In his works on physics Stevin was again a fount of new and innovative ideas. His *De Beghinselen der Weeghconst* (The Elements of the Art of Weighing, 1586) outlines the study of statics of rigid bodies. It contains the fabulous '*clootcrans*' or 'wreath of spheres' theorem, a most ingenious thought-experiment by which one can find the condition of equilibrium of weights on different inclined planes. This theorem enabled Stevin to obtain the composition law of two concurrent forces by the parallelogram rule. In *De Beghinselen des Waterwichts* (The Elements of Hydrostatics, 1586) Stevin gave an improved demonstration of Archimedes' law about the upward force acting on a body immersed in a liquid. He also succeeded in calculating the force exerted by a fluid on the bottom and walls of the vessel in which it is contained. And this led him

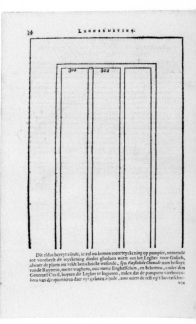

Design method for army camps, in *Castrametatio, dat is Legermeting* (Castrametatio, or the Marking out of Army

to formulate the so-called hydrostatic paradox many years before Blaise Pascal, to whom it is usually attributed. In 1586 Stevin published his experiment in which two spheres of lead, one ten times as heavy as the other, were dropped from a church tower in Delft and fell 30 feet, according to his account, in the same time. Stevin's report preceded Galileo's first treatise on gravity by 3 years and his theoretical work on falling bodies by 18 years.

In the service of Maurits and the Republic

From 1590 onwards Stevin worked mainly in the service of Prince Maurits. Here the recent exhibition *Maurits, prins van Oranje* (Maurice, Prince of Orange) at the Rijksmuseum in Amsterdam has been very helpful, contributing to a better understanding of the interaction between Stevin and Maurits. The exhibition catalogue goes into considerable detail about their relationship. It would seem that from 1590 on most of Stevin's publications were on topics of interest to Maurits or to the nation. In 1590 he published a pamphlet entitled *Vita Politica, Het Burgherlick Leven* (Civic Life) in which he sets out how a citizen, as a good subject, should comply with the rules laid down by the authorities. This was the time when the Republic of the Provinces of the Netherlands was being set up, and Stevin wrote his pamphlet *inter alia* in order to promote order and regularity. In the same spirit he published two books of practical use for the defence of the country and the expansion of the fleet. In *De Stercktenbouwing* (The Building of Fortresses, 1594) he modified the new Italian system of fortification to suit the geographical conditions and available means of the Low Countries, with the result that his name is still associated with what is known as the 'old Dutch' method of fortification. This book was probably used as course material by the engineering school in Leiden. In the second book, *De Havenvinding* (The Haven-Finding Art, 1599) Stevin described how to determine a place's location on the earth's surface by knowing its geographical latitude and the magnetic variation of the compass needle. This method proved extremely valuable to the ships of the VOC (The Verenigde Oost-Indische Compagnie, the Dutch East India Company), which had established a monopoly of trade between the (Far) East and Western Europe. Between 1605 and 1608 the textbooks he had produced for Prince Maurits in numerous sciences (algebra, geography, astronomy, bookkeeping, statics and hydrostatics, perspective etc.) were collected and published under the title *Wisconstige Gedachtenissen* (Mathematical Memoirs). His last publication, in 1617, was a double volume: in *Castrametatio, dat is Legermeting* (Castrametatio, or the Marking out of Army Camps) he describes how to set up and equip a well-organised military camp, and in *Nieuwe Maniere van Sterctebou door Spilsluysen* (New Manner of Fortification Using Spindle-Sluices) how to use special sluices he had just invented in defensive works, mainly to maintain an appropriate depth of water in moats.

As well as the well-known aspects of his work, Stevin's less generally known contributions are now attracting increasing interest and appreciation. In his *Van de Spiegeling der Singconst* (Theory of the Art of Singing) – the manuscript of which was discovered in 1884 by Bierens de Haan – he was the first to propound a correct theory of the division of the octave into twelve equal intervals. In *Van de Verschaeuwing* (On Perspective), part of the *Wisconstige Gedachtenissen*, he was the first to build on the pioneering work of Guidobaldo del Monte. He devised new and fundamental theorems on

fabulous '*clootcrans*' or 'wreath of spheres' theorem. Photo courtesy of De Biekorf, Brugge.

Camps, 1617). Koninklijke Bibliotheek, Den Haag. Photo courtesy of De Biekorf, Brugge.

projections, some of which can be found attributed to him in the works of celebrated mathematicians. Considerable attention is also being paid to the influence of Stevin's ideas on architecture, house-building and town planning. His thoughts on these subjects are set out in *Van de Oirdening der deelen eens huys* (House Planning) and *Van de Oirdening der Steden* (Town Planning) included in *the Materiae Politicae, Burgherlicke Stoffen* (Civic Matters, 1649) published by his son Hendrik. This material is only a small part of a projected much larger work entitled *Huysbou* (House - Building) that Stevin planned but never published. Sections of the hand-written manuscript of *Huysbou* were partially reproduced in the Journal of Isaac Beeckman and discovered in 1905 in the Rijksarchief (Public Record Office) of the Province of Zeeland in the Netherlands. They show the importance of Stevin's ideas for the history of civil architectural techniques in his time.

Stevin published most of his works in Dutch, his mother tongue, rather than in Latin. His aim was to bring science and technology to people outside academic circles, who knew no Latin but had some understanding of the sciences or of technology. In the introduction to *De Thiende* he lists the categories of people for whom he wrote the pamphlet: star-gazers, surveyors, carpet-makers, wine-gaugers, mintmasters and merchants of all kinds. In his *Uytspraeck vande Weerdicheyt der Duytsche Tael* (Discourse on the Worth of the Dutch Language) written as an introduction to the *Beghinselen der Weeghconst*, Stevin outlined his views on his native language in some detail. In his opinion 'Nederduytsch' was exceptionally well-suited to expressing ideas, particularly scientific ideas, because of its short words and the readiness with which it formed word-combinations. Stevin deserves great credit for enriching the Dutch language by introducing new words or combining existing ones to translate their Latin counterparts. A typical example is the modern Dutch word for mathematics, '*wiskunde*', which derives from Stevin's '*wisconst*'. In 1992 M. Kool published a careful analysis of the neologisms and semantic neologisms introduced by Stevin in the field of arithmetic.

Stevin was highly esteemed not only by famous scientists but by his contemporaries, as is clear from the writings of Willebrord Snellius, William Gilbert, Isaac Beeckman, Constantijn and Christiaan Huygens and Adrianus Romanus (Adriaan van Roomen). This last praised Stevin for his statics and for his sailing chariot. Beeckman reproduced some of Stevin's manuscripts, which he had borrowed from Stevin's widow, in his Journal. Hugo de Groot or Grotius, the 'father of international law', was another who expressed great admiration for his work. In later times no lesser personages than Lagrange in his *Traité de Mécanique analytique*, Ernst Mach in *Die Mechanik in ihrer Entwicklung historisch-kritisch dargestellt* and Feynman in the famous *Feynman Lectures* referred admiringly to Stevin's work.

In short, it is very clear that Simon Stevin occupies an important place in the history of the Low Countries and in the realms of science and technology, civic matters and also of music.

JOZEF T. DEVREESE and GUIDO VANDEN BERGHE

The authors of this article have also written a book on Stevin, which will be published in the course of 2002 by the Flemish Davidsfonds publishers.

Scientific and technical Dutch

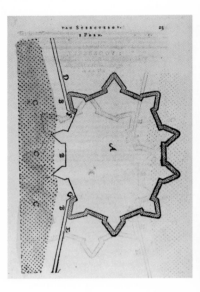

A design for the use of spindle-sluices, as pictured in *Nieuwe Maniere van Sterctebou door Spilsluysen* (New Manner of Fortification Using Spindle-Sluices, 1617). Photo courtesy of De Biekorf, Brugge.

ohan

Goudsblom: More than a Sociologist

The most interesting cultural figures are often the most difficult to catego-
rise. A man like Johan Goudsblom (1932-) would be described in *Who's
Who* as a sociologist. That description is not incorrect, it is merely incomplete. Readers of his work will get to know not only a sociologist but also a
poet, a historian of ideas, a cultural historian, and more. That is why someone such as myself, whose main interest is not sociology, can write about
this intellectual from Amsterdam in a publication not primarily intended for
sociologists. That context allows me the freedom to focus on Goudsblom's
more general writings rather than on his sociological work. However, in
comparing the two types of work I shall be tempted to make one or two critical remarks about certain pretensions inherent in the discipline of sociology.

To begin with that last point: at a gathering of academics I once heard
another academic sociologist – he was a student of Goudsblom's, so this is
not really a digression – claim that the history of Siena in the late Middle
Ages could be explained in three ways. It could be explained in terms of the
transition from a feudal to a city state; it could be interpreted in the manner
of Norbert Elias, and it could be considered from a Marxist perspective. The
sociologist then went on to relate the history of Siena in a way that prompted me to wonder which of the three approaches he was using. A pointless
question, of course, because the speaker had only intended to make a me-
thodologically-correct gesture. The rest of his argument dealt with the subject itself, namely the description and interpretation of documents and objects in archives and museums. He was careful not to give his interpretations
in triplicate, although this would have been consistent with his introduction.

What sociologists appear to be trying to do is not simply to provide historical accounts (this would not distinguish them from historians), but to see
historical events as 'instantiations' of general sociological laws. Sociologists of various persuasions debate the nature of those laws, while non-so-
ciologists wonder if any purely sociological law has ever been formulated at
all. If it has, then there must be sociological analyses – of the history of universal suffrage, for example – that have a greater capacity to explain, and
provide greater insight than purely historical descriptions of the same process. But I do not believe that such analyses exist.

The unbearable lightness of 'figuration'

Goudsblom's readers are confronted with the same problem. Take, for example, his work *Fire and Civilization* (Vuur en beschaving, 1992), a history of how man has learned to control and use fire. Goudsblom sees this as a *sociological* subject because '*in order to subdue fire, they had to subdue each other and themselves*'. He succeeds in convincing the reader that the one is not possible without the other, but the extent to which sociology contributes to the historical argument is less clear. I am afraid that contribution is merely a verbal one, as I shall attempt to show with an example.

A number of terms used by Goudsblom are borrowed from Norbert Elias, in particular from his work *The Civilizing Process* (1939). Goudsblom's description of the history of the use of fire is a variant on Elias' description of the history of etiquette. Both developments were made possible by man's increasing ability to conquer his impulses, and the increasing social regulation of individual behaviour. The use of fire involves a third form of control also referred to by Elias: the control of nature.

Johan Goudsblom (1932-). Photo by Klaas Koppe.

The Eliatic term most frequently used by Goudsblom in *Fire and Civilization* is 'figuration'. Let us consider whether this term is really necessary to explain something that could not be expressed without it. The answer to that can help us answer another, more general question: do theories such as those in *Fire and Civilisation* contain elements that cannot be classified under a non-sociological discipline such as history?

What is figuration? The cover of the Dutch edition of Goudsblom's *Sociology in the Balance* (Balans van de sociologie, 1974) introduces the concept: '*The photo used in the cover shows an inflatable cushion of the type you may find in a children's playground. This is a large plastic cushion filled with water, which can hold a great many climbing, jumping, dancing children at the same time. The weight of each child makes an impression in the surface of the cushion, causing an increase in outward pressure at other points on the cushion. The children move over the cushion in ever-changing groups, causing movements that none of them can control for long. They are therefore continually forced to adapt to those movements. This mercurial scene is a graphic and lively illustration of the social figurations between people*'. Here, Goudsblom has found a fine metaphor for the interdependencies that characterise human society. But the metaphor also tells us a great deal about the status of the concept of figuration. The *physical* figurations can be translated into differential equations that exactly express how the upward pressure increases at a particular point, as forces change in size and direction at other points. It is virtually impossible to describe this physical analysis without using technical terms from physics (such as 'force', 'acceleration', etc.) and mathematics ('derivative', 'integral', etc.). The analysis cannot be expressed in everyday language without losing some of its substance. And that is where this type of language differs from the language of sociology: in using the image of the cushion to illustrate sociological phenomena, there is *nothing* than can only be expressed by using technical terms such as 'figuration'. What I am arguing here on the basis of a single passage from *Sociology in the Balance* is equally true for every passage in that book, and also in *Fire and Civilization*, that contains the term 'figuration'.

What Goudsblom, following Elias, refers to as 'figuration' could also be called 'interaction', 'interdependence' and so on. Indeed, Goudsblom himself sometimes uses these and other synonyms. This alone proves that the term is a colloquial one. This does not mean that the word should be avoided, but it does mean that it does not teach us anything new. Neither does it justify the recognition of a separate branch of science known as figurational sociology.

Is does not lead to *ought*

After this general criticism, which is intended to explain how it is possible to like Goudsblom and at the same time dislike sociology, I will now attempt to describe Goudsblom's sociological work. Because that would require more than one or two pages, I will concentrate on three works that mark the beginning, middle and later stages of his academic career. Those works are: *Nihilism and Culture* (Nihilisme en cultuur), the thesis with which the 28-year-old Goudsblom gained his doctorate in 1960; *Sociology in the Balance*, a survey of sociology setting out Goudsblom's own theoretical principles, which he later applied in a wide-ranging context in the third work, *Fire and Civilization*.

Nihilism and Culture is a detailed analysis of nihilism, largely based on the work of Nietzsche, intended to illustrate how 'culturological' research should be done. Talcott Parsons, a leading sociologist in the 1950s, identified three components in human behaviour: a psychological component, a social component and a cultural component. Culturology is the study of the third component: the influence of cultural forms on human behaviour (and is therefore not the same as cultural science, which concentrates on the forms themselves: language, literature, art, religion).

It is not for me to judge whether Goudsblom's analysis of nihilism is useful to sociologists. However, I would say that Goudsblom's first book is still a fine overview of Nietzsche's thought and of nihilistic philosophical issues. The nihilist denies all values, or, rather: he denies that values have any foundation. Hume provided the clearest argument for that: *is* can never lead to *ought*, in other words: values cannot be based on facts. But dyed-in-the-wool nihilists would go a step further: not only are values baseless, truth is baseless too. The much-praised ideal, whereby the whole edifice of knowledge is based on an unquestionable foundation of 'primitive' facts, must be seen as an illusion. Also an illusion, therefore, is the Socratic method: '*that one should make use of all one's faculties to get at the truth*' as the only acceptable guideline for one's acts, as Goudsblom summarises it.

One could ask, in the light of this claim that truth and values are baseless, what is wrong with being permanently willing to review one's own beliefs (provisional truths), and recognising that values are no more than preferences, sometimes passionate and often shared with many other people? Nietzsche's intellectual temperament precluded such an approach. He wrestled, as the Socratic method dictates, with a powerful '*Trieb zur Wahrheit*' ('urge for truth'), which forbade him to give in to the temptation of '*lebenserhaltende Irrtümer*', as they are referred to in *Die fröhliche Wissenschaft*. However, his nihilistic approach did not allow him to reconcile his search for truth with his Socratic desire to see truth as the guiding principle of all human acts.

In nihilism, and in Nietzsche's interpretation of it, the central theme is the relationship between cultural elements (in this case philosophical arguments) and human conduct. The analysis of nihilism is therefore a good example of what Goudsblom would refer to as 'culturology'.

Scope

Strangely, the term 'culturology' does not occur anywhere in *Sociology in the Balance* (English edition 1977), despite the fact that this work is intended as a critical and systematic survey of sociology. There is an explanation for this: while he was writing *Sociology in the Balance,* Goudsblom was greatly influenced by the work of Norbert Elias, for whom the concept of *civilisation* plays a role that renders the concept of culture more or less superfluous. The 'division of labour' between sociology, psychology and culturology ceases to exist in Elias' work, in which the three theories of human behaviour are completely absorbed into the history of civilisation. Although Goudsblom quoted Elias in *Nihilism and Culture*, it was not until the 1970s that he came to recognise Elias's work as formative for the discipline of sociology.

Sociology in the Balance is both a summary of the development of sociology and a critique of it. To achieve this in a clear and systematic way requires criteria by which sociological theories can be assessed. Goudsblom defines four criteria: precision, systematics, scope and relevance (social purpose). Scope is the most important of these criteria, and is not fulfilled if, for example, social phenomena are isolated from their social context. This was the case, for example, in the much-quoted Hawthorne study: '*An industrial sociology which is so narrowly confined to the specific situation within a factory can yield little more than precise factual information of a very limited scope. The same is true of other empirical specialisms: if they are not informed by a broader orientation, their findings are necessarily impaired by the illusion that longer-term developments and further-reaching interdependencies are of no importance.*'

This ties up with the rejection of *reification*, which considers abstractions as facts of nature rather than as human inventions. Reification leads one to see static 'elements' where there are only processes: for example, the concept of bureaucracy as opposed to the process of bureaucratisation. The criterion of scope requires sociology to recognise historical developments, not just study fixed stages. The most all-embracing development is human evolution, even though sociology only deals with the processes – often centuries-long – of social development that have taken place during the most recent phase of evolution.

Notably, Goudsblom not only *uses* the criteria of precision, systematics, scope and relevance to test sociological theories, he also *assesses* them. Precision, systematics and relevance are indeed important, but Goudsblom warns above all against pseudo-precision, pseudo-systematics, and relevance that degenerates into partiality. The opposite applies to the scope criterion: Goudsblom recognises that a broad perspective can result in unacceptable vagueness, but emphasises the need for wide-ranging research and criticises theories that do not meet this requirement. This line of thought again reflects the extent to which Goudsblom has been influenced by Elias, whose work deals primarily with long-term social processes.

Goudsblom deals with one example of such long-term historical development in *Fire and Civilization*. In this book he describes how, from the time *homo erectus* first learnt to use fire – probably some 400,000 years ago – up to the present age of nuclear fission, man's increasing ability to use fire has meant that he also had to learn to control that ability itself. According to Goudsblom: '*As the human capacity to* control *fire has increased, so has people's inclination to* depend *upon social arrangements guaranteeing its regular availability and minimising the hazards it involves.*' Goudsblom's description of this long historical process is an excellent illustration of Elias's three forms of control: control of nature, control of social relationships, and control of man's impulses. *Fire and Civilization* is such a fascinating book and so beautifully written that I do not feel it is necessary to consider whether it should be categorised as a sociological account or, as I suggested earlier, as history.

Saved by style

Goudsblom is a sociologist who writes exceptionally well, which is unusual in a discipline that has long been an object of satire thanks to its proneness to drivel. There are some sociologists, such as Bourdieu, who have nothing to say – and say it in the most exciting way. And there are sociologists who carry out empirical research, but describe their findings in off-putting academic jargon: '*The author thus takes as a point of departure our conclusion from the analysis by Litwak et al. of the relationships between organisations and primary groups, namely the conclusion that inter-organisational networks can be seen as the foundation from which organisations attempt to influence each other*'.[1] This is the prose of a fellow sociologist from Leiden, not light-years away from Amsterdam but a mere 25 km; not separated from Goudsblom by centuries but only by a few years.

If a sociologist who writes well is a *rara avis*, then a sociologist who produces poetry and literary prose is truly unique. Many of Goudsblom's earliest writings, published in the 1950s in the Amsterdam student weekly *Propria Cures*, were miracles of style and ingenuity. They had little to do with sociology – indeed, one might ask: what *were* they actually about? In keeping with *Propria Cures* as it was then, they are best described as stylistic exercises *à la* Queneau. The anthology *Reserves* (1998, containing all of a collection published in 1958) contains good examples of Goudsblom's early work, and the poetry and aphorisms it contains testify to the fact that hidden in the sociologist there has always been the man of letters. This anthology contains less successful pieces, as all anthologies do, but the best of them are so beautiful that they have earned Goudsblom a place in Dutch literature. Gerrit Komrij recognised this – he included one of Goudsblom's poems in his well-known anthology *Dutch poetry of the nineteenth and twentieth century in a thousand and then some poems* (De Nederlandse poëzie van de negentiende en twintigste eeuw in duizend en enige gedichten): '*My higher self and I / fought it out to the end. / My higher self succumbed / – oh, what a godsend.*'

The second volume of *Reserves* contains a number of aphorisms that betray the author's sociological interests, for example '*Work ennobles. A bourgeois expression*', which certainly has no academic pretensions – and needs none. I suspect, however, that the same cannot be said of '*Sociologists saw the rules, historians the exceptions. What next? The system in the exceptions*'. As the reader will realise by now, I cannot determine – either from Goudsblom's sociological work or the work of any other sociologist known to me – whether the first part of that statement is true. As far as the second part is concerned, I expect no clarification at all from sociologists. In so far as Goudsblom and his colleagues have made a contribution to scholarship, it is a contribution to history, with an emphasis on the origins of human relations. However, it is difficult to conceive of history that is not based on this anyway. Sociology as a means to increased historical understanding appears to be as unproductive as that forgotten but once-promising method: the use of psychological theories (such as psychoanalysis) in giving historical explanations.

A sociologist such as Goudsblom is exempt from the scepticism that surrounds sociology. His exceptional erudition and stylistic skills have earned him a place in historiography with work that, in name at least, belongs to the discipline of sociology. The reader of *Fire and Civilization* is not in the least interested in the title of the author's chair. And those who happen to know it will cry: 'that man is too good for sociology.'

PETER WESLY
Translated by Yvette Mead.

NOTE

1. LAMMERS C.J., *Organisaties vergelijkenderwijs*. Utrecht 1998, p. 198. The passage is also a clear example of another characteristic that sociologists have in common with philosophers, namely the tendency to discuss the writings of other sociologists or philosophers instead of solving sociological or philosophical problems.

SOME PUBLICATIONS IN ENGLISH

GOUDSBLOM, JOHAN, *Dutch Society*. New York, 1967.
GOUDSBLOM, JOHAN, *Sociology in the Balance*. A Critical Essay. Oxford, 1977.
GOUDSBLOM, JOHAN, *Nihilism and Culture*. Oxford, 1980.
GOUDSBLOM, JOHAN, *Fire and Civilization*. London, 1992.
GOUDSBLOM, JOHAN, ERIC L. JONES and STEPHEN MENNELL, *The Course of Human History: Economic Growth, Social Process, and Civilization*. Armonk (NY), 1996.

hronicle

Dasein, Empathetic Architecture, or Poetry in Concrete?
The Architecture of Paul Robbrecht and Hilde Daem

In this age of speed and virtualisation, the architecture of Paul Robbrecht and Hilde Daem has a comforting effect. It could even be described as essential, because it creates existential spaces that assert themselves in a globalised world in which everything is reduced to the lowest common denominator. Robbrecht & Daem, who received the Culture Award from the Catholic University of Leuven in 2001, define spaces and give architecture a meaning that draws the mind into a process of awakening.

In a sort of literary encore to the monograph *Works in Architecture / Paul Robbrecht & Hilde Daem* (Werk in architectuur / Paul Robbrecht & Hilde Daem, 1998), the Spanish visual artist Juan Muñoz writes to his friend Paul Robbrecht that his house is essential to him: '*What is important to me, and seems to me the most fundamental thing, is that the house is as vital to me as my rage.*' Here, Muñoz is talking about a garden pavilion: '*I don't want a house to lie low in, like some ridiculous hideaway. I want to walk through this garden at night; I want to walk among the trees towards your building, turning on the lamps, and when I reach it: meet myself.*'

In his letter Muñoz appears not to shy away from the more serious aspects of architecture. On the contrary: he lays bare the very essence of Robbrecht & Daem's entire oeuvre. The architecture of Robbrecht & Daem is just as necessary as Muñoz's house. In their work, one can conveniently assume that the existential need for architecture is bound up with the need for art.

Close cooperation with artists such as Dan Graham, Isa Genzken, Raoul de Keyser, Gerhard Richter, and many others has undoubtedly influenced the work of Robbrecht & Daem. And each relationship produced a series of functional spaces. The design for the extension to the Boijmans van Beuningen Museum in Rotterdam, for example, reveals a unique relationship to art. Together with the museum's director Chris Dercon, the architects redefined their brief: the planned extension to the museum complex had to incorporate a redefinition of the exhibition spaces. The aim of architect and client was to create the museum of the twenty-first century. In the book *Works in Architecture* it is argued that this is a justified aim because: '*in this museum, the visitor and the way in which he experiences the museum are more important than the works of art on display. Because, ultimately, collecting and displaying art, and art history and art criticism too, only have meaning if they add something to our lives, or at the very least change us or help us understand the age in which we live; or if they simply provide a moment of enjoyment – a moment of artistic recreation.*'

Robbrecht and Daem's design embodies all aspects of this vision. Their interventions express two basic principles: the compression of the 'museological organism' and the porosity of the surrounding walls. The new museum is a compression of the building as well as the city. The museum has been made, as it were, more compact, more intelligible to the public.

During the past twenty years, Robbrecht & Daem have built up a consistent oeuvre in which echoes of art constantly resonate: houses for art(ists), integrated art projects, galleries, exhibitions, museums, a museum square in Antwerp, a concert hall in Bruges... Moreover, since 1992 – the year in which they designed the temporary exhibition pavilions for Documenta IX in Kassel – Robbrecht & Daem's oeuvre has acquired an international reputation, as can be seen in the alterations to the Boijmans van Beuningen Museum in Rotterdam and the conversion of the Kunstsammlung Wirt in St Gallen, Switzerland.

Looking back to 1986, when Robbrecht used light-

Robbrecht & Daem, new concert hall in Bruges, 2002. Photo by Kristien Daem.

Robbrecht & Daem's conversion of a railway depot into an exhibition hall, St Gallen (Switzerland), 2000. Photo by Marcel Koch.

weight blocks and a wafer-thin layer of plaster to 'build' *A Wall for a Painting – A Floor for a Sculpture* it would appear that, even then, he was seeking to transform the ephemeral exhibition into a piece of architecture. Today, sixteen years later, this modest intervention has become almost a paradigm for Robbrecht's work, namely to make architecture serve art without renouncing its autonomy or its responsibility to life.

Robbrecht believes that architecture, in contrast to art, hardly needs to prove itself: '*Architecture is accepted. Not only that, there is a permanent demand for it; it is required. That is not so with the visual arts. The energy contained in art is used to perform acts which no-one has asked for. At best, if those acts are powerful enough, they will eventually become incontrovertible facts.*' Robbrecht believes that it is essential to distinguish between art and architecture, because that distinction allows us to combine them to create what he calls '*unforgettable places*'. In this sense he agrees with Muñoz, who claims that unforgettable places do not refer to themselves, nor do they represent anything outside themselves, but they seek an encounter with another individuality. The insistence on such an encounter is indeed a key element in Robbrecht's architecture. An excellent example of this is the concrete gallery that Robbrecht & Daem designed around a bank in a village near Aalst. The porticos bore little or no relation to the function of the bank, but they provided a distinct framework for the nearby bus stop so that the street was immediately transformed into a meeting place. This notion of encounter, of being absorbed into a collective happening, is also expressed in the design for the new concert hall in Bruges (2002). In addition to the central concert hall and conference room, Robbrecht & Daem worked with Van Langen on a design for the chamber-music room. The tower-like structure encloses a cortile – an inner courtyard in the manner of a Spanish or Italian *palazzo* – around which are a series of platforms arranged in a spiral. The staircase-like design allows contact between members of the audience during chamber music concerts or jazz sessions in a single *Gesammtkunstwerk* .

In their work, Robbrecht and Daem take a conscious stand against the modernist obsession with dematerialising architecture and removing the distinction between interior and exterior. Unlike Gerrit Rietveld, the protagonist of the 1920s *De Stijl* movement in the Netherlands who dreamed of architecture without materials, Robbrecht resolutely chooses an architecture that is 'carried by' materials. His design for a garden pavilion in Vosselare, for example, takes the form of an outlandish polyform space, a sort of veiled shrine, the interior of which is shielded by a strongly vertical lattice of brass, a heavy material that also weathers to a patina. This attention to patina, or a phenomenon such as 'wet acoustics', the fascination with wetness of stone in the rain, or the light shining through alabaster or a stained glass window… all are tangible manifestations of an unseen physicality, of sensuality.

The exhibition pavilions for Documenta IX in Kassel are a striking example of Robbrecht's work. These temporary structures were designed to resemble train carriages, arranged in a tangential formation in a romantic park. They present an image of movement stilled, of emptiness, of meeting and parting, and of a tragic dynamism. While the carriage-like spaces were housing works of art, thousands of refugees from the Eastern Block were packed together in crowded trains, waiting to cross the Czech / German border.

The Aue pavilions draw on images of trains, the holocaust and stations, but Robbrecht also likes to draw on architectural history. It is not surprising that he has a deep appreciation for the Baroque, which developed as a theatrical form of 'emo'-architecture. As a newly-qualified architect, Robbrecht used the money from the Godercharle Prize to study the Italian renaissance architect Andrea Palladio. Remarkably, through the use of scrolls and art-historical anecdote, Robbrecht is able to evoke the intrinsic structure of that architecture. He transforms order, light, space, materiality and the theatrical effect of baroque style into contemporary idiom, as can be seen in his recent conversion of a railway depot at St Gallen in Switzerland into an exhibition hall. Within the authoritarian, radial structure of the *Lockremise* (locomotive shed), the exhibition spaces are defined by a new series of walls, some of which reflect the structure of the existing building, while others expressly do not. The sensitivity of this treatment lies in the use of abstract cornices to define the walls. The cornices accentuate the exhibition space, at the same time introducing a sort of 'front and back' hierarchy. The fragile equilibrium that is achieved between a pronounced respect for the soul of the existing building and a formal, resolute intervention produces a mythical sense of wonder.

It could perhaps be said that the architecture of Paul Robbrecht and Hilde Daem is the product of a personal mythology. Whether we refer to it as 'conquering the Baroque' or as 'empathic architecture', the fact remains that at the end of the twentieth century, Robbrecht & Daem create spaces that, as a sort of 'applied mythology', evoke primitive human experience in a way that is completely in keeping with a post-modern culture. That mythology couples the power of construction with the act of art.

KOEN VAN SYNGHEL
Translated by Yvette Mead.

A Temporary 'Naturalisation'
Translators' Houses in Amsterdam and Leuven

Translation does not happen in a vacuum. In other words: a good command of two languages is not enough to produce a good translation. A thorough insight into the cultural context of both source and target languages is vitally important, as the pitfalls are not solely of the linguistic kind. A fine example of this is the American food producer Gerber's venture into Africa. They used the same packaging to sell their baby-food range in Africa as for their home market: a colourful label with a picture of a healthy ruddy-cheeked white baby. They later discovered that African companies normally illustrate the ingredients of a product on the label, because a substantial number of the buyers are illiterate. So it would have been better for Gerber if their marketing team had done some on-the-spot research in advance.

The same applies to the translator of literary texts. When Nelleke van Maaren, Dutch translator and secretary to the Board of the Dutch Literary Production and Translation Fund from 1991 to 2000, spent a few months in Berlin in the 1980s while translating the work of Botho Strauss, she discovered how personally stimulating it could be to live for a while in the environment where the book originated. Some European countries already had at that time a translators' residence for this purpose. In France, for example, this was the old Van Gogh hospital in Arles. Van Maaren asked herself why the Netherlands still had no place where translators of Dutch-language books could stay, to breathe in the local atmosphere and culture. Or as she herself put it: '*No matter how good and grammatically correct the translators' command of Dutch is, an extended stay in the Netherlands is a prerequisite to learning to differentiate between the various manners of speech, understand typical expressions or to reflect the sounds of the streets. You cannot learn that from books, you have to experience it for yourself.*'

It took a lot of effort, but in February 1992 it finally happened. Van Maaren had collected enough subsidy from a number of organisations to open a Translators' House in premises on Anthony van Dijckstraat in Amsterdam-South, where two translators at a time could live and get down to work on Dutch literature. But bigger and better things were dreamed of. That dream was realised in 1995 when the then Secretary of State Aad Nuis allocated an extra million guilders for translation policy. The object was to maintain the momentum of the successful progress made by translated Dutch literature after the 1993 Frankfurt Book Fair, which particularly featured Flanders and the Netherlands. That sizeable sum went to the Production Fund, which in turn advised the Secretary of State to spend the money on a larger, well-equipped Translators' House.

On Tuesday 27 May 1997 the new residence on Van Breestraat opened its doors. The property had been extensively rebuilt to provide five fully-furnished one-room apartments complete with computer, printer, radio and telephone. On the ground floor is a comprehensive library with Dutch literature, dictionaries, CD-ROMS and a computer with internet access. In a communal kitchen on the first floor the translators can get acquainted with their host country by watching television. Also available in the Translators' House are a fax machine, photocopier, washing machine, drier and – inevitably, in Amsterdam – three bicycles.

Peter Bergsma, himself an experienced translator, is responsible for the day-to-day running of the residence. Additionally he organises workshops and helps arrange the programme of the annual Translation Days in Nijmegen. Together with the Translators' House committee he also selects which translators are to stay at Van Breestraat and receive a grant for periods varying from two weeks to two months. The conditions of the Residence are strict: '*1. The translator must be engaged on work by a Dutch author. The author concerned must have produced work of proven quality or which at least shows great promise. 2. The translator must supply work of proven quality.*' 'Proven quality' may seem an extremely debatable criterion, but in practice the people at the Translators' House usually get it right. The occupation rate is consistently above ninety percent and in their obligatory reports afterwards the chosen translators generally write in very complimentary terms about their stay. Officially the translators also have to show a contract with a foreign publisher for the translation of a Dutch literary work, but sometimes translators without a contract are provided with accommodation, provided that they are working on a clear-cut literary project such as compiling an anthology, writing a foreword, etc. Since early 1999 the Translators' House has also been available to so-called 'Artists in Residence'. This programme of the Ministry of Education, Culture and Science offers foreign authors the chance to work in the residence for three months a year on a book to which a sojourn in the Netherlands is relevant. Those who benefited in 2000 were the American author Thomas Levine, doing research on Dutch waxwork museums and the works of Rembrandt, and the Austrian Robert Menasse who is working on a book about the seventeenth-century Amsterdam rabbi and printer Menasseh ben Israel.

Flanders too does its best to ensure that translators

The Translators' House in
Van Breestraat, Amsterdam

of Dutch-language literature should not remain cultural outsiders. The Flemish Community offers them the opportunity to stay for a period of one month in the Leuven Begijnhof, where two fully furnished apartments serve as the Flemish Translators' House. Translators here, like those in Amsterdam, are given the opportunity of consulting the authors and/or publishers of the books they are translating. The residence's location in the Low Countries' oldest university city also facilitates access to reliable information. The prerequisite here is that the translator should be engaged in translating a Flemish author. As well as translators, sometimes people are accommodated in the apartments as part of a cultural agreement. For instance, Emmanuelle Roy, the Quebec theatre producer, was a guest at no 91 in February 2000.

The Leuven Translators' House, currently still under the authority of the Flemish Ministry of Culture, will be handed over to the Flemish Fund for Literature in 2003; that, at least, is the present plan.

'Aftercare' is also important to both Translators' Houses. When translators are back home again, they can still get help from the staff with factual questions about texts. This, combined together with their temporary 'naturalisation' can only improve the end result. Thanks to the excellent guidance they receive there, translators more often succeed in letting their own compatriots enjoy a brief taste of the atmosphere of the Netherlands and Flanders, just as they themselves did at the Translators' Houses. Or as Peter Bergsma summarised it: '*The aim is to promote quality. To send translators away wiser than when they arrived.*'

FILIP MATTHIJS
Translated by Derek Denné.

Amsterdam Translators' House: Van Breestraat 19, 1071 ze Amsterdam, The Netherlands / tel. +31 20 470 97 40 / fax +31 20 470 97 41 / verthuis@xs4all.nl

Leuven Translators' House, contact: tel. +32 2 553 69 02 / fax: +32 2 553 69 01 / karine.vanbalen@wvc.vlaanderen.be

The Bookshop of the World

The organisers of the conference that gave rise to this book chose its title as a metaphor for the wide range of subjects that book producers (printers and publishers) have offered their clients (the readers) over the past five centuries. Out of more than fifty papers, twenty-five have been selected for this collection.

The first two contributions provide an introduction. Lotte Hellinga places the emphasis on book producers as *'agents of cultural exchange'* between the Netherlands and Italy and between the Netherlands and England. Ludo Simons gives an overview of the fortunes of publishing in the Southern Netherlands.

The story proper begins on the continent where William Caxton, merchant and governor of the English nation in Bruges, at the request of Margaret of York, the wife of Charles the Bold, completed his translation of Raoul Lefèvre's History of Troy and printed it in Bruges: the first-ever printed book in English. Long after Caxton, the English market continued to be supplied by printers from the Low Countries. National boundaries, unlike language, were of no importance to the publishing world.

At other times in history the focus shifts primarily to the 'forbidden' content of books: the Reformation in the sixteenth century, the Dutch Revolt (or Eighty Years War, 1568-1648) with its thousands of pamphlets and numerous books, printed in the Netherlands and in some cases translated into English. Later there were the English royalist refugees in the mid-seventeenth century who spread the English 'book culture' and later still the so-called *Livres de Hollande*, philosophical (and other) writings, banned in France but published in the Republic and disseminated not only in France but also elsewhere.

Through the ages authors, printers and publishers have learned to live with the phenomenon of edicts and censorship, the underground press and fictitious imprints. It was not only a risky business in itself; it also creates many pitfalls for the bibliographer. Only recently was it discovered that the first English translation of the Bible, by Miles Coverdale, was printed in Antwerp in 1535. Illicit publishing was not without its dangers and for some it led to imprisonment and execution, as in the cases of Christoffel van Ruremund, imprisoned in Westminster for printing English translations of the Bible, and the English Bible translator William Tyndale who was burnt at the stake in Vilvoorde in 1536. The changing régimes in England – Protestant or Catholic – were all grist to the mill for printers on the continent: trade came before all else! [1]

The lion's share of the papers deals with the seventeenth century, the Golden Age of the United Provinces, so the Northern Netherlands naturally receives most attention. Paul Hoftijzer outlines the situation. In the seventeenth century, unlike today, English was barely understood in the Republic, but books were translated into Latin or French and printed there. Furthermore, English books were very expensive because of the book trade's monopolistic practices,

Edward Collier, *Vanitas Still-Life with Books.*
Late 17th century.
Canvas, 50.5 x 60 cm.
Stedelijk Museum
De Lakenhal, Leiden.

which led to a flourishing trade in so-called '*contre-façons*' or pirated editions. English immigrants had their own press (The Pilgrim Press) which supplied the English market clandestinely. The Elseviers, who originally came from Leuven, maintained business relations with English colleagues and authors such as Francis Bacon, George Buchanan and William Harvey from their offices in Leiden and Amsterdam. Journalism takes us briefly to the Southern Netherlands. Paul Arblaster investigates the role of Antwerp, Amsterdam and London in the production and distribution of newspapers. David McKitterick illustrates his contribution on Anglo-Dutch trade in the early eighteenth century by focusing on the compositor and printer Cornelius Crownfield, who originally came from the Netherlands but was for forty years a printer for the Cambridge University Press. As a bookseller without a bookshop, he traded at his own expense and made full use of his Dutch background. Expensive editions were produced by subscription. By the beginning of the nineteenth century the Netherlands' days as '*the low-priced and well-stocked bookshop of the world*' were over, according to Lisa Kuitert. We see the birth of the second-hand book trade and bookshops specialising in unsold stock. In this way, more books now reached the readers for whom they were intended and at a lower price. B.S. Nayler & Co., established on the Dam in Amsterdam, can perhaps be regarded as the forerunner of De Slegte, the modern Dutch chain of bookshops dealing in remaindered stock. Slowly but surely the paths of publisher and bookseller were growing apart; each had their own way of doing business.

Only a few specific aspects of book production are discussed. It is probably not widely known that the original font punches and moulds for Oxford University Press when it was set up in 1670 were made in the United Provinces. Or that Cambridge University Press used a font designed by Christoffel van Dijck. Ilja Veldman describes how Crispijn van de Passe, a Zeelander trained in Antwerp, produced books and, more especially, prints for the English market. According to John H. Astington, emblem books, always popular with the Dutch, also gained a following in England thanks to Thomas Jenner.

The book also describes various other building blocks that contribute to the overall picture. One of them is the unmasking by Karel Bostoen of Johan Radermacher as the editor, publisher and bookseller of M.A. Florio's account of the life and death of England's nine-day Protestant Queen, Lady Jane Grey. Dirk Imhof provides a behind-the-scenes glimpse of the relationship between Balthasar 1 Moretus and the London bookseller Richard Whitacker which switched constantly between mutual trust and mistrust over the loan of a large number of wood print-blocks. The Plantijn archive is far from exhausted. Riccardo Rizza's 'Mariken van Nieumeghen and Mary of Nemmegen: a hopeless case?' is a fine example of textual bibliography.

Book history can be reconstructed from a variety of sources. One important category is the catalogue, whether from libraries, publishers, bookshops or auctions. B.P.M. Dongelmans discusses a ten-year-old project, started by the late Bert van Selm, to record all book sale catalogues in the Netherlands. So far the tally is 4,400 catalogues. Another source is the 1543 inventory of the Leuven bookseller Hieronymus Cloet, which Pierre Delsaerdt uses as convincing evidence that Cloet ran '*a bookshop for a new age*'.

The driving force behind the conference, Dr Jacob Harskamp, is head of the dynamic Dutch and Flemish Section in the British Library, which thanks to him and his predecessors Anna Simoni and Sue Roach is now showing its full potential.[2] He deserves congratulations both for the conference and for this publication.

ELLY COCKX-INDESTEGE
Translated by Chris Emery.

Lotte Hellinga, Alastair Duke, Jacob Harskamp, Theo Hermans, assisted by Elaine Paintin (eds.), *The Bookshop of the World: The Role of the Low Countries in the Book-Trade 1473-1941* (Proceedings of a conference held in London 15-17 September 1999 organised by The Association for Low Countries Studies; University College London, Centre for Dutch and Flemish Culture; The British Library, Dutch and Flemish Section; Wellcome Institute for the History of Medicine). 't Goy-Houten: HES & De Graaf, 2001; 332 pp. ISBN 90-6194-039-7.

NOTES

1. In this connection, readers may be interested in the results of research carried out by Paul Valkema Blouw, much of which has appeared in *Quaerendo: Journal for the History of the Book in the Low Countries*. Revised attributions to printers have led to several new conclusions and even to revised dates.
2. See *The Low Countries* 2000: 264-266.

Film and Theatre

Christ Recrucified The Tegelen Passion Plays

Most of the thirty or so open-air theatres in the Netherlands date from the 1930s. In that period of economic crisis the construction of these theatres was an ideal form of job creation for the working-class unemployed. Neither was it by accident that some of the great traditions of open-air theatre have their roots in the periods just before and after the Second World War – traditions which here and there still survive today. The village of Diever in the eastern province of Drenthe has gained nation-wide fame with its annual production of a play by Shakespeare, an achievement that has earned it the honorary title of 'the Dutch Stratford-upon-Avon' (see *The Low Countries 1995-1996*: 275-276).

No less famous is the quinquennial tradition of passion plays in Tegelen, a village on the River Maas in the southern, predominantly Catholic, province of

The whipping of Christ in the 2000 edition of the Tegelen passion play.

Photo courtesy of Passiespelen Tegelen.

Limburg. The plays are staged in *De Doolhof* (The Labyrinth), a monumental theatre with some 3,500 seats set among trees and bushes. Calvary, the palaces of Pilate and Herod, the Temple and the inn where the Last Supper took place have been a permanent feature of the décor since 1946. Like the Diever pioneers, the original organisers in Tegelen regarded their drama as an important element in the moral and cultural education of the local population. This strong local connection continues to this day, even though, latterly, Jesus has sometimes been recruited from outside the region and on the odd occasion there has even been a Jesus who had to admit to being an unbeliever or at least an agnostic.

In Europe there are about sixty towns that organise passion plays, all of them members of the Europassion umbrella organisation. The plays vary in content, from fairly static representations of the *Via Dolorosa* in Lent to complex mass dramas with hundreds of actors and participants. By far the most important centre for passion plays is Oberammergau. Performances are held there every ten years: in 2000 there were 110 performances in front of over half a million visitors. But after Oberammergau, it is Tegelen that attracts most public interest. Between mid-May and the end of

September 2000, 26 performances were given in *De Doolhof* before a total of 53,000 visitors (according to figures published by the Association of Dutch Open Air Theatres). A respectable number, but nevertheless a source of concern to the organisers since it fell far short of the 64,000 visitors in 1995. Incidentally, in terms of audience figures, the best year was 1955 with 160,000 visitors while 1971, a crisis period for Dutch open air theatre in general, was the worst with 15,000. The history of the plays begins in 1931 when the first series of performances was staged, based on a text by the writer and priest Anton van Delft. Its close relationship with Catholic liturgy was reflected in the liberal accompaniment of Gregorian chant and in the solemn mass that preceded the premiere; this latter practice has been followed ever since. Growing public interest led to further performances in 1932 and 1935 with the same text and musical accompaniment. And despite the outbreak of the Second World War the plays were performed again in 1940, though based on a new script written by Jacques Schreurs, a writer and priest from Limburg whose work was extremely popular in Catholic circles at the time. This script provided the basis for all productions up to and including 1995, although as time went on the various directors had fewer scruples about introducing changes or making cuts. Indeed, the author himself radically revised the text in 1996, the last year of his life.

Since 1975 the plays have been performed regularly every five years. Schreurs' text was finally abandoned in 2000 when Ben Verbong, a native of Tegelen and a well-known film director – his films include *The Girl with Red Hair* (Het meisje met het rode haar, 1982) and *The Indecent Woman* (De onfatsoenlijke vrouw, 1991) – directed the production. The actress and writer Marieke van Leeuwen felt sufficiently inspired by the New Testament to write a fresh script with a more human touch in which, notably, greater prominence was given to the women. The traditional focus on Jesus and Judas was spread more democratically, the mothers of Jesus and Judas were good friends, Mary Magdalen became a self-aware 'modern' woman, and female disciples were present at the Last Supper.

When the steering committee first read the new script, there was so much criticism that the future of the plays seemed to be in jeopardy. And that was only the start of an almost unending series of major and minor conflicts which beset the 2000 production and which possibly contributed to the disappointing attendance. For instance, after reading the script the actor originally cast as Jesus turned down the role – for Tegelen an unprecedented, even subversive act. He was then subjected to so much criticism that in the end he felt that he had, as he put it, '*been nailed to the cross after all*'. From a number of interviews in *De Limburger* newspaper, it is clear that in the past, too, the role of Jesus had often been more of an trial than an honour. The actor who played Jesus in 1995 admitted that on a couple of occasions he almost walked out. He compared the intrigues surrounding the Tegelen plays to those

269

in *Christ Recrucified* (1938) by Nikos Kazantzakis, a novel (also translated as *The Greek Passion*) about a small community in Anatolia in 1922 where daily life and the local tradition of a passion play bring to light all kinds of surprising conflicts.

The national press was moderately positive in its critique of the premiere on Sunday, 14 May 2000. Critics tend to be more restrained in commenting on this kind of event because they feel that the usual artistic criteria should not be applied as strictly as for professional publicly subsidised theatre companies. After all, such a play involves the efforts of large numbers of amateurs, ordinary people who sacrifice a great amount of their free time in order to take part in the spectacle. Residents of Tegelen are happy to recount their personal memories of the passion plays. How at three months old they took part in the entry into Jerusalem, then many years later were promoted to playing a Roman soldier, finally to become a high priest, a scribe or – better still – a disciple. Furthermore, the passion plays are so deeply rooted in the folklore of Catholic Limburg that the rest of the predominantly Calvinist Netherlands doesn't really know what to make of them. Be that as it may, the Tegelen passion plays should be cherished as one of the unusual cultural traditions that abound in the Netherlands.

JOS NIJHOF
Translated by Chris Emery.

How 'Royal' is the Royal Belgian Film Archive?

At the 2001 Cannes Film Festival, the Centre National Français de la Cinématographie organised a meeting of representatives of the most prominent film archives. On the agenda was the dire financial position of the Royal Belgian Film Archive. That this Brussels archive, a bilingual, bicultural institution, attracted international concern should surprise nobody. It is, after all, according to a comparative study by the International Federation of Archives, one of the most important in the world.

The existence of the 'Belgian Cinematheque' is largely the work of Henri Storck (see *The Low Countries 2000*: 270-271), an inspirational filmmaker who built an international reputation for the Belgian documentary school in the 1930s. In 1931, with André Thirifays and Piet Vermeylen, son of the Flemish writer and scholar August Vermeylen, he set up a French-language film club in Brussels, the *Club de l'Écran*. From the outset there were also plans to create a film archive. In 1938, following in the tracks of the French *cinémathèque* which Henri Langlois and the film-maker Georges Franju founded in Paris in 1937, they set up the bilingual *Cinémathèque de Belgique*. This was to become the present-day Royal Belgian Film Archive.

The linguistic balance in the steering committee, three French and three Dutch speakers, was mainly Vermeylen's doing. Furthermore, political balance was also maintained. This double parity, which the institution retains to this day, was rare at that time. The archive was originally housed in Henri Storck's house and contained three films, one of which was Eisenstein's *Battleship Potemkin*. Serious collecting only started after the Second World War.

In 1944 Jacques Ledoux (1922-1988) was appointed as the sole, part-time, employee. Shortly afterwards he became curator and the archive moved to the Palace of Fine Arts, the building where the Queen Elizabeth music competition is now held. Ledoux did not only collect films. His engineering background enabled him to play a pioneering role in their preservation. He saved thousands of pre-1951 nitrate films, which are particularly flammable and liable to deterioration, by transferring them to an acetate base. Nowadays a polyester base is used. Ledoux also discovered a way of preventing colour films from fading by storing them in specially adapted units at a temperature of 6°C and a humidity level of 30%. The various cinematic events that he organised rapidly made Belgium – which in relative terms had always had the largest number of cinemas – the 'viewpoint' of cinema culture: the World Film Festivals in Brussels (1947) and Knokke (1949), the 'Confrontation with the Twelve Best Films of All Time' during the 1958 World Exhibition in Brussels, the international festivals of experimental film (*Experimentl* five times between 1949 and 1975, and the *L'Age d'Or* awards annually since then). Jacques Ledoux, who was awarded the Erasmus prize posthumously in 1988, was without peer in the way he not only collected and preserved films from all periods and from all countries, but also restored and reconstructed them (including Abel Gance's *Napoleon*).

After his death his colleague Gabrielle Claes took over as curator. Together with a limited number of staff she is responsible for running this now internationally famous archive.

At the present time, the Belgian film archive houses 280 million metres of film, 44,000 titles and about 100,000 copies. In contrast to other archives it holds international titles, past and present, in addition to the whole national production. Unlike printed works, Belgium has no 'statutory depository' of visual materials so the archive has to request copies from the film distributors. Usually it obtains four copies of which the best, with the negative whenever possible, is preserved, while the others are used or lent out for non-commercial viewing.

The annual stream of acquisitions is enormous: the average is 2,000 films per annum, but in 2000 alone there were 6,000. In addition to that, the archive also has a library of 37,000 books, 2,400 journals and a documentation centre with 70,000 files of press cuttings dating from the turn of the last century. A major problem is that this 'royal' collection of film information has to be made accessible to the public by means of costly digitisation. Public access had always been part of Ledoux's policy, which is why in 1962 he set up the 'Film Museum', a projection room for films from the collection. For many years now, five films

Stephen Fry, Flora
Montgomery and Greg
Wise in Jeroen Krabbé's
The Discovery of Heaven
(2001).

have been shown each day, three sound films and two silent films with piano accompaniment. This film museum provided a foundation for works by French filmmakers like François Truffaut, Claude Chabrol and Bertrand Tavernier. Important Flemish film-makers such as Dominique Deruddere (*Everybody Famous – Iedereen beroemd*) and Marc Didden (*Brussels by Night*) as well as numerous film critics owe much of their cinematic education to the museum.

Unfortunately, the film museum, the library and even the work of the archive itself are seriously threatened by a lack of funds. The limited space is in a sorry state and far from 'royal'; the beleaguered staff is underpaid; the temperature control system in the storerooms is long out of date, which is adversely affecting the condition of the films. That is why the present curator, Gabrielle Claes, once again sounded the alarm and why her plea for more financial resources resounded in Cannes.

But this time it has had some effect. Under pressure from the film world, from such names as Kusturica, Bertolucci, Scorsese (who called the archive '*one of the finest collections on the planet*' and stressed the fact that it holds over 100 American silent movies that exist nowhere else) and, last but not least, the French actress Catherine Deneuve, the Belgian government has decided to increase the funding for the archive by 70% from 2002. This means that Gabrielle Claes will be able to take on more staff and give them better conditions, pay off some of the debts incurred when more storage space had to be bought, and finally make a start on digitising the 'paper' archive.

WIM DE POORTER
Translated by Chris Emery.

Film Museum: Hortastraat 23 / 1000 Brussel / Belgium /
tel. +32 2 507 83 70
Film Archive: Ravensteinstraat 23 / 1000 Brussels / Belgium /
tel. +32 2 507 83 70

Where Angels Fear to Tread
The Discovery of Heaven

Whatever else you may think about *The Discovery of Heaven*, any film-maker who embarks on such a project must be a brave man; and particularly when his experience as a director can at best be described as modest. Jeroen Krabbé is best known as an actor, playing such roles as the bad guy in the James Bond movie *The Living Daylights*. *The Discovery of Heaven* is only his second film as director but its scale is far greater than his relatively small-scale debut, *Left Luggage* (1998). However, courage alone is not sufficient to guarantee a successful film, especially when it is based on a novel that from the outset poses a hundred and one problems for the film-maker.

Harry Mulisch' universally acclaimed novel is long (900 pages), stretches over a period of about twenty years, is firmly rooted in the second half of the twentieth century, and takes the whole of western cultural history as its frame of reference. The structure and plot are complex. Anyone who has read the book will realise that the trickiest problem in adapting it for the screen is the two-part division into a heavenly and an earthly perspective. How should one depict heaven? What do angels wear? How does one win over the audience? Should it be done with humour? Krabbé has not found a satisfactory solution. His angels, for instance, inhabit stage sets based on Piranesi's famous *Carceri* (Prisons) etchings. Using these drawings of romantic ruins may be defensible in theory, but in practice, surprisingly, when recreated three-dimensionally in cardboard and chipboard Piranesi's visions seem fairly banal. One gets a sense of *déjà vu*, of having seen this kind of décor before in ghost films and gothic horror fantasies. Also the way in which Krabbé represents the angels as grotesque creatures, weighed down by practical problems and worried about their careers, is unconvincing and rather corny. (Mulisch must naturally take some responsibility for this.)

What is it about? To put it briefly, God the Father is fed up with humanity. He can no longer bear to watch the mess that human beings are making of earth and decides to revoke his divine contract with them and abandon them to their miserable fate. That contract is the Ten Commandments, carved in the two tablets of stone that He had once given to Moses. God Himself never appears on screen; he leaves the dirty work to two angels, one of whom is Krabbé himself. The angels are not permitted to intervene personally. They may give fortune a forceful nudge, which they regularly do, but that is all. To retrieve the stone tablets, a son, born of human parents but with a divine ponytail, will be chosen – a new type of Christ. The young man is called Quinten and is born in the Netherlands. The details of his birth, like that of his predecessor, are somewhat unclear. Is Quinten the son of Onno, the bohemian and once influential linguist who becomes a politician, or of his soulmate Max, the compulsive womaniser and brilliant astronomer? The fantastical course of their lives, their complicated early backgrounds and their love for the same woman provide the earthly component of the book. We are taken from the Netherlands to Cuba, Israel, Italy and Poland, and from the 1960s to the eighties. Along the way, in classic Mulisch style, the entire cosmos is explained.

The three people behind this English-language production, director Jeroen Krabbé, script-writer Edwin de Vries and producer Ate de Jong, the same team that produced *Left Luggage*, have created a clear and balanced résumé of the book. Entire chapters are compressed into a few lines of dialogue that reflect, more or less, the essence of the original. The choice of British actor Stephen Fry (Onno) and Greg Wise (Max) for the leading roles is appropriate, and most of the other actors put in satisfactory performances. Mulisch' pedantic tone has been lightened somewhat, but its hurried, compressed rhythm makes one feel one is watching summarised highlights.

In *Left Luggage*, Krabbé proved himself capable of producing a film that could run smoothly without the audience hearing the engine sputter. But it also showed that he was not a particularly original film-maker, and worked more readily with sentiment than emotions. In *The Discovery of Heaven* too, the imagery and narrative interventions come straight out of the fast food section of the Hollywood kitchen. But when one gets the chance to work with more exotic ingredients, such as a novel by Harry Mulisch, it seems a shame to cover them with the bland sauce of uniformity.

ERIK MARTENS
Translated by Chris Emery.

Selective Affinities Anglo-Dutch Relations, 1780-1980

The publication of *Unspoken Allies* marks the rediscovery of Anglo-Dutch relations as an interesting and fruitful topic for historical investigation. The book is the outcome of academic cooperation across the North Sea led by professors Nigel Ashton (LSE) and Duco Hellema (Utrecht University). Its starting point is the Gaullist view that the Netherlands and Britain are different from the continental Europeans, since both are Atlantic nations and have been shaped in large part by their maritime and colonial past.

With their introduction and postcript the editors provide a frame for the various well-documented contributions, written by ten Dutch and five British historians, which focus on the role of international relations in the history of Anglo-Dutch contact over the past two centuries. The order of presentation is chronological, and the book closes in the 1980s – so it is slightly odd to see a picture of Tony Blair and Wim Kok on the cover, when inside the book these two labour party modernisers are hardly mentioned at all.

The colonial theme figures prominently in the book. From the end of the eighteenth century the Dutch colonial empire was sheltered under the British umbrella, and safeguarded by the British in order to maintain the European balance of power. In the twentieth century the colonial issue comes up again in the chapter on Anglo-Dutch relations during the Second World War – momentous years, when the future of the Dutch colonies was in peril, and the Netherlands itself depended on Great Britain for the restoration of its sovereignty. This is followed by an extensive chapter on Anglo-Dutch relations during the Indonesian revolution (1945-1950), which concedes that the political assessment of the situation on Java by the British officer Laurens Van der Post had been '*essentially correct*' – something he himself did not fail to advertise in his memoirs, *The Admiral's Baby* (1996).

There are, surprisingly, no British contributions on the colonial theme, and this may explain why for example Sir Thomas Stamford Raffles, the founder of Singapore, is only mentioned in passing. From both sides, though, Anglo-Dutch colonial relations deserve much further study, along the lines of Bromley and Kossmann's *Britain and the Netherlands in Europe and Asia* (1968). Thus, it would be very interesting to find out how the treaties which the Dutch concluded with native rulers were assessed in Whitehall and the India Office. Many other colonial episodes are waiting to be explored in the rich archives and libraries of London. Jaap Harskamp's recent catalogue of British Library holdings, *The Indonesian Question,* offers a good starting point here.

The other contributions in the book focus on Anglo-Dutch relations in Europe, especially in the twentieth

Unspoken Allies
Anglo-Dutch Relations since 1780

century. During the First World War the neutral Dutch performed an uneasy balancing act between Germany and Britain, and were subject to very strong pressures on matters of trade and security. At the end of that war there was the high drama and theatre of diplomatic bluff and counterbluff over the German Kaiser Wilhelm, who had sought asylum in the Netherlands. The inter-war period was dominated by trade problems. There is a very interesting chapter on security issues in the run-up to the Second World War – a well-told tale, based on a lot of original archival material from the Public Records Office. This is followed by an extensive chapter on the political and military contacts between the Dutch and the British during the Second World War, although there is no mention of the *Englandspiel*.

After the war Anglo-Dutch relations moved into a different key, and the issue of European cooperation and integration took centre stage. The enlargement of the European Community to include Britain was one of the key priorities of Dutch post-war foreign policy. The unsuccessful first and second British applications to join the European Community are discussed in detail here, and we learn not only to what lengths Dutch diplomats went in order to assist the British, but also that for Britain they '*were not necessarily the most useful ally to have*'. The book ends with a contribution on the very different views of the Dutch and the British on the Middle East during the oil crisis of the 1970s.

In their postscript Ashton and Hellema conclude that '*Anglo-Dutch relations have lost a considerable part of the meaning they had in the past*'. The two countries no longer possess colonial empires, and Anglo-Dutch relations today are firmly embedded in the multilateral frameworks of EU and NATO. But there still is '*an underlying, unspoken alliance in terms of ideology and interests*' between the two countries, in particular in their long traditions of parliamentary democracy and their liberal views on international matters. True as this may be, there have often been ten-

sions, conflicts and crises too – most recently when Dutch Euro-diplomacy seriously underestimated the strength of British Euro-scepticism and was defeated in the run-up to Maastricht.

Unspoken Allies is a stimulating book, well-supported with extensive archival evidence, and one hopes it will be followed by further research on topics that have not been covered here. In the field of contemporary international politics, it would be interesting to have a study of the special relationship between recent Dutch and British prime ministers, first Mrs Thatcher and Ruud Lubbers, today Tony Blair and Wim Kok. In the field of business the success of Anglo-Dutch joint ventures merits closer study, for example the purchase by ING of Baring's Bank. Beyond this, it would be interesting to broaden the scope of investigation to the field of social policy, and to investigate on the one hand how the Dutch are adopting British privatisation in public transport and other sectors of their 'polder model' economy, while conversely, the British are debating the relevance for their own society of the legalisation of soft drugs, prostitution and euthanasia, as well as the Dutch approach to public housing and urban development.

REINIER SALVERDA

Nigel Ashton and Duco Hellema (eds.), *Unspoken Allies. Anglo-Dutch Relations since 1780*. Amsterdam: Amsterdam University Press, 2001; 310 pp. ISBN 90-5356-471-3 (Publication sponsored by the Dutch Foreign Office).
Jaap Harskamp (ed.), *The Indonesian Question. The Dutch / Western response to the struggle for independence in Indonesia 1945-1950. An annotated catalogue of primary materials held in the British Library*. Introduction by Peter Carey. London: The British Library, 2001; XX-210 pp. ISBN 0-7123-1127-0.

A Passionately Dutch English King
The Tercentenary of the Death of William III

On 24 February 1702 William III was thrown from his horse as it stumbled on a molehill. A broken collarbone, combined with a lung infection, killed him a fortnight later, though in popular tradition 'the mole' has always remained the culprit, 'fatal' for his followers but 'providential' for his opponents whose toast at once became '*To the little gentleman in black velvet*'.

In the year 2002 it is worth recalling what both Britain and the Netherlands owe to this remarkable man who was born at The Hague on 4 November 1650, eight days after the death of his father from smallpox. His mother was Charles I's daughter Mary, who in 1641 at the age of 10 married the 14-year-old Stadholder Prince William II of Orange. Their posthumous son William III, having lost his mother in 1660 when he was 10, was a half-English orphan. Having been barred from the succession by the Act of Seclusion suggested by Cromwell, he became Stadholder only in 1672, the Dutch '*Rampjaar*' or 'year of disaster' when Louis XIV of France invaded the United Provinces.

This resulted in William's being raised to the rank of Captain-General of the Dutch forces and restored to the Stadholderate.

In Dutch and English history, his brilliant campaigns against the French, ending in 1678, should be as well-known as the bloodless Revolution of 1688 which in April 1689 brought the coronation of William III and his English wife Mary II as joint Sovereigns of Britain.

William and Mary were both homesick for Holland, especially William in spite of his early psychological drawbacks. His mother had hated the United Provinces and his education had been farmed out to a series of stern tutors, the Guardianship proving a bitter bone of contention between his mother and his strongminded grandmother, Amalia van Solms. William's mother was only interested in her exiled English relatives and was often away. From his ninth year onwards William's upbringing, strictly Protestant in spirit, took place at Leiden under an exhausting program of tutorials, official mealtime-receptions and hardly any sport or recreation. He was lonely – a situation echoed in the little rhyme later ascribed to him:

As I walked by myself
And talk'd to myself
Myself said to me:
Look to thyself,
Take care of thyself,
For nobody cares for thee.

When his mother went to England in 1660 to attend the Restoration, she, too, fell victim to an attack of smallpox. To everybody's surprise William was inconsolable, in spite of the emotional neglect he had suffered in her lifetime. It was a youthful visit to his German step-uncle, the Elector of Brandenburg, that started his passion for horses, dogs and falcons, with the chase developing into a ritual that became one of his chief pursuits for the rest of his life and was largely responsible for his renowned military prowess.

William's education and style of living were radically altered in 1666 when the brilliant Grand Pensionary Johan de Witt and the States General became his 'Super-Guardians'. Although physically unimpressive (his wife was at least a head taller than he was) William could be charming: a courteous, polyglot, art-loving and basically extremely tolerant and intelligent adult. At the same time he was a pragmatist, politically unassailable and singleminded. When called upon to play his hereditary part in the defence of his country against the invading French he proved both brave and astute, pinning Louis' armies down by battle after battle in present-day Belgium. Fagel, the new Grand Pensionary, laconically recorded: '*His Highness never rests, eats little, and is good cheer.*' While sometimes accused of homosexuality, though openly having a mistress, he chose to surround himself with a small band of trusted military colleagues and fellow-huntsmen, led by his coeval, the Dutch country-gentleman Hans Willem Bentinck, who was in many respects his Royal friend's physical and psychological opposite.

P. van den Berge,
William III's Fall from his
Horse, 1702.

Made Earl of Portland, he was succeeded on his retirement by Joost van Keppel who became Earl of Albemarle.

William had met Mary during a visit to London in 1676. He was very impressed by this attractive 15-year-old daughter of Charles II's brother James. However, their marriage in the following year was not so much based on passion as on politics, although after a few years their feelings for each other had grown to such an extent that when in November 1688 they had to say good-bye when William embarked for England in his huge fleet, Mary wrote in her diary that their last dialogue was '*unforgettable in its tenderness*' and that if her husband were to succumb she would never want another since she could never find his equal. To William's immense sorrow she died in 1694, also of smallpox.

In 1688 King James II of England had been presented with a baby son by his second wife, Mary of Modena. This was immediately considered a grave threat to religious peace. In consequence a secret invitation by seven influential nobles was carried to William to come over with an army to save England from lasting Catholic tyranny and restore its laws and liberties. His acceptance implied the return of Protestantism, the creation of a basis for democratically constituted Parliament and, ultimately, the restoration of the balance of power in Europe.

Unwilling to fight William's army, James threw the Great Seal of State into the Thames and fled the country in the night of 22 December 1688 to join his wife and son (already refugees in France) and the English throne was consequently vacant. Out of this situation the Bill of Rights was born in Parliament, an unparalleled document that was to function ever after as the British Constitution and a model of democratic thinking far and wide. In fact, thanks to William III the relationship between Britain and Europe changed radically – a change which, often rooted in the Low Countries examples, was beneficial in more respects than is usually realised today. William's victory in 1690 at the Battle of the Boyne over the largely French invading army of James II threatened again to revive the slogan 'popery or slavery'. But the present situation in Ireland cannot be laid at William's door.

Throughout his career William's political initiatives and inspiring 'Grand Alliances' were always based on the defence of Protestantism and the preservation of Dutch independence, which he saw as the cornerstones of any balance of power in Europe and achievable only by beating French Catholic imperialism with English support.

What finally must be acknowledged is the foundation under William of the Bank of England and Lloyd's Insurance which functioned as the country's economic kedge anchors. According to Daniel Defoe the Dutch ruler's lack of popularity with his English councillors was more their fault than his. Writing about him in his soon famous poem 'The True-born Englishman', he said:

We blame the King that he relies too much
on strangers, Germans, Huguenots, and Dutch;
and seldom would his great affairs of State
to English Councillors communicate.
The fact might very well be answered thus:
He had so often been betrayed by us,
he must have been a madman to rely
on English gentleman's fidelity.

William indeed remained passionately Dutch to the end and to the island race largely a stranger, but he prepared the way for England's coming economic greatness in the next century and consolidated the country of his birth in a newly stabilised Europe.

FRED G.H. BACHRACH

The Commemoration of a Multinational Four Hundred Years of the Dutch East India Company

On 20 March 1602 the Dutch United East India Company was founded. The Vereenigde Oost-Indische Compagnie, or VOC as we shall refer to it from now on (both for brevity's sake and to distinguish it from its English and French rivals) was, in effect, a trading cooperative which in a relatively short space of time built up an empire of settlements and trade relations along the coasts of South and East Africa and in Asia.

During the century following the discovery of America Western European trade networks had rapidly expanded over ever-greater distances. Merchants collaborated to create companies to trade in, for example, Turkey (the Ottoman Empire) and Russia. In London, the English East India Company had already been set up in 1600, so the Dutch company was the second of its kind. (The French followed their example in 1664.) In 1621, the Dutch West India Company was also established in the Republic. In both cases the state provided important support, hoping to break the Spanish and Portuguese monopoly of a large part of the New World. The Dutch companies themselves were monopolistic, so that only merchants who were members could trade legally in any area where a base had been established. The search for new markets and new commodities was as important a motivation as gold and silver, or the valuable spice trade .

The seventeenth century was the age of Holland's sea power. In 1600, about 10,000 ships flew the Dutch flag and almost all sea-trade along the coasts of Western Europe from Bordeaux to Spitsbergen, as well as in the Baltic Sea, was in the hands of Hollanders. Holland also had military control of the seas. A special feature of the VOC was not only that it had full government backing for its undertakings, but also that it remained a private limited company. The 17 executive directors, known as the *Heeren XVII*, were elected from a larger body of 73 (later 60). They represented the six 'chambers' of the VOC, based in the six ports of Amsterdam, Enkhuizen, Hoorn, Rotterdam, Delft and Middelburg. In practice there was very little control over the *Heeren XVII*; and certainly from 1610, when a governor-general was appointed, the board had virtually unlimited freedom of action. Beyond the borders of the Republic, the VOC was a single large company with far more power than any modern multinational. On its ships and in its overseas trading settlements, the VOC itself laid down the rules. It had its own army and its own fleet, on its own authority it could sign treaties, declare war and make peace, and it minted its own coins.

The early years in particular were extremely successful. The main goal was to drive the Portuguese out of India and Indonesia. In 1619 Batavia (present-day Jakarta) was founded, a fortified trading post on Java which for two centuries was the most important VOC settlement in Asia and was later to become the colonial capital of the Dutch East Indies. In 1623, after a clash with the English, the Dutch also took over Ambon, and with it control of the spice-trade. In the course of the seventeenth century the remaining seaports in the archipelago and the island of Java were brought under VOC control. The first Dutch ship arrived in Japan in 1600, and when the Japanese closed their territory to all westerners in 1641 the VOC was alone in being allowed to keep a small trading post on the artificial island of Deshima in Nagasaki harbour. In 1652 the VOC captured the Cape of Good Hope and established a base

Hendrik van Schuylenburgh, *The Factory of the Dutch East India Company in Houghly,*

Bengal. 1665.
Canvas, 203 x 316 cm.
Rijksmuseum, Amsterdam.

there whose main purpose was to supply fresh food and water to ships plying the long route round Africa to Asia. The settlement that grew up next to it was to become the modern city of Cape Town. The VOC also established itself in Ceylon (Sri Lanka), and between 1623 and 1765 it also had a trading post in Persia (Iran).

Despite this commercial success, however, there was also much that went wrong. The centralised organisation could exercise little effective control over itself, and this soon gave rise to corruption at all levels. Employees of the company were poorly paid and so felt entitled to skim off a substantial proportion of the turnover for their own profit. In the early years, this practice did not prevent the VOC from distributing large dividends to its shareholders. However, it did become a problem later and in the course of the eighteenth century the company went into decline and had to eat increasingly into its capital. Growing corruption and the collapse of its monopoly position all played a part, but equally important was the fact that the Republic lost its command of the seas to Great Britain. After 1781 the VOC could no longer pay dividends to its shareholders and debts started to mount. In a last-ditch effort to save the company, the management was radically reformed in 1795, but all to no avail. On 17 March 1798, the VOC was formally wound up. All its possessions, territories and debts were taken over by the state, which at that time was the Batavian Republic.

It is important to remember that the VOC was a maritime trading power, never a colonial power. No attempt was ever made to bring extensive territories under the direct authority of the company and the Dutch government itself had absolutely no say in the matter. There were only trading posts with strong fortifications and often a narrow hinterland, and these settlements formed a network in which trade was coordinated and conducted not only between South Asia and Holland but also directly between the territories around the Indian Ocean and the China Seas. Incidentally, opium played a not unimportant role in this 'regional' trade. Just as the British did later, the VOC, and then the Netherlands government in Indonesia, exploited this addictive substance to maintain the balance of trade. Naturally, the VOC also pursued a deliberate policy of keeping the local potentates weak and divided so that they were unable to damage its commercial interests. Only after 1815 did the Kingdom of the Netherlands lay claim to a number of former VOC possessions and begin the process of building a colonial empire.

In 2002 the Netherlands remembers the VOC, both its achievements and its failures. Official commemorations, special educational programmes, a scholarly conference and numerous exhibitions should ensure that nobody is left unaware that four hundred years ago an enterprise was set up that, for over a century, played a major part in making the Netherlands one of the richest and most powerful countries in Europe. A number of large exhibitions trace its history down to the present time. The Netherlands Ship Museum in Amsterdam and the Maritime Museum in Rotterdam will jointly house the *National Jubilee Exhibition VOC*

1602-2002. From mid-March until the end of September Amsterdam's Rijksmuseum will mount a major exhibition entitled *The Dutch Encounter with Asia, 1602-1950*, as well as smaller exhibitions that will include *Photos from Distant Lands*, the Gordon Atlas with maps of South Africa, and Japanese porcelain. An important attraction is the *Duyfken*, a replica of a VOC sailing ship. Built in Australia, she set sail from Sydney for the Netherlands in May 2001, following the original route taken by the spice traders. During the summer months of 2002, the *Duyfken* will make 'guest appearances' at maritime events and pay visits to the original VOC towns.

LAURAN TOORIANS
Translated by Chris Emery.

Celebration 400 Years VOC: P.O. Box 93002 / 2509 AA The Hague / The Netherlands / tel. +31 70 349 0144 / fax +31 70 349 0287 / www.voc2002.nl

Language

Languages in Competition

With his new book *Words of the World* the Amsterdam sociologist Abram de Swaan makes an important contribution to the political economics of language rivalry in the global language system.

All over the world we see the rise of English, in many different domains (politics, trade, the law, science, the internet, sports, infotainment and the media) and in many different countries, including the Netherlands and Belgium, where – as Tom McArthur observed in *The English Languages* (1998) – English is now no longer a foreign language. The other side of this coin is the threat of language death. According to Nettle and Romaine's book *Vanishing Voices* (2000), ninety percent of the world's 6,000 languages will die out in the present century. For this reason, over the past ten years many linguists have joined the call for action to preserve linguistic diversity (see Uhlenbeck in *The Low Countries* 1993-94: 25-32), and in 2000 Tove Skutnabb-Kangas called for an international campaign for linguistic human rights in her book *Linguistic Genocide in Education – or Worldwide Diversity and Human Rights?*

Here De Swaan takes a different position. For him the key issue is that of language and power. In a global context language groups are in unequal competition, and their exchanges proceed on very unequal terms. In the first part of his book De Swaan presents a theoretical framework for the analysis of competition between languages. Using mathematical models from game theory and economic decision-making he constructs a formula for calculating the so-called Q-value of a language, which reflects its economic and cultural weight and its consequent social desirability. The many advantages of English, for example, greatly enhance its Q-value, and as a result we see a stampede into English by millions of people all over the world. The theory of Q-values is certainly the most original and important part of De Swaan's book. It would be very interesting to link it to Peter Nelde's work in conflict linguistics. De Swaan's theory also has important implications for a language such as Dutch – which he labels 'Netherlandish', perhaps because he does not discuss the case of Dutch and Dutch language policy in Belgium and Flanders – and poses a clear challenge to the Dutch language authorities in the Low Countries: is it possible to raise the Q-value of Dutch by developing / implementing an effective and attractive language policy and by investing in the future, in teaching Dutch as a second language, and in Dutch speech and language technology?

De Swaan then goes on to present five highly informative case studies of language competition in multilingual societies – in India, Indonesia, Central and South Africa, and in the European Union (EU). While these chapters provide a solid empirical basis, the analysis will need to be extended to, among other things, competition between English and Spanish or Arabic; to cases of urban multilingualism caused by globalisation in e.g. London and Amsterdam; and to the web, where, according to David Crystal in his latest book, *Language and the Internet* (2001), linguistic diversity is alive and well and about a quarter of the world's languages have some form of presence today.

A very interesting case in De Swaan's book is that of Indonesia, which unlike India has not retained the language of its former coloniser. To explain why, De Swaan analyses both the demise of Dutch and the surrender of Javanese in competition with Malay. Under De Swaan's Q-formula, the choice of Malay was both realistic and rational, for, as demonstrated in Groeneboer's *Gateway to the West* (1998; see *The Low Countries 1999-2000*: 277-278), Malay was used as *lingua franca* throughout the archipelago, by the colonial administration and the army in their contacts with the native population, in schools and hospitals, in markets, plantations and factories, in the press, in politics and literature.

Similarly, many Dutch people today would consider it just as rational and realistic to adopt English as the single official language of the European Union. The EU today has twelve official languages, two of which – English and French – are used as working languages. In addition, the European Charter of Fundamental Rights of December 2000 has for the first time defined the basic language rights of European citizens. But what will happen when the EU expands still further? The key thesis De Swaan presents in chapter 8, on the basis of extensive statistics, is that the more languages are officially recognised, the more this will work to the advantage of English. Indeed, given that today ninety percent of all European schoolchildren are learning English, we may already have passed the point of no return. It would be simplistic, however, to assume that knowing English is sufficient by itself, as if other languages now no longer matter. Indeed, an important feature of De Swaan's book is its consistent focus on the position of bilinguals as intermediaries whose linguistic skills provide the necessary interconnections in the global language system. The EU would therefore do well to consider the economic potential of its multilingual service sector, and to expand and improve the programmes for foreign language learning and translation in all its member states.

A more socio-cultural reason for such a European investment in learning each others' languages has to do with the European Year of Languages (2001), which has considerably raised awareness of the continent's linguistic diversity. Thus, in her recent travel book *Mother Tongues* (2001) Helena Drysdale recounts her visits to the linguistic minorities in Europe, noting that quite a few are seriously at risk of dying out in the near future. De Swaan, however, has little to say about these languages and refers only in passing to the European Charter for Regional or Minority Languages of 1998. He also says little about the situation of immigrant languages, which are the subject of Extra & Gorter's stimulating volume on *The Other Languages of Europe* (2000).

De Swaan's well-documented book makes very clear what is at stake in matters of language choice. His discussion, however, is predominantly framed in terms of free choice versus protectionism, and this does not seem entirely adequate, since many other factors – such as cultural values, social traditions, political ideologies and personal attachments – appear to play a role as well. In any case, if, as De Swaan claims, language constellations are indeed first and foremost a matter of power relations, then we have to ask how, in a democratic Europe, the ongoing competition between languages can be regulated and managed fairly.

The French novelist Amin Maalouf has made an important suggestion here. In his prize-winning essay *On Identity* (2000) he proposes a three-pronged language strategy for Europe: first, '*to preserve the language of one's own identity, and never let it be so neglected that those who speak it have to turn elsewhere for access to what is offered them by the civilization of today*'; second, '*to make the teaching of English as a third language a matter of course everywhere, and without repining, but explaining to the younger generation that while it is necessary it is not sufficient*'; and third, '*to encourage linguistic diversity so that there are many people in every country familiar not only with Spanish, French, Portuguese, German but also with Arabic, Chinese, Japanese and a hundred other languages that are more rarely studied.*'

REINIER SALVERDA

Abram de Swaan, *Words of the World. The Global Language System.* Cambridge: Polity Press / Blackwell, 2001; 253 pp.
ISBN 0-7456-2748-X.

The Ageless Writings of Bart Moeyaert

Bart Moeyaert (1964-) made his debut in 1983 when he was 19 years old, with a typical novel for teenagers called *Duet, Out of Tune* (Duet met valse noten). It was an ingeniously constructed record of a burgeoning idyll involving Lander and Liselot, who take turns to recount their view of events and their feelings for each other. Moeyaert distilled the story from notes in his own diary, addressed to an imaginary girl. The book struck a chord among young readers and was soon awarded the Prize of the Flemish Children's juries. With this first novel Moeyaert instantly established himself as a youthful star in the gallery of established Flemish children's writers.

In *Back to Square One* (Terug naar af, 1986), the result of having to repeat a year's study, something Moeyaert found hard to come to terms with, he cautiously tried to employ a less wordy rhetoric than in his first novel. The thesis he wrote on the British youth writer Aidan Chambers for his graduation project at the teacher training institute in Brussels set him firmly on a new course. His contacts with Chambers taught him that writing for young readers demanded attention to literary qualities too: composition, style and psychological depth are quite as important, if not more so, as a readable, exciting story.

The first fruit of these new insights was the novel *Suzanne Dantine* (1989). This was the first time Moeyaert had carefully built up an oppressive atmosphere that pushed the actual action into the background. He ingeniously interwove the past and present of the 14-year-old narrator Suzanne Dantine. It is only very sparingly, and in calculated doses, that the author supplies his readers with the pieces of the puzzle that explain the unspoken conflicts and distorted relationships. In the recently published revised version entitled *Hornet's Nest* (Wespennest), the book was purged of its superfluous detail and elaboration and sometimes vague storylines.

According to Moeyaert himself, *Suzanne Dantine* was a pivotal book. The youth writer became an author (for young people and readers in general). In everything that followed he successfully explored new styles, subjects and structures. Unity of time, place and action made the novella *Kiss Me* (Kus me, 1991) an intriguing and gripping tragedy. Four adolescents, three girls and a boy, play their game of secrets by a lake one hot afternoon. In this superb book Moeyaert handles words and narrative motifs with genuine economy. As a result, it requires attentive readers with a degree of literary competence. The pent-up emotions have to be plucked from between the lines. In this work Moeyaert presents us with an uncommonly physical, sensual sort of literature.

In *Bare Hands* (Blote handen, 1995) the compact

structure, sharply defined character sketches and, most particularly, the breathtakingly oppressive atmosphere of *Kiss Me* become Moeyaert's brilliant trump cards. Here the plot is simple and spans only a few hours. Ward and Bernie, two boys of about ten, are running across the bare fields with their dog Elmer on a chill winter's afternoon just before New Year. They are being chased by the cursing Betjeman, with his plastic hand '*which strikes everything that has a heart*'. He is furious at the death of his duck and takes his revenge on Elmer. Because of its ingenious composition, restrained use of language and incredibly evocative power, this simple story develops into an obsessive epic packed full of nameless and unspoken feelings. By guesswork and intuition the attentive reader reconstructs for himself what it is all about. The inevitability of what *has* to happen, the powerful emotions, the whole staging – it seems to possess all the ingredients of a Greek tragedy. The angle from which the story is told – everything is seen and related by the main character, Ward – means that the great drama is set in a childlike microcosm.

In the story *Mansoor, or How We almost got Stina Killed* (Mansoor of hoe we Stina bijna doodkregen, 1996), virtually the same elements are compressed into barely 32 pages: secrets, oppressiveness and pure tragedy in a story about a typical Flemish family reunion. Just as in *Kiss Me*, *Bare Hands* and *Suzanne Dantine*, power and powerlessness are played off against one another. No one wins or loses absolutely, it seems. The reader decides.

In *It's Love We Don't Understand* (Het is de liefde die we niet begrijpen, 1999), a novel for adolescents, Moeyaert leaves behind the bleak Flemish fields and suffocating villages. In a setting reminiscent of American road movies and British social dramas he juxtaposes people in a complicated web of relationships and emotions. The stories in the book, composed like films, are about homesickness that never fades, the yearning for happiness in a loathsome world, and most of all about the love which, in all its forms, keeps people going.

Bart Moeyaert takes *all* his readers seriously. This is also apparent in the little books he wrote for young children beginning to read. In spite of the limitations imposed by the language used for this age group, he succeeds in creating penetrating stories with pronounced characters. Not a word too many here either. In *For Ever, Always* (Voor altijd, altijd, 1992), *Gone Away is not so Far* (Echt weg is niet zo ver, 1993) and *That Alley of Ours* (Die steeg van ons, 1995) Moeyaert tackles such subjects as death, missing people and alcoholism in an original and moving way.

Moeyaert is not an author who cherishes the isolation of his study. Together with the Swedish writer and illustrator Anna Höglund he has produced a striking picture book called *Africa through the Gate* (Afrika achter het hek, 1995) about intercultural tolerance. In *Luna in the Tree* (Luna van de boom, 2000), an extraordinary multimedia picture book, he retells an old Slovak fairytale in his own inimitable style. This book, for which Gerda Dendooven did the illustrations and Filip Bral the music, was awarded the 2001 Golden Owl Prize for Children's Literature. In the meantime Moeyaert has also made his name in the theatre world: as the author of the play *Highwayman Lush* (Rover Dronkeman) and *Uncouth* (Ongelikt), a highly individual adaptation of *King Lear*, and as the author of and actor in *Bremen Is Not Far Away* (Bremen is niet ver), inspired by *Die Bremer Stadtsmusikanten*. He appears as a performer with increasing regularity, for instance with the witty and recognisable stories from his collection entitled *Brother* (Broere) and also in a successful tour with the Dutch writer and illustrator Joke van Leeuwen.

In recent years Bart Moeyaert has made his way, modestly but with stubborn independence, into the first rank. His work has repeatedly been honoured with Flemish, Dutch and German prizes and nominations and is much translated.

He is occasionally labelled 'highbrow'. The implicit and literary nature of his ageless books makes serious demands on the reader. Nevertheless, among the youngsters who read them they undoubtedly tap new and unknown depths and awaken interesting new needs.

ANNEMIE LEYSEN
Translated by Gregory Ball.

Bart Moeyaert (1964-).
Photo by David Samyn.

Bare Hands (Tr. David Colmer). New York, 1998.
Hornet's Nest (Tr. David Colmer). New York, 2000.
It's Love We Don't Understand (Tr. Wanda Boeke). New York, 2001.

Amsterdam, The Netherlands' Big Apple

Travel guides. They come in all shapes and sizes. There are travel guides for the package tourist who is passing through and is satisfied with no more than the comforting clichés; there are guides for the more selective traveller looking for food, love, museums, etc. And then there are the literary guides; those which evoke a landscape by spinning stories around it, or by setting their stories in that landscape. Things become even more interesting when the landscape is that of a city, with its haphazard juxtaposition of houses, squares and public buildings, all charged with history, with that dizzying piling up of events and actions, the unpredictable encounters among the teeming masses of people, the glances and the imagined parallel lives.

Whereabouts Press has already devoted volumes in its *Traveler's Literary Companions* series to Costa Rica, Prague, Vietnam, Israel, Greece and Australia, and now it is the turn of Amsterdam. In the eye of the foreign beholder Amsterdam is a city of canals and bicycles, of a tolerance which spills over into a mild permissiveness of coffeeshops and red lights, a city where gays do not stand out, a city which is at once provincial and cosmopolitan, a city which is civilised, reasonable and open-minded, outspoken and republican.

The *Companion* opens with a fine text by the Dutch writer Cees Nooteboom, who relates how the water invented a city. The novelist J.J. Voskuil and the columnist Simon Carmiggelt are then allowed to fill out the sketch of the city and its people, though the short piece by Carmiggelt, whose indefatigable wanderings through the streets and bars of Amsterdam were matched by his enthusiastic consumption of alcohol, might have been a little less bland. In the introduction to the *Companion* the compiler, Manfred Wolf, describes this oh-so-Dutch genre, which he himself terms a '*column*', very nicely as '*the narrative with a point, the essay with a little story*'. Under the vague title 'Canals' we are presented with stories about a lonely artist in the grip of the gallery-owners, a young couple from the affluent society who venture into a restaurant for the first time since the birth of their first child, with lamentable results, and the tragic demise of a poet who puts off writing his masterpiece whilst sinking into an alcohol-induced decline. We are inside the '*Grachtengordel*', the streets bounded by concentric circles of canals where writers and publishers, artists and art brokers continually rub shoulders and everyone is 'in the know'. Truly typical of Amsterdam is the story by Maarten 't Hart, 'Living in the Red-Light District', in which the writer, who has just been demolished by a feminist in a popular talk show hosted by the politically correct Sonja Barend, is treated to a cup of coffee by a prostitute who wrote a paper on his work whilst in college and who gives him moral support. Although ultimately the sober commercial spirit of the Dutch will prevail.

Two surprising stories by Gerrit Komrij and Bas Heijne about 'Gay Amsterdam' were almost *de rigeur*

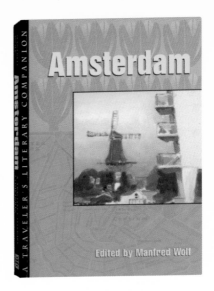

in a book conceived in San Francisco.

The fragment from *The Assault* (De aanslag, 1982) by Harry Mulisch is somewhat strangely placed under the heading 'South'. Strange, because the story does not take place in South Amsterdam at all, but in Haarlem, a small town some 20 kilometres west of Amsterdam. If the compilers wanted to include a fragment from Mulisch' work – and there is plenty to choose from – why not the 1960s marriage of Onno and Ada from *The Discovery of Heaven* (De ontdekking van de hemel, 1992)? Perhaps the scene where the informal bridal couple arrive at the town hall on their bicycles, with the canals exuding an atmosphere of the New Left and Cuba-mania.

The strongest part of the book is the triptych dedicated to Jewish Amsterdam. Just as the heart of Rotterdam was brutally ripped out by a single Luftwaffe bombing raid on a sunny day in May 1940, so the Jewish population of Amsterdam evaporated within the space of five years. Three stories sketch this Decline and Fall of a community. The pre-war years, which now seem idyllic because we know that they never returned ('Business' by Lizzy Sara May); the war years themselves, with the gaps appearing in the community, the slashed wrists, the poisoned chalices being raised to the lips (the classic 'The Decline and Fall of the Boslowits Family' by Gerard Reve: the only remaining item of furniture of the Bobrowmitsky family, friends of Reve who disappeared during the Second World War, is a mirror, which can be seen in an exhibition about Gerard Reve in the Literary Museum in The Hague); and, when everything is over, the return of a few souls to a city which would never be the same because the people in it had disappeared and because '*Le cœur des villes change plus vite que le cœur des hommes*' ('The Return' by Marga Minco).

The soul of a city lies in the details. Homeless people near Central Station compare the quality of the food proffered by the Hare Krishna movement and the

Salvation Army in Geert Mak's 'Rambling about Centraal Station'. But *'everyone agreed that by far the best meal is served once a month at a place called De Wallen by a minister. "You can get a good meal there, three courses, and you even get a bag of oranges and a roll of peppermints as you leave," our tablemate across from us said. "But you do have to first sit through a church service, at which his daughter plays the guitar."'*

A young Amsterdam woman, for her part, thinks it necessary to sexually re-educate her Moroccan new-comer-lover Hafid Bouazza. The didactic genius of a city which regards itself as the most free-and-easy of all cities ultimately forces the lover literally onto his knees. Apolline, tall, blonde, self-confident and unassailable, merges with the city itself. The lover will lose her for ever, and is left behind pregnant: *'On my drunken lurchings across Amsterdam I keep thinking I see Apolline. Her words, the shake of her hair, and the tap of her heels are the seams of recognition that holds the city together for me.'*

Look for her while you're walking through Amsterdam.

LUC DEVOLDERE
Translated by Julian Ross.

Manfred Wolf (ed.), *Amsterdam, A Traveler's Literary Companion.* San Francisco: Whereabouts Press, 2001; 238 pp. ISBN 1-883513-09-X.

The Middle Dutch Arthur in his Rightful Place at the Round Table

Old kings never die, and some do not even fade away. That is certainly true of King Arthur who continues to be in the limelight, not only as an easily recognisable icon for film and cartoon makers but also for scholars and students everywhere. And there is still quite a lot of room for expansion. A recent, and excellent, series of publications which aims to set King Arthur in the context of some national cultures, such as for instance, *The Arthur of the English* (Cardiff, 1999), *The Arthur of the Welsh* (Cardiff, 1991) was recently enriched with a further sturdy volume: *The Arthur of the Germans. The Arthurian Legend in Medieval German and Dutch Literature*, Arthurian Literature in the Middle Ages III, (eds. W.H. Jackson and S.A. Ranawake, Cardiff: University of Wales Press, 2000). One of its nineteen chapters is dedicated to Medieval Dutch Arthurian material and written by Bart Besamusca, an Arthurian scholar who has amply earned his spurs in this field. The editors make a very convincing case for the inclusion of the Middle Dutch material in this volume, which incidentally also encompasses Bohemian and Czech material. Besamusca's contribution is an excellent survey of the surviving material and of the various traditions in Middle Dutch Arthurian literature, with special attention paid to the indigenous romances: *Walewein, Moriaen, Riddere metter mouwen, Walewein ende Keye*. This is however not a new departure:

it is worth pointing out that Dutch scholars, Besamusca himself included, have been exerting themselves for quite a long time to put their Arthur on the European map; and a glance at the bibliography in the survey and the selected bibliography in the new *King Arthur in the Medieval Low Countries* confirms that Dutch Arthurians have publicised their treasures, in various languages, in international journals and volumes of essays. Non-Dutch scholars too have taken the medieval Dutch legacy on board and done much to make others aware of the richness of the Arthurian tradition in the Low Countries.

So, what's new; what makes the present volume such a welcome addition to the existing scholarly research, written in other languages than Dutch, with regard to the medieval Dutch Arthurian tradition?

First of all, it fills a scholarly gap in the map of European Arthurian literature by presenting a more detailed survey of the rich textual tradition in the Low Countries and a plethora of articles presenting the state of research in Arthurian studies in the Netherlands and Dutch-speaking Belgium, in that it pays ample attention to the textual tradition in its European context and discusses translations, adaptations and the indigenous romances which are so prominent in the Middle Dutch tradition. Regrettably but not unexpectedly, the promise in the title *King Arthur in the Medieval Low Countries* does not mean that the presence or absence of texts originating from the French- or German-speaking areas of Belgium is discussed. And, as so often, it would have been very helpful to have a map of the medieval Low Countries, even though, or because, they were such a fluid entity. But those are practically the only quibbles I have, for the volume is immensely helpful both as a whole and in its individual parts.

Moreover, the editors of this volume have thoughtfully provided non-Dutch readers with summaries of the texts themselves. This is particularly timely since we are now also able to read those texts in English translations, a gigantic undertaking. In the series 'Arthurian Archives' (Woodbridge, Suffolk: Boydell & Brewer) a sub-series now exists of which the first two volumes have already appeared: Dutch Romances, Volume I, *Roman van Walewein*, Arthurian Archives Volume 6, (2000) and Dutch Romances, Volume II, *Roman van Ferguut*, Arthurian Archives Volume 7, (2000). The *Walewein* is a revised edition of an earlier translation by David F. Johnson (Garland, 1992) and has fortunately retained its bilingual format: the Middle Dutch text, now fully punctuated in line with modern editorial practices, is printed opposite the English translation. In the case of *Ferguut* we are presented with the first-ever English translation, also with the Middle Dutch text. More translations will follow, and if they are as good as these access to the riches of the Middle Dutch tradition will have been amply ensured.

Thus, the translations and the present volume of articles are a substantial addition to what seems a veritable campaign to accord the Middle Dutch Arthur his rightful place at the Round Table of European Arthurian heroes.

In the Introduction Claassens and Johnson lead us safely through the complexities of the manuscript and compilation traditions and thereby clarify the position of the medieval Dutch material in the European tradition.

Four of the articles discuss texts in which Walewein, '*the father of adventure*', features, and no wonder: he and his French, English and German alter egos Gauvain, Gawain and Gawein, are lastingly important characters in the various traditions. In the Low Countries, Walewein not only appeared in adaptations or translations, he was made the subject of a very long indigenous romance which became known as the *Roman van Walewein*. Equally he is the subject of a shorter indigenous text in which the Perfect Knight is, somewhat unfairly it would seem, the opponent of the hapless seneschal Keye who, here as in other Arthurian traditions, gets hopelessly lost in the impenetrable thickets of a Perilous Forest of his own making, as M. Hogenbirk shows in her contribution. B. Veldhoen compares *Sir Gawain and the Green Knight* with the *Roman van Walewein*, shedding light on the social context in which these texts were produced and, almost as an afterthought, pointing to another fascinating set of religious doctrinal aspects; more work on that would clearly be a valuable addition to existing interpretations of these texts. L. Jongen shows that Walewein in the Dutch tradition becomes the epitome of all that is most excellent, a very different fate from that meted out to his French counterpart; Jongen focuses on one aspect in particular, that of Walewein in the role of confessor, in a scene reminiscent of the *Queste del Saint Graal*, where Gauvain refuses to confess and do penance. K. van Dalen-Oskam considers one of the most intriguing aspects of the *Roman van Walewein*, the episode of the Flying Chessboard, and interprets that marvellous and costly object as a sophisticated worldly counterpart of the Holy Grail

Naturally, Sir Lancelot and the immense Middle Dutch *Lancelot Compilation* are extensively represented in articles by Brandsma, who goes in pursuit of the corrector of the *Lancelot Compilation* and concludes, somewhat wistfully, that that interfering personage becomes more elusive the longer one chases after him. Never mind: as in any true Quest, the voyaging is the fascinating part, whatever the point of arrival. Besamusca follows the vicissitudes of the Damsel of Montesclare in the *Compilation*; this lady does not invite pursuit, on the contrary, her unfortunate '*manners and appearance did not calculate to please*' but Besamusca shows convincingly that this secondary character brings consistency and cohesion to an otherwise very diverse narrative cycle. The presence of another not so very prominent character also sheds light on the constitution of the *Lancelot Compilation*, as Oppenhuis de Jong shows in a veritable archeological investigation tracing Acglovael's varying adventures. Claassens discusses the narrator in one of the indigenous romances which have been interpolated into the *Lancelot Compilation*, the *Lanceloet en het hert met de witte voet*, a text very similar to the *Lai de Tyolet* and mis-

KING ARTHUR
IN THE MEDIEVAL
LOW COUNTRIES

LEUVEN UNIVERSITY PRESS
2000

leading in its title: here too it is Walewein who takes the starring role, whilst Lanceloet is depicted in a rather sorry state.

One of the intriguing indigenous romances also inserted into the *Lancelot Compilation*, the story of the black knight *Moriaen*, is discussed by Norris Lacy whose frustration with the existing text, and longing for the lost Flemish original, results in a very lively and interesting contribution with the kind of conclusion which scholars come to only as a last resort: this is '*a deeply flawed adaptation*', '*a hermeneutic conundrum that the present state of our understanding will not permit us to solve*'. Claassens' article about the *Queste van den Grale* shows that the Götterdämmerung mood which is so pervasive in the *Queste del Saint Graal* is largely absent in its Middle Dutch counterpart, which seems to aim at delaying as long as possible the inevitable decline and fall of the Arthurian empire. Pallemans takes up the sword and prepares to do battle, armed with his conviction that '*the Middle Dutch "Wrake van Ragisel" can directly contribute to a better understanding of its French model "La Vengeance Raguidel"*'. He wins that combat and in doing so not only shows the fascinating nature of the French and Middle Dutch texts but also demonstrates the complex interventions of translators, adapters and compilers who have their own hidden agendas.

Schlusemann's contribution brings the Middle Dutch and the Middle German Arthurian material together. As with other medieval Dutch texts, Arthurian tales too were often translated into German dialects. The Dutch material, Arthurian or otherwise, thus forged a link between Romance and Germanic cultures. Schlusemann shows that the linking was not merely a question of translating but also of transforming, and that some of the preoccupations of the three cultures can be identified by their presence or absence in the various texts.

Indeed, that is true of this volume too: *King Arthur in the Medieval Low Countries* presents us with much that is unique, distinctive and characteristic in Dutch medieval Arthurian literature, but it also allows us different perspectives of the Arthurian culture of the surrounding countries; like the eponymous hero of the *Roman van Walewein*, we tumble from one exciting adventure into the next. Walewein is presented with precious white silk clothes by King Wonder. '*I do believe*', says the narrator, '*that never before had such costly clothes been seen. So many marvels had been embroidered on them that one could not have bought their like for 1000 pounds. There is not a clerk in all Paris, so learned and so wise, who could have read or interpreted what was embroidered on those garments.*' Well, our assembly of clerks have had a very succesful go at it.

ELSA STRIETMAN

Geert H.M.Claassens and David F. Johnson (eds.), *King Arthur in the Medieval Low Countries*. Medievalia Lovaniensia, Series 1, Studia XXVIII. Leuven University Press, 2000; 274 pp. ISBN 90-5867-042-2.

Music

Music of the People, for the People
Peter Benoit, a Hundred Years On

Composer, conductor and teacher Peter Benoit (1834-1901) was widely commemorated in 2001, the one-hundredth anniversary of his death. The leading light of musical Flanders in the nineteenth century, he left behind an impressive oeuvre and laid the foundations for important innovations in musical life.

Benoit studied at the Conservatoire in Brussels where the director, Fétis, was his most influential teacher. Having completed his studies, Benoit was appointed conductor of the Flemish Theatre in Brussels. In 1857 he won the prestigious Prix de Rome for composition. The award included a scholarship that enabled him to spend two years in various large musical centres in Germany, followed by several years (1859-1863) in Paris. There he made a name for himself as a composer of piano music and was for a while the conductor of the Bouffes Parisiennes, Offenbach's operetta company, with which he also appeared in Vienna, Brussels and Amsterdam. By that time he had found success in Brussels too, not least with his *Quadrilogie Religieuse* (Christmas Cantata, High Mass, Te Deum and Requiem). On his return to Belgium he was hailed as the most promising composer of his generation. A new triumph followed in 1866 with his oratorio *Lucifer*. Contrary to all logic, he wrote the oratorio to a text in Dutch, and this marked the beginning of his years of work for the revaluation of the 'Flemish' language and 'Flemish' music.

In 1867 he became director of the Ecole de musique d'Anvers, which he renamed the 'Vlaamse Muziekschool' or Flemish Music School. From then until his death he would remain a zealous advocate of his nationalistic musical principles. He believed composers should draw on the rhythm and melody of folk song and use their mother tongue, since that too is a source of national culture. In this respect his aspirations ran parallel to the so-called 'national schools' of (among others) Grieg in Norway and Smetana in Bohemia. In his educational theory, Benoit regarded his school as a centre for total music education, embracing all strata of society: from family music-making and brass bands to the virtuoso and the composer, everything was geared towards general cultural education and raising the cultural level of the Flemish people. To this end he organised large-scale music festivals, developed cultural cooperation with the Netherlands and campaigned for opera in Flemish. Benoit thus became the leading light of the Flemish national school in the field of music. Yet he was certainly not narrow-minded: he also defended the Walloon composers and as a conductor he promoted compositions by other national schools in Europe and organised festivals at which work by his friends Gounod and Liszt was performed. From his base at the music school, through his public

Edouard de Jans, *Portrait of Peter Benoit*. 1916.

appearances as a conductor, his compositions and numerous publications, he received ample support both from musicians and literary figures and gradually reached the masses as well. Partly thanks to that huge following, in 1897 his school was raised to the official status of Royal Flemish Academy of Music (Koninklijk Vlaams Muziekconservatorium). At a time when not only every institute of higher education, but also the judicial authorities, the army, ministries, etc. used French as the official language of communication, this was a major step towards the cultural autonomy of Flanders. A hundred years after his death, his influence is still apparent: directly in the two institutions he established – the academy and the opera house in Antwerp –, but also indirectly in the fruits of his ideas: the Flanders International Festival, the cultural agreements with neighbouring countries, cultural federalism, the broad-based musical life in the form of choirs, brass bands and wind and percussion ensembles.

As a composer Benoit was a child of his time, and his work is very much part of the romantic movement. Yet we can clearly distinguish two different periods in his oeuvre. With his work up to and including *Lucifer* he established himself as a composer with a personal but contemporary European style. His religious music, his piano compositions and his contribution to the revival of the secular oratorio can be considered valuable, even from an international standpoint. He continued along that road for the next ten years, but then gave his full attention to the national movements. Here, too, he wrote successful works in a romantic-realistic style, which were described by his contemporaries as modern: oratorios (*The Scheldt* – De Schelde, *The War* – De Oorlog), lyric dramas (*The Pacification of Ghent* – De Pacificatie van Gent), piano work and songs (*Love Drama* – Liefdedrama) and religious music (*Drama Christi*). But in campaigning for an art that would have popular appeal – typical of nineteenth-century nationalism – he wanted to embrace first and foremost ordinary people. From 1877 and the *Rubens Cantata* (Rubenscantate) he saw his work mainly as a socio-cultural, educational medium. He simplified his style into an art for the masses: straightforward melodies, large choirs, strong orchestration. For example, he wrote several cantatas that pay tribute in broad frescos to his people and his native country. In so doing, Benoit deliberately stagnated as a composer, but as a cultural leader he was well able to enthuse the public at large and could thus realise his ambitions for Flemish national culture. Since his death, it has been those popular works that have kept his name alive. His centenary, which coincides with a European revival of the romantic stylistic period, is a splendid opportunity to reassess his valuable work from the years 1857-1877.

HENDRIK WILLAERT
Translated by Alison Mouthaan-Gwillim.

Peter Benoit, *Music from Flanders, part I.* CD Harmonia Mundi, 1999.

A Pioneer in Electronic Music The Tonal Art of Jan Boerman

In 1999 Donemus brought out *The Complete Tape Music of Jan Boerman*, a boxed set of five CDs and a book, which many welcomed as a long-overdue tribute to a composer whose voice has for some four decades been internationally acknowledged as an original and innovative force in electronic music. The CD set, which features key works from a formidable oeuvre beginning with *Musique concrète* (1959) and concluding on *Ruin* (Ruïne, 1997), is beautifully produced, and was the 1999 recipient of the annual Edison award for Dutch recorded music.

A piece of particular fascination, and displaying the quintessential qualities associated with Boerman's mature work, is *Unchainment II* (Ontketening II) of 1984, a thirty-minute, large-scale composition scored for percussion, electronics, and tape. Live electronics, and the integration of electronic and instrumental – including vocal – elements have been central to the composer's work since the mid-seventies. The result is not easy to describe. In the case of *Unchainment II*, the opening consists of a wonderfully elusive, mysterious tape episode, which is soon augmented by a no less entrancing sound from Slagwerkgroup Den Haag – for whom the piece was written – playing an eclectic assembly of instruments that among others things includes crotals, cymbals, dobachi, gongs, tam-tams, temple blocks, maracas, bongos, congas, large and small tympanum, kettledrums, and marimba. Two years before the completion of *Unchainment II*, in 1982, Boerman received the premier Dutch award for contemporary music, the Matthijs Vermeulen Prize, in recognition of his work as a whole.

Vocalise 1994, also featured on the CD set, which was awarded the 1994 Willem Pijper Prize for the outstanding composition of the year, is the culmination of a process of experimentation with electronics and the human voice which began in 1976, with *Preparatory Study for a Vocalise* (Vocalise – voorstudie; not featured), in the course of which Boerman also wrote for choir, brass and tape.

Boerman has always set his own parameters and steadfastly gone his own way, pushing the limits of whatever captures his interest until he feels he has exhausted all its possibilities. Thus he continued to work with tape until 1989, well after most composers had abandoned this medium. From the 1960s onwards, he has been absorbed in uniting concrete acoustic and constructed synthesised sounds, and in intensive exploration of the relationship between tone length and timbre-movement, creating 'music spaces' at the intersection of 'tone and noise', in which 'dead' tones are metamorphosed into living, breathing sounds. To structure and order this tonal world of his creation, Boerman applied the principle of the Golden Section, or Divine Proportion – the mathematical system whereby the lesser part is to the greater as is the greater to the whole – which occupied so important a place in Renaissance painting, architecture and music. Out

Jan Boerman (1923-).
Photo by Co Broerse.

of this has come music of rare emotional and intellectual intensity.

In awarding Boerman the Willem Pijper Prize in 1994, the jury made a special point of emphasising that in his tonal (electronic) art, Boerman 'places himself within the great instrumental and vocal tradition'. Boerman himself has never perceived electronics as a repudiation of the classical tradition in which he first established his name as a composer during the decade from 1950 to 1960. Throughout his career, moreover, he has remained loyal to the piano, his first instrument, producing a body of work for two pianos that tends to be overshadowed by his electronic work. During Holland Festival 2000 he was granted the honour of devising a programme pairing two compositions of his own with earlier masterworks to which he acknowledges a debt. Boerman's choice was to couple, in order of performance, the purely electronic works *Composition 1972* (Compositie 1972) and *Cycle I* (Kringloop I) – both featured on the CD set – with the Jacob Obrecht mass *Sub tuum praesidium confugimus* and Joseph Haydn's *Oxford Symphony* respectively. To Obrecht, declared Boerman, he owed the idea of applying the Golden Section. His debt to Haydn he described in terms of a musical approach which was light and optimistic and at the same time profound in feeling.

Jan Boerman was born in 1923 in The Hague, where he still lives, and studied at the Royal Conservatory of Music. His first subject was piano with Léon Orthel, after which, from 1945, he also took composition with Hendrik Andriessen. From 1956 onwards he worked in the electronic studios of the Technical University of Delft, the University of Utrecht – which was to become the Institute of Sonology, his shared domain with Dick Raaymakers – and of The Hague Royal Conservatory. At the Conservatory he also taught piano and, from 1974, electronic composition.

Preparatory Study for a Vocalise (1976), as mentioned earlier, marked Boerman's first venture into combining electronics and natural, live sound. His next

work, *Composition 1979* (Compositie 1979) was an electronic tape work, but there then followed a succession of compositions for a variety of live electronic, tape, and instrumental combinations. Another facet of Boerman's work up to 1970 was his interest in the stage. During this period he composed both for the theatre and, notably, for ballet. His *Monument for a Dead Boy* (Monument voor een gestorven jongen), an electronic score commissioned by the Royal Netherlands Ballet, has remained part of the company's permanent repertory since it was premiered in 1965.

According to composer-musician Michael Waisvisz, a co-director of STEIM (Studio for electro-instrumental music) in Amsterdam, Boerman single-handedly represents the entire genre of electro-acoustic music in The Netherlands. Waisvisz calls him a loner, who has existed in relative isolation from his foreign colleagues. The landscape of electronic music is in itself an isolated landscape, but even within this Boerman counts as a clever enough but isolated composer, with the advantage, incidentally, that this isolation has nourished the alchemical nature of his music.

To this Waisvisz adds that though Boerman today receives every recognition as a tonal master, he had to wait a long time for this, and sometimes life was bitter. '*He is a master of nuances. But in the past, other people playing his tapes could sometimes be a bit slapdash – which in places where those nuances play an important role, was, of course, quite unfortunate.*'

Michel Waisvisz regards Jan Boerman as an authentically tonal composer. '*Sound is what matters to him most, and he has a gift for transcending the purely technical. Boerman is always out to create a wholly individual narrative in sound. Pierre Henry and other electronic composers as a rule turn to literary motifs as contexts to give substance to their work, but Boerman doesn't need that. He virtually exists in a universe of sound. Through the years he has worked with specific sets of sound families, or relationships, that are very recognisable, and it's through this that he creates his highly individual particular sound culture.*'

Boerman himself would never assert that he has been an innovator in a technical respect, but for all that it is established fact that from 1962 he was, together with Dick Raaymakers, one of the first exponents of electronic music to develop electronic musical concepts and techniques that are now part of the common language. Over the decades the two of them never stopped amending and rebuilding their studio equipment to extract completely new sounds. Waisvisz: *'It's precisely because Boerman achieved such technical mastery that he was able to see his way to producing the superior musical utterances he does. And as a teacher he never failed to turn out people of absolutely solid professional quality.'*

In an illuminating commentary on the Donemus CD set, Fritz van der Waa observes that the composer has always regarded the phenomenon of electronic music as an intermediary phase, a forerunner of what will one day be a truly new music performed on instruments yet to come. Like the French composer Edgar Varèse he cherishes a vision of *'the liberation of a sound*, and sees the emergence of keyboards as a step backwards rather than forwards. Neither, for that matter, does he want anything to do with computers.

Ruin of 1997, which is featured on the 1999 CD set, is Boerman's last completed composition. He was seventy-four when he finished it, and had sadly been finding increasingly that his hearing was no longer up to the high frequencies he so much loves to work with. Besides, according to Van der Waa, he feels that he has gone as far as he can and wants to with electronics, though not with music as such. Currently he is working on a large-scale choral work and a new set of piano pieces.

For a keener insight into a composer and his music, it is always worth going to the source. Asked in interview whether he thought that applying the classical mathematical relationships of the Golden Section evokes a heightened emotional response to his music, Boerman answered that: *'Music is invariably about emotion, but equally all music is based on rational principles. The two cannot be divorced from one another. Naturally, I do want to express something in my work, but not outside of the music itself. In this connection I would mention "The Sea I" (De Zee I, 1965), because this has a particular kind of dramatic power and impact. However, this does not mean to say that I was out to mimic the sound of the sea.'*

Of the works on CD, *The Sea I* and *Composition 1972* may perhaps be accounted the purest, most uncompromising, in terms of the sharpness of articulation. Especially *The Sea* is composed almost exclusively of 'noise' sounds dissolving into the rise and fall of motions whose internal movements and dynamics are governed by the ratios of the Golden Section.

JAN RUBINSTEIN
Translated by Sonja Prescod.

The Complete Tape Music of Jan Boerman. (NEAR / Donemus, CV NEAR 4/5/6/7/8, 1999).

The Queen and the Violin Fiftieth Anniversary of the Queen Elisabeth International Music Competition

The Belgian Queen Elisabeth International Music Competition, which celebrated its fiftieth anniversary in 2001, is unique of its kind, not so much because it comprises four disciplines – violin, piano, singing and composition –, but because it is regarded as one of the most exacting in the world. It has been won by such renowned virtuosos as Fleisher, Ashkenazy, Laredo and Repin. The Competition venues include the Royal Brussels Music Conservatory, the Queen Elisabeth Music Chapel in Waterloo and the Brussels Palais des Beaux-Arts.

The inspiration for the competition came from Eugène Ysaÿe, after Charles de Bériot and Henri Vieuxtemps the third in an illustrious line of soloists to emerge from the Belgian violin school. As a young soloist starting out on his career, Ysaÿe had experienced for himself just how difficult it was to make it onto the international concert stage. So he toyed with the idea of giving young musicians a faster and more dignified start to their careers through healthy competition with the very best of their contemporaries.

He felt very strongly, however, that any cliquishness or rivalry between different schools should be avoided at all costs. He elaborated on that view in a letter to Théodore Dubois, director of the Paris Conservatoire in 1904, in which he set out his reasons for declining to sit on a jury that judged and awarded prizes for the higher grades of violin at the conservatory.

'Alas', he wrote, *'long experience has taught me that the competitions tell us more about the teachers than the students'.* In the same document Ysaÿe suggested organising an examination for musicians at university level. Candidates would spend eight to ten days in isolation studying a concerto in manuscript form of which they would be required to give an interpretation without having been coached on the piece by a teacher. Another point on which Ysaÿe felt very strongly was the absolute objectivity, integrity and strictness of the jury.

In the end, it was thanks to none other than the Belgian Queen Elisabeth, the wilful, non-conformist Bavarian who had inherited from her father, Karl-Theodor von Wittelsbach, a passion for everything to do with medicines and music, that these ideas became reality. After the tragic death of her husband, King Albert I, in Marche-les-Dames on 17 February 1934 it was Jacques Thibaud who raised her spirits, not with words but with his violin, her favourite instrument.

The concrete result of the cooperation between the Queen and the virtuoso was the Concours International Eugene Ysaÿe, which took place in 1937. The Liège engineer and composer Charles Houdret was responsible for organising the event. And it proved a resounding success. Its format then was very similar to that of the Queen Elisabeth Competition today: the selection procedure (preliminary round, semi-final and final involving twelve short-listed musicians) and the jury

Queen Elisabeth of
Belgium in 1949. Photo by
Paul van den Abeele.

system (in which the prestigious members judge individually rather than collectively) have remained unchanged.

Nearly all the prizes were scooped up by Russians. Five of them took part, five made it through to the final round and all five ranked among the first six! The overall winner was David Oistrakh. Buoyed up by the success of the event, Charles Houdret came up with the idea of establishing a four-year cycle with a competition for violin, followed by one for piano and then for orchestral conducting, and then a year's break. So, in 1938 there would be a competition for piano, in 1939 one for conductors, nothing in 1940 and then in 1941 a violin competition again, in 1942 a piano competition and in 1943 a competition for conductors.

With the discrete support of the Queen, Houdret pressed ahead and proved he was right, for the 1938 piano competition was even more favourably received than the violin competition. The Concours Ysaÿe would have had a dazzling future had the war not come along (and Charles Houdret misappropriated the funds), bringing down the whole carefully erected structure.

The idea of a competition was not resurrected until the fifties. And, of course, again it was the Queen who instigated it. But rather than Ysaÿe's name, the new organisers – Count Paul de Launoit and Marcel Cuvelier – decided to name the competition for Elisabeth, not least because it would now comprise several disciplines (violin, piano and composition).

When on Monday 21 May 1951 – twenty years after the death of Eugène Ysaÿe – the first finalist mounted the stage in what would officially be called the 'Concours musical international reine Elisabeth de Belgique', it was the twenty-four-year-old Russian violinist, Alexej Gorokov, who had the honour of performing

the world première of the composition written for the competition, the *Violin Concerto* by the Belgian René Defossez.

Fifty years later to the day, on 21 May 2001, another twenty-four-year-old Russian violinist, Boris Brovtsyn, stood before the jury, this time to perform the world première of *Qilaatersoneq* by the Dane Soren Nils Eichberger, chosen as the compulsory concerto from the ninety-five entries for the international competition for composition.

It is no accident that the fiftieth anniversary fell in the very year of a violin competition; rather this was the result of an earlier change in sequence. In 1975, when it would normally have been the turn of the violin, the organisers arranged for the piano competition to go ahead first so that they could move the violin competition to 1976, the one-hundredth anniversary of the birth of Queen Elisabeth.

Later on the singing competition was introduced and since then the cycles have been scrupulously respected. They always begin in an odd year with the piano competition, continue in an even year with the singing and end in an odd year with the violin, followed by a year's rest.

So as a result of delaying the violin session for a year and introducing the singing contest, the competition's golden jubilee in 2001 conveniently coincided with a competition for the violin, the instrument with which it had all begun.

VIC DE DONDER
Translated by Alison Mouthaan-Gwillim.

http://www.queen-elisabeth-competition.be

Face to Face with the *Dalton Terror*
Philosophy between University and Journalism

The *Dalton Terror* is one of the newest attractions in the Belgian theme park Six Flags, just south of Brussels. You are strapped into a chair, hoisted to a height of sixty metres and then dropped, sitting in the chair, like a stone to the ground. Some people find it awful; others find it a fantastic experience. For the Flemish author and philosopher Patricia de Martelaere the *Dalton Terror* is first and foremost an exercise in dying.

As is usually the case with De Martelaere, you should not take this too straightforwardly or literally. Of course a fall of sixty metres has something to do with being scared to death, but that is not what she means. It is more the unpredictability of her own reaction, waiting in the queue with her children for the attraction, that makes her think about dying. After all, you do not know how you will behave in your last hours either. Only the experience itself can count as a touchstone of character.

From this everyday scene of queuing for a theme park attraction De Martelaere glides smoothly, in her newest collection of essays *Unworldliness* (Wereldvreemdheid, 2000)*,* into a philosophical reflection in which the Stoics, Nietzsche and the *Tibetan Book of the Dead* criss-cross as a matter of course. The common-or-garden is not a springboard to the eternal, exalted realm of philosophy, a badly camouflaged attempt at seducing the reader. Philosophy *exists* for De Martelaere first and foremost in the commonplace. Her essays belong there too; like those from her earlier collections *A Longing for Inconsolability* (Een verlangen naar ontroostbaarheid, 1993) and *Surprises* (Verrassingen, 1997) they had previously been published in newspapers, weeklies and popular magazines. She understands the gift of letting everything melt into one logical amalgam, in which the commonplace leads to something less than banality and directness of speech to something less than simplicity.

In this De Martelaere belongs to the small group of Dutch-speaking philosophers (she teaches at the universities of Brussels and Leuven) who realise that philosophy cannot afford to remain locked up in academic institutions. Not only does philosophy have – like any other science – the task of becoming *real*, which it can only do by addressing a public that itself belongs to the broadest social reality, but she cannot imagine her own intellectual activity without the questions and problems which society puts to philosophy and which ultimately provide its final source of inspiration and its *raison d'être.*

That is a role that philosophers have to get used to but few are really successful in. In the past, it was theologians rather than philosophers that traditionally conducted philosophical discussion, particularly in the Netherlands. In Flanders too only a few philosophers

The *Dalton Terror* at Six Flags, Wavre. Photo courtesy of Six Flags.

have managed to play the public role traditionally fulfilled, especially in France, by philosophers. With the diminishing influence of the Church and religion, the field has gone untilled in both countries and increasingly over the last decade the public has looked hopefully towards philosophy as the most suitable discipline to fill this gap.

Philosophical periodicals like the Dutch monthly *Filosofie Magazine* have achieved circulation figures that until recently were unthinkable and philosophers are much sought-after speakers in a continuously expanding circuit of lectures and discussion forums with a philosophical bias. The journalist Antoine Verbij, who recently described this development in his book *Thinking behind the Dykes* (Denken achter de dijken, 2000), subtitled the book: *The Advance of Philosophy in Holland.* Verbij refuses to see philosophy as a sort of substitute for a diminished religion. Although on the ragged edges of this very diversified terrain the necessary mystical woolliness and neo-religiosity can be found, he noticed on his travels that most of the people involved draw a very clear distinction between clear philosophical rationality and the grubbier desires of the philosophical underbelly.

Verbij writes this with a noticeable sigh of relief, which is justified because in general the academic world largely ignores this 'wild' interest in philosophy and does little to give it proper guidance. The universities have put all their money on pure scholarship, which means they expect their philosophers to converse mainly *amongst themselves* and publish articles (nearly always in English) in international journals. This soon puts paid to any exchange of ideas with the wider public, all the more so because such activity yields hardly any credits in the university points system, even if it does not immediately discredit any academic who engages in it.

Thus we are faced with the paradoxical situation that philosophy in the Low Countries is more popular than ever, but the institutions where it traditionally belongs make every effort to steer clear of or even frustrate this popularity. The place where philosophy carries out its social function and duty is thus gradually shifting to a sort of philosophical midfield where philosophically-trained publicists, authors and journalists congregate together with the odd academic who does not care about the universities' stuffy attitude.

De Martelaere is one of those philosophers who know how to combine scholarship with social presentation. Just how welcome this is, can be seen from the fact that some of her volumes of essays (a genre which seldom makes for a large circulation in the Dutch language-area) even appeared in paperback. But then De Martelaere is a hybrid figure; she also writes novels, and so is by nature attuned to the broader literary readership.

In this she has a counterpart in the Flemish author Stefan Hertmans, an emphatically *non*-academic poet and novelist, who has likewise achieved success in the field of the philosophical essay. His impressive collection *Fugues and Blue-Tits (about current events, art and criticism)* (Fuga's en pimpelmezen (over actualiteit, kunst en kritiek)), published in 1995, gained a sequel in a book-length essay *Dubious Matters* (Het bedenkelijke, 1999). In this Hertmans embarks on a quest – inspired by present-day French philosophy – for the paradoxes of the obscene and enigmas of the indecent that we usually prefer to hide under the carpet – a quest as uncomfortable as it is profound.

Hertmans' essay appeared in the series with which the philosophical publishing house Boom has recently sought to give this suspect genre a wider forum and more prestige in the Netherlands. The increasing popularity of philosophical reflections written for a wider public and linked to topical subjects formed the starting-point for this series, in which Boom stretched the 'essay' concept to a generous hundred pages. Besides Hertmans, others published in the series included the philosophers Hans Achterhuis, with *The Politics of Good Intentions* (Politiek van goede bedoelingen, 1999), a critical audit of NATO's intervention in Kosovo, Harry Kunneman, in a personal reckoning with his tutor Jürgen Habermas entitled *Postmodern Morality* (Postmoderne moraliteit, 1998) and Henk Oosterling with *Radical Mediocrity* (Radicale middelmatigheid, 2000) a reflection on globalisation, new media and post-modern philosophy.

The question is, whether all these attempts succeed as philosophical *essays*. The genre demands much of philosophers, who sometimes still find it hard to distance themselves from jargon and philosopher's style. Thinkers who can write well, express themselves in simple terms and who also have their own ideas, are rare at present. However, the future of a vigorous philosophy in the Low Countries is more crucially dependent upon this than university governors want to recognise. Slowly it is taking shape, defying the oppression, as a new genre, halfway between journalism and science. This kind of essay embodies a 'wild thinking' and writing in which philosophical *passion* continues, even – or perhaps precisely – when face to face with something as improbable as the *Dalton Terror*.

GER GROOT
Translated by Derek Denné.

No Half-Measures Peter Piot Leads the Struggle against Aids

The 1st of December is World Aids Day. Since 1996, on the initiative of UNAIDS, the victims of this disease have been remembered on this day. At the moment it is estimated that the number of people infected with the HIV virus is 40 million; 90% of them live in the third world and about half of these in Africa. The United Nations founded UNAIDS in 1996 with the aim of setting in motion a world-wide campaign against Aids. From the beginning it has been headed by Peter Piot (1949-), a doctor from Flanders .

Piot studied medicine at Ghent University and microbiology in Antwerp and specialised in sexually-transmitted diseases at the University of Washington in Seattle. From 1980 to 1992 he worked at the Institute of Tropical Medicine in Antwerp. During this period he spent a good deal of time in African countries including Burundi, Ivory Coast, Kenya, Tanzania and Congo. He was one of those who discovered the Ebola virus in 1976. He has written more than 500 articles and 15 books.

Following research at a Kinshasa hospital in 1983, he wrote a study of the transmission of the HIV virus by heterosexual contact. It met with much scepticism; people continued to assume that the HIV virus was not transmissible between men and women. In 1984 the renowned medical journal *The Lancet* published his study. Piot also focused attention on the significant consequences of Aids for the social and economic development of Africa. Since 1987 he has worked on the World Health Organisation's Aids programme, and in

1996 he was appointed the first executive director of UNAIDS by the Secretary-General of the United Nations. He was chosen partly for his scientific knowledge, but also for his political insight. He often meets political leaders whom he has to convince of the need for radical action, and his diplomatic talents are a considerable help.

UNAIDS is based in Geneva; with 180 staff and a budget (in 2000-01) of $140 million it is not a large UN organisation. Nevertheless, it has succeeded in getting Aids onto the political agenda of such important meetings as those of the G8, G77 and the European Union.

In June 2001 an assembly of the UN met especially to discuss Aids. It was the first time the UN had organised this sort of meeting to deal with a health problem. In late 2001 there was also an international conference in Dakar, organised by France to discuss access to medicines to combat Aids. At the September 2001 Racism Conference at Durban in South Africa Piot complained that Aids sufferers laboured under an excessive burden of shame and fear. He also explicitly linked the disease to racism, poverty, intolerance and inequality. In his view, the HIV epidemic is *the* tragedy of the twenty-first century. Piot has received several awards for his efforts and consistent action. In 1995 he was honoured with the title of baron by King Albert II of Belgium. In October 2000 he was elected one of the 56 foreign members of the American Institute of Medicine. Probably his finest award is the one he received before the start of the Durban conference. It was there that he was handed the Mandela Award by Secretary-General Kofi Annan. Annan praised Piot because he '*brings to this fight a blend of authority and commitment that only comes from long and first-hand experience. He has rightly pointed out that half-measures do not work against this epidemic*'. In his speech of thanks Piot said that millions of dollars are needed every year for the poorer countries and that a Fund for Aids Control, which is soon to be set up, is intended to help the countries most affected.

Peter Piot sees Aids as one of the world's most important problems, but he is absolutely convinced that a solution does exist. If we do not believe that, he thinks, his work is pointless.

DIRK VAN ASSCHE
Translated by Gregory Ball.

www.unaids.org

Peter Piot (1949-). Photo courtesy of UNAIDS.

perfect man for the job, as other European countries have acknowledged. During Kok's period in office, the Dutch 'polder model' has become known worldwide as a method of government that combines economic success with social and political stability. The basic rules of this model are: practice politics in a businesslike way, seek consensus with social organisations and defer decisions until all the cards have been shuffled. Kok can also take credit for founding the Third Way – the new, somewhat vague political ideology that has returned the social democrats to the centre of the political stage in England, Germany and Spain.

How did Kok reach the top? This is an interesting question because until well into the 1980s there was little to indicate that he would become a prominent politician. As a young man, Kok's ambition was to become a newspaper correspondent. More or less by chance he joined the trade union movement and in 1972, at only 33 years of age, he was appointed president of the largest Dutch trade union federation, the Nationaal Vak Verbond (NVV), later renamed the Federatie van Nederlandse Vakverenigingen (FNV; Federation of Netherlands Trade Unions). Fourteen years later, when Kok was almost 50, the Dutch Labour Party (Partij van de Arbeid or PvdA) approached him to lead the social democrats in the Netherlands.

What special qualities convinced the PvdA that Kok should be their leader? Kok is Dutch through-and-through, a 'boy from the polders'. He is the son of a carpenter from Bergambacht in the province of South Holland. Sheltering behind the dykes, Bergambacht is a village of relatively well-off, orthodox Protestant farmers, joinery workshops and a working-class community. Such a mixture can be extremely volatile, as experience has shown in some parts of the Netherlands: in neighbouring Ammerstol, for instance, which became known as Moscow-on-the-Lek. Not so Bergambacht. Its workers were reformists; aware of differing opinions, but equally aware that the only realistic approach was practical, piecemeal reform. Calvinist

Society

Wim Kok, the Prime Minister from the Polders

Since 1994, Wim Kok (1938-) has been not only a successful Prime Minister of the Netherlands but also the

Wim Kok (1938-).

Socialism is characterised by its austerity, work ethic, and incredibly deep-seated loyalty to the party and the labour movement. Kok has always remained loyal to this form of socialism; he was born to it.

The young Kok was a quiet, studious boy who liked to remain in the background. At weekends he preferred to immerse himself in the headmaster's books rather than going out on the tiles. His school grades were excellent, and he attended an advanced elementary school (then known as 'MULO') before moving up to high school (then known as 'HBS'). In this he was unusual among working-class children, who usually attended technical school. Kok did not go to university; it was too expensive and took too long. Instead, he took a two-year management course at the somewhat elite Nijenrode institute. They were not the happiest days of his life, but he gained a good grounding in languages and learned to survive in a completely different environment.

Kok decided to work for the trade union movement, which was going through turbulent times. It was an era of almost revolutionary fervour, which the old union framework was struggling to cope with. In all this turmoil Kok was a peaceful, unifying influence of considerable importance. His plans for reform were anything but impetuous, and he remained loyal to the idea that a common-sense approach yields the best results. This approach won him the presidency at the youthful age of 33. Kok, with his common-sense views, proved that he could read the signs of the times better than the PvdA, which thought it could win a majority by diametrically opposing the other parties. Although this resulted in the most left-wing cabinet in Dutch history (the Den Uyl cabinet, 1973-1977), the party achieved nothing like its hoped-for majority. This taught Kok that in a country with as many political currents as the Netherlands successful reform could only be achieved if it was built on a foundation of social co-operation, or consensus.

In 1982 events proved him right. The Dutch economy was experiencing its worst-ever recession. The centre-right Lubbers cabinet was about to take office. Kok nevertheless decided to adopt a cooperative stance. With Chris van Veen, president of the employers' organisation, he signed the historic Wassenaar Accord: wage moderation in return for shorter working hours and job security. The accord encapsulated what later came be known as the Polder Model, or Dutch Model.

In the years that followed the Accord proved successful, though it was the Lubbers government that reaped most of the benefits. Joop den Uyl was nevertheless convinced that Wim Kok was the only man who could succeed him as leader of the Labour Party. After a great deal of hesitation – he is hesitant by nature – Kok took up the gauntlet, knowing that he had a long way to go before the party stalwarts could be persuaded to adopt a more practical approach. Kok did not make himself popular. In 1993, as Minister of Finance in the third Lubbers cabinet, he brought his party to the brink of disaster by voting in favour of the cabinet's proposed cutbacks in social services.

Eventually, though, the 'lonely cyclist' won support. His party lost a great many seats in the 1994 elections, but the Christian Democratic party (CDA; Christen-Democratisch Appel), torn by an internal power struggle, suffered even more . Kok's PvdA ended up as the largest party, and consequently was responsible for forming the cabinet. Kok used this opportunity to form a coalition with the liberal- conservative VVD party, the former adversaries of the PvdA. He became Prime Minister of a cabinet that, for the first time since 1918, contained no Christian Democrats; and because the economic tide was with him it was a success. In 1998, Kok signed up for a second 'Purple Cabinet'.

Kok will not be standing for re-election in May 2002; but it is expected that he will continue to play a prominent role in Europe. Kok will go down in history as the champion of the polder model, with which he achieved an era of hitherto unknown prosperity and peace. The worst one can say of him is that he has remained very much the 'boy from the polders'. His down-to-earth approach, level-headedness and tendency to wait until all the cards are shuffled have reduced Dutch political debate to nothing.

WILLEM BREEDVELD
Translated by Yvette Mead.

The Lambermont Agreement: Another Step in Belgian State Reform

State reforms in Belgium always follow the same pattern: the federal state loses elements of its authority and financial resources in favour of the regions and communities. In June 2001, by the necessary extraordinary majorities, the federal parliament approved the Lambermont Agreement, which reduced the powers of the federal state even more. From now on, the three regions – Flanders, Wallonia and Brussels – exercise authority over internal affairs, agricultural policy, foreign trade and parts of development cooperation. Together with these new powers, the regions and communities are to receive the necessary financial resources (about 100 million Euro) and a limited form of fiscal autonomy. When new powers are granted certain significant items are almost always excluded, these being the sensitive areas on which the Flemish and French-speakers have found it so hard to compromise in the past. These items usually remain in federal hands.

From 1 January 2002, the regions have wide-ranging authority to organise their internal affairs. They are able to modify or replace the federal laws on local authorities and provinces. This means they can determine for themselves the composition, organisation and powers of local and provincial bodies. The Flemish government has already let it be known that it plans to have mayors directly elected. Those Flemish local authorities around Brussels which have language facilities for both communities, even those where French-speakers hold a majority on the council, will also come under the supervision of the Flemish government. But their boundaries must not be altered, nor may any changes be made to the language arrangements. French-speakers in the Flemish outskirts of Brussels will have easier access to the Council of State if they feel the Flemish authorities are discriminating against them. The federal government will retain authority in matters relating to the police and fire services.

Virtually every aspect of agricultural policy will from now on be a matter for the regions. The federal minister of agriculture can throw away his name-plate. Previously, only limited elements of agricultural policy had been regionalised. Now everything is being reversed: the whole of this policy area is now a regional matter, with just a few exceptions. For example, the federal government retains its authority over hygiene policy through the Federal Agency for Food Chain Safety, which was set up as a consequence of the dioxin crisis (in 1999 public health was threatened by traces of dioxin in the food chain). Prices and incomes policy also remains a federal matter. Offshore fishing, on the other hand, is entirely a matter for the regions (in practice this involves only the Flemish region). The sizeable representation of federal Belgium in the EU Councils of Ministers has also been sorted out: the three regions will try to adopt a common stance, which will be conveyed by the federal Secretary of State for Foreign Affairs. If no common stance is arrived at, Belgium will abstain.

Large parts of foreign trade had already been entrusted to the regions. Marketing and export policy has now been added. The Belgian Department of Foreign Trade has been abolished. In Flanders the *Export Vlaanderen* service has gained more powers and resources. The Lambermont Agreement does not go quite so far when it comes to development cooperation. It has been arranged that a working party will prepare for the regionalisation that should be largely complete by 2004.

Previously, the regions have had virtually no say regarding the present regional taxes (e.g. TV and radio licence fees, inheritance tax, etc.). This is now changing completely. In fact, the regions are to have full authority to regulate tax bases, allowances and exemptions. The regions will also pocket the whole of this revenue. The Flemish government has already decided to abolish TV and radio licences completely. From now on the regions will also be able to allow deductions on personal tax, though it will still be collected by the federal government. However, limits have been set on this fiscal autonomy so as not to endanger the economic and monetary unity of federal Belgium. The communities will also be funded in a different way by the national treasury. The French-speakers in particular had insisted on this, and because of the principle of reciprocity the Flemish will receive extra income. In contrast to the regions, the communities are not able to grant tax allowances. This would have led to serious problems in Brussels, where the two communities live alongside each other.

Brussels' position as a third region has been reinforced, with the Brussels government being given the same powers as those of Flanders and Wallonia. The financial resources of the Brussels region have also been increased. In order to raise the number of elected Flemish members of the Brussels parliament to a viable level, 17 seats were guaranteed for Flemish members, as opposed to 72 for the French-speakers. This increase should also prevent the far-right Vlaams Blok party from gaining a blocking majority. In exchange for more money for each of the 19 Brussels boroughs, at least one Flemish person must be elected as an alderman or as chairman of the OCMW (local Social Security Service).

One of the important things about this state reform, the fifth since 1970, is that the regions are now able to go their own way in financial matters (e.g. taxation). The first steps towards fiscal autonomy have been taken. Everyone expects more to follow in the years to come, especially in social security, in which the regions wish to put different emphases on such areas as family allowances and pensions. Lambermont will, in other words, be followed by yet more state reforms.

JOS BOUVEROUX
Translated by Gregory Ball.

Pieter Bruegel the Elder: The Master Drawer's Comeback

The picture art historians paint of Pieter Bruegel the Elder (c.1528-1569) has changed quite dramatically in recent decades. He was long dubbed 'Peasant Bruegel', a man thoroughly familiar with the country life he depicted so well. However, the emphasis gradually shifted and Bruegel became a typical city-dweller who

looked down on, and to some extent poked fun at, country life. The most recent studies have elevated him almost to a man of learning, one who moved in Antwerp's humanist circles. However, we should not lose sight of the fact that we know few concrete biographical details about him and that the preservation of his oeuvre has been fragmentary. Moreover, most of the hypotheses about Bruegel are based on his oeuvre as a painter, even though he was also a keen and talented draughtsman. In fact, we know of no paintings by Bruegel from the period before 1557, only drawings and designs for engravings.

In an exhibition at the Boijmans Van Beuningen Museum in Rotterdam in the Summer of 2001, Bruegel the master drawer was rehabilitated. This exhibition, which showed 55 of the 61 drawings attributed to Bruegel and a complete overview of his designs, then moved on to the Metropolitan Museum of Art in New York.

A brief biographical sketch would seem indispensable if we are to put this work in its proper context. Though the details are scanty, it is possible to trace Bruegel's life story reasonably well. In the late 1540s-early 1550s we find him in the Antwerp studio of his teacher, the painter Pieter Coecke. In 1552 Bruegel crossed the Alps heading for Italy, where he spent time in Calabria, Naples and Rome. It is not clear if he also went to Venice, but there is no doubt he was strongly influenced by Titian. After his return from Italy in 1554 Bruegel often received commissions from the

Pieter Bruegel the Elder,
The Painter and the Connoisseur. c.1565.
Drawing, 25.5 x 21.5 cm.
Graphische Sammlung
Albertina, Vienna.

Pieter Bruegel the Elder,
Skaters near St Joris Gate.
c.1559.
Drawing, 20.8 x 29.3 cm.
Private collection.

Antwerp print-publisher Hieronymus Cock. In 1562 he moved to Brussels and a year later married Mayken Coecke, the daughter of his former teacher. Judging by the now famous works, it was in this period that he really began to blossom as a painter. Yet he also continued to draw.

Bruegel's career was closely bound up with that of

Hieronymus Cock, a pioneer of professional print-publishing in Northern Europe. Like his counterparts in Italy, Cock contracted out to specialised craftsmen the various stages in the process of producing books of prints (e.g. creating the design, engraving the composition on the copper plate and printing from the plate). This modernised production process and Antwerp's development into an important printing centre enabled Cock to publish his books of prints in editions of a size hitherto unknown.

Bruegel was Cock's preferred designer and initially supplied him mainly with landscapes. With his flair for large compositions in which every detail nevertheless comes into its own, his unerring feel for the right perspective and for light effects, Bruegel excelled in this genre. The subjects of some drawings (a diminutive village amidst imposing mountains, a southern landscape) and a flamboyant use of lines betray the influence of his Italian sojourn. In terms of workmanship, the twelve compositions marketed by Cock under the collective name 'The large landscapes' mark a high point in his career. The combination of biblical subjects, southern views and scenes of the Flemish countryside guarantees magnificent drawings, which might even be said to anticipate the great landscape art of the seventeenth century.

From 1556 the tastes of Flemish print collectors began to change, at least if we can judge from the commissions Bruegel received from Cock: few if any landscapes, but numerous allegorical drawings. Village and town took centre stage and the human figure now played a lead role. The allegories often conceal a moral lesson, but Bruegel presented them in an extraordinary setting overflowing with symbolism, absurd humour and bizarre fantasies. One of the most famous is *The Big Fish Eat the Small*, but in the cycles *The Seven Deadly Sins* and *The Seven Virtues*, separated by a loose sheet depicting *The Last Judgement*, he also attained new artistic heights. These sort of drawings earned Bruegel the title of 'the second Bosch' even during his lifetime. It is doubtful if Bruegel ever actually saw the original work of Hieronymus Bosch, the great master of the fantastic; but he must have seen various copies of Bosch's compositions, for large numbers of them were in circulation in the early sixteenth century.

Bruegel did not, however, restrict himself to landscapes and allegories. Some of his very best drawings are of ships and fairs or religious scenes. During his 'Brussels period' (from 1562), besides some of his most famous paintings, he also produced successful drawings such as the intriguing *The Painter and the Connoisseur*. The two people depicted here are each other's opposites: a confident, stern painter and a gullible-looking patron, who already has his hand in his purse. Though probably not a self-portrait, this drawing is seen as an expression of Bruegel's longing for artistic independence.

Bruegel died in 1569. In a posthumous ode one of his greatest friends, the map-maker Abraham Ortelius, described him as '*the most perfect painter of his time*'.

Ortelius was probably right, but he did not go far enough. Bruegel was not only an excellent painter, he was also a highly gifted draughtsman.

HANS VANACKER
Translated by Alison Mouthaan-Gwillim.

Nadine M. Ohrenstein (ed.), *Pieter Bruegel the Elder: Prints and Drawings*. New Haven (CT): Yale University Press, 2001; 320 pp. ISBN 0-300-09014-5.

An Enduring Fascination The Boom in Bosch

On 1 September 2001 a major Bosch exhibition opened at the Boijmans Van Beuningen Museum in Rotterdam. It was followed two weeks later by the opening of a parallel exhibition, *The World of Bosch*, in 's-Hertogenbosch. A Bosch colloquium was held in Bruges between 13 and 15 September and an international Bosch congress in 's-Hertogenbosch between 5 and 7 November.

2001 was clearly a Hieronymus Bosch year and inevitably this went hand in hand with the publication of a whole series of books. First came several novels, including *A Darkness More Than Night*, a thriller by the American Michael Connelly in which Bosch's paintings play a not insignificant role. Only after that did the non-fiction begin to appear.

Quickest off the mark when it came to anticipating the demand for Bosch literature was the Flemish art-historian Roger-Henri Marijnissen. Marijnissen enjoys international fame, not least because of the monograph he wrote in cooperation with Peter Ruyffelaere in 1987, which has been translated into five world languages. *Bosch: the Complete Works* is still a standard work, not only because of its magnificent, detailed colour illustrations, but also because of the soundness of its views on Bosch and the flair and understated humour with which they are presented. Recently Amsterdam University Press produced a reprint; a must for every Bosch lover, it is only to be regretted that the Bosch titles which have appeared since 1987 were not added to the (nevertheless impressive) bibliography in this new edition.

According to Marijnissen and Ruyffelaere, Bosch's message is religious and moralistic. In essence Bosch's works are about the repudiation of sinful worldly vanities, about resisting the ruses of the devil and striving for a blissful journey's end in the life to come. The texts dating from his time – in the first place the Middle Dutch, but also the (still insufficiently researched) Latin – are essential to a thorough understanding of the symbolic way Bosch put this message across.

Reading between the lines, we note that Marijnissen is sometimes critical of Paul Vandenbroeck, a Flemish art-historian whose essay in the catalogue that accompanies the Bosch exhibition in Rotterdam *Hieronymus Bosch. The Complete Paintings and Drawings* runs to no fewer than ninety-four pages. In fact, the controver-

Hieronymus Bosch and / or workshop, *The Conjurer*. c.1502. Panel, 53 x 65 cm. Musée Municipal, Saint-Germain-en-Laye.

sy that resurfaces here dates back to 1987, when Vandenbroeck also published an impressive Bosch monograph; Marijnissen and Vandenbroeck then reviewed each other's books and did not mince their words in the process. Vandenbroeck called into question Marijnissen's assertion that Bosch's oeuvre is fundamentally religious. In a new French monograph published in 2001, Marijnissen repeats that Bosch's oeuvre consists chiefly of triptychs and that these served as cult objects, i.e. as retables, in the Low Countries of the late Middle Ages.

In the past Vandenbroeck, Curator of the Koninklijk Museum voor Schone Kunsten in Antwerp and of the exhibition in Rotterdam, has referred more than once to the existence of profane late-medieval triptychs (albeit smaller in size). He believes that Bosch did paint such profane works, but that they have gone missing and we only know of them from copies or references to them in old inventories.

In no fewer than twenty places in his catalogue text Vandenbroeck discusses representations believed to go back to lost compositions by Bosch. To my mind, this is a weak element in his argument. How, in the year 2001, is it possible to determine beyond all doubt whether a work from the sixteenth-century Bosch school is in fact a Bosch original and whether the authors of sixteenth-century inventories really were in a position to distinguish an original Bosch from a copy? Yet Vandenbroeck does have a point with his emphasis on the profane content of Bosch's oeuvre, because while it is difficult to deny that the authentic Bosch works contain what is in essence a religious theme, panels such as *The Conjurer* and *The Cure of Folly* (whose authenticity is in any case doubtful) nev-

ertheless seem to suggest that Bosch sometimes made profane themes the main subject of a painting. This is corroborated by the clear presence of profane themes *within* Bosch's religious triptychs (think for example of the eroticism in the *Garden of Earthly Delights*).

If one reads Vandenbroeck's contribution to the catalogue very carefully, his views about Bosch and those of Marijnissen prove to be considerably less far apart than they at first appear. According to Vandenbroeck some Bosch triptychs, such as *The Temptations of St Anthony* in Lisbon and *The Adoration of the Magi* in the Prado, were indeed altar retables, but the *Garden of Earthly Delights* and *The Haywain* were not. In the case of the two latter works, Vandenbroeck speaks of *profane* triptychs, which is a very unfortunate and confusing choice of words. What he actually means is that these triptychs never stood on an altar. They do indeed contain a religious message, but – in a way that was unique for its time – Bosch used this religious frame of reference to air his views on mankind, the world and society. Vandenbroeck's quite strongly developed basic proposition is that this view was very much part of the late-medieval urban-bourgeois mentality, which on the one hand condemned intemperance, sexual passions, aggression, social unrest, idleness, squandering and greed and on the other considered a zest for work and a well-ordered family life of paramount importance.

These findings certainly do not resolve the differences in opinion between Marijnissen and Vandenbroeck, but if we also read the two other contributions to the Rotterdam catalogue, written by Jos Koldeweij and Bernard Vermet, we note that this is not the only occasion when opinions about Bosch are divided. Even

Hieronymus Bosch, *The Garden of Earthly Delights* (detail of central panel). 1480-1490. Museo del Prado, Madrid.

in the introduction, Koldeweij points out that the three-man exhibition research team sometimes held differing views and that no attempt was made to narrow the gap. This might sound like an admission of defeat, but anyone familiar with the Bosch exegesis will know that this is not a one-off occurrence. It must nevertheless be rather confusing for the interested layman to read in Koldeweij's article that Bosch's oeuvre reflects the influence of the Modern Devotion movement and that the main figure on the outside panels of the *Haywain* triptych is not a pedlar, while in his article Vandenbroeck claims precisely the opposite.

Koldeweij is at his best when he shows Bosch's work in its cultural-historical context (i.e. that of 's-Hertogenbosch around 1500). Furthermore, he presents with verve the interesting hypothesis that Bosch painted the *St John the Baptist* (Madrid) and the *St John on Patmos* (Berlin) shortly after 1489 at the request of Jan van Vladeracken as part of the Our Lady Brotherhood retable in the Church of St John in 's-Hertogenbosch. Vermet elaborates on the results of the dendrochronological research carried out by the German Peter Klein (who explains his method of determining the age of wooden panels in *Hieronymus Bosch. New Insights into his Life and Work*, a collection of scientific essays).

Though – as Klein and Vermet are keen to emphasise – the findings of the dendrochronology should be treated with the greatest caution, there seems little doubt that the (nevertheless magnificent) *Christ Crowned with Thorns*, now in the Escorial, can only have been painted some fifteen years after the death of Bosch and that the Rotterdam Pedlar tondo formed the outside panels of a triptych with the *Ship of Fools* (Paris) and the *Death of a Miser* (Washington) on the inside. A particularly fascinating and plausible hypothesis (to be further investigated in future technical research) is that much of Bosch's oeuvre is the product of cooperation between Bosch and his studio, which was staffed not only by pupils and assistants, but also by close family members.

It is a pity that the Rotterdam catalogue is not really a catalogue, in other words a book in which all the objects on show were included systematically and provided with detailed, expert commentary. There is a concise exhibition appendix at the back of the catalogue listing all the works of art and objects shown in Rotterdam, but, for example, the work of modern artists influenced by Bosch is illustrated only by tiny black and white photographs. There are plenty of fine colour illustrations of the work of Bosch and his followers, but perhaps it would have been better to include the separate contributions by Koldeweij, Vermet and Vandenbroeck (which, there is no denying, are worthwhile) in the volume of essays referred to above.

The World of Bosch (De Wereld van Bosch), which accompanied the exhibition of the same name in the North Brabant Museum in 's-Hertogenbosch, is not really a catalogue either. Once again it is a beautifully illustrated and, in terms of style, very accessible publication, in which five historians and one art-historian (Koldeweij) restore Bosch's oeuvre to its most immediate cultural-historical context: the city of 's-Hertogenbosch in the late Middle Ages. Here you will find no original new insights into Bosch or revelatory points of view, but a large quantity of material known to us from elsewhere, brought together in an attractive and well-ordered fashion. The last chapter in particular (by Jan van Oudheusden), about the rather lukewarm way in which 's-Hertogenbosch has treated its most famous son over the last five hundred years, leaves us wanting more and longing for a history of how Bosch has been received through the centuries, and not only in his birthplace.

The scholarly monograph *In search of Jheronimus of Aachen alias Bosch* (Op zoek naar Jheronimus van Aken alias Bosch) by the 's-Hertogenbosch historian G.C.M. van Dijck is a more in-depth work and a real asset to Bosch studies. After thirty years of research in the archives of Den Bosch and Nijmegen, Van Dijck sets out all the known historical facts about Bosch and his paintings in a well-ordered manner and adds a few new ones. These are not really revolutionary, but they nevertheless serve to fill a few gaps in the none too abundant documentation about Bosch and his family. For example, it appears from the archives that Bosch's mother was born out of wedlock (nothing exceptional in those days), that several of his in-laws had studied at university, that he may have died during an epidemic in the city and that he left no great (financial) legacy. Another interesting discovery is that the *Ecce Homo* triptych from Boston (a work from the Bosch studio) was commissioned by the town secretary of 's-Hertogenbosch, Pieter van Os, and painted shortly after 1500.

In the three-day conference *Jheronimus Bosch Revealed? The Painter and his World* ('s-Hertogenbosch, 5-7 November 2001) Bosch specialists from the Netherlands, Belgium, Germany, Austria, Italy and the United States exchanged views on the Rotterdam exhibition and its research findings, but above all on various iconographic and technical aspects of Bosch's oeuvre. As was only to be expected, agreement was not reached on all questions, but this makes the study of Bosch a phenomenon almost as fascinating and remarkable as the oeuvre itself.

ERIC DE BRUYN
Translated by Alison Mouthaan-Gwillim.

Michael Connelly, *A Darkness More Than Night*. New York: Little Brown & Company, 2001; 418 pp. ISBN 03-16154-075.
Roger-Henri Marijnissen and Peter Ruyffelaere, *Bosch*. Amsterdam: Amsterdam University Press, 2000; 516 pp. ISBN 90-5356-436-5.
Jos Koldeweij, Paul Vandenbroeck, Bernard Vermet, *Hieronymus Bosch. The Complete Paintings and Drawings*. Ghent: Ludion / Rotterdam: NAi Publishers (distr. Harry N. Abrams, Inc., New York), 2001; 207 pp. ISBN 0-8109-9064-4.
Jos Koldeweij, Bernard Vermet, Barbera van Kooij, *Hieronymus Bosch: New Insights into his Life and Work*. Rotterdam: Museum Boijmans Van Beuningen, 2001; 216 pp. ISBN 90-5662-214-5
G.C.M. van Dijck, *Op zoek naar Jheronimus van Aken alias Bosch*. Zaltbommel: Europese Bibliotheek, 2001; 246 pp. ISBN 90-2882-687-4.

Flexible Materials with Backbone
The Duality of Sibyl Heijnen's Objects

There is a great temptation to describe the work of Sibyl Heijnen (1961-) as monumental textile art. But her art is difficult to classify, and so one is in constant danger of blurring and confusing ideas. This is mainly because of the degree of latitude she insists on; everything in her work revolves around exploring, overstepping and redefining boundaries and disciplines, and therefore one has to be flexible in applying existing classifications. Most of them are simply inadequate.

Those who associate textiles with woven materials or traditional textile art will almost certainly find themselves in difficulties when confronted by Heijnen's recent work. For she reserves the right to use materials that are only indirectly associated with textiles. These materials in their turn demand applications that deviate from what is usual in textile art, and different treatments lead in turn to new forms. As a result, most of

what she produces cannot simply be classified as 'textile art'. The link with textile art lies in the way the materials have been used. It is impossible to define Heijnen's field of activity precisely. Nor, in view of the modest size and ease of handling of many objects, is 'monumental' really an appropriate term. Consequently, the monumentality that is clearly present in her work has nothing to do with its dimensions. True monumentality cannot be measured in terms of volume or dimensions.

Anyone seeking to describe Sybil Heijnen's work both accurately and comprehensively has to realise that her mercurial approach produces objects and installations with chameleon-like traits. Textile no longer has exclusive rights, and rubber, plastic and other synthetic materials have become increasingly prominent over the years. Fortunately, the monumental quality has remained proudly intact.

While Sibyl Heijnen's objects may appear highly varied, they display common features of both theme and execution. Her preference for flexible materials expresses itself in varying forms, and the phenomenon of 'two-sidedness' manifests itself in a range of different areas and ways. The artist's endeavours are constantly focused on transforming the weaker aspects of soft and pliant materials so that they become models of solidity. By stitching layers of material together or rolling them up, she transforms flexible pieces into sturdy volumes that are able to stand alone without any form of support. Make your weakness your strength. Heijnen has adopted this attitude in a very literal sense and applied it to her objects. Again and again, her time-consuming experiments result in objects that suggest solidity, volume, strength and weight, but which in reality are light and vulnerable. With great zeal and patience Heijnen applies the procedures that give soft material a backbone. But at the same time, by cutting into the materials or folding or pleating flexible materials, she discloses their duality. Affinities with unbending trees or columns and similarities to growing organic structures are the rule rather than the exception. The effect of these layers of material cut with a Stanley knife is reminiscent of the growth rings that become visible once a tree has been felled. A Stanley knife and a saw are indispensable tools for revealing cyclical processes. The link with repeated patterns, rhythm and system, articulation, accumulation and other recurring natural phenomena plays an important role, even though this kinship is never emphatically displayed.

Another aspect that deserves attention is the artist's ability to manipulate a space. With her characteristic urge for expansion she conquers the space, helped by her non-conformist attitude and hunger for new images. She makes the spectators conscious of their location, a place which under normal circumstances they would consider only slightly, if at all, special. Heijnen finds filling and defining a place a rewarding starting point. She does not like leaving things to chance; everything must be carefully studied, for everything there is a time and a fixed purpose. Her objects demand their space. Although their physical presence is obvious they never force themselves upon you. Nevertheless, however modestly they may position themselves, they do not allow themselves to be ignored, pushed aside or overlooked. They help to define the surroundings. Here too their dualism is clearly visible.

Nobody has two faces. Without the vibrating or passionately beating inner self, the outside is no more than an empty shell. Anyone who seeks a confrontation or combination of male and female in the duality of her art will meet with no objection from Sibyl Heijnen. In her view the theme of duality is elastic, applicable in all manner of sub-areas and infinitely extensible.

In her later work the painterly approach to skin, colour and texture becomes ever more marked. The particular effects of colour transitions are consciously exploited and become an inalienable part of the image-forming process. Openings in the compact mass reveal seductive layers of colour, which give the objects a painting-like aspect. These incisions are reminiscent of notches carved in a tree or black wax crayon scraped away to magically reveal the colourful layer beneath. Duality is present throughout Sibyl Heijnen's work. She also examines the friction that exists between sculpture and painting. One of the ways she does this is by a thorough review of the eternal dilemma of front and back. One simple folding movement reveals the

Sibyl Heynen, *Gate* (and the artist). 2000. Rubber and sheet copper, 260 x 300 x 130 cm.

hidden reverse side, which then defines the appearance of the work. The artist cherishes such self-evident adjustments, if only to emphasise that small, seemingly insignificant actions can have important consequences, or that there are two signs to every coin. What appears to be subordinate or concealed can become significant, literally, with a flick of the wrist.

An accent placed slightly differently from normal can, for example, reveal the tension between introvert and extrovert. The exuberant glow of copper and flaming colours can be tempered, differentiated or put in perspective by being combined with a colourless reverse side. Nowadays the surface of the paint has become more important in Heijnen's work. The layers of paint look as if they have been damaged by time and circumstances, thus emphasising the transient nature of things.

Human relationships frequently translate into the association of opposites. Dynamic personalities that draw all the attention in a group often flourish alongside the inconspicuous who deliberately seek the shadows. These and other experiences, characteristics and behaviour can be convincingly connected with Sibyl Heijnen's work. Although she starts from a complex creative process in which intuitive action and conceptual thinking coincide, the results of her way of working are always comprehensible and applicable at different levels. Views and ideas on the contrast between people's inner and outer selves find their visual counterpart in objects with a glowing, warm interior and sombre, dull or colourless exterior.

Oppose. Question stagnated viewing habits. Do away with prejudice. Show that nothing is as clear and simple as it often seems at first. This is what Sibyl Heijnen likes to do, and she does it a lot. More than this, in fact: she derives from it the right to her artistic existence. Her works of art are anything but noncommittal. International recognition of her work is based mainly on the subtle way she captures in images such abstract concepts as weakness and strength, elasticity and firmness, pliability and identity, dualism and fusion, disarming openness and dark secretiveness, the incompatibility of characters and synthesis.

In 1992 she was the first and only Dutch artist ever to be awarded the Excellence Award by the Municipal Museum of Modern Art in Kyoto (Japan). Two years previously she had received the Jugend Gestaltet Preis in Munich. And in 2001 Sotheby's announced that they would promote Heijnen's work in galleries in New York and Tel Aviv. Her clear and universal imagery guarantees an accessible approach to generally unfathomable phenomena that are hard to analyse. Very few artists have built walls in order to demolish walls. Heijnen did this with her *Two Sides of the Same Coin,* a paradoxical wall of rolls of textile that unites extremes.

In a former industrial building in a suburb of Almelo, the artist examines the possible effects of her work on an environment. Here her monumental objects are literally given all the space they need. Extremely heavy pieces of rubber hang from the studio's ceiling

Rineke Dijkstra, *Polish Girl*

and walls. Pulleys can be used to raise or lower vertical forms as desired. As the artist lowers the heavy load, various changes of shape appear in consecutive stages, enabling her to determine precisely which height produces the greatest degree of tension.

Raising and lowering. Folding and rolling. Cutting and pasting. Sibyl Heijnen does little else. Experimenting, twisting and turning, she seeks the maximum return. A tour of her working area, in which a few smaller rooms have been partitioned off, makes it very clear that her work defies any simple categorisation. Artistically speaking, she has reached a fork in the road. She is using all manner of tests to discover how different materials react to changing conditions. The material demands a lot of her but she gets back as much as she puts in, if not more. Without this interaction there would be no surprising discoveries and no unexpected results. The magic word is: dialogue.

Initially Heijnen combined many metres of patterned fabric to form rough blocks of textile. In a subsequent stage this basic form was sculpted so that the inside was partly exposed. Later on she worked with rubber and plastic, and has now added aluminium and ceramics to the list. The first results are still experimental, however. Again and again she forces herself to look at things from a different angle. Her approach and way of seeing, together with the other constituent parts, form a logical whole. Each image derives its coherence from a cluster of interactions and cross-fertilisations, transformations and metamorphoses.

Sibyl Heijnen is constantly looking for new and unusual forms. She adds a third dimension to two-dimensional materials by folding, pleating, twisting, cutting and building up in layers. A notable new item in her armoury is transparency. Another development that is becoming increasingly evident is a preference for simple manipulations. There are times when a single effective movement is enough to delineate a form that renders any further additions unnecessary. This produces images which, although formed in the twinkling of an eye, stay with you for eternity.

WIM VAN DER BEEK
Translated by Gregory Ball.

Variations on the Ordinary
The Photographs of Rineke Dijkstra

At last we have a book of photographs by the Dutch photographer Rineke Dijkstra. It is a small book, with only 37 small photos. They are colour photos and they look ordinary. More ordinary than the photos in most books of photographs, with the subject bang in the middle of the picture. They are pictures of fairly ordinary people looking straight at the camera and usually posed in front of a none too striking background. Which might give the impression that these photos are crude, the work of a naive photographer, a novice.

It is only on closer inspection that we notice that the photos are highly professional. Not just because many of them have been taken with a heavy specialised camera, but above all because great attention has been paid to every detail of the image: the light, the pose, the balance between what is in focus and out of focus, the colour, the background. Nothing in these photos is accidental. Here the ordinary is exceptional.

The book contains four series of photos, 'Bathers', 'Almerisa', 'New Mothers' en 'Videostills', and one further small series of four photos. The largest and best-known series is the 'Bathers': twenty photos of young people posing singly or in groups of two or three in front of the sea. Rineke Dijkstra worked for six years on this series. She took photographs in Liverpool, Montemor (Portugal), South Carolina, Kolobrzeg (Poland), De Panne (Belgium), Yalta, Dubrovnik, Odessa, Brighton, Ostend and Long Island. From this whole period and after all these far-flung journeys, she only picked out the odd photo here and there. The care that Rineke Dijkstra puts into her work is a matter not only of meticulous framing but also of unremitting selection. Evidently Rineke Dijkstra is not easily satisfied; she exhibits very little, and only the best of the best.

The young people know they are posing. That is inevitable; Rineke Dijkstra works with a large camera.

The thing stands on a heavy tripod, which digs deep into the sand. She and her camera are very conspicuous. Rineke Dijkstra asks the young people to pose for her, to stand in front of the camera and strike a pose. She does not direct this pose, asking them to stand or look this way or that, no, she lets things happen. And what happens is something strange. The young people – surprised, yet a little proud – choose a natural pose. They prepare for the limited immortality of a photograph. Sometimes they let their arms hang down, sometimes they cross their hands, sometimes they stand slightly askew, always they are touchingly uncertain.

Rineke Dijkstra even goes so far as to make a test exposure using instant film. Thus the young people could see roughly what the photo would look like. The image appeared fairly ordinary and they were reassured, but they probably couldn't imagine how later, enlarged and in a big edition, those photos would take on a life of their own. For at the end of the day they were not taken as casual holiday souvenirs, they would be exhibited and printed in books about photography. They are so-called art photographs, they will show not only the body of a young girl standing by the sea but, ultimately, the vision of Rineke Dijkstra.

The photos were taken using a heavy tripod and a powerful flash. This makes it possible to take photos that are razor-sharp and retain an impression of sharpness when enlarged to more than life-size. The flash freezes all movement, only the body is brightly lit, the background (the sea and sky) which are further away from the light are sombre, so that we can still see the sea but it is less eye-catching. It is only a vague presence.

The girls are between childhood and womanhood. Thirteen years old or thereabouts. The boys of the same age are even less mature, a bit comic even. One could describe this as a beautiful but vulnerable age. The fact that they can strike a fixed pose, that they have not yet learned how to put up a protective front for the camera, makes these photos especially striking. The observer notices that something is going on, the ordinary photo is a bland one, the photographer is a young woman, but she is and remains a stranger, the relationship between model and photographer is a little tense, and all this together makes the photo naked, open. Humanity laid bare.

These photos made Rineke Dijkstra famous. But since then she has made several more series, always on the same theme. She photographed people at a vulnerable moment, she showed seemingly ordinary photos, in which people pose, on the sidelines of an event. Such are the four photos of Almerisa. The girl was photographed four times, at two-year intervals, between 1994 and 2000. Almerisa is a Bosnian girl who becomes visibly westernised. Each time she is photographed seated, firstly still in her little frock and red ribbon, like any other girl from the region, later in more colourful dresses and finally as a long-haired teenager. The four images cannot be separated; they are not just a documentary series, they also tell four stories and

Rineke Dijkstra,
Bullfighter, Portugal.

show four aspects of a girl growing up.

In line with this penchant for seeking out the vulnerable are two photos of Portuguese bullfighters: they were photographed immediately after the fight, unwashed, with injuries still visible and slightly torn and bloody clothing. The men who are the very symbol of inviolability and masculine behaviour look fragile and at the same time rough and alluring. They are only very small photos in the book, but they are among Dijkstra's better work.

Then of course there is also the series of New Mothers; they stand naked against a blank wall and pose with their new-born babies in their arms. The mothers have come straight from the delivery room, they are still trembling, still overwhelmed by their emotions. On one of the mothers (Tecla) we can see blood trickling down her legs. I have always felt that these photos go to the very brink.

Indeed, the significance of these photos lies in their variations on the ordinary. In the fact that the observer gets the impression that he already knows the picture, and only notices on closer examination how staggering things are, how the body of a recognisable human being becomes a revelation. But in the end what strikes me most about the photos of Rineke Dijkstra is their calm. How she isolates the people, flashes them out of the tumult of existence into an image never to be forgotten.

Translated by Derek Denné.

Rineke Dijkstra. Portraits. Stuttgart: Hatje Cantz Publishers / Boston: Institute of Contemporary Art, 2001; 112 pp. ISBN 3-7757-1015-9.

'A talent for art and a liking for mathematics' The Sculpture of Norman Dilworth

The artist Norman Dilworth, who was born in Wigan, England, in 1931, has been firmly established in the centre of Amsterdam since 1982. With his cooperation his permanent gallery in Amsterdam, Art Affairs, published a book in 2001: *Norman Dilworth 12131*. The figures refer to his date of birth, a good seventy years ago. The book with its many photographs, both in black and white and in colour, has been meticulously produced.

After a strict education with the Jesuits Norman Dilworth attended Wigan School of Art (1949-1952) and then, until 1956, the Slade School of Art, part of London University. At the Slade he studied two disciplines, painting and sculpture, which was unusual. He was rewarded with a scholarship for a year in Paris. There he sought contact with Alberto Giacometti, whose work and personality fascinated him. In 1965 he produced his first systematic works, which show no

affinity with the work of Giacometti, and in 1970 he held his first solo exhibition in the Netherlands, in The Hague.

Personal photographs, photographs of exhibition openings, of colleagues, of two- and three-dimensional work accompany the text by Cees de Boer. The latter is associated with the Art Affairs gallery, but is nonetheless an independently-minded author. He relates Dilworth's structural work in the 1960s and 1970s to structuralism in language, sociology, psychology and other branches of knowledge of the period.

Personally I would have preferred to see a book dealing with an artist focus more closely on the *work*, particularly in the case of a constructive artist like Norman Dilworth, and devote fewer pages to personal photographs of colleagues such as Carl André, Daniel Buren, François Morellet, Richard Serra, who for the most part were more famous. It is true, though, that this approach allows something of the influence of formal and constructive art in the Netherlands to be shown implicitly in this way, and also the influence exerted by Riekje Swart's gallery in Amsterdam. The latter relentlessly brought artists who worked systematically, such as Ad Dekkers, Norman Dilworth and Peter Struycken, into the public eye. The design of *Norman Dilworth 12131* enabled attention to be paid to the activities of the gallery which published it. The gallery was started by Antoinette de Stigter in 1975 in a bathhouse in Gorinchem, an old city in the province of South-Holland. In 1989 the Bathhouse Art Centre relocated to Amsterdam as the Art Affairs gallery, where it grew into one of the leading galleries in the Netherlands. Like the Riekje Swart gallery, Art Affairs, with its preference for systematic and conceptual art, has never been primarily interested in making easy sales.

Cees de Boer's introduction to Norman Dilworth 12131 is followed by a selection of the most important articles about Dilworth's work, in the original language of the critic and in the original layout of the newspaper or periodical where the article appeared. This selection also helps to build up a picture of the times.

One of the critics contributing is Bert Jansen. He writes in 1995 that '*the image constructs itself according to a predetermined formula*'. Thus a circulating polygon from 1983, *Circular Progression,* shows a system whereby the length of a line element is consistently shortened by one unit. The inward movement, which is what the sculpture is all about, has to be undertaken in ever-decreasing line elements, because of the systematic progression. This is why the circulating form shows an increasingly lively zigzag profile.

Dilworth's early '*talent for art and a liking for mathematics*', which have remained with him throughout his life, continually enter into a pact with his delight in play. He loves to make calculations and sur-

Norman Dilworth, *Circular Progression I*.1983, wood stained black, 70 cm.
Photo by Christine Cadin.

Norman Dilworth,
1,2,3,4,5. 1997, wood
stained black,
49 x 118 x 49 cm.
Collection of the University
of East Anglia. Photo by
Christine Cadin.

prises himself on occasion with the sometimes over-powering three-dimensional presence of the work of art. This is why, as far as I am concerned, the figures following the title of the book can be read as something of a joke.

'*My work is close to nature, it deals with growth and progression*' writes Dilworth. And Ulrich Grevmühl adds: '*The rhythms and harmonies that occur are created by the underlying structure of the system. The use of number and proportion are the means and the components of the resulting image.*' The term systematic art can be distilled from this text. Van Doesburg tried to get the denomination 'concrete art' accepted instead of this.

The sculpture entitled *1,2,3,4,5* from 1997 is a composite of several forms. It was executed in wood that was stained black. The constructive, mathematical premises for all its parts can be seen at a glance. That convinces the onlooker and gives him or her confidence in how well thought out the image is. The artist' s use of different forms, or of the same forms differently presented, creates an impression of liveliness. No chance here for visual monotony, which is so often a danger to systematic art, and which Dilworth's art too does not always escape. This is partly a consequence of choosing the right size: the generous proportions give an impression of monumentality. The sculpture with the unimaginative title convinces us by its forcefulness.

JOSÉ BOYENS
Translated by Sheila M. Dale.

Norman Dilworth 12131. Amsterdam: Art Affairs, 2001; 204 pp.
ISBN 90-73985-04-8.

Short takes

In around 1580, as we have seen in the themed section of this yearbook, the iconoclasm swept through the Low Countries. It was only following the bloody intervention of Spanish troops that the Counter-Reformation could begin its difficult task. A crafty 'shepherd' who drives out the devil from women by putting his tongue in their mouths, another man who is skilled in making medicinal poultices of the consecrated host for women with gynaecological problems, a village priest-farmer who allows his poultry to scratch around in his church to their hearts' content… some of the many priceless tales of knavery that landed on the desk of Mathias Hovius, Archbishop of Mechelen until 1620.

In *A Bishop's Tale* Craig Harline and Eddy Put have written Hovius' biography. In it they have convincingly brought to life not so much the bishop himself but his work and his beliefs. The whole is a fascinating tale of the many worries that beset a man trying to purge his diocese of the abuses that had made it a breeding-ground for Protestantism. But when a friend tries to convince the bishop that he should exchange his silver goblet for one of pewter, Hovius decides that the struggle against worldly vanity can go too far.

Craig Harline and Eddy Put, *A Bishop's Tale. Mathias Hovius among his Flock in Seventeenth-Century Flanders*. New Haven (CT): Yale University Press, 2001; 387 pp. ISBN 0-300-08342-4.

In his memoirs *Farewell to Europe* (Afscheid van Europa, 1969) the Dutch author Jan Greshoff wrote: '*It was the fateful year 1914 that put an end for ever to the possibility of regarding and experiencing life as a ballet, as a many-sided feast, as a complicated and mischievous game.*' But while much of Europe was the scene of ghastly slaughter, the Netherlands escaped the *danse macabre* of the First World War. In *The Netherlands and World War I. Espionage, Diplomacy and Survival* the American historian Hubert van Tuyll van Serooskerken investigates why, exactly, it was able to stay out of the war. The Netherlands did indeed mobilise, but otherwise made itself as unobtrusive as possible. The belligerents had nothing to gain from dragging that small country into their large-scale military operations; and on top of that the Netherlands' foreign policy was so obsessively neutral that it gave the combatants no excuse to occupy the country.

Van Tuyll puts this neutrality into perspective, however. The Netherlands may have regarded itself as neutral, but Britain, France and the United States saw things rather differently; in their view, the Netherlands was making a great deal of money from its trade with Germany. The Germans for their part thought that the Dutch were far too sympathetic to the British. The book describes the Dutch Minister for Foreign Affairs, Jonkheer John Loudon, as a master of postponement and delaying tactics whose approach to the principle of neutrality was highly pragmatic. In addition, the Dutch army was considerably better organised than was generally thought. The Hague maintained an excellent espionage network which provided it with advance information of plans for German offensives; and right up to 1918 it was aware of the military intentions of potential enemies. This foreknowledge bore fruit in the Dutch army's extremely rapid mobilisation in 1914, which sent a clear signal of the armed forces' high state of readiness. Van Tuyll convincingly demonstrates that the Netherlands, '*the mouse that roared*', did not merely sit passively waiting to see if it would become

a victim, but with exceptional skill made the most of every possibility available to it.

Hubert P. van Tuyll van Serooskerken, *The Netherlands and World War I. Espionage, Diplomacy and Survival* (History of Warfare, 7). Leiden: Brill Academic Publishers, 2001; 381 pp. ISBN 90-04-12243-5.

Another clash of arms, this one from a much earlier date: in 2002 Flanders celebrates the 700th anniversary of the Battle of the Golden Spurs. Ever since the publication of Hendrik Conscience's historical novel *The Lion of Flanders* (De Leeuw van Vlaanderen, 1838) this battle has been one of the 'invented traditions' of the struggle for Flemish emancipation.

The County of Flanders was a fief of the French crown. At the end of the thirteenth century the Count of Flanders was imprisoned in Paris by King Philip IV of France. Flanders itself was governed by one of the King's relations, Jacques de Châtillon de Saint-Pol. He was extremely unpopular among the Flemish people; moreover, the French occupation intensified social divisions. Both the Flemish nobility and the guilds wanted the French out and, each seeking their own advantage, they joined forces. The revolt that followed was a well-organised campaign which culminated in a confrontation between the rebellious Flemings and French punitive forces at the Groeningebeek in West-Flemish Kortrijk in the summer of 1302. And there the unthinkable happened: for the first time in history footsoldiers succeeded in putting an imposing army of knights to flight.

Flemish chroniclers related that 500 pairs of golden spurs belonging to fallen French knights were collect-

The Battle of the Golden Spurs, as pictured in *Grandes Chroniques de France*. Koninklijke Bibliotheek, Brussels.

ed after the battle. The effect of the defeat in France was considerable; the prestige of Philip the Handsome was badly dented and he was faced with serious disturbances in his own country. In Flanders too the consequences were notable. The trade associations, who had provided the bulk of the troops, very soon gained political power. And the Flemish nobles managed to conquer sizeable areas of Zeeland and Holland. In 1305 Flanders once again became a French vassal state. 11 July, the day of the remarkable victory by the Groeninge stream, is remembered and celebrated in Flanders as a national holiday.

Unlike the Netherlands, Belgium did not escape the horrors of the First World War. 'Brave Little Belgium', doggedly doing battle with the German invader from the trenches of West Flanders, even became an established concept of the time.

Many Flemish artists fled to Great Britain in 1914 to escape the war. The largest group, some fifty artists including Edgar Tytgat and Emile Claus, ended up in London, and four others – George Minne, Edgar Gevaert, Valerius de Saedeleer and Gustave van de Woestijne – in Wales. At the outbreak of war a Welsh family with a particular love for the arts and a grave concern about the dubious quality of Welsh art had sent a number of agents to seek out Flemish artists who wanted to get out of Belgium. And so the four found themselves in Wales. Works produced by them before, during and after their exile will be on show from 22 June to 15 September 2002 in the National Museum and Galleries of Wales in an exhibition entitled *Art in Exile: Flanders, Wales and the First World War*. The exhibition also contains various paintings and sculptures by Welsh artists of the period; regrettably, it is clear from these that the Flemish artists failed to inspire the work of their Welsh colleagues with new elan. In fact there was very little contact between the two, and the Flemings themselves made little if any effort to develop their own work during their sojourn in foreign parts.

After the Second World War a great many books from the Ets Haim Library returned to Amsterdam from Germany in a battered condition. This small circular library – Ets Haim, meaning 'Tree of Life', was a Jewish educational institute which trained its people for lower, middle and senior management – houses thirty thousand printed volumes and five hundred manuscripts, the nucleus of which were sent to the Jewish National Library and University Library in Jerusalem in the late 1970s on long loan. The core of the world's oldest still functioning Jewish library has now returned home and the task of restoring the books is slowly nearing completion. They include many rare and valuable pieces: Plantijn's *Biblia Regia*, manuscripts by Grotius on Jewish settlement in the Dutch Republic dating from 1616, Hebrew translations of Handel libretti and an Amsterdam *hagada* of 1712. This prayer book, read at the annual service marking Pesach, is covered with wine-stains, but that is as it should be: it is a sign of intensive use and only enhances the book's value. The aim of the collection's curator and librarian Abraham Rosenberg, who is supervising its restoration and also producing an electronic catalogue, is to return the books to their original purpose as objects to be used. And stains are then a necessary evil.

Ets Haim Library / Mr. Visserplein 3 / 1011 RD Amsterdam / The Netherlands / tel. +31 20 622 818 8 / Fax +31 20 625 468 0

On 16 July 2001 the Fleming Jacques Rogge (1942-) was elected President of the International Olympic Committee. This set the crown on a rich and varied career. Rogge studied medicine in Ghent, was ten times selected for the national rugby team and competed in three separate Olympics as a yachtsman – in which sport he was also once world champion. He worked as an orthopaedic surgeon, lectured in sports medicine and several times headed the Belgian Olympic delegation. From 1989 he was president of the National Olympic Committees of Europe. As a member of the IOC he also headed the coordination commission for the Sydney Olympics.

While delighted at his election, the new President immediately showed that he had plans of his own: '*The IOC has important tasks ahead. We must continue to defend the high values of the sport: the fight against doping, corruption, washing out commercialisation (…).*' The Games must also be slimmed down, for they are now too large, too expensive and too sophisticated: '*Africa, South America and other Asian countries than China, Japan and Korea must be given the opportunity to organise the Games.*'

Art from the Golden Age is a major Dutch cultural export. On 13 February 2002 an exhibition of the work of Aelbert Cuyp, one of the most important seventeenth-century Dutch creators of paintings and drawings, opened at the National Gallery in London. Cuyp is known mainly for his splendid views of the countryside, but he also painted impressive panoramas of the rivers around his home base of Dordrecht. And among his drawings, along with still more landscapes, one finds highly intimate studies of people, animals and plants.

The exhibition surveys Cuyp's career from 1640 to 1665, from his early Dutch landscapes to the mature Italianate works. The latter offer a unique combination of elements from Dutch landscape and the warm golden light of the Mediterranean. After 12 May this outstanding collection of 43 paintings and 27 drawings will move on to Amsterdam's Rijksmuseum (7 June).

Until 20 May 2002 this same Rijksmuseum plays host to an 'obscure' Master: Michael Sweerts, one of the most creative and mysterious of Golden Age artists. After Amsterdam this exhibition will also visit the Fine Arts Museum in San Francisco (8 June) and the Wadsworth Atheneum in Hartford, CT (19 September).

Michael Sweerts, *Drawing Class*. c.1660. Canvas, 76.5 x 109.9 cm. Frans Hals Museum, Haarlem.

Little is known of Sweerts' life. As a result of his travels around Holland, Flanders and Italy artistic and cultural elements from Northern and Southern Europe are united in his works. He painted the people of the streets with sympathy and respect, but also produced portraits of wealthy gentlemen. In addition to that, he was first and foremost a teacher. Throughout his life he demonstrated a particular interest in the teaching of art; many of his paintings are of studios full of pupils busily painting and drawing. The presence in his paintings of many plaster and marble fragments attests to the inspiration he drew from classical antiquity. An intriguing feature of his oeuvre is the surprisingly small number of religious paintings it contains, for Sweerts was known as an extremely devout man, who fasted and took Communion regularly.

Arthur K. Wheelock (ed.), *Aelbert Cuyp*. London: Thames & Hudson, 2001. ISBN 0-5005-1057-1. / Peter Sutton *et al.*, *Michael Sweerts*. Amsterdam: Rijksmuseum / Zwolle: Waanders Publishers, 2002.

In summer 2001, at the request of the Tervuren Royal Museum of Central Africa, the Belgian King Baudouin Foundation bid successfully at Christie's for a collection of archives belonging to the nineteenth-century explorer Henry Morton Stanley. As a result, the Museum now holds the complete archive of this remarkable man. It contains valuable information on Stanley's four expeditions into Central Africa: the search for Livingstone, the transcontinental expedition, the services he rendered to the Belgian King Leopold II and the attempt to free Emin Pasha. But there is also a manuscript telling of his experiences in the American Civil War (in which Stanley took the

Confederate side) and letters from Queen Victoria, King Edward VII, Chancellor Bismarck, Chamberlain, Baden Powell and Mark Twain.

The complete archive will now be intensively studied. As well as an inventory of it, in 2004 there will be a publication and an exhibition to mark the centenary of Stanley's death. And after conservation all the documents will be made accessible to the public.

Royal Museum of Central Africa / Leuvensesteenweg 13 / 3080 Tervuren / Belgium / tel. +32 2 769 52 11 / fax +32 2 769 56 38 / www.africamuseum.be

'*A delicious satire about business, greed, ambition and cheese – Edam's great moment in world literature*': thus the description of *Cheese*, the translation of Willem Elsschot's novella *Kaas* (1933), on its back cover. Paul Vincent has been sitting on his excellent translation for some time – an extract from it appeared in the eighth issue of *The Low Countries* – but now the whole text has finally reached the shops. And a good thing too, for otherwise Vincent's work would have suffered the same fate as the cheese of the title. The main character Frans Laarmans, a middle-aged clerk, is unexpectedly offered a job as chief agent for a Dutch cheese company. Suddenly the pen-pusher finds himself '*in charge of distribution throughout Belgium and the Grand Duchy of Luxembourg*'. Laarmans decides to try his hand at business and takes a month's sick leave. But he is more concerned with the externals of his new position, and meanwhile the three hundred cases of red-waxed full-cream Edam cheeses sit in his cellar going nowhere. His incompetence as a businessman proves greater than his ambitions to climb the social ladder and the whole enterprise fails lamentably.

This satirical fable of capitalism and dreams of riches is not only extremely enjoyable, at a time of so many dot.com bankruptcies it is also highly relevant. And at the same time it is, to quote the back cover again, '*a delightful period piece*', a lively evocation of 1930s Belgium.

Willem Elsschot, *Cheese* (Tr. Paul Vincent). London: Granta Books, 2002; 153 pp. ISBN 1-86207-481-X.

Intercities (Steden, 1998), by the Flemish poet, essayist and novelist Stefan Hertmans, is an erudite collection of travel stories in which the author 'encounters' great figures from world literature in Brussels, Amsterdam, Dresden, Trieste, Venice, Vienna and Sydney. They are essays about the feeling of losing oneself and by doing so enriching oneself. The building-blocks of Hertmans' cities are the books on his shelves, and the objects of his musings include Walter Benjamin, Robert Musil, Milan Kundera and Claudio Magris.

For his part, Cees Nooteboom writes travel books of a more classic variety. He is one of the most translated contemporary authors writing in Dutch, and many of his travel stories, novels and poems are available in English. But J.M. Coetzee's *Stranger Shores. Essays 1986-1999* (2001), which praises that other famous Dutch writer Harry Mulisch as someone who knows how to tell a story, gives Nooteboom short shrift. His celebration of 'old Spain' in *Roads to Santiago: A Modern-Day Pilgrimage Through Spain* (De omweg naar Santiago, 1992) is dismissed by Coetzee as an – albeit unintentional – contribution to the tourist industry. Nooteboom's melancholy laments merely encourage his readers to follow the author's example, head off in droves to see for themselves the sights he describes and so further accelerate the destruction of 'old Spain'.

Stefan Hertmans, *Intercities* (Tr. Paul Vincent). London: Reaktion Books Ltd., 2001; 235 pp. ISBN 1-86189-093-1 / J.M. Coetzee, *Stranger Shores (Essays 1986-1999)*. New York: Viking, 2001; 295 pp. ISBN 0-6708-9982-8.

In 2001 the Dutch painter, writer and photographer Henk van Woerden became the first foreigner to receive South Africa's Alan Paton Award. The prize is named for the author of the literary monument *Cry the Beloved Country*, and previous winners include Breyten Breytenbach and Nelson Mandela.

Van Woerden, who spent part of his youth in South Africa, has written three books about that country: *Moenie kyk nie* (1993), *Tikoes* (1996) and *A Mouthful of Glass* (Een mond vol glas, 1998). Described by André Brink as 'a must-read', the latter novel tells the story of Dimitros Tsafendas, the illegitimate son of a Greek father and a Mozambican mother who stabbed the South African premier and architect of apartheid Hendrik Verwoerd to death in 1966. Van Woerden, who visited Tsafendas in Sterkfontein psychiatric clin-

ic, sees the murderer as a metaphor for South Africa, and more specifically for the ambiguous position of people of mixed race. Tsafendas was accepted neither by whites nor blacks and so grew up without a country he could call his own. His rage and frustration at this situation culminated in the murder of Verwoerd, with which according to Van Woerden he sought to rip the heart from the apartheid system. It was not an act of madness, but the only gesture possible to someone like Tsafendas in a country torn apart by racial insanity.

Henk van Woerden, *A Mouthful of Glass* (Tr. Dan Jacobson). London: Granta Books, 2000; 168 pp. ISBN 1-86207-383-X.

In May and June 2002 the National Library of Ottawa will hold an exhibition of 'Early Belgian cartography and authentic documents in Canada'. The material dates from before 1800 and comes from the National Library itself and the National Archives. In her press release its compiler Claire Carbonez explains the background to the exhibition: '*In the fifteenth, sixteenth and seventeenth centuries engravers, arctographers and atlas publishers from the southern part of the Low Countries systematically gathered geographical information, including the new knowledge from actual overseas exploration, both coastal and interior, and played a major role in disseminating and sharing that information among the interested circles in Europe, thus furthering the spread of knowledge and, most important, promoting trade.*' Such priceless pieces as Cornelius Wyfliet's maps of Canada and the *Novum Belgium* or New Netherlands map by Johannes de Laet will draw the visitor's attention to the early contacts and connections between the Low Countries and Canada.

www.nlc-bnc.com

Learning Dutch doesn't have to be hard work. *Hippocrene's Illustrated Dutch Dictionary* proves that. English-speaking five- to ten-year-olds can pick up Dutch vocabulary with no trouble at all. Each page contains between four and eight words, each furnished with a large illustration and an English translation. The lay-out of the book allows the young reader to focus on each separate word and its accompanying illustration. The words selected mostly relate to people, animals, flowers, colours, numbers and objects the children use every day. And, of course, there is the indispensable accompaniment: a simplified phonetic transcription of each word.

Hippocrene's Illustrated Dutch Dictionary (English-Dutch / Dutch-English). New York: Hippocrene Books, 2001; 94 pp. ISBN 0-78180-888-X.

In *Nynke* the Dutch film-maker Pieter Verhoeff has brought to the screen the life of the children's writer Nynke van Hichtum (1860-1939), whose best-known

A design by Jurgi Persoons.

book, *Afkes Tiental* (1903) was published in English in 1936 as *Afke's Ten*. Nienke, in real life Sjoukje Bokma de Boer, married the socialist leader Pieter Jelles Troelstra in 1888, but the marriage was not a success. In the film, which has Frisian dialogue, Verhoeff sketches the life of a woman wrestling with conflicts between motherhood and ambition, love and dependence, and who eventually sinks into depression. But not everything is trouble and affliction; the film also does full justice to her success as a writer. After her divorce from Troelstra she continued to publish until she died in 1939, a free woman with a powerful will and an equally strong spirit.

For his debut as a director the Fleming Hans Herbots chose *Falling*, from the book of the same name by the Flemish author Anne Provoost. This novel for adolescents is a denunciation of nationalism, racial intolerance and fundamentalism. That's a lot to handle, but Herbots manages to bring it off. His film – with French and English dialogue and a number of English actors in the lead roles – shows how young people in today's world are exposed to the temptations of political and racial intolerance. Among the issues dealt with are both the persecution of the Jews in the Second World War and the present diaspora of foreign asylum-seekers.

The Netherlands enjoys a solid international reputation in the field of design, from the austerity of De Stijl to today's audacity. The end of 2001 brought the first issue of the new yearbook *Apples and Oranges*, devoted to the most outstanding Dutch graphic designers. The book contains a wealth of images from posters, flyers, websites and the like, which demonstrate an infectious enthusiasm for daring forms and an inventive use of image and humour.

One of the members of the editorial selection committee is Thonik's Nikki Gonnissen. The minimalist work of this designer-duo first achieved a monograph in the series *Young Dutch Design*; subsequently there has been a second part on DieTwee, a designers' collective that began by producing party flyers and annual reports and is currently known mainly for its bizarre website designs.

More design, but this time from Flanders and of a different kind, can be found in *Forms from Flanders*. This is concerned with 20th-century industrial design, from an elegant art nouveau chair by Victor Horta (1900) to the sturdy chip-pans of the Nova team (1960) and Kipling's trendy little back-packs (2000).

In *Young Belgian Fashion Design* Veerle Windels has written a book on the latest generation of designers in Belgium. While not all of them are Belgians, they all work in Brussels or Antwerp and so are following in the footsteps of the Antwerp Six, the designers who won international fame in the 1980s. Windels visited each of the designers individually, and the result is a varied series of stories about the passion for fashion. Refreshingly, the whole thing is told in a clear and lucid style, and the designers themselves come across as very spontaneous, with no taste for trendy insider 'newspeak'. Or as one of them, Jurgi Persoons, puts it: *'Don't get me wrong, my stories are still here, but now I let the clothes speak for themselves'*. Hopefully the same will go for MoMu, the new Museum of Fashion due to open its doors on 21 September in Antwerp.

Gert Staal *et al.* (ed.), *Apples & Oranges 01 (Best Dutch Graphic Design)*. Amsterdam: Netherlands Design Institute, 2001; 176 pp. ISBN 90-72007-83-2 / *Thonik (Young Dutch Design 1)*. Amsterdam: Netherlands Design Institute, 2001; 235 pp. ISBN 90-72007-92-1 / *Dietwee (Young Dutch Design 2)*. Amsterdam: Netherlands Design Institute, 2001; 235 pp. ISBN 90-72007-91-3 / Moniek E. Bucquoye *et al.*, *Forms from Flanders*. Ghent: Ludion, 2001; ISBN 90-5544-355-7 / Veerle Windels, *Young Belgian Fashion Design*. Ghent: Ludion, 2001; 144 pp. ISBN 90-5544-346-8.

In Roddy Doyle's novel *The Woman who Walked into Doors* the phrase *'I walked into the door'* is a battered wife's standard excuse for her cuts and bruises. The Flemish composer and musician Kris Defoort and director Guy Cassiers turned the book into 'an opera for soprano, actress and video screen'. What they produced was an inventive many-voiced mix of sung and spoken texts on the stage and images of houses, cigarette-smoke and text balloons ('WHACK' in large letters as the woman is hit yet again by her husband) on the screen. The result was a divided image of the protagonist Paula, emphasised still more by the music which is played alternately by a classical ensemble and a jazz band. The whole is a gripping portrait of a woman who is the victim not just of her husband, but also of the latent violence of society.

The Dutch stage- and prose writer Herman Heijermans (1864-1924) believed that the writing of literary work was justified only if said work related directly to reality and sought to influence it. In other words: art must fulfil a function in society. Among the opposing attitudes of his day Heijermans opted for socialism and in his own work he consistently spread the socialist word. His best-known play, *The Good Hope* (Op hoop van zegen, 1900) is an excellent example of this. It is set in a fishing village on the North Sea coast, where a shipowner quite deliberately sends an unseaworthy vessel to sea. The boat goes down, and now he can claim the insurance. Heijermans' indictment of this use of 'floating coffins' made such an impression in the Netherlands that nine years after the play's premiere a stricter Shipping Law was introduced – a 'justified' literary work, indeed.

In the early years of last century *The Good Hope* made a triumphal progress through all the capitals of Europe. It was performed in London in 1903, with the celebrated actress Ellen Terry in one of the leading roles. In the *Saturday Review* the eminent critic Max Beerbohm wrote how exceptional the piece was. No drawing-room stereotypes but real people, hardly a love story but still very lively: English playwrights, he said, would do well to take it as a model. Four years later the play travelled to the United States, again with Ellen Terry.

Around the turn of 2001-2002, after a gap of more than 50 years, *The Good Hope* at last returned to the London stage. Bill Bryden, who had directed it at the Dutch RO Theater back in 1989, repeated the venture with a number of splendidly old-fashioned, melodramatic, almost folk-theatre (black smudges on the faces of the poor fisherwomen!) performances at the National Theatre. '*Superb ensemble acting, wonderful folk music (...), and a palpable sense of community and humanity*' – so said *The Daily Telegraph*. Shifting the action to the little Yorkshire fishing town of Whitby posed no problems, for the piece's theme is both timeless and universal: maintaining one's dignity in the midst of injustice and the eternal conflict between profit and public safety in a capitalist system.

FILIP MATTHIJS
Translated by Tanis Guest.

Bibliography

of Dutch-Language Publications translated into English (traced January-November 21, 2001)

Access
Access for all ages!: ten examples from everyday life / [text and ed.: Annet Huizing text & editing; text introductory chapter: Annelies de Vries; transl. from the Dutch: Anna Neervoort; text and ed. (English version): S.M. van der Werff-Woolhouse; photogr.: Edgar van Riesen]. Utrecht: National Age Discrimination Office; Utrecht: National Bureau for Accessibility, cop. 2000. 50 p.
Transl. of: Toegang voor alle leeftijden! 1999.

Amsterdam
Amsterdam: a traveler's literary companion / ed. by Manfred Wolf. San Francisco: Whereabouts Press, 2000. XIII, 238 p. Contains translations of: Cees Nooteboom, J.J. Voskuil, Simon Carmiggelt, J. Bernlef, Martin Bril, Remco Campert, Marion Bloem, Maarten 't Hart, Geert Mak, Hermine Landvreugd, Gerrit Komrij, Bas Heijne, Lizzy Sara May, Gerard Reve, Marga Minco, Harry Mulisch en Hafid Bouazza.

Appel, Hans
Doing business in the new millennium: strategic use of technology in the E-commerce world / Hans Appel; [ill.: Joep van Opstal; pre-production ed.: Ward van Beek; transl. from the Dutch: The Localizers]. 399e pr. Groningen: Gopher, 2000. 248 p.
Transl. of: Zakendoen in het nieuwe millennium: strategische inzet van technologie in een E-commerce-wereld. 2000.

Baantjer, A.C.
DeKok and the sorrowing tomcat / by Baantjer; transl. from the Dutch by H.G. Smittenaar. New York: St. Martin's Minotaur, 2001. 256 p. (Minotaur books)
First English ed.: Fairfax Station, VA: Intercontinental Publishing, 1993.
Transl. of: De Cock en de treurende kater. 1977. (Fontein paperbacks).

Baarda, Frits
Rotterdam / Frits Baarda; [transl. from the Dutch: Concorde Vertalingen; rev.: Van Lierop tele-editing; photogr: Frits Baarda; cartogr.: Mairs Geographischer Verlag]. Houten: Van Reemst, cop. 2001. 96 p. (Marco Polo)
Transl. of: Rotterdam. 2000. (Marco Polo).

Babel
The Babel guide of Dutch and Flemish fiction / red. Theo Hermans. Oxford: Boulevard/Babel, 2001. 208 p. (The Babel guide series)
Contains: quotations from English translations of Dutch literature.

Backker, Vera de
Coco makes music / ill. by Vera de Backker; written by Karen van Holst Pellekaan; [English text, transl. from the Dutch, by Jo Ann Early Macken]. 1st ed. Milwaukee, WI: Gareth Stevens Publ., 2000. 29 p.
Transl. of: Koosje maakt muziek. 1998.

Backker, Vera de
Coco the koala / written and ill. by Vera de Backker; [English text, transl. from the Dutch, by Jo Ann Early Macken]. 1st ed. Milwaukee, WI: Gareth Stevens Publ., 2000. 29 p.
Transl. of: Koosje Koala. 1997.

Backker, Vera de
Coco's surprise / ill. by Vera de Backker; written by Karen van Holst Pellekaan; [English text, transl. from the Dutch, by Jo Ann Early Macken]. 1st ed. Milwaukee, WI: Gareth Stevens Pub., 2000. 31 p. Transl. of: Koosje is boos. 1998.

Baehr, Peter R.
Human rights: universality in practice / Peter R. Baehr. Basingstoke [etc.]: MacMillan Press; New York, NY: St. Martin's Press, 1999. VIII, 178 p. Transl. of: Rechten van de mens. 1998.

Bakhuis, Paula
Feeling good and getting better: a remarkable Indian herbal remedy rediscovered / Paula Bakhuis; [transl. from the Dutch by Merel Reinink]. Amsterdam: Parole Publishing, cop. 1999. 204 p. Cover title. Transl. of: Je hoeft niet ziek te zijn om beter te worden. 1997.

Bakker, Kees
Inventory of the Joris Ivens Archives / by Kees Bakker; [transl. from the Dutch]. Nijmegen: European Foundation Joris Ivens; Nijmegen: Municipal Archives Nijmegen, 1999. 105 p. Transl. of: Inventaris van het Joris Ivens archief. 1998.

Beer, Hans de
Good times with the Molesons / stories by Burny Bos; ill. by Hans de Beer; transl. [from the Dutch] by J. Alison James. New York: North-South Books, 2001. 48 p. Transl. of: Familie Mol-de Mol: hartelijk gefeliciteerd: zes nieuwe verhalen. 2001. (Hoera ik kan lezen).

Blaisse, Mark
The repositioning of Jerusalem / Mark Blaisse, Edmond Rinnooy Kan; [fi-nal ed. Ben Herbergs ... et al.; English transl. from the Dutch Maureen Shepstone ... et al.]. Amsterdam: Pan Area Publishers, cop. 2000. 76 p. Transl. of: De herpositionering van Jeruzalem. 2000.

Bokhoven, Esmé van
Water & playing / Esmé van Bokhoven, Eddo Hartmann; [text Toon Tellegen; transl. from the Dutch W.P.B. Willemsen; composition/ed.: Aad Speksnijder]. Rotterdam: Duo/Duo, 2000. 109 p. (Water in the Netherlands; 8) Publ. in cooperation with and in order of Tauw BV. Transl. of: Water & spelen. 2000.

Bont, Chris de
Delft's water: two thousand years of habitation and water management in and around Delft / Chris de Bont; [ill. Hans Emeis; transl. from the Dutch by Paul Gretton]. Delft: IHE; Zutphen: Walburg pers, cop. 2000. 136 p. Transl. of: Delfts water. 2000.

Boonzajer Flaes, Rob
Brass unbound: secret children of the colonial brass band / Rob Boonzajer Flaes; [transl. from the Dutch: Donald Gardner; photo's: Rob Boonzajer Flaes ... et al.]. 2nd, rev. ed. Amsterdam: Royal Tropical Institute, cop. 2000. 165 p. + CD Transl. of: Bewogen koper: van koloniale kapel tot wereldblaasorkest. 1993.

Bovenkerk, F.
Policing a multicultural society / F. Bovenkerk, M. van San, S. de Vries; [transl. from the Dutch]. Apeldoorn: LSOP Police Training and Knowledge Centre; Beek-Ubbergen: Tandem Felix [distr.], cop. 1999. XII, 191 p. Transl. of: Politiewerk in een multiculturele samenleving. 1999.

Braay, C.P.
Windmills of Holland / [text: C.P. Braay; comp.: Herman Scholten ... et al.; photography: Herman Scholten; transl. from the Dutch]. Koog a/d Zaan: Kooijman International Trade, [2001]. 32 p. Transl. of: Molens in Nederland. [1994].

Brink, H.M. van den
On the water / H.M. van den Brink; transl. from the Dutch by Paul Vincent. London: Faber and Faber, 2001. 134 p. Transl. of: Over het water: novelle. 1998. (Meulenhoff editie; 1663). Other ed.: New York: Grove Press, 2001.

Buitenen, Paul van
Blowing the whistle / Paul van Buitenen; [transl. from the Dutch by Lorna Dale]. London: Politico's, cop. 2000. VIII, 262 p. Transl. of: Strijd voor Europa. 1999.

City
The city of Utrecht through twenty centuries: a brief history / Renger de Bruin, Tarquinius Hoekstra, Arend Pietersma; [transl. from the Dutch by Donald Gardner ... et al.; English ed. Cathy Brickwood; photographs: Fotodienst of het Utrechts Archief]. Utrecht: SPOU; Utrecht: Het Utrechts Archief, 1999. 104 p. Transl. of: Twintig eeuwen Utrecht: korte geschiedenis van de stad. 1999.

Close-up
Close-up / Szabinka Dudevszky; photographs: Pieter Kers; transl. [from the Dutch]: Wanda Boeke. 1st ed. Asheville, North Carolina: Front Street & Lemniscaat, 1999. 125 p. Transl. of: Close-up. 1998.

Complete
The complete letters of Vincent van Gogh: with reproductions of all the drawings in the correspondence / [transl. from the Dutch and French by J. van Gogh-Bonger ... et al.]. 3rd ed. Boston [etc.]: Little Brown and Company, 2000. 3 vol. (559, 625, 625 p.). First ed.: 1958.

Craenen, J.G.
The constitution of the kingdom of Belgium: coordinated text of February 17, 1994 / [transl. (unofficial) from the Dutch and French:] J.G. Craenen, G.J. Craenen. 2nd rev. ed. Leuven; Amersfoort: Acco, cop. 2000. 47 p. Transl. based on: De Belgische grondwet: de tekst van de grondwet van 17 februari 1994 en het werk van de constituante 1991-1994 = La constitution Belge: le texte de la constitution du 17 février 1994 et les modifications apportées par la constituante 1991-1994. 1994.

Cramer, J.M.
Towards sustainable business: connecting environment and market / J.M. Cramer; [transl. from the Dutch]. The Hague: SMO, Society and Enterprise Foundation, 1999. 61 p.: ill.; 21 cm. (SMO) Transl. of: Op weg naar duurzaam ondernemen: koppeling van milieu en markt. 1999.

De Bode, Ann
Could you leave the light on? / Ann De Bode [ill.]; and Rien Broere [story; English text transl. from the Dutch by Su Swallow]. London: Evans Brothers Limited, 1999. 33 p. (Helping hands) First English ed.: 1997. Transl. of: Mag het licht nog even aan? 1996. (Harten-boeken).

Dealing
Dealing with human rights: Asian and Western views on the value of human rights / edited by Martha Meijer. Bloomfield, CT: Kumarian Press, 2001. 192 p. Transl. of: Grondrecht en

wisselgeld: Aziatische en westerse visies op de waarde van de rechten van de mens.1998.

Dekker, Rudolf M.
Humour in Dutch culture of the Golden Age / Rudolf M. Dekker; [transl. from the Dutch]. New York: Palgrave, 2000. 187 p.
Transl. of: Lachen in de Gouden Eeuw: een geschiedenis van de Nederlandse humor. 1997. (Historische reeks).

Dekkers, Midas
Dearest pet: on bestiality / Midas Dekkers; transl. [from the Dutch] by Paul Vincent. London: Verso Books, 2000. 208 p.
First English ed.: 1994.
Transl. of: Lief dier: over bestialiteit. 1992.

Delfos, Martine F.
Are you listening to me?: communicating with children from four to twelve years old / Martine F. Delfos; [transl. from the Dutch by Eef Gravendaal]. Amsterdam: SWP, cop. 2001. 159 p.
Transl. of: Luister je wel naar mij?: gespreksvoering met kinderen tussen vier en twaalf jaar. 2000. wesp-publicatiereeks).

Dokkum, Marius van
Bethlehem revisited / [ill.: Marius van Dokkum]. Aduard: Art Revisited, cop. 1999. 18 p.
Text: Lukas 2:1-20 (Revised Standard Version of the Bible).
The first text on each page is an paraphrase of the original text by Hans and JoAnn van Seventer, the second text is taken from the RSV.
Transl. of: De beste wensen uit Bethlehem. 1999.

Dolmans, D.
Problem construction / D. Dolmans en H. Snellen-Balendong; [transl. from the Dutch: Mereke Gorsira]. Maastricht: Maastricht University, Department of Educational Development

and Research, cop. 2000. 56 p. (A series on Problem-Based Medical Education; pt. 1)
Transl. of: Constructie van taken. 1995. (Een reeks voor Probleem Gestuurd Medisch Onderwijs; 1).

Donkers, Jan
The American dream in the Netherlands 1944-1969 / Jan Donkers; [transl. from the Dutch by Sheila Gogol]. Nijmegen: SUN Publishers; Arnhem: National Heritage Museum, cop. 2000. 144 p. Transl. of: De Amerikaanse droom in Nederland 1944-1969. 2000.

Dorrestein, Renate
A heart of stone / Renate Dorrestein; transl. from the Dutch by Hester Velmans. New York: Viking, 2001. 243 p.
First English ed.: London [etc.]: Doubleday, 2000.
Transl. of: Een hart van steen. 1998.

Draaisma, Douwe
Metaphors of memory: a history of ideas about the mind / Douwe Draaisma; transl. [from the Dutch] by Paul Vincent. Cambridge: Cambridge University Press, cop. 2000. XIV, 241 p.
Transl. of: De Metaforenmachine: een geschiedenis van het geheugen. 1995.

Duijker, Hubrecht
Burgundy / Hubrecht Duijker; [transl. from the Dutch]. Rev. ed. London: Mitchell Beazley, 2000. 144 p. (Touring in wine country)
First English ed.: 1993. (A wine lover's touring guide).
Transl. of: Bourgogne: een wijn- en fijnproeversgids. 1993. (Hubrecht Duijker's wijnbibliotheek).

Duijker, Hubrecht
Touring in the wine country Bordeaux / Hubrecht Duijker; [transl. from the Dutch]. New ed. London: Mitchell Beazley, 2000. 144 p. (Touring in wine country)

First English ed. entitled: Bordeaux. 1994. (A wine lover's touring guide).
Transl. of: Bordeaux: een wijn-, reis- en fijnproeversgids. 1994. (Hubrecht Duijker's wijnbibliotheek).

Duijker, Hubrecht
The wines of Chile / Hubrecht Duijker; [transl. from the Dutch]. Utrecht: Het Spectrum, 1999. 240 p. Transl. of: Charmante wijnen van Chili: een smaakvolle reis door de vele wijnstreken van Chili. 1999.

Durable
Durable and sustainable construction materials / authors Ch.F Hendriks ... [et al.]; final ed.: C. van de Fliert; transl. from the Dutch Margaux van de Fliert ... et al.; drawings F. Smink; photogr. B. de Ruiter]. Best: Aeneas, 2000. 656 p.
Transl. of: Duurzame bouwmaterialen. 1999.

Dutch
Dutch cooking today / [recipes: Clara ten Houte de Lange ... et al. ; ed.: Chantel Veer; transl. from the Dutch: Lynn George; photogr.: De Studio; commissioning ed.: Inmerc]. Wormer: Inmerc, 2001. 69 p. Publ. in collab. with Het Nederlands Zuivelbureau (the Dutch Dairy Board). Transl. of: Koken op z'n Hollands. 2001.

Dutch
Dutch romances / ed. by David F. Johnson and Geert H.M. Claassens. Cambridge: Brewer, 2000- ... . .. vol.
Vol. 1: Roman van Walewein. 2000. 541 p. (Arthurian Archives; 6).
Vol. 2: Ferguut. 2000. 263 p. (Arthurian Archives; 7)
Text in Middle Dutch with English translation.

Eggels, Elle
The house of the seven sisters / Elle Eggels; transl. from the Dutch by David Colmer. London [etc.]: Picador, 2001. 229 p.

Transl. of: Het huis van de zeven zusters. 1998.

Essential
The essential guide to Dutch music: 100 composers and their work / Jolande van der Klis (ed.); [ed. board: Louis Peter Grijp ... et al.; transl. from the Dutch: Robert Avak ... et al.]. Amsterdam: Amsterdam University Press; Amsterdam: Muziekgroep Nederland, cop. 2000. XIV, 437 p.
Transl. of: Het honderd componisten boek. 1997.

Everything
Everything you need to know about Zeeland / [editorial office: Province of Zeeland, Office of Information: Robbert Jan Swiers; ill.: Kelvin Wilson; photos: Jaap Wolterbeek; transl. from the Dutch]. 1st ed. [Middelburg]: Province of Zeeland, [1999]. 32 p. Transl. of: Wat je gewoon moet weten over Zeeland. 1997.

Faries, Molly
The Madonnas of Jan van Scorel 1495-1562: serial production of a cherished motif / Molly Faries and Liesbeth M. Helmus; with contributions by J.R.J. van Asperen de Boer; [contents and ed. of the technical documentation J.R.J. van Asperen de Boer ... et al.; English transl.: David Alexander ... et al.]. Utrecht: Centraal Museum, cop. 2000. 101 p.
Publ. on the occasion of the Exhibition: "De madonna's van Jan van Scorel 1495-1562: serieproductie van een geliefd motief", in the Centraal Museum, Utrecht (April 8, 2000 - July 2, 2000).
In cooperation with the Netherlands Institute of Art History.
Transl. of: De madonna's van Jan van Scorel 1495-1562: serieproductie van een geliefd motief. 2000.

Flashback
A flashback to the future:
10 years of Samenspel /
[compilation and text: Julia
Dotulong; contributions:
Marleen de Jong; ed.: Roel
Copier; photogr.: Jan Suys
... *et al.* ; transl. from the
Dutch: Red Publishing and
Secretarial Services].
Rotterdam: Samenspel op
Maat, [2000]. 24 p.
Publ. within the framework
of the tenth anniversary of
Samenspel.
Transl. of: Een terugblik
naar de toekomst. 2000.

Fokkelman, Jan
Reading biblical narrative:
a practical guide / Jan
Fokkelman; transl. [from
the Dutch] by Ineke Smit.
Leiden: Deo Publishing,
cop. 1999. 216 p. (Tools for
biblical study; 1)
Transl. of: Vertelkunst in de
bijbel. 1995.

Fosterchildren
(Foster)children and odd
behaviour!?: on 13 themes:
foster anxiety, adoption,
loyalty, ancestral anxiety,
attachment, mourning,
sexual abuse, ADHD,
borderline, depression,
bullying, autism, social
awkwardness / ed.
Martine F. Delfos, Nelleke
Visscher; [transl. from the
Dutch: Pauline Winkelaar-
Swann]. Amsterdam: SWP,
cop. 2001. 159 p.
Transl. of: (Pleeg)kinderen
en vreemd gedrag!?. 2001.

Frank, Anne
The diary of a young girl:
the definitive edition / Anne
Frank; ed. by Otto H. Frank
and Mirjam Pressler;
transl. [from the Dutch] by
Susan Massotty. London
[etc.]: Penguin Books,
2000. 368 p. (Penguin
modern classics)
First English ed.: New York
[etc.]: Doubleday, 1995.
Transl. of: Het Achterhuis:
dagboekbrieven 14 juni
1942-1 augustus 1944.
Rev. and enl. ed. 1991.

Frissen, P.
Politics, governance, and
technology: a postmodern
narrative on the virtual state
/ P.H.A. Frissen; transl.
[from the Dutch]: Chris
Emery. Cheltenham [etc,]:
Edward Elgar, cop. 1999.
XII, 299 p. (New horizons
in public policy)
Transl. of: De virtuele staat:
politiek, bestuur,
technologie. 1996.

Gaal, Frans van
's-Hertogenbosch within
the walls, a historical
exploration / Frans van
Gaal and Peter Verhagen;
[transl. from the Dutch:
Hilde Young-ten Hacken;
ed.: Ton Kappelhof ... *et al.*;
final ed.: Yke Schotanus].
's-Hertogenbosch: Heinen;
['s-Hertogenbosch]:
Stichting Archeologie,
Bouwhistorie en Cultuur
's-Hertogenbosch, 2001.
132, [12] p. (ABC of history; 3)
Transl. of: 's-Hertogenbosch
binnen de veste: een
historische verkennings-
tocht. 2001.

Gerritsen, Jan-Willem
The control of fuddle and
flash: a sociological history
of the regulation of alcohol
and opiates / Jan-Willem
Gerritsen; [transl. from the
Dutch by Beverley
Jackson]. Leiden [etc.]:
Brill, 2000. VI, 279 p.
(International studies in sociology and social
anthropology; vol. 76)
Transl. of: De politieke
economie van de roes: de
ontwikkeling van
reguleringsregimes voor alcohol en opiaten. 1993.
Thesis Amsterdam.

Ginkel, Dirk van
Ben Bos: design of a life-
time / Dirk van Ginkel and
Paul Hefting; [transl. from
the Dutch Jan Willem
Reitsma].
First ed. Amsterdam: BIS
Publishers, 2000. 191 p.
Transl. of: Ben Bos: design
of a lifetime. 2000.

Greve, Ruud
Ganesha: the Hindu God
with the elephant's head /
Ruud Greve; [transl. from
the Dutch: R. Wetselaar ...
et al.]. Terschuur:
Zevenster, cop. 2001. 128 p.
Transl. of: Ganesha: de
hindoegod met het
olifantenhoofd. 1998.

Groen, Els de
No roof in Bosnia / Els de
Groen; transl. [from the
Dutch] by Patricia
Crampton. Barnstaple:
Spindlewood, 2001. 191 p.
First English ed.: 1997.
Transl. of: Tuig. 1995.

Groot, Stefan de
The retroflash / by Stefan
de Groot; [transl. from the
Dutch]. Groningen: Gopher
Publishers, 2000. [48] p.
(Kwab and the World of
Whatif?; 1)
Transl. of: De retroflits.
1999. (Kwab en de Wereld
van Watals?; 1).

Grunberg, Arnon
Silent extras / by Arnon
Grunberg; transl. from the
Dutch by Sam Garrett. New
York: St. Martin's
Minotaur, 2001. 320 p.
First English ed.: London:
Secker & Warburg.
Transl. of: Figuranten.
1997.

Gulik, Willem van
A distant court journey:
Dutch traders visit the
shogun of Japan / Willem
van Gulik; [ed. Eymert-Jan
Goossens; transl. from the
Dutch]. [Amsterdam]:
Stichting Koninklijk Paleis
Amsterdam, cop. 2000. 84 p.
Translator: Icette Roosen-
berg.
Publ. on the occasion of the
Exhibition: "Een verre reis:
Nederlanders op weg naar
de shôgun van Japan", in
the Koninklijk Paleis,
Amsterdam (June 24, 2000
- September 24, 2000).
Transl. of: Een verre
hofreis: Nederlanders op
weg naar de shôgun van
Japan. 2000.

Heitink, Gerben
Practical theology: history,
theory, action domains:
manual for practical theology / Gerben Heitink; transl.
[from the Dutch] by
Reinder Bruinsma. Grand
Rapids, Michigan [etc.]:
Eerdmans, cop. 1999. XIX,
358 p. (Studies in practical
theology)
Transl. of: Praktische theologie. 1993. (Handboek
praktische theologie).

Hendriks, Ch.F.
The building cycle /
authors Ch.F Hendriks,
A.A. Nijkerk, A.E. van
Koppen; [final ed.: C. van
de Fliert; transl. from the
Dutch: Margaux van de
Fliert ... *et al.*; drawings:
F. Smink; photogr.: B. de
Ruiter]. Best: Æneas, cop.
2000. 233 p.
Transl. of: De bouwcyclus.
1999.

Hertmans, Stefan
Intercities / by Stefan
Hertmans; transl. from the
Dutch by Paul Vincent.
London: Reaktion Books,
2001. 240 p.
Transl. of: Steden: verhalen
onderweg. 1998.
(Meulenhoff editie; 1662).

Hertzberger, Herman
Space and the architect:
lessons in architecture 2 /
Herman Hertzberger;
[comp. by Jop Voorn;
transl. from the Dutch by
John Kirkpatrick].
Rotterdam: 010 Publishers,
2000. 292 p.
Continuation of: Lessons
for students in architecture.
3rd rev. ed. 1998. First ed.:
1991.
Transl. of: De ruimte van de
architect: lessen in
architectuur 2. 1999.

Hieronymus
Hieronymus Bosch: new in-
sights into his life and work
/ ed. by Jos Koldeweij,
Bernard Vermet; with
Barbera van
Kooij. Rotterdam [etc.]:
Museum Boijmans Van
Beuningen [etc.], cop.
2001. 216 p.
Publ. on the occasion of the
"Hieronymus Bosch"-
Exhibition in the Museum
Boijmans Van Beuningen,
Rotterdam (September 1,
2001 - November 11, 2001).

Hinterding, Erik
Rembrandt the printmaker / Erik Hinterding, Ger Luijten and Martin Royalton-Kisch; with contributions by Marijn Schapelhouman, Peter Schatborn and Ernst van de Wetering; [transl. from the Dutch Beverley Jackson ... et al.; Dutch texts ed. by Dorine Duyster]. [Zwolle]: Waanders; Amsterdam: Rijksmuseum, cop. 2000. 384 p.
Publ. to coincide with the exhibition shown in two parts at the Rijksmuseum, Amsterdam (July 22, 2000 - October 8, 2000 and October 14, 2000 - January 7, 2001), and in one exhibition at the British Museum, London (January 26, 2001 - April 8, 2001).

Hogeweg, Margriet
The God of Grandma Forever / Margriet Hogeweg; transl. [from the Dutch] by Nancy Forest. Asheville, NC: Front Street, 2001. 112 p.
Transl. of: De God van oma Vanouds. 1999.

Hooft, H.G.A.
Patriot and patrician: to Holland and Ceylon in the steps of Henrik Hooft and Pieter Ondaatje, champions of Dutch democracy / Hendrik Hooft; [transl. from the Dutch].
1st ed. Canton, Mass.: Science History Publications, 1999. 253 p.
Transl. of: De burgher en de burgemeester. 1994.

Huizinga, Johan
Erasmus and the Age of Reformation / Johan Huizinga; [transl. from the Dutch]. Mineola, NY.: Dover Publ., 2001. 214 p.
First English ed.: London: Phaidon Press, 1924
Transl. of: Erasmus. 1924.

Huizinga, Johan
The waning of the Middle Ages / Johan H. Huizinga; transl. [from the Dutch]. London [etc.]: Penguin Books, 2001. 352 p.
First English ed.: London: Arnold, 1924

Transl. of: Herfsttij der middeleeuwen: studie over levens- en gedachtenvormen der veertiende en vijftiende eeuw in Frankrijk en de Nederlanden. 1919.

Huygen, Wil
Gnome life: a monthly celebration of secrets, tales, and whimsy / Wil Huygen; ill. by Rien Poortvliet; [transl. from the Dutch; ed.: Amy L. Vinchesi]. New York: Abrams, 1999. [28] p.
Transl. of: De wereld van de kabouter. 1988.

Ibelings, Hans
Meyer en Van Schooten Architects / Hans Ibelings; [transl. from the Dutch]. Rotterdam: NAi Publishers, 2001-... .. vol.
Vol. 1 / [transl. Victor Joseph ... et al.]. cop. 2001. 223 p.
Transl. of: Meyer en Van Schooten Architecten. Vol. 1. 2001.

Iens
Iens independent index: Amsterdam restaurants / [general ed. Iens Boswijk; ed. Amber van Rijn; editorial assistants Gabriëlle Stein ... et al.; transl. from the Dutch Liz Waters]. Amsterdam: Forum, 2000. 176, XXXI p.
Transl. of: Iens independent index: restaurants van Amsterdam. Ed. 2001. 2000.

Interrupted
An Interrupted life: the diaries 1941-1943 and Letters of Etty Hillesum, 1941-1943 / [transl. from the Dutch by Arnold J. Pomerans; forew. by Eva Hoffman; introd. and notes by Jan G. Gaarlandt]. London: Persephone Books, 1999.
First English ed. of 'Interrupted life' entitled: Etty: a diary 1941-1943. 1983.
First English ed. of: 'Letters from Westerbork': 1986.
Transl. of: Het verstoorde leven: dagboek van Etty Hillesum 1941-1943. 1981,

and: Het denkende hart van de barak: brieven van Etty Hillesum. 1982.

J.
J.J.P. Oud: poetic functionalist, 1890-1963: the complete works / [written and ed. by:] Ed Taverne, Cor Wagenaar, Martien de Vletter; with contributions of: Dolf Broekhuizen ... [et al.; ed.: Marianne Lahr ... et al.; transl. from the Dutch: Robyn de Jong-Dalziel ... et al.]. Rotterdam: NAi Publishers, cop. 2001. 575 p.
Publ. on the occasion of the Exhibition: 'J.J.P Oud: poëtisch functionalist, 1890-1963' in the Netherlands Architecture Institute (May 18, 2000 - September 9, 2001).
Transl. of: J.J.P Oud: poëtisch functionalist, 1890-1963. Rotterdam: NAi Uitgevers, 2001.

Jan
Jan Huygen van Linschoten and the moral map of Asia: the plates and text of the 'Itinerario' and 'Icones, habitus gestusque Indorum ac Lusitanorum per Indiam viventium' / with a study by Ernst van den Boogaart. London: Printed for presentation to the members of The Roxburghe Club, 1999. XIII, 282 p. + Icones, habitus gestusque Indorum ac Lusitanorum per Indiam viventium ([30] L.)
Number of copies printed 300.
Contains the English transl. of the: 'Itinerario' by William Philip (London: John Wolfe, 1598); the plates and maps of the Dutch ed.: (Amsterdam: Cornelis Claesz, 1596) with an English transl. of the Latin texts by C.L. Heesakkers and P. Mason; and the plates of the 'Icones'. (Amsterdam: Cornelis Nicolai, 1604).
The plates and maps are taken from the copy in the Brenthurst Library, South Africa.
Original Dutch title: Itinerario, voyage ofte schipvaert van Jan Huygen

van Linschoten naer Oost ofte Portugaels Indien inhoudende een corte beschrijvinghe der selver landen en de zeecusten ... 1596.

Japin, Arthur
The two hearts of Kwasi Boachi: a novel / Arthur Japin; transl. from the Dutch by Ina Rilke. 1st ed. New York: Knopf, 2000. 384 p.
First English ed.: London: Chatto & Windus, 2000.
Transl. of: De zwarte met het witte hart. Amsterdam: Arbeiderspers, 1997.
Other ed.: London: [etc.]: Vintage, 2001.

Kaper, B.
Mathematics with applications in micro-economics / B. Kaper & H. Hamers; [ed. by Christy de Back]. Schoonhoven: Academic Service economie en bedrijfskunde, cop. 2000. 225 p. Transl. of: Wiskunde met toepassingen in de micro- economie. 2000.

Kiers, Judikje
The glory of the Golden Age: Dutch art of the 17th century: painting, sculpture and decorative art / [authors: Judikje Kiers and Fieke Tissink; with contrib. by Jan Piet Filedt Kok ... et al.; ed.: Bart Cornelis ... et al.; transl. from the Dutch: Sam Herman ... et al.; photogr.: Department of photography, Rijksmuseum: Henk Bekker ... et al.]. Zwolle: Waanders; Amsterdam: Rijksmuseum, cop. 2000. 366 p.
Publ. on the occasion of the Exhibition: "De glorie van de gouden eeuw: Nederlandse kunst uit de 17e eeuw: schilderijen, beeldhouwkunst en kunst-nijverheid" in the Rijksmuseum, Amsterdam (April 15, 2000 - September 17, 2000).
Transl. of: De glorie van de Gouden Eeuw: Nederlandse kunst uit de 17e eeuw: schilderijen, beeldhouwkunst en kunstnijverheid. 2000.

Koldeweij, Jos
Hieronymus Bosch: the complete painting and drawings / Jos Koldeweij, Paul Vandenbroeck, Bernard Vermet; [i.s.m. Matthijs Ilsink; eindred. Barbera van Kooij]. New York: Harry N. Abrams, 2001. 208 p.
Publ. on the occasion of the Exhibition: "Jheronimus Bosch" in Museum Boijmans Van Beuningen, Rotterdam (September 1, 2001 - November 11, 2001).
Transl. of: Jheronimus Bosch: alle schilderijen en tekeningen. 2001.

Kranenburg, Ronald
Compact geography of the Netherlands / [text Ronald Kranenburg; with contributions by Henk Meijer; transl. from the Dutch Writing consultance international Interface; photos Henk Berendsen ... et al.; maps KartLab ... et al.]. Utrecht: KNAG, Royal Dutch Geographical Society, cop. 2001. 48 p.
Transl. of: Kleine geografie van Nederland. 2000.

Lange, Frits de
Waiting for the word: Dietrich Bonhoeffer on speaking about God / Frits de Lange; transl. [from the Dutch] by Martin N. Walton. Grand Rapids, Michigan [etc.]: Eerdmans, cop. 2000. VII, 154 p.
Transl. of: Wachten op het verlossende woord: Dietrich Bonhoeffer en het spreken over God. 1995.

Lauwen, Toon
Otto Treumann / [text Toon Lauwen; ed. Kees Broos ... et al.; transl. from the Dutch John Kirkpatrick]. Rotterdam: 010 Publishers, cop. 2001. 129 p. (Graphic design in the Netherlands) Transl. of: Otto Treuman. 1999. (Grafisch ontwerpen in Nederland).

Leijerzapf, Ingeborg Th.
Henri Berssenbrugge: passion, energy, photography / Ingeborg Th.
Leijerzapf and Harm Botman; [transl. from the Dutch: Rudy L. Leyerzapf]. Zutphen: Walburg Pers, 2001. 349 p.
Publ. on the occasion of the Exhibition: "Henri Berssenbrugge" in the Kunsthal, Rotterdam (January 13, 2001 - April 22, 2001).
Transl. of: Henri Berssenbrugge: passie, energie, fotografie. 2001.

Leeuwen, Joke van
Sontjeland / Joke van Leeuwen; [transl. from the Dutch: Jan Michael]. Amsterdam: Stichting Culturele Manifestaties NANA; Tilburg: Zwijsen, cop. 2000. 36 p.
Publ. on the occasion of the Kinderboekenfestival 2000. Transl. of: Sontjeland. 2000. (Serie Spetter).

Lieshout, Ted van
Brothers / Ted van Lieshout; transl. [from the Dutch] by Lance Salway. London: CollinsFlamingo, 2001. 154 p.
Transl. of: Gebr. 1996.

Linders, Clara
The very best door of all / Clara Linders & Marijke ten Cate; [transl. from the Dutch]. 1st ed. Asheville, North Carolina: Front Street, Lemniscaat, 2001. [28] p.
Transl. of: De mooiste deur van overal. 2000.

Lindwer, Willy
The last seven months of Anne Frank / [compiled by] Willy Lindwer; transl. from Dutch by Alison Meersschaert. London: Macmillan, 1999. XIII, 204 p, [32] p. pl.
First English ed.: New York: Pantheon Books, cop. 1991.
Transl. of: De laatste zeven maanden: vrouwen in het spoor van Anne Frank. 1988.

Loo, Bert van
Holland / [Bert van Loo; transl. from the Dutch by Helen Dupuis]. [Baarn:
Tirion]; Houten: Van Loo, [2001]. 96 p.
Other ed. in English-Hebrew: [Baarn: Tirion]; Houten: Van Loo, [2001].

Loo, Tessa de (pseud. of J.M. Duyvené de Wit)
The twins / Tessa de Loo; transl. from the Dutch by Ruth Levitt. London: Arcadia Books, 2001. 392 p.
First English ed.: London: Arcadia Books, 2000.
Transl. of: De tweeling: roman. 1993.

Loon, Corey van
The power of affirmative prayer: healing thoughts and affirmations throughout the year / Corey van Loon; [transl. from the Dutch]. Maastricht: Omni Publishers, cop. 2000. 187 p.
Transl. of: Handleiding voor een gelukkig leven. 1987.

Loon, Corey van
You are a reflection of perfection / Corey van Loon; [transl. from the Dutch]. Maastricht: Omni Publishers, cop. 2000. 176 p.
Transl. of: De kracht van de gedachte: over hoe gedachten jouw leven beïnvloeden. 1998.

Magic
The magic of M.C. Escher / with an introduction by J.L. Locher; designed by Erik Thae; [transl. from the Dutch by Marjolein de Jager]. New York: Abrams, 2000. 200 p. "Joost Elffers books".

Mak, Geert
Amsterdam: a brief life of the city / Geert Mak; transl. from the Dutch by Philipp Blom. Rev. ed. London: Harvill Press, 2001. XIII, 338 p.
First English ed.: 1999.
Transl. of: Een kleine geschiedenis van Amsterdam. 1994.

Mander, Karel van
The lives of the illustrious Netherlandish and German painters; preceded by the lineage, circumstances and
place of birth, life and Works of Karel van Mander, painter and poet and likewise his death and burial / ed. by Hesel Miedema. Doornspijk: DAVACO, 1994-1999. 6 vol.
From vol. 3 without subtitle. Transl. of: Het leven der Nederlandtsche en Hoogduytsche schilders. Originally part of Het Schilder-boeck... 1604. Later separate publication.
Vol 6: Commentary on lives: fol. 291v01-end / transl. [from the Dutch]: Derry Cook-Radmore. 1999. XXXIV, 237 p., [63] p. pl.

Marees van Swinderen, Elisabeth de
Peter loves Uncle John / written by Elisabeth de Marees van Swinderen; [transl. from the Dutch]. Hilversum: Schreeuw om Leven (Cry for Life), cop. 1999. 49 p.
Transl. of: Peter houdt van oom Hans. 1999.

Masters
Masters of the margin / [ed. Jos ten Berge; contributing authors Ans van Berkum ... et al.; fotogr.: Hans Versteeg ... et al.; transl. from the Dutch]. Zwolle: De Stadshof, museum of naïve and outsider art; Amsterdam: Coen Sligting Bookimport [distr.], [1999]. 120 p.
Publ. on the occasion of the Exhibition: "Meesters uit de marge" in De Stadshof, Zwolle (October 9, 1999 - March 6, 2000).
Transl. of: Meesters uit de marge. 1999.

Meer, Frits van der
Imaging quality in X-ray diagnostic systems: tools for clinical practice in medical physics / Frits van der Meer; transl. from the Dutch by C.M.H. Harrisson. [S.l.: s.n.], 1999 (Wijk bij Duurstede: Addix). 174 p. Transl. of: Afbeeldingskwaliteit van röntgendiagnostische systemen: gereedschappen voor de klinisch fysische

praktijk. 1997. Thesis
Rotterdam.

Möring, Marcel
In Babylon / Marcel
Möring; transl. from the
Dutch by Stacey Knecht.
London: Flamingo [etc.],
2000. 416 p.
First English ed.: London:
Flamingo, 1999.
Transl. of: In Babylon.
1997.

Mooij, Bart
Amsterdam, Amsterdam,
Amsterdam: with city map!
/ [photogr.: Bart Mooij &
Piet van der Meer; transl.
from the Dutch].
Amsterdam: Suurland,
1999. 51 p. English ed.
First Dutch ed.: 1995.

Moor, Margriet de
The Duke of Egypt /
Margriet de Moor; transl.
from the Dutch by Paul
Vincent. London: Picador,
2001. 243 p.
Transl. of: Hertog van
Egypte. 1996.
Other ed.: New York:
Arcade, 2001.

Moor, Margriet de
First gray, then white, then
blue / Margriet de Moor;
transl. from the Dutch by
Paul Vincent. New York:
Overlook Press, 2001. 218 p.
First English ed.: London
[etc.]: Picador, 1994.
Transl. of: Eerst grijs dan
wit dan blauw. 1991.

Mortier, Erwin
Marcel / Erwin Mortier;
transl. from the Dutch by
Ina Rilke. London: Harvill,
2001. 176 p.
Transl. of: Marcel: roman.
1999.

Moust, Jos H.C.
Problem-based learning:
a student guide / Jos H.C.
Moust, Peter A.J. Bouhuijs,
Henk G. Schmidt; [transl.
from the Dutch]. Groningen:
Wolters-Noordhoff, cop.
2001. 94 p.
(Hoger onderwijs reeks)
Transl. of: probleem-
gestuurd leren: een
wegwijzer voor studenten.
1989. (Hoger onderwijs
reeks).

Mulisch, Harry
The discovery of heaven:
a novel / [Harry Mulisch;
transl. from the Dutch by
Paul Vincent]. London
[etc.]: Penguin Books,
2001. 736 p.
First English ed.: New
York: Viking, 1996.
Transl. of: De ontdekking
van de hemel. 1992.

Mulisch, Harry
The procedure / Harry
Mulisch; transl. [from the
Dutch] by Paul Vincent.
London [etc.]: Viking,
2001. 230 p.
Transl. of: De procedure.
Amsterdam: Bezige Bij,
1998.
Other ed.: London [etc.]:
Penguin Books, 2001.

Muller, Wim
Order and meaning in de-
sign / Wim Muller; [transl.
from the Dutch]. Utrecht:
LEMMA, 2001.
354 p. (Series in industrial
design)
Transl. of: Vormgeven: or-
dening en betekenisgeving.
2nd rev. ed. 1997. First ed.:
1990.

Netherlandish
Netherlandish art in the
Rijksmuseum / [transl. from
the Dutch: Michael Hoyle.
Zwolle: Waanders;
Amsterdam: Rijksmuseum,
2000-... . .. vol.
Vol. 2: 1600-1700 / Jan Piet
Filedt Kok ... [et al.]; with
contributions by Jan Daan
van Dam ... [et al.]. cop.
2001. 275 p.
Transl. of: Nederlandse
kunst in het Rijksmuseum.
Vol. 2: 1600-1700.

Netherlands
The Netherlands: a practical
guide for the foreigner and
a mirror for the Dutch /
[partly transl. from the
Dutch by Sam Garrett ... et
al.]. Amsterdam:
Prometheus; Rotterdam:
NRC Handelsblad, 2001.
114 p.

Netherlands
The Netherlands in brief /
[ed. board: Foreign
Information Division

(DVL/VB), Erika Koehler;
transl. from the Dutch].
Den Haag: Ministerie van
Buitenlandse Zaken,
Directie Voorlichting
Buitenlandse Zaken,
Afdeling Voorlichting
Buitenland, cop. 2000.
51 p., [2] l.
Publ. by the Ministry of
Foreign Affairs, and
produced with the coopera-
tion of the other ministries.
Transl. of: Nederland in
kort bestek. 2000.

Nijkerk, Alfred Arn.
Handbook of recycling
techniques / by Alfred Arn.
Nijkerk and Wijnand L.
Dalmijn; [transl. from the
Dutch]. 5th, [rev. and ex-
panded] pr. The Hague:
Nijkerk Consultancy,
2001. 256 p. Written within
the framework of the Dutch
National Re-use of Waste
Research Programme
(NOH).
Publ. in collab. with
NOVEM and RIVM.
First English ed.: 1994.
Transl. of: Handboek der
recycling technieken. 1994.

Noordwijk, Jacob van
Dialysing for life: the development of the
artificial kidney / by Jacob
van Noordwijk; [transl.
from the Dutch]. Dordrecht
[etc.]: Kluwer Academic
Publishers, cop. 2001. XII,
114 p.
Transl. and adapt. of: De
omwenteling die in
Kampen begon: de ont-
wikkeling van de kunst-
matige nier. 1998.

Nooteboom, Cees
All souls' day / Cees
Nooteboom; transl. from
the Dutch by Susan
Massotty. New York:
Harcourt, 2001. 352 p.
Transl. of: Allerzielen.
1998.
Other ed.: London: Picador,
2001

Nooteboom, Cees
Roads to Santiago: a mod-
ern-day pilgrimage to Spain
/ Cees Nooteboom; transl.
from the Dutch by Ina
Rilke; [photogr. Simone

Sassen]. New York:
Harcourt, 2000. 352 p.
(Harvest in translation)
First English ed.: New
York: [etc.]: Harcourt
Brace, 1996.
Transl. of: De omweg naar
Santiago. 1992.

Parents
Parents teach teachers: an
account of a project / L.E.T.
Hulshof ... [et al.]; photogr.
Tom Pilzecker; transl.
from the Dutch Jean
Vaughan]. Delft: Stichting
Forsa Zuid-Holland;
Rotterdam: SBWR; Rotter-
dam: FOCR, cop. 1999. 32 p.
Transl. of: Ouders in-
formeren leerkrachten.
1999.

*Petri, Catharose de (pseud.
of H. Stok-Huyser)*
The living word / Catharose
de Petri; [transl. from the
Dutch]. Haarlem: Rozekruis
Pers, 2001. 269 p.
Transl. of: Het levende
woord. 1989.

Pierik, Perry
From Leningrad to Berlin:
Dutch volunteers in the service of the German
Waffen-SS 1941-1945: the
political and military history of the legion, brigade and
divison known as
'Nederland' / Perry Pierik;
[transl. from the Dutch:
D.E. Butterman-Dorey].
1st English pr. Soesterberg:
Aspekt, 2001. 287 p.
(Aspekt non-fiction)
Transl. of: Van Leningrad
tot Berlijn: Nederlandse
vrijwilligers in dienst van
de Duitse Waffen-SS
1941-1945: geschiedenis
van het legioen, de brigade
en de divisie 'Nederland'
in politieke en militaire
context. 2nd compl. rev. ed.
2000. First Dutch ed.: 1995.
(Ciceroreeks; 1).

Pleij, Herman
Dreaming of Cockaigne /
Herman Pleij; transl. [from
the Dutch] by Diane Webb.
New York: Columbia
University Press, 2001.
544 p.
Transl. of: Dromen van
Cocagne: Middeleeuwse

fantasieën over het volmaakte leven. 1997.

Porck, Henk J.
Rate of paper degradation: the predictive value of artificial aging tests / Henk J. Porck; [transl. from the Dutch]. Amsterdam: European Commission on Preservation and Access, 2000. 40 p.
Transl. of: Snelheid van papierverval: de betrouwbaarheid van prognoses op basis van kunstmatige verouderingstests. 1999.

Rhytm
Rhythm, a dance in time / ed. by Elisabeth den Otter; [photogr.: Paul Romijn ... et al.; transl. from the Dutch]. Amsterdam: Royal Tropical Institute, cop. 2001.
196 P. + CD
Publ. on the occasion of the Exhibition: "Ritme, dans van de tijd" in the Tropenmuseum, Amsterdam (December 16, 1999 - January 14, 2001). Transl. and adapt. of: Ritme, dans van de tijd. 1999.

Rona, Jutka
An imaginary life: Hungarian photo album / Jutka Rona; [transl. from the Dutch Dimitri Frenkel Frank]. Amsterdam: Rap; Budapest: Interart Stúdió, cop. 2000. 191 p.
Transl. of: Een denkbeeldig leven. 2000.

Rotterdam
Rotterdam / composition and photogr. Herman Scholten; text Frederik Wiedijk; [transl. from the Dutch]. Almere: Bears Publishing, [2001]. 48 p.
Transl. of: Rotterdam. 2001.

Royal
Royal Cabinet of Paintings Mauritshuis: guide / [contributions Ben Broos ... et al.; ed. Quentin Buvelot; transl. from the Dutch Beverley Jackson]. The Hague: Friends of the Mauritshuis Foundation,

cop. 2000. 152 p.
Transl. of: Koninklijk Kabinet van Schilderijen Mauritshuis: gids. 2000.

Royen, Heleen van
The happy housewife / Heleen van Royen; transl. [from the Dutch] by Liz Waters. London: Virago, 2001. 359 p.
Transl. of: De gelukkige huisvrouw. 2000.

Ruebsamen, Helga
The song and the truth / Helga Ruebsamen; transl. from the Dutch by Paul Vincent. London: Harvill Press, 2001. 356 p.
First English ed.: New York: Knopf, 2000.
Transl. of: Het lied en de waarheid. Amsterdam [etc.]: Contact, 1997.

Ruiter, Erica de
Tejido huave and beyond: easy pick-up patterning on two, three or four shafts / Erica de Ruiter; graphics: J. van Krieken; [transl. from the Dutch by the author]. 1st print. Nijmegen: De Ruiter, 1999. 37 p.
Transl. of: Tejido: weefsels in vrije patronen met doorlopende patroondraad. 3th pr. 1999.

Rulof, Jozef
The bridge to eternal life / Jozef Rulof; transl. from the Dutch by W. Peebles-Den Held. 2nd ed. Apeldoorn: Wayti publishing House Foundation, 2000. 214 p.; 23 cm.
First English ed.: The Hague [etc.]: Foundation Society for Spiritual Consciousness 'The Age of Christ', 1986. Transl. of: Zij, die terugkeerden uit de dood. 1937.

Rulof, Jozef
The cycle of the soul / Jozef Rulof; [transl. from the Dutch by: M. Briggs-Feenstra]. 2nd ed. Apeldoorn: Wayti Publishing House Foundation, cop. 2000. 330 p.
First English ed.: The Hague: Foundation Society for Spiritual Consciousness

'The Age of Christ', 1988.
Transl. of: De kringloop der ziel. 1938.

Rulof, Jozef
The origin of the universe / Jozef Rulof; transl. from the Dutch by C. Damman. Apeldoorn: Stichting Wayti Uitgeverij, 2000. 564 p.
Transl. of: Het ontstaan van het heelal 's-Gravenhage: Geestelijk Wetenschappelijk Genootschap 'De eeuw van Christus', 1952.
First Dutch ed. in 3 vol.: 1939.

Rulof, Jozef
A view into the hereafter / Jozef Rulof. [transl. from the Dutch by P. Rypkema; ed.: C. Damman]. Apeldoorn: Wayti Publishing House Foundation, 2000. 3 vol.
Vol. 1.: 1st ed. 2000. 238 p., [4] p. pl.
Vol. 2.: 1st ed. 2000. 255 p., [2] p. pl.
Vol. 3.: 1st ed. 2000. 246 p., [2] p. pl.
Transl. of: Een blik in het hiernamaals. 3 vol. 1933-1936.

Schatborn, Peter
Drawn to warmth: 17th-century Dutch artists in Italy / Peter Schatborn; with an essay by Judith Verberne; [ed. Ger Luijten ... et al.; trans. from the Dutch Lynne Richards]. Zwolle: Waanders; Amsterdam: Rijksmuseum, cop. 2001. 223 p.
Publ. on the occasion of the Exhibition: 'Tekenen van warmte: 17de-eeuwse Nederlandse tekenaars in Italië' in the Rijksmuseum, Amsterdam (June 30, 2001 - September 30, 2001).
Transl. of: Tekenen van warmte: 17de-eeuwse Nederlandse tekenaars in Italië. 2001.

Scheers, Don
M(a)stering the future services: the wholesale trade is facing a strategic choice / Don Scheers; [transl. from the Dutch]. [S.l.]: Cap Gemini, [2000]. 28 p.

Transl. of: M(a)stering the future services: de groothandel staat voor een strategische keuze. 2000.

Schogt, Philibert
The wild numbers / by Philibert Schogt; [transl. from the Dutch]. London: Weidenfeld & Nicolson, 2001. 171 p.
First English ed.: New York: Four Walls Eight Windows, 2000.
Transl. of: De wilde getallen. 1998.
Other ed.: New York: Plume Books, 2001

Scholten, Patty
Elephants in love and other poems / Patty Scholten; transl. [from the Dutch by James Brockway]. London: London Magazine Ed, 2001. 96 p.
Transl. of a choice of her poems.

Schubert, Dieter
Where's my monkey? / Dieter Schubert; [transl. from the Dutch]. 1st board book ed. Asheville, North Carolina: Front Street, Lemniscaat, cop. 2000. [24] p.
Transl. of: Monkie. 1986.

Schubert, Ingrid
Bear's eggs / Ingrid and Dieter Schubert; [transl. from the Dutch]. London: Andersen, cop. 1999. 32 p.
First English ed.: Asheville, NC: Front Street, Lemniscaat, cop. 1999.
Transl. of: Dat komt er nou van... 1999.

Schubert, Ingrid
Beaver's lodge / Ingrid and Dieter Schubert; [transl. from the Dutch]. 1st ed. Asheville, NC: Front Street, Lemniscaat, 2001. [28] p.
Transl. of: Samen kunnen we alles. 2000.
Other ed.: London: Andersen, cop. 2001.

Snellen-Balendong, H.
Block construction / H. Snellen-Balendong and D. Dolmans; [transl. from the Dutch: Mereke Gorsira]. Maastricht: Maastricht University, Department of

Educational Development and Research, cop. 1999. 59 p.
(A series on Problem-Based Medical Education; pt. 2)
Transl. of: Constructie van blokken. 1996. (Een reeks voor Probleem Gestuurd Medisch Onderwijs; vol. 2).

Sonneveld
The Sonneveld House: an avant-garde home from 1933 / text Elly Adriaansz ... [et al.]; photogr. Jannes Linders; [copy ed. Hermien Hamhuis ... et al.; English transl. Peter Mason ... et al.; image ed. Ingrid Oosterheerd ... et al.; drawings Molenaar & Van Winden Architecten].
Rotterdam: NAi Publishers, cop. 2001. 159 p.
Publ. on the occasion of the restauration and the re-establishment of the Museum The Sonneveld House.
Transl. of: Huis Sonneveld: modern wonen in 1933. 2001

Stevens, Harm
Shades of Orange: a history of the Royal House of the Netherlands / [author: Harm Stevens; transl. from the Dutch: Lynne Richards; photography: Department of Photography Rijksmuseum ... et al.].
Amsterdam: Rijksmuseum; Zwolle: Waanders, cop. 2001. 47 p.
(Rijksmuseum-dossiers)
Transl. of: Wonderspiegel van Oranje: een geschiedenis van het Nederlandse vorstenhuis. 2001.

Stokvis, Willemijn
Cobra 3 dimensions: work in wood, clay, metal, stone, plaster, waste, polyester, bread, ceramics / Willemijn Stokvis; [translation from the Dutch: Lynn George, Nicoline Galehouse, Sam Herman]. London: Lund Humphries Publishers, 1999. 176 p.
Transl. of: Cobra 3 dimensionaal: werk in hout, klei, metaal, steen, gips, afval, polyester, brood, keramiek,... 1998.

Publ. on the occasion of the Exhibition: "Cobra en de beeldhouwkunst" in the program of the "Cobra 50 Manifestatie" in the Cobra Museum voor Moderne Kunst, Amstelveen (November 8, 1998 - January 10, 1999).

Strijbosch, Clara
The seafaring Saint: sources and analogues of the twelfth-century Voyage of Saint Brendan / Clara Strijbosch; transl. [from the Dutch] Thea Summerfield. Dublin [etc.]: Four Courts Press, cop. 2000. X, 325 p.
Transl. of: De bronnen van De reis van Sint Brandaan. 1995. (Middeleeuwse studies en bronnen; 44).
Thesis Utrecht.

Tongeren, Louis van
Exaltation of the Cross: towards the origins of the Feast of the Cross and the meaning of the Cross in early medieval liturgy / Louis van Tongeren. Leuven [etc.]: Peeters, 2001. X, 342 p. (Liturgia condenda; 11)
Transl. of: Exaltatio crucis: het feest van Kruisverheffing en de zingeving van het kruis in het Westen tijdens de vroege middeleeuwen: een liturgie-historische studie. 1995. (TFT-studies; 25).
Thesis Katholieke Universiteit Tilburg.

Valk, Jeroen de
Ben Webster: his life and music / Jeroen de Valk; [transl. from the Dutch by Laura Jennings-Blijleven]. Berkeley, Cal.: Berkeley Hills Books, cop. 2001. XI, 280 p.
Transl. and adapt. of: In a mellow tone: het levensverhaal van Ben Webster. 1992.

Valk, Jeroen de
Chet Baker: his life and music / Jeroen de Valk. Berkeley, Cal.: Berkeley Hills Books, 2000. XI, 294 p.
Transl. of: Chet Baker: herinneringen aan een lyrisch trompettist. 1989.

Van Genechten, Guido
Flop-Ear and Annie / Guido Van Genechten; [transl. from the Dutch]. London: Cat's Whiskers, 2000. 32 p.
Transl. of: Rikki en Anni. 2000.

Van Genechten, Guido
Floppy / Guido Van Genechten; [transl. from the Dutch]; Turkish transl. by Kelâmi Dedezade. London: Mantra, cop. 1999. [28] p.
Transl. of: Rikki. 1999.
English and Turkish text.

Van Steenberghe, Etienne
Belgian winegrowers in France / Etienne Van Steenberghe. Tielt: Lannoo, 2000. 252 p.
Dutch ed.: Belgische wijnbouwers in Frankrijk. 2000.

Veldkamp, Tjibbe
The school trip / Tjibbe Veldkamp; pictures by Philip Hopman; [transl. from the Dutch]. 1st ed. Asheville, NC: Front Street, Lemniscaat, 2001. [22] p.
Transl. of: Het schoolreisje. 2000.

Velmans, Edith
Edith's story / Edith Velmans. New York [etc.]: Bantam, 2001. 256 p.
First American ed.: New York Soho. 1999.
First English ed. publ. as: Edith's book. London: Viking, 1998.
Based on diaries and letters from the period: February 6, 1946 - December 27, 1946.
Subtitle on the cover: The true story of a young girl's courage, love and survival during World War II.
Dutch ed.: Het verhaal van Edith. 1997.

Velthuijs, Max
Frog and the very special day / Max Velthuijs; [transl. from the Dutch]. London: Andersen, 2001. 32 p.
Transl. of: Kikker en een heel bijzondere dag. 1999.

Verhagen, Mila
Paris restaurants and their recipes / [author Mila Verhagen; transl. from the

Dutch Henriëtte Straub; transl. ed. Helen Williams; directing ed. Joyce Enthoven ... et al.; photogr. Linda Maas ... et al.].
Breda: Mo'Media, cop. 2001. 141 p.
Transl. of: Unieke restaurants van Parijs en hun lekkerste recepten. 2001. (The right guide).

Verstegen, Ton
Tropisms: methaphoric animation and architecture / Ton Verstegen; [ed.: Els Brinkman; transl. from the Dutch: Peter Mason].
Rotterdam: NAi Publishers, cop. 2001. 112 p.
Transl. of: Tropismen: metaforische animatie en architectuur. 2001. (Fascinaties; 10).

Vincent
Vincent van Gogh. 1: Paintings: Dutch period 1881-1885, Van Gogh Museum / Louis van Tilborgh, Marije Vellekoop; [red.: Sjraar van Heugten ... et al.].
Burlington, VT: Lund Humphries, 1999. 160 p.
Transl. of: Vincent van Gogh. 1: Schilderijen: Nederlandse periode 1881-1885, Van Gogh Museum. 1999.

Volunteering
Volunteering worldwide / Margriet-Marie Govaart ... [et al.] (ed.); [with the co-operation of: Norbert Broenink ... et al.; with contributions of: Ken Allen ... et al.; transl. from the Dutch: Tolkagentschap; photogr. Hollandse Hoogte ... et al.]. Utrecht: NIZW, cop. 2001. 276 p.
Transl. of: Vrijwilligerswerk wereldwijd. 2001. ([Vrijwilligerswerk en vrijwilligersbeleid]).

Vons, Geert-Jan
Sam and the Black-and-white-creatures / Geert-Jan Vons; [transl. from the Dutch by Geert-Jan Vons]. Amersfoort: Whale Weirdo Foundation, cop. 1999. [28] p.
Cover title.

Transl. of: Sam en de zwart-met-witte-beesten. 1999.

Vons, Geert-Jan
Sam and the Isle of Poeke / Geert-Jan Vons; [transl. from the Dutch by Geert-Jan Vons]. Amersfoort: Whale Weirdo Foundation, cop. 1999. [28] p.
Cover title.
Transl. of: Sam en het eiland van Poeke. 1999.

Vons, Geert-Jan
Sam and the sleeping-snow-bank / Geert-Jan Vons; [transl. from the Dutch by Geert-Jan Vons]. Amersfoort: Whale Weirdo Foundation, cop. 1999. [28] p.
Cover title.
Transl. of: Sam en de bewegende-berg-van-sneeuw. 1999.

Vons, Geert-Jan
Sam and the strange-thing-made-of-string / Geert-Jan Vons; [transl. from the Dutch by Julia Murphy]. Amersfoort: Whale Weirdo Foundation, cop. 1999. [28] p.
Cover title.
Transl. of: Sam en het rare-ding-van-touw. 1999.

Vries, Anne de
Journey through the night / by Anne de Vries; [transl. from the Dutch by Harry der Nederlanden]. Neerlandia, etc.: Inheritance Publ., 2001. 373 p.
Previous ed.: St. Catharines [Ontario]: Paideia Press, 1978.
Transl. of: Reis door de nacht. 1960.

Walraven-Raming, M.G.V.
Surveying your stutter / M.G.V. Walraven-Raming; transl. from the Dutch by J.E. Klok, J. Terpstra. Rotterdam: Vredeberg Foundation, cop. 1999. 17 p.
Transl. of: Stotteren je kan het overzien. 1989.

Wang, Lulu
The lily theatre / Lulu Wang; transl. [from the Dutch] by Hester Velmans.

London: Hodder & Stoughton General, 2001. 366 p.
First English ed.: New York [etc.]: Nan A. Talese, 2000, and: London: Little, Brown, 2000.
Transl. and adapt. of: Het lelie theater. 1997.

Water
Water colours of Delft: the past, present and future / International Institute for Urban Environment; [ed.: Tjeerd Deelstra ... et al.; transl. from the Dutch].
Delft: International Institute for the Urban Environment, cop. 1999.
Transl. of: De vele kleuren van Delfts water: het verleden, het heden en de toekomst. 1999.
Includes: Grey; Green; Blue; The history; The future; Poster.

Water
The Water project: a nineteenth-century walk through Rotterdam / comp. by Fransje Hooimeijer and Mariëtte Kamphuis; photogr. Daniël Nicolas; [ed. Hetty Berens ... et al.; maps Gemeentewerken Rotterdam, afd. Landmeten en Vastgoedinformatie; transl. from the Dutch John Kirkpatrick]. Rotterdam: 010 Publishers, 2001. 192 p.
Publ. as part of the event Waterproject 1854-2001, a component of Rotterdam 2001, Cultural Capital of Europe.
Transl. of: Het Waterproject: een negentiende-eeuwse wandeling door Rotterdam. 2001.

Wetering, JanWillem van de
The empty mirror: experiences in an American Zen community / Janwillem van de Wetering; [transl. from the Dutch]. New York: St. Martin's Press, 1999. 160 p.
First English ed.: Londen: Routledge & Kegan Paul, 1973.
Transl. of: De lege spiegel. 1972.

Wijnen, Gert
Managing unique assignments: a team approach to projects and programmes / Gert Wijnen and Rudy Kor. Aldershot, Hampshire,: Gower, 2000. 403 p.
Transl. of: Het managen van unieke opgaven: samen werken aan projecten en programma's. 1996.

Wind, Anneke
Old Woody builds a house / [ill.: Michel de Boer; transl. from the Dutch]. London: Candle Books, [1999]. [32] p.
(Woody books) Text Anneke Wind. A story based on Luke 6: 46-49.
Transl. of: Opa Knoest bouwt een huis. 1999. (Knoest serie).

Wind, Anneke
Old Woody gets help / [ill.: Michel de Boer; transl. from the Dutch]. London: Candle Books, [1999]. [32] p.: (Woody books) Text Anneke Wind.
A story based on Luke 10: 25-37.
Transl. of: Opa Knoest gaat vissen. 1999. (Knoest serie).

Wind, Anneke
Old Woody goes sowing / [ill.: Michel de Boer; transl. from the Dutch]. London: Candle Books, [1999]. [32] p.
(Woody books) Text Anneke Wind. A story based on Luke 8: 4-15.
Transl. of: Opa Knoest gaat zaaien. 1999. (Knoest serie).

Wind, Anneke
Old Woody loses his cat / [ill.: Michel de Boer; transl. from the Dutch]. London: Candle Books, [1999]. [32] p.
(Woody books) Text Anneke Wind. A story based on Luke 15: 1-7.
Transl. of: Opa Knoest gaat vissen. 1999. (Knoest serie).

Witvliet, Theo
Broken tradition: plurality and identity in Christianity / Theo Witvliet; transl.

from the Dutch by John Bowden.
London: SCM, 2000. 288 p.
Transl. of: Gebroken traditie: christelijke religie in het spanningsveld van pluraliteit en identiteit. 1999.

Woerden, Henk van
The assassin: a story of race and rage in the land of Apartheid / Henk van Woerden; transl. [from the Dutch] and ed. by Dan Jacobson. [S.l.]: Publ. Group West, 2000. 256 p.
First English ed. entitled: A mouthful of glass: the man who killed the Father of Apartheid.
London: Granta, 2000.
Transl. of: Een mond vol glas. 1998.
Partially previous published in: Granta, no. 69.
Other ed.: New York: Metropolitan Books, 2001.

Woodboro, Ted
Yours and mine / Ted Woodboro; [transl. from the Dutch: Tony Burrett]. Groningen: Gopher Publishers, 2001. 222 p.
Transl. of: Een daad van liefde. 2000.

World
World fairs: selected plans / [ed. L. van Duin ... et al.; transl. from the Dutch]. 1st ed. Delft: DUP Blue Print, 2000. 95 p. (TUDelft series on architecture)
Transl. of: Plannenmap wereldtentoonstellingen. 2e uitg. 2000. (TUDelft series on architecture).

World
The world of Bosch / ed. Jan van Oudheusden, Aart Vos; writers Ronald Glaudemans ... [et al.; English transl. from the Dutch: Tony Burrett ... et al.; image ed. Jac Biemans ... et al.]. 's-Hertogenbosch: Heinen; ['s-Hertogenbosch]: Stichting Archeologie, Bouwhistorie en Cultuur 's-Hertogenbosch; ['s-Hertogenbosch]: Stadsarchief 's-Hertogenbosch, 2001. 161, [3] p. (Historisch ABC; 4)

In cooperation with the Noordbrabants Museum. Transl. of: De wereld van Bosch. 2001.

Zweers, Wim
Participating with nature: outline for an ecologization of our world view / Wim Zweers; [transl. from the Dutch: Janet Taylor]. Utrecht: International Books, cop. 2000. 400 p. Transl. of: Participeren aan de natuur: ontwerp voor een ecologisering van het wereldbeeld. 1995. ([Serie milieufilosofie]).

Zwetsman, Melchert
My first art book / [comp. by Melchert Zwetsman and Josette van Gemert; transl. from the Dutch]. [Amsterdam: Van Gogh Museum, 2000]. [16] p. Cover in blue. Transl. of: Mijn eerste kunstboek. 2000.

Zwetsman, Melchert
My first art book / [comp. by Melchert Zwetsman and Josette van Gemert; transl. from the Dutch]. [Amsterdam: Van Gogh Museum, 2000]. [16] p. Cover in yellow. Transl. of: Mijn eerste kunstboek. 2000.

Zwijnenberg, Robert
The writings and drawings of Leonardo da Vinci: order and chaos in early modern thought / Robert Zwijnenberg; transl. [from the Dutch] by Caroline A. van Eck. Cambridge [etc.]: Cambridge University Press, 1999. VIII, 232 p.

Editor:
Dutch Book in Translation
Koninklijke Bibliotheek
The Hague
The Netherlands

Contributors

Dirk van Assche (1955-)
Editorial secretary
Ons Erfdeel
Murissonstraat 260,
8930 Rekkem, Belgium

Fred G.H. Bachrach (1914-)
Emeritus Professor of English Literature (University of Leiden)
55 Cole Park Road, Twickenham TW1 1HT, United Kingdom

Wim van der Beek
Art critic
Prinses Margrietlaan 41,
8069 AV Wezep,
The Netherlands

Guido Vanden Berghe (1945-)
Professor of Numeral Mathematics (University Of Ghent)
Krijgslaan 281 S9,
9000 Ghent, Belgium

Rieta Bergsma (1954-)
Lecturer in Art History
Linnaeushof 88 11,
1098 KT Amsterdam,
The Netherlands

Lori van Biervliet (1944-)
Free-lance researcher
Sint-Annarei 11,
8000 Bruges, Belgium

Jos Bouveroux (1947-)
Chief editor News (VRT Radio)
A. Reyerslaan 52,
1043 Brussels, Belgium

José Boyens
Art critic
Hogewaldseweg 33,
6562 KR Groesbeek,
The Netherlands

Willem Breedveld (1945-)
Journalist *Trouw* / Lecturer in Mass Communication and Politics (University of Leiden)
Waardsedijk 102,
3421 NH Oudewater,
The Netherlands

Hugo Brems (1944-)
Professor of Modern Dutch Literature (Catholic University of Leuven)
Huttelaan 41,
3001 Heverlee, Belgium

Eric de Bruyn (1955-)
Teacher
Venwei 20,
2990 Wuustwezel, Belgium

Elly Cockx-Indestege (1933-)
Librarian (retired)
Ninoofsesteenweg 5,
1700 Dilbeek, Belgium

Hans Cools (1969-)
Researcher (University of Leiden)
Elandstraat 265,
2513 HW The Hague,
The Netherlands

Brigitte Dekeyzer (1966-)
Assistant lecturer in Art History (Catholic University of Leuven)
Stijn Streuvelslaan 40,
3010 Kessel-Lo, Belgium

Jozef Deleu (1937-)
Chief editor / Managing director 'Stichting Ons Erfdeel'
Murissonstraat 260,
8930 Rekkem, Belgium

Peter Derkx (1951-)
Senior Lecturer in the History of Humanism (University for Humanist Studies)
P.O. Box 797,
3500 AT Utrecht,
The Netherlands

Luc Devoldere (1956-)
Deputy editor 'Stichting Ons Erfdeel'
Murissonstraat 260,
8930 Rekkem, Belgium

Jozef T. Devreese(1937-)
Professor of Theoretical Physics (University of Antwerp)
D'Oultremontlei 24,
2930 Brasschaat, Belgium

Vic de Donder (1939-)
Editor *de Standaard*
Ortolaanstraat 10,
1731 Zellik, Belgium

Marc Dubois (1950-)
Architecture critic / Lecturer (St Lucas Architecture Institute, Ghent)
Holstraat 89,
9000 Ghent, Belgium

Th. van den End (1940-)
Staff member of the Gereformeerde Zendingsbond
Daendelsweg 3,
7315 AH Apeldoorn,
The Netherlands

Kees Fens (1929-)
Emeritus Professor of Modern Dutch Literature (Catholic University of Nijmegen)
Keizersgracht 245 A,
1016 EB Amsterdam,
The Netherlands

Cees van der Geer (1931-)
Art critic *Haagsche Courant*
Vlaardingerdijk 306,
3117 ZV Schiedam,
The Netherlands

Joris Gerits (1943-)
Lecturer in Dutch Modern Literature and Language (UFSIA, Antwerp)
Ter Rivierenlaan 57,
2100 Deurne, Belgium

Ger Groot (1954-)
Lecturer in Philosophy (Erasmus University, Rotterdam)
Hobbemastraat 69,
1000 Brussels, Belgium

Hans Ibelings (1963-)
Architecture critic
Javakade 542,
1019 SE Amsterdam,
The Netherlands

Lammert G. Jansma (1943-)
Director Fryske Akademy, Leeuwarden
Achterweg 66,
9269 TP Veenwouden,
The Netherlands

Jan Kerkhofs S.J. (1924)
Emeritus Professor of Theology (Catholic University of Leuven)
Waversebaan 220,
3001 Leuven, Belgium

C.G. Kok (1948-)
Director, Stichting Leerhuis & Liturgie, Amsterdam
Groenendaalstraat 48",
1058 LH Amsterdam,
The Netherlands